THE SANTURCE CRABBERS

THE SANTURCE CRABBERS

Sixty Seasons of Puerto Rican Winter League Baseball

by

THOMAS E. VAN HYNING

WITH A FOREWORD BY
Herman Franks

McFarland & Company, Inc., Publishers
Jefferson, North Carolina, and London

To Pedrín Zorrilla (1905–1981),
founder and owner of the Santurce Crabbers (1939–1956),
known as "Mr. Baseball" and "El Cangrejo Mayor"

On the cover: Juan "Igor" González swinging at a pitch against San Juan
during the 1993-1994 season (courtesy of Angel Colón)

British Library Cataloguing-in-Publication data are available

Library of Congress Cataloguing-in-Publication Data

Van Hyning, Thomas E., 1954–
    The Santurce Crabbers : sixty seasons of Puerto Rican Winter
League baseball / by Thomas E. Van Hyning.
        p.   cm.
    Includes bibliographical references (p.   ) and index.
    ISBN 0-7864-0662-3 (case binding : 50# alkaline paper) ∞
    1. Santurce Crabbers (Baseball team)—History.   2. Puerto
Rico Winter League (Baseball league)—History.   3. Baseball—
Puerto Rico—History.   I. Title.
GV875.S363V36   1999
796.357'64'097295—dc21   99-23513
                                                     CIP

Manufactured in the United States of America

McFarland & Company, Inc., Publishers
  Box 611, Jefferson, North Carolina 28640

ACKNOWLEDGMENTS

Diana Zorrilla facilitated baseball photos and historical information on Pedrín Zorrilla. She was a magnificent hostess at her Santurce home during my five-day trip to Puerto Rico in November 1997. Thanks, Diana, and for suggesting that Herman Franks prepare the Foreword. Thank you, Herman Franks.

Enriqueta Marcano Zorrilla duplicated and sent *El Imparcial* and *El Mundo* articles from Santurce's first three league seasons. Enriqueta also assisted me with copying baseball photos.

Reinaldo "Poto" Paniagua, owner of the Santurce Baseball Club, provided a wealth of historical and current information on this franchise. Poto's ties to Pedrín Zorrilla made this research project more special and meaningful. Former Santurce General Manager Frankie Thon was also helpful in providing a "behind-the-scenes" scenario of running a winter league franchise.

José Crescioni Benítez and Eduardo Valero were very cooperative by filling in statistical and historical gaps. Crescioni has taken the lead in securing Puerto Rico Winter League data and publishing it. Valero is a top-notch historian of Caribbean baseball.

Ismael Trabal shared anecdotes and recollections covering a forty-year period, 1939–1979. He has a keen mind for baseball history and writes very well.

Heriberto Ramírez de Arellano, a.k.a. "Don Guindo," knew Pedrín Zorrilla before there was a semi-pro or a professional team in Santurce. Don Guindo, who came up with the idea of a "City Championship" for the San Juan–Santurce rivalry, was a godsend in highlighting and sharing information for the early years.

Guigo Otero Suro, a confidante of the Zorrilla family for some 50 years, conversed with me for over an hour on matters pertaining to Santurce from the time Josh Gibson was signed by Pedrín to a host of other historical anecdotes.

Luis Alvelo allowed me to use a postcard of Willard Brown from his personal collection. Héctor Barea sent me several of his baseball books and articles on former Santurce players. Ubaldo Bernier kindly mailed a "care package" full of historical clippings. Rai García and Yuyo Ruíz facilitated photos.

Benny Agosto, Executive Director of the Liga de Béisbol Profesional de Puerto Rico, authorized credentials for the 1997–98 season. Benny sent me the 1995–96 and 1996–97 *Recuentos Cronológicos* for the league. Angel Colón, an official with the Puerto Rico Professional Baseball Players Association, allowed me to use some photos from his collection.

Rafael Bracero, a renowned television sportscaster, conversed with me about the section of Santurce where he grew up, his admiration for Rubén Gómez, the glory years of the Santurce franchise between the early and mid–1950s, and other matters.

Luis R. Mayoral, the Texas Rangers' radio announcer for Spanish transmissions, shared some of his articles. Eddie Napoleon, a coach with Texas, provided tidbits on the Caribbean and InterAmerican Series from a Panamanian perspective.

The sports editors of *El Nuevo Día* (Erick Rodríguez) and *The San Juan Star* (Marcos Pérez) provided assistance, as did Gabrielle Paese and Eric Edwards of *The San Juan Star*.

Manuel Junco alerted me to the book *Cangrejos* and what the Crabbers and Santurce symbolize for him. Charles Ferrer shared humorous anecdotes about the Crabbers. Luis Maldonado, another Santurce fan, brought a 1990s perspective of the Crabbers to the table. Miguel A. Gaud and Mara T. Patermaster, former co-workers in Puerto Rico, provided background about the sectors of Santurce where they grew up.

Freddie Thon, Jr., now living in South Bend, Indiana, shared pertinent recollections on his days as a San Juan fan and batboy during the 1940s when he saw some of the world's best baseball players, including Josh Gibson, Monte Irvin, Willard Brown and Roy Campanella. Dickie Thon, one of Freddie's sons, deserves thanks for his insights on the Puerto Rico Winter League, having played for the Bayamón/San Juan franchise prior to completing his league career with Santurce. The Thon family is a class act.

Tony Gwynn, a former teammate of Dickie Thon with Bayamón and San Juan, shared his memories of the rivalry with Santurce. Tom McCraw, a Houston coach, recalled moments from the 1960s when he played for Caguas and San Juan.

Houston's Assistant General Manager, Tim Purpura, provided winter league insights from a big league perspective. So did Tony Menéndez, an Account Executive with the Florida Marlins.

Thanks to media/public relations officials John Blake and Amy Gunter of the Texas Rangers, and Rob Matwick and Darrell Simon of the Houston Astros for facilitating major league game credentials. And thanks to Aaron Lombard of the New Orleans Zephyrs, class AAA, as well as Bill Blackwell, General Manager of the Jackson Generals, class AA, for facilitating access to their players. Charlie Brenner, interlibrary loan manager, Eudorah Welty Library, Jackson, Mississippi, helped me secure *The San Juan Star* microfilm from other libraries.

This book would not have been finished without the editorial and word processing assistance of my mother, Paula Van Hyning. She turned 80 during this ordeal and kept plugging. My wife, Donna, read some of the earlier drafts. Our dog, Sam, provided early morning support near the computer.

And finally, to all those current and former Santurce players, managers and coaches: you have my gratitude for your time. There was not enough space to include all of your quotes. Your names are listed alphabetically at the end of this section.

Notes on Research

I used some taped conversations and survey responses between 1991 and 1994 for my first book, titled *Puerto Rico's Winter League: A History of Major League Baseball's Launching Pad*, to supplement conversations and survey responses between 1997 and 1998. The one mail survey conducted between August and October 1997 of 50 former Santurce players or managers, resulted in a 36 percent response rate, as 18 players/managers returned usable instruments. This was a one-page (front side only) form focusing on their Santurce experience in terms of their season(s), the fans, and the rivalry with San Juan.

That feedback was combined with information gleaned from face-to-face conversations at big league, minor league and winter league stadiums. I spoke with former Santurce managers, coaches and players at the Houston Astrodome on May 16, 1998, and at The Ballpark in Arlington, Texas, three weeks later. Between June 30, 1997, and May 18, 1998, I talked to former and current Santurce players and managers at minor league stadiums in Jackson, Mississippi and New Orleans, Louisiana. My conversations prior to Santurce games took place at Hiram Bithorn Stadium on November 19–20, 1997.

The conversations were conducted in Spanish or English. Here is the list of former and current Santurce managers, coaches and players with whom I spoke or corresponded between 1991 and 1994, and then between 1997 and 1998: Kyle Abbott, Luis Aguayo, José Alberro, Gary Allenson, Sandy Alomar, Jr., Sandy Alomar, Sr., José Alvarez, Manolo Alvarez, Craig Anderson, Luis Aquino. Scott Bailes, Jim Beauchamp, Fred Beene, Derek Bell, Jay Bell, Vern Benson, Paul Blair, Dennis "Oil Can" Boyd, Jackie Brandt, Tom Bruno, John Burgos, Pete Burnside, Iván Calderón, Casey Candaele, Ramón Castro, Danny Cater, Orlando Cepeda, Ron Cey, Dennis Colón, Edwin Correa, Terry Crowley, José "Cheo" Cruz, Mike Cuéllar, Jerry DaVanon, Ted Davidson, Leon Day, Ken Dayley, Iván de Jesús, José de Jesús, Miguel de la Hoz, Steve Demeter, Mike Devereaux, Mario Díaz, Jim Dickson, Scott Elarton. Eduardo Figueroa, Gil Flores, Tony Fossas, Eric Fox, Herman Franks, Roger Freed, Matt Galante, Bob Gibson, Leo Gómez, Rubén Gómez, Juan "Igor" González, Julio Gotay, Bill Greason, Mike Grzanich, Chris Gwynn, Larry Haney, Bill Harrell, Elrod Hendricks, Tom Henke, Earl Hersch, Jack Howell, Dick Hughes, Luis Isaac, Hal Jeffcoat, Russ Johnson, Kevin Kennedy, Bill Krueger, Tom Lasorda, Jack Lazorko, Charlie Leibrandt, Dave Leonhard, Carlos Lezcano, José "Chico" Lind, Pedro López, Sam McDowell, Jack McKeon, Mark McLemore, Rick Mahler, Dennis Martínez, José Martínez, Brian Maxcy, Willie Mays, Orlando Mercado, Orlando Merced, Ray Miller, Balor Moore, Jerry Morales, Angel Morris, Pedro Muñoz, Jaime Navarro, Julio Navarro, David Nied, Melvin Nieves, Otis Nixon, Reinaldo "Pochy" Oliver, Francisco Javier Oliveras, Mako Oliveras, José Olmeda, Luis R. Olmo, Adalberto "Junior" Ortíz, José "Polilla" Ortíz, Bob Patterson, Julián Pérez, Mike Pérez, Tany Pérez, Juan "Terín" Pizarro, J.W. Porter, Jamie Quirk, Milton Ramírez, Merv Rettenmund, Steve Ridzik, Germán Rivera, Germán "Deportivo" Rivera, Frank Robinson, Eliseo "Ellie" Rodríguez, Victor Rodríguez, Sr., Octavio "Cookie" Rojas, Luis "Papo" Rosado, Vern Ruhle, José G. "Pantalones" Santiago, Al Severinsen, Mike Sharperson, John Shelby, Rubén "El Indio" Sierra, Dwight Smith, Zane Smith, Marv Staehle, Pat Tabler, José Tartabull, Dickie Thon, Frankie Thon, Bob Thurman, Otto Vélez, Héctor Villanueva, Billy Wagner, Bob Walk, Dave Wallace, Earl Weaver, Turk Wendell, John Wetteland, Jerry Willard, Gerald Williams, Artie Wilson, Ed Wojna, Robin Yount, Don Zimmer.

CONTENTS

FOREWORD
by Herman Franks

The Santurce ball club I managed in 1954–55 was a great club. Here are some facts about Pedrín (Pete) Zorrilla and the Santurce Crabbers Baseball Club. I met Pedrín Zorrilla through his association with the New York Giants. He was the person responsible for the Giants acquiring Rubén Gómez and he made many trips to New York visiting Rubén and the owner of the Giants, Horace Stoneham. Pedrín was one of the finest men I ever met in baseball or out of baseball. We ended up being very dear friends and our family is still very close today to the Zorrilla family.

Pedrín was one of the most knowledgeable men about baseball talent and the game itself that I ever knew. He and his two or three friends would sit next to the dugout and I would sit on a chair in the middle of the dugout by the little cubby hole. I'll never forget one time the bases were full and I said I'm going to walk this hitter. Pete immediately said, "The bases are full — where are you going to put him?" I said, "In back of the pitcher," which got a real big laugh. After every game we would have a great time talking about the ball game and sometimes these talks would get very heated.

Pete had some great ballplayers play for him and I enjoyed the stories he used to tell of the old Negro players, and the stories he told about Josh Gibson. He told us Josh might have been greater than Babe Ruth if they had allowed him to play in the major leagues.

The 1954–55 Santurce club with a little more pitching depth could have won it all in the major leagues. Rubén Gómez, Sam Jones and Bill Greason were three terrific starters. Can you imagine the power on that Santurce club with George Crowe, Buster Clarkson, Bob Thurman, Roberto Clemente and Willie Mays? The old Sixto Escobar Stadium had some distant fences, but it wasn't anything for that gang. Santurce's fans and the old stadium were just great. I don't think the new stadiums had or will ever have the feeling of Sixto Escobar Stadium.

Willie Mays was the best baseball player I ever saw; he made unbelievable plays all the time. Clemente belonged to the Brooklyn Dodgers and was with Montreal that (1954) season and at the end of the season he was eligible for the major league draft. The New York Giants, whom I coached for in 1954, didn't have a chance to draft him as we had won the pennant and World Series. Branch Rickey of Pittsburgh came to Puerto Rico looking

1

for ballplayers. Pedrín and I told him to draft Clemente and you know his story at Pittsburgh. If I had to pick a ballplayer outside of Willie Mays, it would be Roberto.

Willie and Roberto led us to the 1954–55 Puerto Rico Winter League championship and a trip to Caracas, Venezuela, for the seventh Caribbean Series. I had managed the Magallanes Navigators in Caracas the winter before, so when we arrived there for the championship series, they asked me what I was doing there. They said, "We didn't have a chance to win," as Almendares from Cuba would take it all. I told them the only reason I brought this team there was for them to see Willie Mays. Willie started the series going without a hit in his first 12 at-bats. Then, facing Ramón Monzant (a pitcher that had pitched for me in Venezuela the year before) and with Clemente on first base, Willie got his first hit, a homer, winning game three of the series. I think Willie got 10 hits in the next three games. Santurce went on to win that Caribbean Series over the teams from Cuba, Panama and Venezuela. It was great to win Santurce's third Caribbean Series title under Pedrín Zorrilla.

Pedrín asked me to manage Santurce in 1955–56 and we had another fine team with Roberto Clemente, Bob Thurman, Bill White, Don Zimmer and many other good players, but we didn't make it to the Caribbean Series after winning the regular season title. I stayed in touch with Pedrín over the years since he was a scout for the New York and San Francisco Giants while I was a coach and manager of the Giants. Then the Chicago Cubs hired me as their manager in 1977 and Pedrín became a scout for the Cubs for a few years.

I really miss my good friend, Pedrín. However, we talk to his widow, Diana, all the time and that helps.

Herman Franks,
Salt Lake City, Utah

Former player, St. Louis Cardinals,
Brooklyn Dodgers, Philadelphia A's, New York Giants;
Santurce Crabbers Manager, 1954–55 and 1955–56;
San Francisco Giants Manager, 1965–68;
Chicago Cubs Manager, 1977–1979

PREFACE

The Santurce Crabbers became part of my childhood between the early– and mid–1960s when I lived in a Santurce neighborhood. My Estrella Street friends, with the exception of three brothers who rooted for the arch rival San Juan Senators, were all Santurce fans. We followed the exploits of Orlando "Peruchín" Cepeda, Rubén Gómez and Juan "Terín" Pizarro, and had lively discussions about the games and seasons which lasted from about mid–October through the following January.

From the mid–1960s through the mid–1980s I attended Puerto Rico Winter League games at Hiram Bithorn Stadium in Hato Rey, and Juan Ramón Loubriel Stadium in Bayamón. The level of play was between AAA baseball in the states and the big leagues. I saw the gamut of players from Santurce's Orlando Cepeda and San Juan's Roberto Clemente to those of the next generation such as Sandy Alomar, Jr. and Rubén Sierra of Santurce; Tony Gwynn and Dickie Thon of Bayamón/San Juan.

In the summer of 1985 I moved to the U.S. mainland and lost touch with the Puerto Rico Winter League for a few years. But in 1989 I became a member of the Society for American Baseball Research, and then got involved with the Latin America Committee. Between 1991 and 1994 I did extensive research for my first book, *Puerto Rico's Winter League: A History of Major League Baseball's Launching Pad*, published in May 1995.

Two years transpired when I decided to write this book. A story needed to be told about the Santurce Crabbers Baseball Club. And who better to do this than someone who had lived in Santurce for 10 of the 25 years he spent in Puerto Rico, and who cared deeply about Winter League baseball history. My fluency in Spanish also enabled me to converse and correspond with many baseball players, managers and coaches, as well as some officials and sportswriters from Puerto Rico.

The Santurce franchise is to the Puerto Rico Winter League what the New York Yankees are to the major leagues (a franchise with a rich history and a winning tradition). When Santurce does well on the field, it bodes well for the rest of Puerto Rico's Winter League in terms of attendance, enthusiasm and what U.S. baseball fans call winter "hot stove league" discussions. And the Santurce Crabbers existence and tradition began with Pedro "Pedrín" Zorrilla.

Pedrín Zorrilla scouted and signed Roberto Clemente, Orlando Cepeda, Rubén Gómez and Juan Pizarro, to name a few, to their first professional baseball contracts with Santurce. He did much of the legwork with major league organizations during the 1950s which resulted in Roberto Clemente initially signing with the Brooklyn Dodgers as well as Rubén Gómez and Orlando Cepeda doing likewise with the New York Giants. Pedrín had a special rapport with many Negro Leaguers.

"It Began with Pedrín" (Chapter 1) focuses on the formative years of the Santurce Crabbers between the 1939–40 and 1945–46 seasons. Pedrín Zorrilla was a remarkable human being with a passion for baseball who signed Josh Gibson (Joshua Gibson to Puerto Rico fans) as a Santurce "import" in their 1939–40 maiden season, and Roy Campanella in 1944–45. This chapter covers the origin and importance of the "City Championship" series between San Juan and Santurce.

Santurce was "A League Anchor" (Chapter 2) in terms of having a loyal fan base who flocked to Sixto Escobar Stadium between the 1946–47 and 1953–54 seasons. They saw the one-two punch of Willard Brown and Bob Thurman do for the Crabbers what Babe Ruth and Lou Gehrig did for the Yankees circa 1925–1934. The Crabbers became the first team from Puerto Rico to win a Caribbean Series in 1951, and followed this triumph with another one in 1953, as "Puerto Rico's Team."

"Rubén Gómez, #22" (Chapter 3), pitched for Santurce during 28 seasons and managed them in two other campaigns. He made Pedrín look good with sterling performances in the 1951 and 1953 Caribbean Series as well as a win in the 1954 World Series. Rubén usually prevailed over the San Juan Senators in those eagerly awaited contests. He was one of the stars on the 1954–55 Santurce team considered by many writers and players to be the best Winter League Baseball team of all time.

"From Caracas to Caracas" (Chapter 4) chronicles the epic 1955 Caribbean Series in Caracas, Venezuela, won by Santurce, who featured Roberto Clemente and Willie Mays. This chapter begins with Pedrín's efforts to secure Willie Mays for Santurce and ends with a return trip by Santurce to the 1959 Caribbean Series which was also held in Caracas. The close ties between Santurce and the New York Giants are discussed. Ditto for the sale of the Santurce franchise by Pedrín in late 1956.

Chapter 5 covers the transition from Sixto Escobar to Bithorn Stadium as Santurce's home field. Special attention is given to the 1961–62 championship season and the Inter-American Series held at Escobar in February 1962, plus the 1964–65 season when Santurce won another league title. Santurce had some outstanding imports between the early and mid–1960s including Bob Gibson, Sam McDowell, Tany (Tony) Pérez, to complement Orlando Cepeda, Rubén Gómez and Juan Pizarro.

"Baltimore Comes to Town" (Chapter 6) documents some more glory years for Santurce from 1966–67 to 1972–73, a period in which the Crabbers won three league titles and played in two Caribbean Series events. Earl Weaver and Frank Robinson managed Santurce throughout this period with the exception of 1971–72. Weaver and Robinson benefited from their Santurce managing stints, as did Baltimore Orioles players including Don Baylor, Paul Blair, Elrod Hendricks and Jim Palmer.

Chapter 7, "The Dry Spell Begins," focuses on a transition period between 1973–74 and 1981–82 when the San Juan franchise moved to Bayamón, and Orlando Cepeda, Rubén Gómez and Juan Pizarro retired. Frank Robinson became the first African-American big league manager upon signing a player-manager contract for the 1975 Cleveland Indians following his sixth season as Santurce's skipper. Reinaldo "Poto" Paniagua emerged as Santurce's new owner during this transition period.

"The Dry Spell Continues" (Chapter 8) highlights the 1982–83 through 1989–90 seasons, a period where Santurce had some good ballclubs, but did *not* win the league title.

Santurce moved their home games to Bayamón's Juan Ramón Loubriel Stadium in 1982–83 in an effort to spur attendance. Tany Pérez made 1982–83 his farewell season for Santurce. The Los Angeles Dodgers had a working agreement with Santurce for three seasons from 1986–87 to 1988–89.

The 1990s were "A New Decade" (Chapter 9). Santurce recaptured some of its past glory by winning league titles in 1990–91 and 1992–93, and claiming the 1993 Caribbean Series crown. Puerto Rico Winter League baseball took a turn for the better in terms of attendance when established big leaguers such as Juan González and Dickie Thon played for the Crabbers in 1992–93 and 1993–94. Santurce had informal working agreements with the Atlanta Braves and Houston Astros in the 1990s.

Recollections of trips to minor league, big league and winter league ballparks plus Santurce-related thoughts comprise Chapter 10. Conversations with current and former Santurce players, managers and coaches account for most of the chapter. Emphasis is placed on feedback from Houston Astros prospects and big leaguers who conversed with me in Jackson, Mississippi; New Orleans, Louisiana; and, Houston, Texas. Ditto for comments made by some Texas Rangers players and Tony Gwynn of the San Diego Padres.

This book does not attempt to compare or contrast other winter league teams with the Santurce Crabbers. Some of those clubs are Arecibo, Caguas, Mayagüez, Ponce and San Juan (now the Carolina franchise) in Puerto Rico; Almendares, Cienfuegos, Havana and Marianao of the former Cuban Winter League; Aguilas Cibaeñas, Escogido and Licey in the Dominican Winter League; Culiacán, Hermosillo and Mexicali of the Mexican Pacific League; Caracas, Magallanes and Zulia in the Venezuelan Winter League; Carta Vieja, Chesterfield and Marlboro of the old Panama Winter League; and, Boer plus Cinco Estrellas in Nicaragua's former Winter League. The same holds true for ballclubs in the former Colombian and Hawaii Winter Leagues and the current Australian Winter League.

This is a 60-year history of the Santurce Crabbers, Roberto Clemente's first professional team. It has featured sluggers from Josh Gibson to Juan González, with Roy Campanella, Willard Brown, Bob Thurman, Willie Mays, Orlando Cepeda, Tany Pérez and Reggie Jackson part of that mix. Some of Santurce's talented native and imported hurlers over the years have included Luis Raúl Cabrera, Satchel Paige, Rubén Gómez, Juan Pizarro, Bob Gibson, Jim Palmer, Luis Tiant and Dennis Martínez. Lee Smith, major league baseball's all-time saves leader, pitched for Santurce, as did other big league closers such as Gene Garber, Tom Henke, Troy Percival, Billy Wagner and John Wetteland. Robin Yount plied his trade with Santurce. Earl Weaver and Frank Robinson experienced success in managing the Crabbers.

1. It Began with Pedrín

*The Santurce Baseball Club was created by Pedrín, with the help of
other sports-minded people who were not in it for the money.*
— Panchicú Toste, historian/statistician

Pedrín Zorrilla's Santurce ballclub made their Puerto Rico Winter League debut in 1939–40 when teams played Sunday double-headers. The franchise overcame much adversity in joining the league and earned two final series appearances in 1941 and 1943. Josh Gibson, Roy Campanella, and Clarence Palm were three of Santurce's best imports between 1939–40 through 1945–46. Luis Raúl Cabrera a.k.a. "Cabrerita" or "El Tigre" was the team's top local star.

A Person of Culture and Stature

Pedrín Zorrilla was nearly 34 years old when Santurce opened the 1939–40 season against the Aguadilla Sharks. Pedrín was born in Manatí, Puerto Rico, on November 9, 1905 to Enrique Zorrilla and Josefa Porrata.[1] His father was a poet, not a sports aficionado. Pedrín had a well-rounded education at Harrisburg Military Academy and Baltimore's Rock Hill College, and excelled in baseball and basketball.

Baseball remained Pedrín's passion when he began his career as an executive with the Shell Oil Company in Puerto Rico circa 1927. From 1927 to 1933 he spent his free time playing amateur baseball for the Buick and Wrigley teams.[2] Heriberto Ramírez de Arellano was in his late teens and a member of the All-Santurce amateur team when he first met Pedrín in 1931. Hiram Bithorn, the first Puerto Rican big leaguer, also played for All-Santurce. Santurce comprises part of San Juan, Puerto Rico's capital.

"I became friends with Pedrín in the early 1930s when his Buick team played their home games at the Las Casas Racetrack in Barrio Obrero," said Ramírez de Arellano. "There were several other amateur teams in Santurce — the Cubs and the Stars ... baseball had become very popular throughout Santurce. Our All-Santurce club became known as the 'Cangrejeros' (Crabbers) since some of us lived in the Condado section known as 'Cangrejo Arriba' … others were from Santurce's Loiza Street area, 'Cangrejo Abajo.'"

It was Ramírez de Arellano who coined the nickname "Cangrejeros" for the Santurce franchise when it joined Puerto Rico's Semi-Pro League in 1939–40, the league's second season. He had been born in Santurce and spent his childhood in the Condado section before moving to Stop 20 near a trolley stop. Ramírez de Arellano commuted to and from the university on the trolley. Stop 20 has been Santurce's hub for various generations and close to movie theaters, restaurants, shops, government offices, Central High School, a farmers' market, among other places.

"Rafael Muñiz, Mike Pasarell, Héctor Nevares, Toño Palerm, and I were among those who assisted Pedrín with fund raising, staffing, and other operational aspects for the Santurce franchise and we went to board meetings, but Pedrín ran the show," said Ramírez de Arellano, who later took the nickname "Don Guindo" in honor of a racehorse. "We liked Pedrín very much and did whatever was possible to make his dream a reality."

Panchicú Toste, a long-time resident of Santurce's Miramar section, helped contact area businesses for promotional assistance and sold season tickets or "abonos" to companies and individuals. Toste later developed a penchant for statistics and wrote three booklets on Puerto Rico's league.

"The Santurce Baseball Club was created by Pedrín with the help of other sports-minded people who were not in it for the money," said Toste. "That was nearly 60 years ago and a different era … a special time for us."

Toste might have added that Santurce's catalysts did not have huge cash reserves to cover the team's costs. Carlos Pieve, who later became a General Manager and a baseball columnist, recalls that his mother did the pertinent alterations and sewing for Santurce's first uniforms pro bono. Mrs. Pieve and her husband were rabid San Juan fans who lived in the Puerta de Tierra section of the city, an enclave that predominantly supported the San Juan Senators ballclub.

Pedrín and Rafael Muñiz stopped by the Pieve household one day with two huge boxes full of uniforms, outfits without the team name or numerals. Pedrín had a list with the players' sizes, and felt to be used for the team name and numerals. Carlos Pieve later pointed out that his mother truly enjoyed that experience, and that it brought her closer to the game of baseball.[3]

1939–40: The "Softball Team"

League rules allowed for three imports per team, and Pedrín secured Billy Byrd, Josh Gibson, and Dick Seay. Pedrín's sincerity and warmth came through to the Negro Leaguers who barnstormed in Puerto Rico during the mid–1930s. It was there that he first met and interacted with Gibson, Seay, Satchel Paige, Ray Dandridge, and other ballplayers who later played for Santurce. Pedrín finally had his ballclub.

Pedrín called Josh Gibson the "Bambino of the Caribbean" for the hitting prowess he displayed in Puerto Rico and in the Dominican Republic. Gibson's other nickname in Puerto Rico was "Trucutú," named after a popular cartoon hero. Dick Seay had played for the Humacao Oriental Grays in 1938–39, and began the 1939–40 season as Santurce's player-manager. Josh Gibson took over as player-manager after his arrival in Puerto Rico.

Santurce opened the 56-game season with an October 1, 1939 twin-bill at Aguadilla, the other expansion team. They would end the season on April 7, 1940 against the same team.[4] Aguadilla's home games were at Parque Colón with seating capacity for 2,500 fans.[5] Leon Day blanked Santurce in the Sunday morning opener before the Crabbers came back to win game two. Day shared some memories of that season with me two years before his passing.

"Aguadilla paid me $20 a week ... it was a lot of fun living on the beach," said Day. "There were good rivalries ... Ponce had [Juan] Guilbe; Satchel Paige and I had a few duels; Partlow was with San Juan ... Cabrera and Billy Byrd could throw the ball for Santurce."

Byrd and Cabrera worked in tandem with one starting the Sunday morning game and the other toiling in the afternoon. Sportswriters made predictions in their pre-game columns as was the case when *El Mundo*'s Vibrián T. Sana stated that Ponce would sweep Santurce in week two.

"I am sorry for Don Guindo, who will be saddened by the onslaught of the Pirates," wrote Sana. "Beware of a shutout."[6]

The Ponce-Santurce games took added meaning since the Crabbers' third baseman, Tingo Daviú, had piloted and played for Ponce in 1938–39. Daviú was the first Puerto Rican to play organized baseball in the States, having joined Allentown of the Eastern League in the late 1920s.[7] He was one of Santurce's oldest players, and played a key role in getting fellow Ponce native Luis Raúl Cabrera to sign with Santurce.

Ponce management passed up on signing "Cabrerita" prior to the 1939–40 season since they felt the youngster was too frail and did not have an overpowering delivery.[8] But Daviú begged to differ and suggested that Pedrín sign the sidearm hurler. Santurce's current owner, Reinaldo "Poto" Paniagua, remembers Cabrera's delivery and his emergence as the team's franchise player of the 1940s.

"Cabrerita became the nemesis of San Juan and the franchise player because it took Santurce a few years to develop a larger following," said Paniagua. "His fingers would touch the dirt after those sidearm pitches; his knuckleball and slider were hard to hit ... he had great success...."

Cabrera struggled his rookie season, but was given a helping hand by Josh Gibson. Gibson missed the first three Sundays of the season, but did arrive at the Isla Grande Airport via a Pan Am clipper on October 20, 1939. Among those to greet him were Pedrín, Cabrerita, Don Guindo, Rafael Muñiz, and Mike Pasarell.[9] The 27-year-old slugger worked out the next day and then caught both games of Santurce's October 22, 1939 twin-bill against San Juan. Fans had eagerly awaited this moment for over a month since reading an *El Mundo* column by Arturo Gigante on Gibson's clouts at Griffith Stadium in Washington, D.C.; Pittsburgh's Forbes Field; and Yankee Stadium.

San Juan and Santurce split their twin-bill at Escambrón Stadium, with Raymond Brown winning the opener for the Senators, and Billy Byrd returning the favor in game two. Some Santurce fans put it best: "They defeated us, 3–2, in the morning with Brown, and we beat them, 3–2, in the afternoon, with Byrd."[10]

Escambrón Stadium was later renamed Sixto Escobar Stadium in honor of Puerto Rico's first world boxing champion, a bantamweight. Santurce and San Juan shared this stadium for 23 seasons. It was located across from the statuesque Normandie Hotel, and a few bus stops from historic Old San Juan, the oldest city under the U.S. flag. Escambrón/ Escobar Stadium could seat about 13,000 fans between its grandstands, box seat chairs,

Pedrín Zorrilla greets Josh Gibson upon his arrival at Isla Grande on October 20, 1939 (courtesy of Diana Zorrilla).

and the bleachers. It was a comfortable stadium where one could feel the presence of the Caribbean trade winds. A large scoreboard and some pine trees in the background were stadium fixtures for many years.

Santurce's line-up in their first game against San Juan featured Oscar Mangual in right; Dick Seay at short; third baseman Tingo Daviú; Josh Gibson catching; Billy Byrd in center; Monchile Concepción in left; Guillermo Angulo at first; Fellito Concepción playing second; and Luis Raúl Cabrera on the mound. San Juan had shortstop Millito Martínez; third baseman Rafael Quintana; Gene "Bicicleta" Benson in center; Clarence Palm behind the plate; Pepe Santana at first; Raymond Brown pitching; Nenené Rivera at second; Georgie Calderón in right; and, Rafael Polanco in left.[11]

The inspiration behind this "City Championship" was Don Guindo.

"I created Santurce's first banner," said Don Guindo. "It then occurred to me that a battle for the city's supremacy would stimulate fan interest and attendance. Pablito Albanese from the Sport Shop gave me a special 'City Champ' banner ... and San Juan won it [in 1939–40]. I gave it to either Billo Torruella or Benjamín Acosta at the end of that season."

A lot of the excitement from that first double-header against San Juan was tempered by a 23–0 loss to Guayama and their ace, Satchel Paige, on November 5, 1939.[12] It was the worst defeat ever suffered by a Santurce team in its 60-year history, and Paige's first of 19 regular season wins, the most ever in league play.[13] Guayama cracked 28 hits in this rout. Baseball historian Eduardo Valero and Poto Paniagua recalled that Santurce was called a "Softball Team" during their first few years of existence. The team was ridiculed by the sportswriters and fans alike for a time.

Santurce stalled San Juan's first half pennant run by sweeping a December 10, 1939 twin-bill, giving Santurce three wins in eight meetings with their arch rivals, but more importantly, much needed respect. Poto Paniagua noted that Santurce's strong showing against San Juan in future seasons was poetic justice due to obstacles put in place by San Juan officials vis-à-vis the inception of Santurce's franchise.

Sportswriters played a major role in building up the rivalry. Carlos García de la Noceda, the league president through 1944–45, wrote for *El Mundo* under the pseudonym "Manolo El Leñero." He dissected Santurce's sweep of San Juan like a coroner would do an autopsy. Cabrerita had won his first game versus San Juan and earned a great ovation at game's end.

"The admiration and goodwill was for the kid who had left Ponce three months earlier … Cabrera's faith was shown by his constant smile," wrote Manolo El Leñero. "San Juan fans were disappointed … and from the middle of the game began treating and respecting Santurce as worthy opponents … the muscular Josh Gibson cajoled Cabrerita on to victory."[14]

Gibson captivated the crowd with a game-winning 475-foot homer to left center in game one and scored the only run in game two to break up a scoreless pitching duel between Hiram Bithorn and Billy Byrd. San Juan's fans lamented not clinching the first half title, but witnessed baseball that "is worth more than a title."[15]

Rafael Pont Flores wrote a classic piece on Santurce's ups and downs shortly after Christmas 1939. The team's "headquarters" were at Stop 20, and they were the "ugly duckling" of the Semi-Pro League, a second division team, a softball team. Josh Gibson, or "Crustaceo Monumentalis," was the team leader. Santurce got plaudits for "intoxicating" San Juan.[16]

Santurce tied Aguadilla for the fourth spot in the second half after finishing sixth when the first half ended. Aguadilla faced more serious problems, which required them to put up a $175 guarantee through a local realtor to cover second half-game expenses. Concern was expressed by some officials and fans about the post season. They felt more teams should be eligible for post-season play with a payoff being better attendance. Extra revenues could be used for increasing player salaries that were about $10–$15/week for the native players, and perhaps $20-$30/week for the imports.

Josh Gibson and Leon Day left their clubs just before season's end to play in Venezuela. Gibson had finished second in the batting chase to Perucho Cepeda of Guayama prior to joining Centauros of Caracas. Juan Vené, the veteran baseball writer and commentator from Venezuela, got first-hand looks at Gibson in Caracas circa April 1940. Vené's godfather was Miguel Antonio Rivas, the owner of San Agustín Stadium in southern Caracas where Centauros played their home games.

"I was 11 at the time and we would see Gibson and other American players at a hotel in Caracas," said Vené. "Gibson was a joy to watch … he could hit the ball a mile."

1940–41: Santurce Reaches the Finals

Santurce reached the league championship series by winning the second half title, but lost a seven-game series to Caguas. Clarence Palm took over the catching when Josh Gibson became unavailable. Raymond Brown replaced Billy Byrd when Byrd opted to sign with Caguas. Dick Seay returned and Pedrín Zorrilla managed the team. Luis Cabrera was the league MVP.

Pedrín did everything possible to sign Josh Gibson, but found an adequate replacement in Clarence Palm. Raymond Brown had posted a 14–0 record with San Juan over the past two winters with Palm as his catcher. The Crabbers signed former Aguadilla infielder Efraín "Pee Wee" Merced and ex-San Juan flychaser Georgie Calderón. Mayagüez outfielder Pedro Jaime Reyes was obtained in a trade for Monchile Concepción.

Don Guindo entertained *El Mundo*'s readers with a pre-season piece. He called Santurce "El equipo de las mil emociones" (the team of a thousand emotions) and predicted a title with the one-two punch of Raymond Brown and Cabrerita. The outfield was better with Pedro Jaime in left, Manuel Archeval in center, and Georgie Calderón in right. Wichie Calderón and Tingo Daviú manned the infield corners with Fellito Concepción and Dick Seay as the middle infielders.[17]

The signing of Raymond Brown was a coup since Pedrín outbid team owners in Cuba and Mexico for the hurler. Pedrín had departed for the States on August 31, 1940, nearly two months before the regular season opener, to sign Brown for a reputed $50 a week.[18] Josh Gibson could not be contacted at the time since he was playing in Mexico.

Santurce's 42-game season began with a split against San Juan. The Crabbers went into a tailspin and finished the first half dead last. Raymond Brown was not effective and neither were the hitters. Rafael Muñiz wrote a detailed article on Santurce's repeated efforts to contact Josh Gibson. Dick Seay finally got hold of Mrs. Gibson via phone around Thanksgiving time and was told that Josh was working on home repairs and might be available in a month. But shortly after Christmas she told the Santurce brass that Josh's "extended vacation" would continue.[19]

Efforts were made to sign James "Cool Papa" Bell, Ray Dandridge, and Leroy Matlock. Dandridge was playing in Cuba and required two round trip plane tickets, one for himself and one for his wife. This could not get done by January 29, 1941, the deadline for making roster changes. Neither Bell nor Matlock could be reached.

Santurce responded in the abbreviated second half to win 11 of 14 games and advance to the finals. Raymond Brown got things started by shutting out San Juan, 1–0, and inducing Monte Irvin to hit into a bases loaded fielder's choice to end the game.[20]

"I recall the enthusiasm of the San Juan and Santurce fans when we played each other," said Irvin. "They made it fun for us...."

The Crabbers swept San Juan to clinch the City Championship and won three of their next four games, including a sweep of Humacao. Pedrín received a commemorative banner from Santurce's fans prior to the Humacao contests for winning the city title. Raymond Brown hurled another shutout and Cabrera won game two. The defensive gem was made by Humacao outfielder Fellé Delgado on a long drive to left center by Manuel Archeval. Luis Rosario, Jr., *El Imparcial*'s sports editor, wrote, "Santurce went from being the most erratic team to a top club."[21]

Fellé Delgado recalled those days as a fun time when we conversed at Hiram Bithorn

Stadium some 52 years later. Delgado played with the New York Cubans in the summer of 1941, and found the brand of Puerto Rico baseball to be of high quality like the Negro Leagues, yet fun with the games played on Sundays.

Santurce fans went bonkers when they swept Caguas on March 2, 1941, to give the Crabbers a one-game lead in the second half. Raymond Brown pitched a 15-inning shutout to win game one, 1–0, before Cabrera's 6–0 victory in game two.[22] Angel "Mickey" Armada, who became a bank executive and one of Puerto Rico's foremost baseball statisticians, was there.

"My family lived and died with Caguas," said Armada. "We lived near the Caguas ballpark, but those games were at Escambrón. Raymond Brown drove in the only run of the first game … went out to have a late lunch and back to see Cabrerita shut us out in game two … it was the first and only time in league history that a team did not score in 24 innings in one day!"

Cabrera won against Mayagüez the following Sunday, before polishing off Guayama and their ace, Satchel Paige, in the final regular season game. Santurce had clinched their final series berth and Cabrera swayed the sportswriters in winning league MVP honors. Luis Rosario, Jr. noted that Cabrera's consistency was a plus in helping Santurce "rise from the ashes just like the Phoenix."[23]

The finals opened at Escambrón on March 23, 1941. U.S. Federal Court Judge Robert Cooper threw out the first pitch. He was flanked by Carlos García de la Noceda, Caguas owner Rafael Delgado Márquez, Pedrín, and Rafael Muñiz. Raymond Brown then pitched a 12-inning shutout in a 1–0 morning win over Billy Byrd. Caguas won the afternoon game, 8–1.[24]

Caguas hosted two games a week hence when Byrd bested Brown in game one and Cabrera outpitched Rogelio Wiscovitch that afternoon. Caguas fan Pedro Montañez, Puerto Rico's boxing "Champion Without a Crown," was at the ballpark along with former world boxing champ Kid Chocolate from Cuba.[25]

Both teams rested during the week before renewing the series at Escambrón on Saturday. Puerto Rico's governor, Guy J. Swope, threw a strike at 3 p.m. prior to the single game, but neither Brown nor Byrd were sharp in Santurce's 9–6 win. Pedrín hoped that Cabrera would win game six the next morning.

Cabrera took a 2–0 lead into the last of the fifth when he unraveled after Manolo García tripled and scored on a fielder's choice. Caguas player-manager Pepe Seda reached first when Dick Seay's throw home was wide. Seda gave the bunt sign to Leonard Pearson and Luis Olmo, and both bunted for hits to load the bases. The 19-year-old Roy Campanella hit a sidearm curve ball over the left field fence to put Caguas ahead, 5–2. Caguas fans took up a collection for Campanella and ran to the area near home plate to give him the cash before hoisting him up on their shoulders.

Caguas scored four more times off a dejected Cabrera plus five additional runs to take a 14–2 lead. The 14 runs in one inning have never been duplicated in a league regular nor post-season game.[26] Héctor Barea was the Caguas batboy and not quite nine years old at the time.

"After the morning game I went with my dad, Salvador, and the Caguas President, Mr. Delgado Márquez, to have lunch at the house of Don Heraldo Lizardi, a family friend and a brother-in-law of Luis Olmo," said Barea. "We were on the verge of winning a title … and we did win it."

Caguas center fielder Manolo García got things going in game seven with a triple off

Raymond Brown. The Criollos scored four runs en route to a 6–2 win. Billy Byrd went the distance on less than 24 hours rest. [27] Pepe Seda and utility player, Pito Alvarez de la Vega, had clutch hits.

1941–42: Josh Gibson Hits Them Out

Josh Gibson hit a circuit-leading .480 with 13 homers in garnering League MVP honors. Vidal López, the Venezuelan pitcher-outfielder, did well, but the Crabbers lost a lot of close games. Ponce shined with Juan Guilbe and Raymond Brown on the mound, and the hitting of Pancho Coímbre, Howard Easterling, and Sammy Bankhead. They won both halves to win it all.

Pedrín was confident that Josh Gibson would arrive in Puerto Rico by the third week of October 1941. Gibson had completed a summer season in Mexico and needed to take care of some legal business with the Homestead Grays. Pedrín also had to contend with an unhappy Raymond Brown, whose asking price went up to more than $50/week plus a furnished apartment in Santurce with all the trappings and round trip air or steamship fare.[28] Brown became Santurce's first holdout and Pedrín opted to sell him to Ponce for $500, an unheard of sum at the time.[29] Brown finalized his travel plans a few weeks into the season, and upon his arrival, Ponce owner Martiniano "El Lider" García, sent Pedrín the $500.[30]

Vidal López, a.k.a. "El Muchachote de Barlovento," did not create any problems for Pedrín. López arrived in San Juan on the steamship *Cuba* the Friday before the 1941–42 season began. He cleared Customs and went to the offices of El Imparcial to meet with Luis Rosario, Jr., and with Santurce's treasurer, Luis F. Torres. Rosario and Torres commented that López had the same skill levels as Alejandro Carrasquel and would be in the majors if darker-skinned players had a chance to play there.[31]

Juan Vené told me that López had a swarthy complexion and was a shade over six feet tall. Barlovento was in the northeast part of Venezuela, and hence, Vidal's nickname. Vené had seen him pitch for Magallanes many times in the "Estadio Miranda," the stadium where López won pitching duels with Alejandro Carrasquel, Venezuela's first big leaguer and the uncle of Chico Carrasquel. Alejandro Carrasquel once told López that "I lament not being able to take you to the U.S. so you can play in the big leagues."[32]

Santurce lost twice to Aguadilla to open the season, but Pedrín was not concerned. Vidal López had a bad first inning in his outing, but came back to fan 11, including the side in the fourth when Juan Sánchez and Willie Wells were two victims.[33]

Josh Gibson's arrival on October 21, 1941, created excitement. He was greeted at Isla Grande by Pedrín, Don Guindo, Clarence Palm, Cabrera, and others. When asked how he felt, Gibson responded, "I'm in good shape, having played in Mexico. I come to help Santurce win the Professional Baseball Championship." [34]

Gibson made a good point, since the league was no longer called a Semi-Pro one. Hand and finger injuries sustained in a Santurce practice precluded Gibson from making his debut against Ponce the next Sunday. Clarence Palm filled in and caught Vidal López's shutout against the Lions in game one, a game where Dick Seay hit his only Santurce homer (an inside-the-park one). Vidal López also homered in that win.[35]

Island baseball fans eagerly read an *El Imparcial* feature on October 29, 1941, listing Cum Posey's top two Black All-Star teams for 1941. "First team" members in Puerto Rico, or on their way there, included Josh Gibson, Ray Dandridge, Howard Easterling, Monte Irvin, and Bill Wright. Posey had built the Homestead Grays into the premier Negro Leagues team.

Santurce swept San Juan on the first Sunday in November without Josh Gibson. A good crowd was on hand to see Vidal López face Terris McDuffie in game one. Crabber fans roared when López fanned Irvin and got McDuffie to hit into an eighth inning double play to preserve the 2–1 lead. López had driven in both Santurce runs with a single, while Irvin's sacrifice fly accounted for San Juan's only run.[36]

Vibrián T. Sana of *El Mundo* alluded to the enthusiasm prevalent that day. Many of San Juan's fans had bet that the Senators would sweep Santurce with both games decided by one or two runs. Georgie Calderón made the play of the day when he robbed Rafael Polanco of a hit in game one. Vidal López was carried off the field by the Santurce fans after his win.[37]

Gibson sprung into action on November 9, 1941 when Santurce was swept by Guayama. Clarence Palm was inactivated and made a coach, prior to his signing with Humacao. Gibson homered in game one against Barney Brown and had an RBI single in game two versus Rafaelito Ortíz.[38]

Santurce took two games from Mayagüez the next Sunday behind the pitching of López and Cabrera.[39] Buster Clarkson was Mayagüez's best hitter and they also had catcher William Perkins, Millán Clara at second, and pitcher-outfielder Tite Figueroa. Ismael Trabal, Mayagüez's first batboy who later became a sportswriter, broadcaster, and public relations officer with that franchise, noted that Clarkson had hit two homers in one inning for Mayagüez in 1940–41, and that his range and arm at shortstop were good.

Puerto Rico's newspapers were running Marín Rum ads at this point with either Cabrera or Don Guindo, Vidal López, and Josh Gibson in the photo. Gibson might be holding the bottle, which represented the fourth "ace" in poker. The Marín Rum Company was Santurce's first corporate sponsor. This explained the use of the term Santurce-Marín in press clippings of the early 1940s. Ismael Trabal recalled that Manuel Marín opened his rum company or "licorería" on the road going past Mayaguez's current ballpark, Isidoro García Stadium, en route to Joyudas. Mr. Marín had first owned a Mayagüez drugstore before getting into the rum business.

Don Guindo remembers that Josh Gibson loved various brands of Puerto Rican rum as well as "batata dulce" (similar to sweet potato). Gibson made some trips to Manatí during the week to enjoy the hospitality of Pedrín and his relatives. Enriqueta Marcano Zorrilla, Pedrín's niece, fondly recalls the time a car got stuck in a ditch and marveled at Josh Gibson's strength in single-handedly lifting the car out of it.

"Pedrín was a bachelor at the time," said Enriqueta. "The Santurce players would come to Pedrín's house in Manatí ... I would see them from the time I was a young girl ... they were my heroes and they all loved Pedrín, whose generosity knew no bounds."

One player Pedrín wanted to sign was Ray Dandridge. He dispatched Luis F. Torres to the States in early December 1941 to finalize terms with him. When Dandridge arrived at Isla Grande via Pan Am clipper on December 9, 1941, he was met by Josh Gibson, Dick Seay, and team officials. Seay was made a coach so that Dandridge could take his roster spot.[40]

Seay's final games that season came in a December 7, 1941 twin-bill against Caguas. Roy Campanella, the Caguas catcher, was reading a newspaper and listening to the radio that morning, when a bulletin in Spanish suddenly interrupted the music. Pearl Harbor had been bombed by the Japanese Air Force. League games were played that Sunday, and Campanella recalls that Caguas won both contests.[41]

The season's first half ended two weeks later with Santurce four games off the pace set by Guayama, Ponce, and San Juan. They had lost six games by one run.[42] Four Santurce players were selected for the league All-Star games played on January 1, 1942. It had been three years since the league's first All-Star game took place in 1938–39.

Both All-Star games pitted the Northeast team of Caguas, Humacao, San Juan, and Santurce, against the Southeast team with Aguadilla, Guayama, Mayagüez, and Ponce players. Luis Cabrera, Ray Dandridge, Josh Gibson, and Vidal López were the Santurce quartet. They were joined by Caguas stars Byrd, Campanella, Sammy Céspedes, Manolo García, and Luis Olmo; Monte Irvin, Gerardo Rodríguez, Freddie Thon, Sr., and Bill Wright of San Juan; and, Willard Brown of Humacao. The Southeast squad featured Sam Bankhead, Barney and Raymond Brown, Buster Clarkson, Pancho Coímbre, Leon Day, Quincy Trouppe, Willie Wells, among others.[43]

Cabrera started game one, a 7–3 win, aided by Bill Wright's homer. Josh Gibson took over for Campanella behind the plate in the eighth, and then caught the second game. Gibson's two long homers in game two paved the way for an 8–3 Northeast win.[44]

Manolo García recalled that the first homer was a towering shot off Leon Day, and that Gibson grinned when rounding the bases. That grin became a laugh after the second blast. Gibson was on a tear.

The next seven weeks belonged to Gibson. Ismael Trabal witnessed a 450-foot shot at Mayagüez's Liga París, which knocked a fan from a tree. Gibson was aggressive in running the bases. When a good base stealer got on, Trabal stated that Gibson would let a pitch drop in front of him and challenge the runner to steal second. [45]

Gibson's best day at the plate was a three-homer display versus Aguadilla on January 11, 1942, according to Víctor Navarro. A long blast in the morning game against Leon Day was followed by two more in game two. Luis Rosario, Jr. compared this display to Gibson's three homers in one game against Cuba's Almendares club some six years earlier at Escambrón.[46] Almendares featured Alejandro Oms, Isidro Fabré, Cocaína García, Lázaro Salazar, among other fine players, in that barnstorming series.

Gibson now had 10 homers, and had surpassed the league record at the time of eight, set by Campanella and Buck Leonard in 1940–41. Gibson's 11th and 12th homers came against San Juan on February 8, 1942.[47] Freddie Thon, Sr. gave up number 11, a three-run shot, that helped Vidal López win game one. Homer number 12 in the afternoon, was hit in a San Juan win. Freddie Thon, Jr. rooted for San Juan, but liked watching Josh Gibson and stars from the other league teams. Thon, Jr. witnessed the longest homer ever hit in Puerto Rico's Winter League (Josh Gibson's 13th homer of 1941–42), and the last one Gibson hit in Puerto Rico.

It was a 600-foot rocket that sailed over Escobar's pine trees on its way to the Escambrón Beach. Arecibo, the former Humacao franchise, was the opposing team on March 1, 1942.[48] Several historians told me that this shot was at least 65 feet longer than Frank Howard's 536-foot homer for Caguas against San Juan at Escobar in the 1960–61 final series.

"Josh Gibson was in his prime and there was no better hitter in Puerto Rico, or perhaps in organized baseball from what dad said," stated Freddie Thon, Jr. "Gibson was just so strong."

Gibson and Dandridge left Puerto Rico on March 5, 1942, so each missed the last Sunday of the season. One of Gibson's final activities was an exhibition basketball game

Josh Gibson, "Bambino of the Caribbean," 1941–42 (courtesy of Diana Zorrilla).

between some of the league's top imports and Arecibo High School. Gibson's hoop team-mates were Buster Clarkson, Howard Easterling, Raymond Brown, Dick Seay, Quincy Trouppe, and Harry Williams. Arecibo's Willard Brown reinforced the high school team.

Guigo Otero Suro, who later became a Santurce official and league president, was a fine university basketball player who recalled playing hoop games with and against Josh Gibson and Dick Seay during the week. "In the early 1940s we played some rough pick-up games," said Otero Suro. "It was a lot of fun … after the games we had some beer and Gibson could down two huge jugs of brew … were times he drank from both at once."

Gibson did not have time to celebrate being named league MVP and getting a huge trophy. It was the high point of his professional baseball career, and the first trophy he had ever received, since the Negro Leagues did not give out trophies.[49]

1942–43 to 1944–45: The War Years

The number of league teams was cut in half, from eight to four, during World War II. No imports graced Puerto Rico's diamonds in 1942–43 nor in 1943–44, but imports returned in 1944–45. Some Caguas players were signed by Santurce as part of a merger or fusion, since Caguas was one of four teams to lose their franchise. Luis Olmo tied Pancho Coímbre for league MVP honors. Santurce faced Ponce in the 1942–43 finals, but fell short. Ponce went on to win the 1943–44 and 1944–45 titles. Santurce's Rookies of the Year those two seasons were "Jueyito" Andrades and Alfonso Gerard.

Austerity was the buzzword. The four-team schedule had 36 games in 1942–43, and 48 games the next two seasons. Mergers/fusions were done for geographical reasons and to create balance, according to Eduardo Valero.

"Guayama and San Juan fused as did Caguas and Santurce," said Valero. "Ponce and Arecibo plus Mayagüez/Aguadilla were part of the fusion."

Valero had a valid point for 1942–43, since only two-and-a-half games separated the four teams by season's end. Santurce earned a final series berth by winning the 24-game first half. Ponce won the 12-game second half on their way to a second straight title.[50]

A trio of former Caguas stars (Sammy Céspedes, Manolo García, and Luis Olmo) came through for Santurce. Player-manager Olmo had a superb all-around season as he led the league in homers; tied for second in RBI; and was third in runs scored. He tied Pancho Coímbre, as the League's Co-MVPs. Olmo then made his 1943 big league debut with the Brooklyn Dodgers.[51]

"It was fun managing and playing for Pedrín," said Olmo. "I was 23 at the time and we had a good season. But the league was not quite as strong then as compared to the earlier seasons with Caguas."

The former Caguas stars played in two league All-Star games for the combined San Juan-Santurce, or North team, sans imports. Mayagüez and Ponce's native players were the South team. Pitching prevailed as the North swept both games, 3–2 and 3–0, on Three King's Day, January 6, 1943. Three King's Day is like a second Christmas and a major Puerto Rico holiday. Olmo had an RBI single in game one before San Juan's Fellé Delgado drove in Perucho Cepeda with the winning run. Freddie Thon, Sr. helped his own cause in game two with sterling pitching and a two-run single. Millito Martínez of Santurce drove in the second game's other run.[52]

Santurce hosted Ponce on Valentine's Day 1943 to open the final series. Luis Olmo received the Santurce MVP trophy prior to the morning game and Senator Allen J. Ellender from Louisiana threw out the first pitch. Ponce took game one, 11–2, behind Rafaelito Ortíz. Santurce retaliated with a 4–2 win in game two. A big moment in that game was when Rogelio Wiscovitch caught Pancho Coímbre looking for a called third strike. Wiscovitch got a standing ovation for this feat, since Coímbre had not struck out in the regular season. Olmo created more applause with an inside-the-park homer.[53]

Ponce swept Santurce at Charles H. Terry Park the next Sunday. The Lions then won game five at Escobar Stadium six days later to win the title. Rafaelito Ortíz was the hero with three of Ponce's four wins. Juan Guilbe got credit for the other win in relief of Planchardón Quiñónes. Pancho Coímbre hit .533 to lead all series hitters. Sportswriter Francisco Soto Respeto gave George Scales a lot of credit, based on how he handled his club during the season's second half and in the finals.[54]

Scales, a former Negro Leagues second baseman, enjoyed Puerto Rico's amenities and hospitality. He led Ponce to a third straight title in 1943–44 when the Lions won 37 of 44 games. Rafaelito Ortíz went 15–0 for Ponce and Pancho Coímbre finished second in the batting chase to Santurce's Tetelo Vargas.[55]

Tetelo Vargas was a 37-year-old veteran from the Dominican Republic and Coímbre's teammate with the New York Cubans in the Negro Leagues. Vargas, known as the "Gamo Dominicano" (Dominican Deer), was at the end of his Negro Leagues career, but played 10 more winters in Puerto Rico.

Luis Cabrera and "Larú" Velázquez pitched well for Santurce in 1943–44 without much run support. Both hurled in the league All-Star game on January 6, 1944. Luis Olmo managed Santurce to a second place finish, but did not play in the regular season nor in the All-Star game. Jueyito Andrades, the Rookie of the Year, made the play of the game in preserving the 6–5 win for the North (San Juan and Santurce) team against the South (Ponce and Mayagüez).

Ponce's Cocó Ferrer hit a shot down the third base line with two outs in the ninth. Andrades robbed Ferrer of an extra base hit in snagging the smash and forcing Fernando Ramos at second. Andrades' prize was a sweater![56] He reminded the writers of his RBI single to drive in the North's first run and his stolen base preceding Tetelo Vargas's RBI hit. Efraín Blassini of Santurce scored the game-winner on a double by Sammy Céspedes. These All-Star games were discontinued for the next five seasons.

An important rule change for 1944–45 was to once again allow three imports per team. Pedrín signed Roy Campanella and Terris McDuffie. But that did not stop Ponce from winning a fourth straight title after roaring through both halves of the season.

Roy Campanella referred to Santurce as the "Shell Oil Team" in his 1959 autobiography. Campanella spoke Spanish quite well, having played summer ball for Monterrey in Mexico and winter ball with Marianao in Cuba.

Puerto Rico's ballplayers would travel in groups of three to five by car to the various ballparks, based on Campanella's recollections of his seasons with Caguas and Santurce. Campanella loved Puerto Rico's beaches, docks, and piers, and the yachts at Santurce's Club Nautico. He fished a lot and listed fried plantains and papaya among his favorite local food.[57]

Terris McDuffie pitched well in spurts, but not as effectively as Cabrera, who defeated Ponce three times in a 24-hour period. He relieved Gerardo Rodríguez in the third inning on Saturday, January 20, 1945, and got credit for the win. Cabrera was summoned to relieve in game one of the next day's twin-bill, and gave up the tying run before Santurce

Left to Right: Pedrín Zorrilla, Luis Raúl Cabrera, Rafael Muñiz, 1944–45 (courtesy of Diana Zorrilla).

Roy Campanella, Santurce's catcher, 1944–45 season (courtesy of Diana Zorrilla).

1944–45 Santurce Crabbers with the Seven-Up logo. *Front, L to R:* Monchile Concepción, Sammy Céspedes, Roy Campanella, Momo Pérez. *Standing, L to R:* Luis Raúl Cabrera, Alfonso Gerard, Pedro Jaime Reyes, Juan Sánchez, Terris McDuffie, Rafael Muñiz, Gina Carmoega (godmother), Pedrín Zorrilla, Gerardo Rodríguez, Heriberto Rivera, Nenené Rivera (courtesy of Diana Zorrilla).

pulled it out. Game two was tied at one when Cabrera came on in the sixth. Santurce scored six times in the home sixth to give Cabrera a "trifecta."[58]

Outfielder Alfonso Gerard made his Santurce debut a good one in 1944–45 by hitting .348 and tying "Canena" Márquez of Mayagüez for Rookie of the Year honors. Juan Sánchez hit .341 and led the league in doubles.[59] Gerard was the first U.S. Virgin Islands player to play for Santurce while Sánchez had proven himself earlier in the decade as a member of the Aguadilla club.

Seven-Up had become Santurce's corporate sponsor in the mid–1940s. Pedrín was not too keen on corporate sponsors and their logos, but these companies did help cover operational expenses.

1945–46

Santurce had their worst season on the field finishing last. Josh Gibson returned, but faltered at the plate and off the field. "Vitín" Cruz picked up some of the slack behind the plate in becoming Santurce's third straight Rookie of the Year. Fernando Zegrí was the new League President, albeit for one season. San Juan won their first championship.

San Juan's happiest fan may have been Freddie Thon, Jr. He traveled with his dad and other San Juan players to Ponce and Mayagüez. The younger Thon was San Juan's batboy, and he relished that role.

"Two of our funniest players were Fellé Delgado and pitcher Francisco Sostre," said Thon, Jr. "They were always joking and telling funny stories ... the real inspiration on that club was Monte Irvin ... he hit a pinch-hit double with a fractured wrist ... nothing can top that."

On the flip side, Josh Gibson was going through some hard times. There were no home runs for him that winter. An aunt of Freddie Thon, Sr. saw Gibson go berserk in the Rio Piedras section of San Juan.

"Gibson ran in front of the tuberculosis center near the 'Oso Blanco' penitentiary," said Freddie Thon, Jr. "It took seven or eight men to hold him down ... this was very sad."

Pedrín was quite concerned about Gibson's frame of mind, and helped him return to Pittsburgh for a long rest prior to his final season with the Homestead Grays. Gibson's replacement with Santurce, Vitín Cruz, did a good job as the catcher in earning Rookie of the Year honors. Luis Cabrera missed Gibson's friendship and presence, but led the league in strikeouts for a second straight season.[60] Tetelo Vargas was Santurce's best hitter.

Perucho Cepeda, Tetelo's former teammate with some great Guayama teams of the late 1930s and early 1940s, played second base and the outfield for the Crabbers. His biggest booster and fan was his son Orlando, also known as "Peruchín."

"I went to Escobar to see dad's first game with Santurce ... it was against Mayagüez and went into extra innings ... 'El Tigre' [Cabrera] pitched very well that day," said Orlando Cepeda. "My formative years were spent in the Tras Talleres section of Santurce ... Cerra and Hoare streets which had many Santurce fans ... the San Juan fans lived in Puerta de Tierra and Old San Juan."

Guigo Otero Suro had come on the scene as an advisor to Fernando Zegrí, the new League President. Pedrín got to know and respect Otero Suro as a bright and down-to-earth person who loved sports. Pedrín liked the fact that this young lawyer from Vega Baja had shown Josh Gibson a thing or two about basketball moves during their pick-up games in the early 1940s.

Some challenges facing Pedrín Zorrilla were shared with me by the current Santurce owner, Poto Paniagua, who noted that the San Juan franchise was one impediment. I was seated in Paniagua's office on November 19, 1997, the 504th anniversary of Puerto Rico's discovery by Christopher Columbus, prior to a San Juan-Santurce afternoon baseball game.

"That city rivalry was the foundation for the first dispute before Santurce's 'birth,'" said Paniagua. "They ridiculed Santurce, stating it was a softball team ... within several years, Santurce grew into the league's premier franchise ... later won the first Caribbean Series for Puerto Rico."

Paniagua stated that Santurce became a team for the capital city's "working masses" from the Barrio Obrero sector to Loiza Street enclaves, as well as Miramar and other sections. San Juan's loyal baseball fans tended to live in the Puerta de Tierra and Old San Juan sections of the city. Orlando Cepeda and Poto Paniagua were on the same page when it came to the Santurce Crabbers. Cepeda and his Tras Talleres buddies lived and died with Santurce just like Paniagua and his Miramar friends did in becoming Santurce fans for life.

2. A League Anchor

Those who wait patiently have their moments of happiness. This is mine.
— George Scales, former Santurce manager.

Santurce emerged as a league anchor in the late 1940s with a loyal fan base and their one-two punch of Willard Brown and Bob Thurman, the most feared tandem in league history. Fans came to the Puerto Rico ballparks in droves from 1946–47 — when Willard Brown first put on the Santurce uniform — through the 1953–54 season, Brown's final full season with the Crabbers. League attendance surpassed the 700,000 mark three times during this period.[1]

Santurce's Neighborhoods, Topography, and Baseball Fans

Santurce's topography ranges from sea level along the coast to 100 feet above sea level at its highest points. It is a peninsula with five elevation areas.[2] Santurce was first shown on a map in 1519 as part of San Juan. Spanish officials called Santurce "Cangrejos" during the 16th and 17th centuries due to its crab-shaped layout on a map. Cangrejos became a key transportation link between San Juan and the rest of the island.[3]

The trolley lines established in Santurce circa 1880 set the tone for its growth.[4] Santurce's population was 5,840 residents according to the 1899 U.S. Census of Population ordered by President McKinley, a census taken the year after Puerto Rico changed from being a Spanish to a U.S. possession, following the Spanish-American War.[5] The Jones Act of 1917 granted U.S. citizenship to Puerto Rico's residents.[6]

Santurce's eastern and western portions were used as training grounds by the U.S. Army in World War I, the first global conflict where Puerto Ricans served in the U.S. military. It was common to see military parades around the Las Casas barracks[7] where Pedrín later played amateur baseball.

Ponce de Leon Avenue was Santurce's main artery, with Fernández Juncos running parallel to the south. To the north of Ponce de Leon were the upper middle class and more affluent sections of Condado, Parque, Sacred Heart, and Monte Flores. Miramar was another affluent area. Working class sections near Fernández Juncos included Gandul, Figueroa, Hipódromo, Bolivar, and Tras Talleres, where Orlando Cepeda grew up.

Santurce's Miramar section, according to Santurce baseball fan Manuel Junco, was called "Alto del Olimpo" (Olimpo Heights) due to its topography. Junco grew up in Miramar, a unique section of Santurce with the older Spanish houses. As a young child, Junco would make the trek by foot to Sixto Escobar Stadium ... passing near the Condado Lagoon, over the Dos Hermanos (Two Brothers) Bridge, and toward the stadium.

"I made this trek with dad and my older brother," said Junco. "Once we crossed the Dos Hermanos Bridge, you could see the caravan of cars filled with Santurce fans going to see their heroes. The ticket line outside the stadium reached the Normandie Hotel ... behind Escobar was the huge [Don Q] scoreboard with living bodies inside it who manually filled in the numbers. It was a moving and touching experience."

Dorothy Thurman, Bob Thurman's widow, lived in Miramar's Refugio Street house several months after her August 1947 wedding.

"It was a big house," said Dorothy Thurman. "A lady by the name of Albertina did the cooking ... went down with Bob a number of seasons ... have a lot of fond memories ... enjoyed it."

Freddie Thon, Jr. told me that the house was located near the Black Angus bar/nightclub and the old Isla Grande Navy Base. Charles Ferrer, the son of Santurce's team doctor — Dr. José Carlos Ferrer Otero — recalled this "Casa Club" had a huge living room and sleeping accommodations for three to five imported players and their spouses, as well as the manager.

Miramar featured and still has huge Spanish-style homes. Mara T. Patermaster, a former co-worker of mine circa 1979, lived in Miramar for six years during the 1960s. She remembers Miramar as a neighborhood with character where extended families lived from generation to generation.

"If you just drive through (Miramar), you will see the old Spanish-style homes with stained-glass windows and interior gardens," said Patermaster. "There is a real strong sense of community."

1946–47: Willard Brown's Santurce Debut

Willard "Ese Hombre" Brown made his Santurce debut and won the first of his three league batting titles. Catcher Johnny Hayes and pitcher-outfielder Roy Partlow joined Brown as Santurce's three imports. Clarence Palm managed the Crabbers to a fourth place finish. Guigo Otero Suro became the team's vice-president. Don Guindo returned from his four years of World War II service in Panama.

Brown's batting title with a .390 mark[8] more than made up for Josh Gibson's disappointing 1945–46 season. Pedrín Zorrilla was impressed by Willard Brown, when he played for Humacao in 1941–42 as their second baseman, and as a hard-hitting outfielder with the Kansas City Monarchs.

Dick Seay's friendship with Willard Brown was one reason why Brown opted to sign with Pedrín's Santurce Crabbers. Seay, who now coached Santurce, got along splendidly with the team's number one fan, Don Guindo.

"I would have a bite to eat with Seay and Brown at the El Picolino Bar and Restaurant," said Don Guindo. "Seay could put down that beer."

Don Guindo had returned from four years of military service in Panama. He and Ismael Trabal — who also served in the defense of Panama and the Canal Zone — were two of many Puerto Ricans who defended the U.S. flag during World War II. Don Guindo rarely got mail from Puerto Rico, and missed the anecdotes and stories about the league.

Pedrín counted on plenty of World War II vets for fan support. He was also fortunate in having Guigo Otero Suro as the team's new vice-president. Guigo's legal and negotiating skills came in handy during league board meetings, and he also drafted Willard Brown's contract.

"Pedrín was not a negotiator, so I helped him with this and drafting player contracts," said Guigo. "We wrote Willard Brown and made his travel arrangements ... remember that Pedrín treated players with tenderness and respect, so even players on other teams left the doors open to play for Santurce at a future time since they liked Pedrín."

Santurce's other two imports were pitcher-outfielder Roy Partlow and catcher Johnny Hayes. Partlow's seasons with San Juan included a 1940–41 batting title and a win over Guayama's Satchel Paige in 1939–40. Historian James Riley notes that Partlow had briefly been Jackie Robinson's teammate with the 1946 Montreal Royals, but did not socialize with him (Robinson).[9] Negro Leagues veteran Johnny Hayes had played for Aguadilla in the early 1940s, but did not produce for Santurce.

Pedrín was always on the lookout for talent. Fellito Concepción, the brother of Santurce coach Monchile Concepción, played on the same New York City team with José "Pantalones" Santiago. Monchile tried to sign Pantalones Santiago for Santurce without success. Santiago wanted a $1,000 signing bonus, but Pedrín would not give in.[10]

Pantalones signed with Ponce and earned Rookie of the Year laurels, prior to pitching for the New York Cubans in the Negro Leagues, and several big league teams in the mid–1950s. Pantalones' friendship with Pedrín resulted in his reinforcing Santurce for the 1951 and 1953 Caribbean Series events. They shared the love of baseball and of horse racing.

"Pedrín was my best friend in baseball despite the fact that I pitched for Ponce," said Santiago. "We maintained this close friendship over the years and once co-owned a stable of race horses, the Establo Cangrejero. Pedrín helped me a lot ... once got me a job as a scout with the Chicago Cubs."

A rookie such as Pantalones Santiago might make $35 per week in Puerto Rico League play in 1946–47. Willard Brown and other league stars probably earned two or three times as much. But money was not their "raison d'etre." Love of the game and pleasing the fans mattered most.

1947–48: A Triple Crown for Willard Brown

Willard Brown clubbed an all-time single-season record of 27 homers on his way to winning his first league Triple Crown. Bob Thurman made his Santurce debut. Pedrín signed Satchel Paige during the latter part of the season. Santurce finished third, but missed out on the playoffs since the winners of each "vuelta" or half, qualified for the finals.

This 60-game season belonged to Willard Brown who had a recent stint with the 1947 St. Louis Browns. His only big league homer was the first American League home run ever hit by an African-American player.[11] Brown was in his mid–30s when he returned for a second season with Santurce.

He had an agenda after his unconditional release by the Browns and secured his first of two Puerto Rico Triple Crown seasons with 27 homers, 86 RBI and a .432 batting average.[12]

Brown's slugging percentage was .906, second only to Josh Gibson's standard (.959) set six years earlier.[13] Rubén Gómez told me Willard Brown was the most dominant player he had ever played with, except for Willie Mays.

Poto Paniagua affirmed that Willard Brown was the most productive import that the Puerto Rico Winter League ever had. Paniagua told me that Brown would have been a big league superstar had he (Brown) been given a chance at a much younger age.

Ismael Trabal had just begun his career as a sportswriter in 1947, and recalls a Mayagüez-Santurce game. Patricio Rosario Fremaint, a.k.a. "Spinball," was Mayagüez's radio broadcaster. Juan "Ratón" Pérez, the league's smallest pitcher at 5 feet, three inches, was on the mound. Spinball:

"We have the battle of David vs. Goliath ... the first pitch is fouled off ... the next pitch is a foul and I tell you, Brown cannot hit a fair ball off Ratón Pérez ... Mayagüez's 'David' is winning the battle ... he's ready, pitches ... and Brown hits it out to [expletive]!"

The nickname "Ese Hombre" (that man) was given to Brown by Rafael Pont Flores. Brown received the red carpet treatment in Puerto Rico and rarely passed up the chance to enjoy a meal or a social drink with fans at various bars. Pedrín usually escorted Brown back to the Miramar house.

Brown was a World War II veteran who visited Santurce hospitals and cheered up children, World War II and (later) Korea veterans, and seniors. Santurce fans "gave back" to Brown when they made collections for him after his Escobar Stadium home runs. Pedrín's niece, Enriqueta, can see Brown receiving the money via his cap. He received the best medical treatment from Dr. Ferrer and dental care from Pedrín's father-in-law.

Charles Ferrer, a cousin of Santurce-born actor and Oscar Award winner José Ferrer, recalled the moments that season when Willard Brown said "Hello Doc and little docs" upon greeting the doctor and his children. The Ferrer clan was among Willard Brown's most avid fans.

Few players wore Santurce's flannels as proudly as outfielder-pitcher Bob Thurman who was 30 years old when he signed his first Santurce contract. He had distinguished himself in World War II with the U.S. Cavalry in New Guinea, but was too modest to brag about his war exploits.

Thurman became known as "El Múcaro" (the owl) after his stellar pitching performances at night. (Escobar was the only stadium with lights at the time.) Thurman won nine games; hit nine homers; stole nine bases; and, hit .411.[14] The interest generated by Brown/Thurman helped set a new league attendance record of 711,638.[15]

Santurce's other outfielder, Virgin Islander Alfonso Gerard, was called a "pesky hitter who could hurt you" by Freddie Thon, Jr. Thon told me that Brown and Thurman were the big guns, but that Gerard did a lot of damage to opposing teams throughout his Santurce career.

John Ford Smith of the Kansas City Monarchs, a.k.a. "El Teniente" (The Lieutenant), won 13 games.[16] His stateside batterymate, Earl "Mickey" Taborn, a.k.a. "Maricutana" in Puerto Rico for his effeminate gait, played his first of three Santurce seasons. This duo plus Brown, Thurman, and Gerard was the team's first "Escadrón del Panico," or Panic Squadron.

Pedrín signed Satchel Paige to a contract during the second half in an attempt to catch Caguas and Mayagüez. Arrangements were made for Paige's flight to the Isla Grande Airport. Pedrín and Guigo waited for Paige to deplane after the aircraft's arrival, but he did

Alfonso Gerard circa 1947–48 (courtesy of Diana Zorrilla).

not come out. So they went on the plane and found Paige seated next to a beautiful woman from St. Thomas, U.S. Virgin Islands. Paige insisted that his friend accompany him, and they enjoyed a fine a meal at a Stop 23 restaurant, El Chevere, before hotel accommodations were made.

Paige pitched well enough in his few outings to impress Bill Veeck, owner of the Cleveland Indians. It was customary for Veeck to make his rounds in the Caribbean during the late 1940s, and he later signed Paige to a contract with the 1948 Cleveland Indians.

Santurce did not make the playoffs despite tying Mayagüez for the first-half lead. Mayagüez was awarded this half due to their better record against Santurce. Caguas won the second-half title and the league finals.

1948–49: A Final Series with Mayagüez

The league implemented an 80-game schedule with the top three teams qualifying for post-season play. League teams were allowed five imports. Santurce tied Ponce for second place and beat them in the semi-finals, but lost the finals to Mayagüez. Santurce had

Satchel Paige signs 1948 contract with Cleveland. Bill Veeck is a happy owner (courtesy of Diana Zorrilla).

the highest home attendance (173,466 fans, or 4,337 per game). The league average was 2,558 per contest.[17] Santurce averaged 11,018 paid fans for their six home playoff games; three apiece against Ponce and Mayagüez.

Pedrín, who had recently married Diana Díaz Gandía of Manatí, once again signed Earl Taborn and John Ford Smith to join forces with Brown and Thurman. Tommy Butts, the shortstop for the Baltimore Elite Giants, was the other import. Butts had played for Almendares in Cuba the prior winter.

Jim LaMarque, a star pitcher with the Kansas City Monarchs, signed with Santurce at mid-season. LaMarque's Puerto Rico nickname was "Libertad" after the famous Argentine singer, Libertad Lamarque.

Santurce's manager, Vic Harris, rested his starters the last weekend. On Saturday, February 5, 1949, he told 21-year-old rookie, Manolo Alvarez, that he would start Sunday's game against San Juan. Alvarez spent that Saturday evening at a hotel near Escobar Stadium and walked to Escobar on Sunday morning rather than take the trolley. He shut out San Juan, 11–0.[18]

Manolo Alvarez exemplified the diversity on Santurce and league rosters from inexperienced local players to quality Negro Leaguers. Alvarez recalled warming up that season at Mayagüez's Liga París ballpark when John Ford Smith told him: "Rookie, you got a nice screwball."

Manolo replied that in Paso Real (the barrio of Manatí he was from) that pitch was called an "in-drop."[19] Alvarez later completed college thanks to the generosity of fellow Manatí native, Pedrín. Diana Zorrilla confirmed this story and many other ones documenting Pedrín's kindness.

The Crabbers then met Ponce in a best-of-five semi-final series. These Lions had Pancho Coímbre, Jorge "Griffin" Tirado, Fernando Díaz Pedroso, Buster Clarkson, Red Lynn and, Pantalones Santiago.

Escobar's lights were turned on for the opener on Tuesday night, February 8, 1949, the first post-season night game in league history. Willard Brown's two-run homer into the 25-cent seats gave Luis Raúl Cabrera the 8–7 win. Ponce evened the series the following night with a 6–2 win. Games three and four were day contests played at Ponce's Charles H. Terry ballpark. Santurce took game three, 4–2, behind Rubén Gómez, but Pantalones Santiago won game four, 4–1. Cabrera, the Ponce native, took the mound at Escobar for game five. He shut out Ponce, 2–0, on a three-hitter.[20]

Rafael Pont Flores noted that Ponce was in mourning, save one native son (Cabrerita) since Ponce had never lost a playoff series. Rubén Gómez, one of Cabrera's best friends, said the knuckles on Cabrera's pitching hand touched the dirt that night after his sidearm pitches.

Mayagüez and Santurce played a day-night twin-bill at Escobar to open the finals on Sunday, February 13. Willard Brown's homer could not offset Alonzo Perry's 8–2 win in the opener. Santurce won the nightcap, 8–7, as Rubén Gómez withstood two solo shots by Luke Easter and Johnny Davis's two-run blast.[21] Bob Thurman's two-run homer won it.

The series moved to Mayagüez for single games on February 14–16. Wilmer Fields pitched Mayagüez to a 6–5 game three win despite Alfonso Gerard's three-run homer. Jim LaMarque hurled a six-hit shutout in game four. Mayagüez's artillery was too much for John Ford Smith in game five. Bob Thurman came to Ford Smith's rescue in the first inning, but Cefo Conde won it with seven relief innings in Mayagüez's 10–5 win.[22]

"Cefo was a good pitcher, he'd pitch for me every day," said Mayagüez player-manager Artie Wilson. "If I wanted to save a pitcher, Cefo said: 'Give me the ball.'"

Mayagüez won game six when Johnny Davis' three-run moonshot off Cabrerita in the first inning started Alonzo Perry on his way to a 6–2 win.[23] Rafael Pont Flores called that homer a poisoned dart that struck "Cabrerita's" heart. Artie Wilson:

"They were good and we beat them and Cabrera. Nobody beat Cabrera in Santurce, but we did and were fortunate enough to win."

Mayagüez went to Cuba for the first Caribbean Series — a six-game round-robin series between winners from Cuba, Panama, Puerto Rico and Venezuela. Almendares, the host team, won the series. This event took place thanks to the behind-the-scenes work of Guigo Otero Suro and others.

1949–50: Willard Brown's Second Triple Crown

Willard Brown secured his place in island sports history with his third batting title and second Triple Crown. Player of the Week awards became a fixture. Brown was the star of the league's first All-Star game in six years. Santurce tied Ponce for second place to qualify for the playoffs. The Crabbers lost to Mayagüez in the semi-finals. Willard Brown and Rubén Gómez reinforced Caguas in the Caribbean Series.

Santurce had a different uniform sponsor — TEK Deluxe Toothbrushes — instead of De Voe Paints, but a cast similar to the 1948–49 one. Tommy Butts and Earl Taborn returned. John Ford Smith was signed by the Havana Reds of the Cuban Winter League after the Crabbers gave up the rights to him via a request from Mike González, manager of the Reds. Pedrín made it clear that Smith was to be returned to Santurce for the next (1950–51) season.[24]

Tommy Butts came with his wife this time. Guigo Otero Suro told me that Pedrín thought it might be better for Butts to have his wife around. But Mrs. Butts loved to party and there were times she wanted her spouse to forsake baseball games for an outing. Butts had an off-year because his wife kept getting rides to parties while the ballplayer suited up for the baseball games.

Leon Day pitched and played second base for skipper Vic Harris. Day did not have his blazing stuff that he showed league fans in the late 1930s and early 1940s. Jim LaMarque picked up the slack later in the season.

Santurce was in first place by mid–December 1949, but faded a bit and Caguas took over first place. The pennant race was a factor for the league setting another single-season attendance record of 781,201.[25]

Poto Paniagua recalled that when Santurce went into a slump, some fans would light candles on the right field side of Escobar to drive away evil spirits. It seemed to work because Santurce started hitting the ball.

"Santurce once lost four straight," said Paniagua. "So Pedrín took the players out partying that Saturday night ... the next day, they won a double-header. Pedrín had his own colorful way of operating the Santurce franchise and he became known as 'El Cangrejo Mayor' (Top Crabber)."

The league's first All-Star game under the lights began at 8:45 p.m. on January 3, 1950 at Escobar. Willard Brown had four hits in the Imports' 11–5 win. Leon Day and Jim LaMarque each pitched an inning while Earl Taborn caught the first five frames. Johnny Logan of the Aguadilla Sharks hit a homer.[26] Doña Inés Mendoza de Muñoz Marín — the wife of Puerto Rico's first elected governor, Luis Muñoz Marín — helped schedule this game after meetings with league officials, sportswriters and broadcasters.[27] Some $10,000 in gate receipts was used to buy Three Kings Day gifts for kids.

Willard Brown edged Bob Thurman in the batting chase, .354 to .353. Brown's 16 homers and 97 RBI gave him another Triple Crown.[28] Brown earned $100 extra for the batting title and $50 each for the home run and RBI crowns.[29] Thurman and Brown also won their share of Player of the Week awards.

Puerto Rico was the first winter league to honor Players of the Week.[30] Kresto Denia, a milk producer, was one of the sponsors. Ballplayers could be feted with a meal and showered with gifts.

Santurce's post season began and ended with their semi-finals versus Mayagüez. Mayagüez's Johnny Davis pitched a 7–5 complete game win in game one. Domingo Sevilla of Santurce won the series' second game.[31] The pivotal game was next. Mayagüez hurler Natalio "Pachy" Irizarry, the league Rookie of the Year, knew that Brown, Thurman, et al. were tough.

"That was a Murderer's Row if I ever saw one," said Irizarry. "[Hank] Aaron later hit a long homer off me in the [1953–54] league All-Star Game, but this was the playoffs."

Irizarry hurled a gem and scored the winning run in the ninth to give Mayagüez a 3–2 win and a two games-to-one series lead.[32] The Crabbers and "Tribe" split their February 11 twin bill. Wilmer Fields, pitching on one day of rest, sent Santurce packing on February 12 with a 6–1 win.[33]

"When I pitched for San Juan, there were incentives for beating Santurce," said Fields. "Mayagüez went after [signed] me after I had pitched well against them. There were rewards for those playoff wins...."

Caguas swept Mayagüez in the finals to reach the Caribbean Series. Fields, Luis "King Kong" Villodas and Bob Wilson of Mayagüez; Ponce's Luis "Tite" Arroyo; and Willard Brown and Rubén Gómez were their reinforcements.

Dan Bankhead and Willard Brown shined against Almendares in game one with Bankhead's shutout and Brown scoring the game's only run. But Panama's Carta Vieja Yankees upset the hosts by beating them three times, including the tie-breaker.[34]

1950–51: The "Trifecta"

Pedrín signed former Ponce skipper George Scales to manage his club. Buster Clarkson and Junior Gilliam were new imports. The Crabbers won the City Championship; defeated Caguas in a seven-game final series; and, won the Caribbean Series in Caracas, to achieve the "Trifecta." Santurce also bested Ponce in the semi-finals prior to defeating Caguas.

The Crabbers now had a huge following, since the 1950 U.S. Census of Population revealed that 195,007 persons resided throughout Santurce, the most in its history.[35] Poto Paniagua was on target when he alluded to the Crabbers becoming the team of Santurce's working class at that time.

John Ford Smith was Santurce's opening day starter, and defeated Ponce, 2–1, in a Montaner Stadium duel with Pantalones Santiago.[36] "El Teniente" did not complete the season, and was replaced by William Powell.

Santurce and Ponce were Caguas' two challengers. That Caguas team, according to Víctor Pellot, was the best one he ever played on with Jim Rivera, Tetelo Vargas and player-manager Luis Olmo in the outfield; league batting champ, George Crowe, at first; Gene Markland at second; Pellot playing third; and Stan Breard at shortstop. Dominican Luis St. Clair, a.k.a. "Gui Gui" Lucas, was the catcher. Manolo Caceres, Roberto Vargas and Mike Clark were the best pitchers for a team that won an all-time regular season record of 57 games.[37]

San Juan qualified for the playoffs. Their outfielders — Babe Barna and Taft Wright — were called "las vacas" (the cows) due to their size and slowness of foot. San Juan's star was outfielder-pitcher Ellis "Cot" Deal.

Nearly 8,500 fans watched the Native players defeat the Imports, 5–1, behind Olmo's two RBI, in the league All-Star game on December 28. New York Yankee prospect and Mayagüez ace, Lew Burdette, started for the Imports. Pedrín called league ump Jim Clegg

EL PELOTERO DENIA

out for not touching first base on a triple in a pre-game contest between local scribes and league umps.[38]

Santurce won another city championship and their fans celebrated two days before the playoffs by walking en masse from Escobar Stadium through portions of San Juan after the Crabbers's February 1, 1951 win over the Senators. This was the first "leg" of the "Trifecta."

Caguas then swept San Juan in their best-of-seven semi-final series. Santurce ousted Ponce in five semi-final games. Rubén Gómez had complete game wins on February 3 and 8, to begin and end it. Ponce broke the ice in game four with a 12-inning, 4–3 win, despite Bob Thurman's complete game.[39]

Caguas visited Santurce February 10–11 to begin the finals before hosting the Crabbers during the next three contests. The finals went back to Escobar for games six and seven. Santurce's home-field advantage was justified by league officials on the grounds that Escobar's seating capacity (13,135) was double that of Caguas' Ildefonso Sola Morales Stadium with its 6,744 seating capacity.[40]

Mike Clark won the first game, 5–4, with relief help from Roberto Vargas. Rubén Gómez evened the score the next night as the Santurce bats woke up in a 15–8 win. Luis Raúl Cabrera won game three in relief of Domingo Sevilla with four plus innings of scoreless relief as Santurce prevailed, 12–5. Caguas then tied the series at two games by rallying for a 6–4 victory. Santurce won game five when Bob Thurman outpitched Mike Clark, 2–1.[41] Junior Gilliam had the key two-run single. This game featured Caguas' Pellot being thrown out at home on an inside-the-park homer bid. Santurce right fielder Juan Sánchez was gunned down by Olmo when trying to score on a base hit by third baseman Pedro Juan Arroyo.[42]

Caguas took game six, 3–1. Guigo Otero Suro had stayed up late that night due to a long meeting at Stop 16 in Santurce. At midnight, there was a knock on his door, and it was Cabrera. He had to find Doña Lala in Ponce, so that she could put a hex on Caguas. Guigo told Cabrera to stay put, and he phoned Pancho Coímbre in Ponce, with instructions to have Doña Lala put in a cab the next day for the trip to Escobar. Guigo :

"Our equipment manager believed in 'black magic,' and he had reserved two seats near the clubhouse. Game seven started ... got word that the cab from Ponce was in Rio Piedras ... she arrived in the third inning and placed some objects inside the clubhouse. Cabrera went in there in the home third and after that, he pitched very well."

Gene Markland got the visitors on the scoreboard first with a third inning home run. Santurce tied it in their half on a triple by Gilliam and Clarkson's RBI fielder's choice. Clarkson put Santurce ahead with a sixth inning homer dedicated to the recently deceased brother of Dr. Ferrer. Caguas pinch-hitter, Pedro Alomar, singled and then scored on Jim Rivera's fielder's choice to tie the game in the eighth. Mike Clark came in to pitch for Caguas and pitched a scoreless eighth.

Cabrerita retired Caguas in the top of the ninth. Clark got Brown on a grounder and struck out Thurman before Pepe Lucas (a .243 regular season hitter with two homers)[43] came up. The first pitch was ball one, but pandemonium broke loose when Clark's next offering was drilled to deep left center field as Tetelo Vargas and Luis Olmo watched the ball sail over the fence. This clout became known as the "Pepelucazo."

Opposite: Postcard of Willard Brown, Triple Crown winner in 1949–50, and a Player of the Week recipient (courtesy of Luis Alvelo).

Santurce fans celebrate the City Championship on February 2, 1951 (courtesy of Diana Zorrilla).

Mike Clark told me it was noisy and that Pepe Lucas became a hero. Clark threw his glove into the stands as he walked off the field. Charles Ferrer was on the stadium roof and ecstatic. Ferrer: "Cabrerita's submarine ball was working. Buster Clarkson hit one [homer] for my uncle and [then] Pepe Lucas hit it out. Olmo just looked up — he didn't move."

Poto Paniagua has vivid memories of the epic homer. Paniagua: "Pepe Lucas hit a line drive that did not rise more than four or five feet. The post-game partying was incredible — as if it was election night."

The record crowd of 16,713 fans did move after that homer as did thousands of fans throughout Santurce who celebrated on the streets. A bedridden Angel Ortíz Cepero got up, picked up a Santurce flag, and walked barefoot from Bayamón toward Santurce. He was cured after the Pepelucazo. Pedrín had this to say: "I made a commitment with our fans 11 years ago to bring them a championship. That commitment has been honored. May God bless you."

Caguas scorer Héctor Barea noted that his team fought until the bitter end. Several Caguas fans stated that they had lost in seven games what had been gained in 77 [regular season] games. George Scales told Rafael Pont Flores that he was the happiest person around and looking forward to playing against Mike González's Havana Reds, since he played for González in the Cuban Winter League circa 1929. Scales said it best: "Those who wait patiently have their moments of happiness. This is mine."[44]

Pedrín reinforced Santurce with Caguas' Olmo, Crowe, Stan Breard, Gui Gui Lucas, Roberto Vargas, Mike Clark, and Ponce's Pantalones Santiago. They all contributed as Santurce won five of the six Caribbean Series games in winning Puerto Rico's title over the Havana Reds, the host Magallanes Navigators and Panama's Spur Cola Colonites. Guigo recalled that Pedrín and Rafael Pont Flores were scared of flying at the time. They held each other's palms during the turbulent flight to Caracas.

Havana had Fernando Díaz Pedroso, Lorenzo "Chiquitín" Cabrera, Pedro Formental and Sandy Amoros. Hoyt Wilhelm was their pitching ace. Spur Cola's veteran lefties, Vibert Clarke and Pat Scantlebury, had Negro Leagues and winter ball credentials. The hosts featured Chico Carrasquel, Johnny Davis, Clem Labine, José Bracho and Vidal López.

Santurce began with a 13–1 win over Havana. Pantalones Santiago went the distance while Wilhelm was knocked out in the seventh inning. Santurce edged Magallanes, 8–7, in game two, thanks to George Crowe's grand slam. The game three win over Spur Cola, 4–3, had Rubén Gómez and Pat Scantlebury going the route. Havana scored four first inning runs off Mike Clark in the only Santurce loss — a 4–3 defeat in game four. The final two games were on February 26. Pantalones Santiago outpitched Magallanes' Clem Labine in the first game for a 6–4 win. Rubén Gómez then beat Spur Cola, 12–1, in an abbreviated six-inning game.[45]

Juan Vené, who covered this Caribbean Series and had dinner with Pantalones during this event, liked him due to his pleasant personality and sense of humor. But Vené was saddened by Santurce's win over Magallanes.

"Pantalones threw hard … but Santurce was losing, 4–3, in the seventh, to Labine," said Vené. "But they scored twice in that inning and again in the eighth … a very sad moment for Venezuela."

Diana Zorrilla was in Caracas that week. She still savors it.

"All week long, the Cuban officials, fans and writers were bragging about how good they were … no other Winter League could come close to them," said Diana. "Pedrín put together the best possible team to represent Puerto Rico. He wanted to win this series for the people of Puerto Rico and Santurce's fans."

Gómez and Santiago were selected as the two pitchers on the series All-Star team. Luis Olmo was the series MVP based on his three homers, 9 RBI and .417 batting mark.[46] Gui Gui Lucas, Stan Breard and Bob Thurman joined Olmo on this select squad. All of Puerto Rico was thrilled.

Juan Vené saw Olmo play center field for Pastora in Maracaibo, Venezuela, circa 1947 and 1948, after Olmo had gone to Mexico to play for the Pasquel brothers. Olmo played those summers in Venezuela since that league did not come under the umbrella of Organized Baseball. Some big leaguers including Olmo were still serving a three-year suspension for having signed contracts to play in Mexico circa 1946.

"I spoke with Olmo during the 1951 Caribbean Series," said Vené. "Many women had their eyes on him … he's good looking and enjoyed the parties. But he was a talented and serious ballplayer."

Arecibo's mayor, Dario Goitía, proclaimed February 27, 1951, a town holiday in native son Olmo's honor. Ponce paid tribute to Pantalones. The team received a hero's welcome from Governor Luis Muñoz Marín, who invited them to a La Fortaleza (governor's mansion) luncheon on February 28, 1951.[47]

1951–52: San Juan Dethrones Santurce

Hiram Bithorn, Puerto Rico's first major leaguer, lost his life after being shot by a policeman in Mexico. Santurce finished third and advanced to the finals against San Juan. Rubén Gómez earned the MVP award. The league allowed six imports on active rosters. Only five teams competed.

Pedrín Zorrilla was presented with three trophies during pre-game ceremonies preceding the club's October 16, 1951 opening game at Escobar against Mayagüez. The trophies were for winning the 1950–51 city championship against San Juan and the league and Caribbean Series titles. Santurce began where they had left off in Caracas by defeating Mayagüez, 7–6, behind Willard Brown's two homers and three RBI.[48]

Santurce featured the hitting of Willard Brown, Buster Clarkson, Junior Gilliam and Bob Thurman, and the pitching of Rubén Gómez, Murray Wall, Johnny Davis and Dan Bankhead. They were playing sub-.500 baseball by mid-December 1951 and struggling in fourth place.

The league All-Star game was played at this time with the proceeds again going to buy holiday season gifts for needy children. Santurce's Murray Wall got the win in the Imports' 2–0 over the Native team. Pre-game activities featured a circling the bases event won by Luis "Canena" Márquez in 13.5 seconds. Junior Gilliam finished second; Carlos Bernier was third.[49]

The Hiram Bithorn tragedy had all Puerto Rico in mourning. Bithorn was shot by a policeman in Mexico on December 29, 1951. He was born and grew up in Santurce before debuting in organized ball with Norfolk in 1936. The New York Yankees shuttled Bithorn between Binghamton, Newark, Kansas City and Oakland in the minors; he joined Hollywood in the Pacific Coast League circa 1940. His 1942 big league debut was with the Chicago Cubs.

San Juan was the only winter league team Bithorn had played for and his last season with them was in 1948–49. All members of the 1951–52 Senators wore a piece of black crepe on their uniform sleeves from January 2, 1952 through the end of the winter season in Bithorn's memory.[50]

Santurce was in fourth place with a 25–27 record, but won 16 of their next 20 games to make the playoffs.[51] Gómez, Wall, (Dan) Bankhead and Davis were unbeatable down the stretch. A loss to San Juan in the last regular season game on February 3, 1952, gave the Senators a one-game edge over Caguas and a two-game margin over Santurce.

Santurce swept Caguas in three straight semi-final games while San Juan had a bye. Willard Brown scored the game-winner in the semi-finals opener. Brown's ninth inning single coupled with his steal of second and a Johnny Davis pinch-hit single gave the Crabbers a 5–4 win on February 5. Santurce won game two, 11–8, despite a grand slam by Víctor Pellot. The series concluded at Escobar on February 7, 1952 with a 12–6 win in which Brown slugged a homer and two singles.[52]

San Juan opened the finals with an 8–2 win on February 9, 1952. A week later they won game six by the same score to wrest the title from Santurce. Homers by George Crowe and Canena Márquez powered the offense. Santurce's two wins were by Rubén Gómez and Johnny Davis. Gómez's 1–0 win in game three was witnessed by New York Yankee manager Casey Stengel.[53]

Buster Clarkson was the only Crabber chosen by San Juan as a 1952 Caribbean Series reinforcement. Havana won five straight games after a tie with San Juan to win this series.

Tommy Fine of the champions provided the event's best performance when he no-hit Cervecería Caracas.[54]

1952–53: Triumph in Havana

Roberto Clemente was signed to his first professional baseball contract by Pedrín. Buster Clarkson did double duty as Santurce's player-manager. Santurce finished second and swept Ponce in the semi-final series. The Crabbers won the finals by defeating San Juan in six games. They flew to Havana and won the Caribbean Series for the second time.

An 18-year-old Roberto Clemente was playing for the Juncos Mules in Puerto Rico's Amateur AA league when Pedrín watched their game against the Manatí Athenians in Manatí. Pedrín was told about Clemente's talent a week earlier by Roberto Marín, a salesman for the Sello Rojo Rice Company, when Marín visited the Zorrillas at their Manatí beach house.[55] Clemente caught Pedrín's eye when he made some great catches and throws.

Pedrín signed Clemente less than a week before the opening of the season. The contract signing took place on October 9, 1952, and called for a salary of $40 per week.[56] Clemente was the 23rd and final player to ink a Santurce contract before the regular season began on October 15, 1952.

The player who Clemente looked up to from the start was Bob Thurman. This was confirmed by Clemente in a newspaper interview several years later when he recalled the time Buster Clarkson called upon him to pinch-hit for Thurman in a game-winning situation. Clemente hit a double off Caguas' Roberto Vargas to win the game and was congratulated by Bob Thurman.[57] Thurman: "He was such a quiet and polite person. I think Roberto knew he had a lot of talent ... but he could [still] learn from us [the veterans]."

Willard Brown, Billy Bruton and Thurman were the three regular outfielders, but Clemente got some playing time. Clarkson, the third baseman/skipper, brought Clemente along slowly. Pepe Lucas handled the first base chores and the double play combo featured Junior Gilliam at second and Billy Hunter at short. Valmy Thomas was the catcher.

Alba "Bobo" Holloman and Rubén Gómez were the staff aces. Lefty Dick Hoover had a cup of coffee with the 1952 Boston Braves as did Buster Clarkson. Johnny Davis came in mid-December and pitched well.

Early season enthusiasm was generated by the pitching duels between Gómez and San Juan's Harvey "El Conejo" (the rabbit) Haddix. San Juan lefty, Don Liddle, had his share of starts against Gómez. Liddle told me that he once found $300 stuffed in his uniform's back pocket after defeating Gómez in a thrilling San Juan-Santurce game.

The stakes were higher than usual in the San Juan-Santurce rivalry. San Juan and Santurce fans took a brief truce to hear the league All-Star game by radio on December 23, 1952. It was played in Ponce and resulted in a 3–1 win by the Imports over the Native team. Bobo Holloman pitched three scoreless innings to win it. Billy Bruton scored twice and stole a base after winning the 100-meter dash in a pre-game competition over Canena Márquez and Carlos Bernier.[58]

Santurce would lose Billy Hunter and Billy Bruton. Hunter was the first to leave when St. Louis Browns' owner Bill Veeck phoned him. The Browns had just acquired Hunter in a deal with the Brooklyn Dodgers and wanted him to return to the States. Hunter balked since he made $1,200 per month with Santurce, the most he had earned in baseball. Veeck arranged a $1,000 pay raise in Hunter's 1953 salary with another $1,000 for returning

Liga Profesional de Baseball de Puerto Rico

Apartado 2467 · San Juan, Puerto Rico

CONTRATO DE JUGADOR #23

Partes.   El _Santurce_ .... BASEBALL CLUB, miembro de la Liga Profesional de Baseball de Puerto Rico, que en adelante se denominará el EQUIPO, y _Roberto Clemente_
                                                                        (nombre)
natural de _Carolina_ .... de _18_ ..... años de edad, que en adelante se denomi-
          (ciudad y país de nacimiento)
nará el JUGADOR, otorgan el siguiente contrato:

_1952-1953_

Convenio.   1.—El Equipo por el presente contrata al Jugador para rendir, y éste conviene en rendir, servicios eficientes y
leales como jugador de baseball durante la temporada de 19_52_ - 19_53_, incluyendo el período de entrenamiento
del Equipo, y todos los partidos de la temporada, inclusive aquellas series post-temporada que auspicie la Liga
Profesional de Baseball de Puerto Rico o la Confederación de Baseball Profesional de Caribe.

Compensa-   2.—Por los servicios mencionados y las promesas más adelante especificadas, el Equipo pagará al Jugador la
ción.   semanales
suma de _Cuarenta_ .... dólares ($_40.00_) quincenales ....
                                                          mensuales

que principiará a devengar tan pronto se inicie la temporada, o a la fecha subsiguiente en que el Jugador empie-
ce a rendir sus servicios, y que seguirá devengando mientras dure la temporada.

Lealtad.   3.—(a) El Jugador se compromete a desempeñar sus servicios diligente y fielmente, en el Equipo contratante
o en cualquiera otro equipo de la Liga Profesional de Baseball de Puerto Rico al cual, de conformidad con su Cons-
titución, fuera transferido, a mantenerse en las mejores condiciones físicas, y a obedecer las reglas de disciplina y
entrenamiento del Equipo, y se obliga y se compromete, además, a observar buena conducta moral y a desempeñar
sus deberes con lealtad y deportismo.

Fomento   (b) En adición a sus servicios como tal Jugador, éste se compromete a cooperar con el Equipo y a participar
del Base-   en todas y en cualquiera de las actividades que, en opinión del Equipo, puedan propender al mejoramiento del Equi-
ball.   po o del baseball profesional, y a observar y cumplir con todos los requisitos o exigencias del Equipo respecto a la
conducta o servicio de sus jugadores, en todo tiempo, ya sea en o fuera del terreno de juego.

Alegaciones   4.—(a) El Jugador expone y conviene en que su destreza y habilidad como jugador de baseball; que los
del Jugador.   servicios que habrá de prestar bajo este Contrato son de carácter especial, excepcional y extraordinarios, lo que
da a tales servicios un valor peculiar que no puede ser razonable o adecuadamente compensado en una acción
judicial ordinaria, y que la falta de cumplimiento de este Contrato por parte del Jugador causará al Equipo graves
e irreparables daños. En tal virtud conviene el Jugador en que, en adición a cualquier otro remedio, el Equipo
tendrá derecho al remedio de Injunction y/o a cualquier otro remedio en equidad para evitar el incumplimiento de
este Contrato por parte del Jugador, incluyendo entre otros el derecho de impedir que juegue baseball para cualquiera otra persona, organización, o corporación pública o privada, durante la vigencia de este Contrato.

Estado físico   (b) El Jugador expone que no tiene defectos físicos o mentales, conocidos por él, que le puedan impedir pres-
del Jugador.   tar sus servicios eficientemente.

Impedimentos.   (c) El Jugador conviene en que, directa ni indirectamente, podrá formar parte de la Junta de Directores de
la Liga ni de la Junta de Directores de ningún equipo afiliado a la Liga Profesional de Baseball de Puerto Rico, ni
tendrá intereses, acciones, etc., de ninguno de tales equipos.

Servicios.   5.—(a) El Jugador se compromete a que mientras se halle bajo contrato y mientras subsista el derecho del
equipo a renovar el mismo, no jugará baseball para ningún otro equipo en o fuera de Puerto Rico, sin permiso
por escrito del equipo.

Otros   (b) El Jugador reconoce y conviene en que su participación en otros deportes y actividades puede menoscabar
Deportes.   o destruir su habilidad como jugador de baseball. En tal virtud conviene en que durante la vigencia de este Contrato no podrá, sin el consentimiento escrito de su Equipo, tomar parte en contiendas o exhibiciones de boxeo, lucha
greco-romana, pancracio, futbol, baloncesto, y otras actividades que puedan afectar su habilidad y eficiencia como
jugador.

Transferen-   6.—(a) El Jugador conviene en que este Contrato puede ser transferido por el Equipo a cualquier otro Equipo
cia de   de la Liga Profesional, y el Jugador se compromete a personarse en el sitio, día y hora que le indique el Equipo
Contrato.   a que hubiere sido transferido.

(b) El sueldo fijado al Jugador en el párrafo 2 de este Contrato por el período establecido en el párrafo 1 no
podrá ser rebajado por tal transferencia.

(c) El Jugador se personará al Equipo al cual hubiere sido transferido inmediatamente después del recibo de
aviso escrito del Equipo de la transferencia de su Contrato. Si dejara de personarse, no tendrá derecho a paga por
el período de la fecha en que reciba el aviso escrito de transferencia hasta que se persone al Equipo al cual ha sido
transferido.

(d) A partir de la fecha de tal transferencia, todos los derechos y obligaciones del Equipo contratante pasarán
a ser derechos y obligaciones del Equipo al cual ha sido transferido el Jugador.

Copy of Roberto Clemente's first professional baseball contract with the 1952–53 Santurce Crabbers
calling for a salary of $40 per week (courtesy of Diana Zorrilla).

home. Veeck had already spoken to Pedrín. Two days later, Hunter and his wife, Bev, flew home.

Billy Bruton's case was different. The Milwaukee Braves wanted Bruton to be their 1953 center fielder and did not want him to get hurt before spring training. Dick Hoover took Bruton's roster spot.

The Ponce Lions were Santurce's obstacle for the final series with San Juan. They featured Tom Lasorda, who had made league history on January 4, 1953, by pitching back-to-back complete games — a 3–1 win in the opener followed by a 2–1 loss in the 10-inning nightcap against Mayagüez.[59]

Ponce was swept by Santurce in three straight semi-final series games. Rubén Gómez won the 11-inning opener, 1–0, on February 6. Santurce won game two, 12–4, behind Bobo Holloman. Pantalones Santiago took the loss and asked his manager, Joe Buzas, for the ball in game three — a 2–1 win by Dick Hoover.[60]

A 14-inning performance by Holloman went for naught in San Juan's 4–3 win in game one of the finals. Cot Deal won it in relief when Nino Escalera's single drove in Canena Márquez. Santurce tied the series the next night when Gómez outpitched Liddle in a 9–6 win. Dick Hoover won game three, 6–3, but Holloman lost game four, a 12–7 win for Cot Deal.[61]

Jackie Robinson was vacationing in Puerto Rico when he and Rachel Robinson took in game five. Robinson asked *El Mundo* sportswriter Elmo Torres Pérez how Junior Gilliam was doing, and was told "Just fine."[62] Gilliam and Robinson visited before the game. Robinson witnessed a 15–5 slugfest won by Santurce as Bob Thurman drove in seven runs with a grand slam homer and several hits.

Santurce made Havana trip plans after their 13-inning win on February 15, 1953. Bobo Holloman went the route and Valmy Thomas clubbed a two-run triple in Santurce's 7–5 win. Cot Deal squelched a ninth inning rally, but took the loss.[63]

Roster moves prior to the Cuba trip included the addition of Cot Deal, Pantalones Santiago, Roberto Vargas, Joe Montalvo, Canena Márquez and Víctor Pellot. Pellot replaced Roberto Clemente on Santurce's roster.[64]

The series favorites were the Havana Reds, winners of three straight Cuban Winter League crowns, a feat this team had last achieved between 1926–27 and 1928–29.[65] Cuban scribes felt that Santurce, Venezuela's Caracas Lions and Panama's Chesterfield Smokers had no chance.

Santurce cooled off the Smokers, 15–6, on February 20, 1953. Rubén Gómez pitched a seven-inning complete game called due to a time limit. Bobo Holloman went seven innings against Caracas the next day, before Cot Deal finished Santurce's 7–4 win. A 21-year-old oil field worker and radio listener from Maracaibo hung himself with a rope from his hammock after this game.[66]

Some 16,700 partisan Cuban fans went bananas when Havana faced Santurce on February 22, 1953. Havana had won 11 straight Caribbean Series games dating to the 1951 series. Sandy Amoros scored the first run in the top of the second frame. Santurce retaliated with a Willard Brown homer and Pepe Lucas' RBI single. Bob Thurman's RBI hit off starter Julio Moreno, a pitcher with the Washington Senators, gave Santurce a 3–1 lead. Havana took the lead with three eighth inning runs and a ninth inning run. Cot Deal relieved in the eighth and cited the last of the ninth from memory. Mario Picone retired Santurce's first two hitters and Deal was the last hope. The Cuban fans joked about Santurce having no one to pinch-hit for a pitcher.

Jackie Robinson visits with Junior Gilliam in the Santurce dugout on February 14, 1953 (courtesy of Diana Zorrilla).

Deal cracked a double and scored on a Canena Márquez single. Hits by Gilliam and Pellot tied the game. Rubén Gómez was next since he had entered the game as a pinch runner for Willard Brown.

"The Cuban fans got all over him [Gómez] ... listed as a pitcher on our roster," said Deal. "When Gómez drove in Gilliam with the winning run on a base hit, they [the Cuban fans] got quiet all of a sudden."

José "Pepe" Seda, a Puerto Rico baseball pioneer, general manager, scout and writer, wrote:

> When the score was 5–3 [in favor of Havana] and with two outs, I accepted defeat like a presidential candidate when the partial number of votes come in...when Cot Deal lit the match and Canena and Gilliam kept it alive, I thought about our battling citizens who struggle to overcome their problems. The game-winning and miraculous hit by Gómez was emotionally satisfying to all Puerto Ricans.[67]

Santurce won their last three series games. Deal went the distance in game four, a 6–3 win over Chesterfield. Holloman defeated Caracas, 9–2, in game five. It ended on February 25, 1953, when Roberto Vargas and Rubén Gómez combined to whip Havana, 7–3.[68] Cot Deal remembers Willard Brown's reluctance to play in the final game despite his chance to set a series home run record. But Brown hit his fourth series homer as a pinch-hitter against the Cuban knuckleball pitcher, Gil Torres, in the ninth.

Deal was the life-saver and Brown the record-setter with his four homers and 13 RBI.[69] Puerto Rico welcomed Brown, Deal and all the other players with open arms. They all thanked Puerto Rico's baseball fans from their hearts. So did Pedrín Zorrilla and other team and league officials.

1953–54: From First to "Worst"

Santurce went from first to "worst" in less than a year. Hank Aaron and player-manager Mickey Owen led Caguas to the league title. Roberto Clemente blossomed, but Willard Brown, Buster Clarkson, Bob Thurman and new import Bobby Balcena had power outages. Tom Lasorda pitched well for the Crabbers as did Rubén Gómez and Bill Greason. Clarkson was suspended for nearly a month after an altercation. Clemente impressed Al Campanis in a tryout.

The Caguas Criollos went from "worst" to first with Hank Aaron leading the league in hitting and tying teammate Jim Rivera for the home run crown.[70] Santurce was a different story.

When Santurce visited Caguas on November 22, 1953, they were dead last and facing Caguas' best pitcher, Bob Buhl. Buster Clarkson was livid when some calls went against Santurce and allegedly spit in the face of umpire William Reagan. The ump demanded that league President Emilio de Aldrey impose a stiff penalty. Clarkson was fined $75 and suspended for four weeks.[71] Ray Dandridge was activated to play third.

Hank Aaron came close to being placed on the Santurce roster. Guigo Otero Suro had spoken with the Milwaukee Braves management about Aaron playing for Santurce, but Caguas had first rights. Aaron almost was released by Caguas due to an early season slump, but began hitting the ball and stayed with Caguas.

Guigo had tried to get other imports, including Ernie Banks and Ted Williams, to sign with Santurce. The Chicago Cubs did not allow Banks to play winter ball. Ted Williams was a different matter.

Emilio de Aldrey and Guigo flew together to see the 1953 Major League All-Star game in Cincinnati. Williams had come back from a tour of duty in Korea, and threw out the first pitch before he and Guigo took the same flight out of Cincinnati. Guigo asked Williams if he would consider playing for Santurce in 1953–54 to stay sharp.

"Williams asked me if there were good golf courses and fishing in Puerto Rico," said Guigo. "I said yes to both, and that Ted would be made an honorary member of all the Puerto Rico Golf Clubs and the Commodore of El Club Nautico. I spoke with Fred Corcoran, Williams' agent, and got the agent's phone number in Pittsburgh … later that summer, a Pittsburgh radio station announced that Ted Williams might play winter ball with Santurce!"

Pedrín was vacationing in Spain when Guigo phoned him about the Ted Williams possibility. The price tag would be $30,000 for signing Williams, and Pedrín was willing to do it. This never happened, since Williams hit the ball at a better than .400 clip with Boston during August and September 1953.[72] The "Splendid Splinter" did not need any more fine-tuning.

Tom Lasorda did pitch for Santurce that winter. Diana Zorrilla recalls that Pedrín liked Lasorda's work ethic and colorful demeanor, but recognized that the pitcher did not have much natural ability. Lasorda and his family enjoyed leisure time at the Zorrilla beach house in Manatí. One lesson that Lasorda learned from Pedrín was that a manager could be friendly with the team's ballplayers without losing their respect. Lasorda considered himself fortunate to have been associated with Pedrín.[73]

Roberto Clemente was the regular left fielder. Santurce's fans wondered about the team's lack of power, since the Crabbers hit 20 home runs in their 80 games, with Brown, Clarkson and Thurman only hitting 12 homers between them.[74]

Al Campanis, a top scout for the Brooklyn Dodgers, was managing the Cienfuegos Elephants, a team in the Cuban Winter League, when he took a break to witness an Escobar tryout organized by Pedrín Zorrilla. Clemente impressed Campanis, by twice running 60 yards in 6.4 seconds and with his arm and bat.[75]

"Clemente was the only guy qualified to meet our [Brooklyn] plans," said Campanis. "He hit them over the left field and right field fence."

Clemente played in his first league All-Star game on December 23, 1953, and got a hit. He ran in the pre-game 100-meter race and finished fourth behind Canena Márquez, Charlie Harmon and Carlos Bernier. Aaron got the ink with his two homers and five RBI in the Imports' 11–1 win.[76]

Bob Thurman showed Aaron he could still pitch when he blanked the Criollos, 6–0, at Escobar on December 28.[77] Crabber fans got more late-season thrills when Santurce pasted San Juan, 21–5, on January 20, 1954, to clinch the city championship.[78]

Roberto Clemente and Rubén Gómez were in the news. Clemente verbally committed to the Dodgers on February 15, 1954 before he signed a contract four days later for a $10,000 signing bonus and a $5,000 salary with the 1954 Montreal Royals.[79] Diana Zorrilla confirmed there were other offers: "Roberto consulted with Pedrín about better offers, like the one with Milwaukee [tendered by scout Luis Olmo], before signing with Brooklyn. Pedrín and Roberto's parents felt that Roberto's word should be honored."

Rubén Gómez reinforced Caguas in the 1954 Caribbean Series at Escobar won by the Criollos. Gómez teamed with Mickey Owen to defeat Venezuela's Pastora Milkers, 3–2, on February 20, 1954. He baffled Pastora's Luis Aparicio, Ed Bailey, Wally Moon and Johnny Temple to earn a spot on the Caribbean Series All-Star team with teammates Mickey Owen (C), Víctor Pellot (1B), Jack Cassini (2B), and Jim Rivera (CF).[80]

The passing of the torch had gone from Willard Brown and Cot Deal to Aaron, Clemente and other league stars. Brown and Deal did a lot for the league between the 1946–47 and 1953–54 seasons to stimulate fan interest. Deal later touched base with Brown in Houston, where "Ese Hombre" lived when he [Deal] was a Houston Astros coach from 1983–1985. Cot Deal told me that Willard Brown was one of the best hitters he ever saw, and that includes Ted Williams and Joe DiMaggio.

"Willard Brown was one of the best hitters I ever saw, and that includes Williams and DiMaggio," said Deal. "As a player, he gave the appearance of loafing, but he was not … very much appreciated in Puerto Rico."

3. RUBÉN GÓMEZ, #22

It was fascinating to see him (Rubén Gómez) throw that screwball.
— Jim Dickson, former Santurce pitcher

Rubén Gómez spent 31 seasons with Santurce: 28 as a player, two as a manager and one as a coach. His screwball, which helped account for 173 career regular season wins for Santurce plus one with Bayamón, made him the "winningest" pitcher in league history. Gómez pitched for nine Santurce league champions. He competed for Santurce in six Caribbean Series events and reinforced Caguas in two others.

1947–48 to 1948–49: The Early Years

Pedrín Zorrilla signed Gómez, a.k.a. "El Loco Divino" (the Divine Madman), to his first professional contract in 1947. It was a close call since Gómez, at the time, was enrolled at the University of Puerto Rico and was hesitant to leave the amateur ranks. He had impressed Pedrín Zorrilla with his hurling against some of Puerto Rico's top amateur teams at the AA level including the Juncos Mules. The university's baseball schedule in the mid to late 1940s included games against AA teams.

Pedrín pulled out all the stops including a visit to the Gómez household in Guayama, located in the southeastern portion of Puerto Rico, where he made his pitch to Gómez's mother, Doña Lola. Gómez reiterated his interest in studying full-time and competing in amateur baseball and track and field. But Pedrín used his psychology by stating that the pitching prospect was scared to play winter ball.

"I signed with Pedrín after he issued the challenge," said Gómez. "Then I told Pedrín to give me the ball."

The rest, as the saying goes, is history. Gómez proved to be the most dependable and durable pitcher in the league over the next 30 years. His superior athletic skills, honed as a university athlete, enabled him to pitch in the league until he was 49 years old. Gómez had earned his University of Puerto Rico athletic scholarship by his success in the 300-meter run, the 4×100 meter relay, the high jump and the pole vault.

When Gómez was 65 years old, he told me that arthritis was not part of his vocabulary nor physique. He had been an avid fisherman in his youth and then took up golf on a regular basis.

"I found a balance between my training and other hobbies," said Gómez. "I lifted weights at home on a daily basis, and at the university made 50 long throws of close to 400 feet from the outfield to home plate. That's why my arm never bothered me."

Gómez, who wore number 22 throughout his Santurce career, recalled that his first Santurce game was a tough 1–0 loss to Caguas in 11 innings. That 1947–48 Caguas team would go on to win the league title with the likes of player-manager Quincy Trouppe, Perucho Cepeda and a 20-year-old rookie named Víctor Pellot. Gómez was thrilled to pitch against those Criollos as well as the fabled Mayagüez Indians with Artie Wilson, Johnny Davis and other stars from the Negro Leagues.

Santurce's imports including Willard Brown, Bob Thurman and John Ford Smith, welcomed Gómez and served as role models. These players would give advice to the younger Puerto Rican players and in some cases, take them under their wing. Gómez was particularly impressed with Willard Brown.

"He still has the record of 27 homers in 60 games," said Gómez. "It was our era ... we had a great time together ... would see each other at the night clubs. Brown, Thurman and the others were very pleasant."

Gómez's best friend on the club was Luis Raúl Cabrera. They made an odd pair, with the college-educated Gómez and the illiterate older pitcher. Cabrera understood that his mantle as the team's "bread and butter" pitcher and San Juan's nemesis would be passed on to Gómez. "El Tigre" passed on his baseball smarts to Gómez and inspired him with his determination.

When I conversed with Gómez in the Bithorn Stadium parking lot, circa January 1993, he recalled that Cabrera's sidearm deliveries were very much like those of Kent Tekulve, a former reliever with the Pirates, Phillies and Reds between the mid–1970s and late 1980s. Gómez told me that Cabrera was the best-dressed ballplayer in Puerto Rico, and that most of his (Cabrera's) salary went for clothing.

Cabrerita and Gómez were two reasons why Santurce advanced to the 1948–49 final series for the first time in six years. The veteran won semi-final series games one and five against Ponce while Gómez earned his first post-season win in game three at the Charles H. Terry ballpark. Gómez kept the Ponce hitters off-balance in silencing the five-time league champions, 4–2.[1]

The Mayagüez bats proved tougher in the league finals, but Gómez hung on for an 8–7 win in game two.[2] Vic Harris, Gómez's manager during his first two seasons, used him in long relief in game five. Gómez allowed two runs in four innings, but did not figure in the decision as Mayagüez prevailed, prior to clinching the series the following night.

"Those Mayagüez hitters (Wilmer Fields, Johnny Davis, Alonzo Perry, Luke Easter, Artie Wilson) were so good," said Gómez. "I had to pitch with my heart as well as my talent."

The 1950s: A Decade to Remember

Rubén Gómez came of age in the 1950s. He won 103 regular season games for Santurce, an average of over 10 per season.[3] Twenty-two of those wins were shutouts and 14 came against San Juan.[4] Gómez led the league in wins three times, was the strikeout king once and earned one MVP award.[5] His screwball, fastball and slider accounted for 20 post-season wins — six semi-final, eight final series and six Caribbean Series triumphs.[6] Gómez pitched in four Caribbean Series events with Santurce and reinforced Caguas twice.

Gómez's vita included seven big league seasons with the New York and San Francisco Giants from 1953–1959. This had a bearing on Santurce's fortunes since it was Pedrín who engineered Gómez's signing with the Giants prior to the 1953 big league season. The success experienced by Gómez for the 1953 and 1954 New York Giants proved invaluable in Pedrín and Horace Stoneham, the Giants owner, signing a working agreement. Gómez helped matters on October 1, 1954, by becoming the first Puerto Rican pitcher to start and win a World Series game.[7]

There was no better pitcher in the Puerto Rico league from 1949–50 through 1952–53, a four-year period when Gómez won 54 league games.[8] Gómez followed his 1949 summer at Bristol (Class B) with a 14–8 mark for Santurce to earn the most league wins while pitching in 26 of Santurce's 80 games.[9] Santurce was bested by Mayagüez in the semifinals. Gómez lost his only start when the Indians rallied for a 3–2 win.[10] But Caguas player-manager Luis Olmo, one of Gómez's best friends and a future golf partner, selected him to reinforce the Criollos for the 1950 Caribbean Series.

Olmo used Gómez in relief in four of the seven games, including the tie-breaker won by Panama's Carta Vieja Yankees. Gómez saved game six against Magallanes of Venezuela with two plus innings of relief work to set up the tie-breaker. When Dan Bankhead was roughed up for six runs in the fourth inning by Carta Vieja, Olmo again called upon Gómez to douse the flames. Puerto Rico's baseball fans had a lot of respect for the 22-year-old competitor, who had pitched 147 regular season, nine semi-final series and 15 Caribbean Series innings.[11]

The 1950–51 season was special because Santurce dethroned Caguas to win their first league title and Caribbean Series. Gómez was proud of Luis Raúl Cabrera for winning game seven of the finals, and of his fishing buddy, Pepe Lucas, for hitting the game-winning homer in the bottom of the ninth. Santurce made it to the league finals by defeating Ponce, four games to one, in a semi-final series where Gómez won the first and final games, and only allowed two total runs.[12] Gómez won game two of the final series while losing the sixth contest.[13]

Gómez's 13–6 regular season mark included his first shutout of San Juan — a 16–0 win — followed by the three wins and four complete games in the league playoffs. He had pitched 178 innings going into the Caribbean Series including three scoreless frames in the league All-Star game won by the Native players over the Imports, 5–1. Gómez's All-Star stint included picking Bob Thurman off second base after working out some signs with San Juan shortstop, Jaime Almendro.[14]

The Caribbean Series included wins in games three and six versus Panama's Spur Cola Colonites and a save against Venezuela in game two.[15] Gómez was rewarded with a berth on the Series All-Star team.

The 24-year-old Gómez was a fan favorite by the time the 1951–52 season got underway. Santurce's fans clamored for Gómez to pitch against San Juan in city championship games. Pedrín saw this as a way to attract more fans. A case in point was a late-season game against San Juan and their ace, Sam Jones. Jones was the league's top winner with 13 wins. Gómez had won six straight starts against San Juan, including three shutouts. This match-up evoked memories of the late 1930s and early 1940s when Paige, Partlow, and Day, among others, hooked up in pitching duels.

Gómez created much excitement when he scored the game's first run on a passed ball by Joe Montalvo. He legged out an infield hit and reached second on a sacrifice by Pepe Lucas. When Montalvo missed a Sam Jones curve ball, Gómez aggressively rounded third and headed home. A close play at the plate resulted in Sam Jones being spiked in the knee and his leaving the game. That play, coupled with Santurce's 7–3 win, helped sway many MVP votes in Gómez's favor.[16]

Tom Greenwade, the scout who had signed Mickey Mantle to a New York Yankee contract in the late 1940s, was in Puerto Rico circa late January 1952 to scout Gómez and Caguas' Víctor Pellot. New York signed them to minor league contracts, but neither would make their big league debut with the Yankees. By season's end, Gómez was 14–7 to lead the league in wins for a second time. Seven of his wins came against San Juan[17] and he completed 15 of his 25 starts in pitching 175 innings.[18] Island sportswriters rewarded Gómez with the MVP award.[19]

"That award was nice, but not the highlight of my Santurce career," said Gómez. "The 1953 Caribbean Series come-from-behind win against Havana was the highlight."

Caguas fell to Gómez in game three of the 1952 semi-finals as Santurce advanced to the finals against San Juan. Casey Stengel took time off from his U.S. Virgin Islands vacation to watch Gómez shut out San Juan, 1–0, in game two on February 12, 1952.[20] That win had a direct bearing on Gómez's signing with the Yankees and being assigned to their minor league club in Kansas City. Gómez was not with the Yankees very long: "I pitched a [1952] game for Kansas City ... they didn't use me for a month. So I went to play ball [with Licey] in the Dominican Republic and the Yankees suspended me. At the end of that season, I bought out my contract with Kansas City for $3,000 by giving money to another person who gave the cash to them."

Gómez was ready for the 1952–53 season and defeated Caguas in Santurce's season opener, 8–3, while hitting a single and a double.[21] San Juan got the best of him three straight times early in the season when Harvey Haddix was virtually unhittable and Don Liddle was sharp.

"Those games against San Juan in the early 1950s were something else," said Gómez. "It was life and death for many of the fans."

One of those fans was 11-year-old Rafael Bracero, a San Juan fan at the time who lived in the Barrio Obrero section of Santurce. Bracero got to know Rubén Gómez quite well, since Gómez lived on the same Barrio Obrero street during the early 1950s.

"I played baseball with Rubén's brother-in-law, 'Nano,' and established a special bond with Rubén," said Bracero. "Rubén was my neighbor and someone who, in effect, represented me when he took the mound ... I was still a San Juan fan, but when Rubén pitched, I felt a special respect for the Santurce ballclub."

Bracero and some of his neighborhood/little league friends would use a stout rope, strong enough to keep a cargo ship moored to the dock, near Sixto Escobar's left field fence to scale it. The kids made it inside Escobar and walked toward the right field area, prior to finding a seat closer to the action so they could watch Rubén Gómez and their other idols.

It was clear that Gómez was San Juan's master. He won eight straight regular season games against San Juan, including four shutouts, after losing his first three decisions to them. One of the wins was a 15-inning effort when he and Ellis "Cot" Deal both went the route. Four of those eight victories were shutouts with the final one coming in a two-hit, 2–0 win on January 30, 1953.[22]

Rafael Bracero recalled that San Juan would usually start their best pitcher against Santurce when Rubén Gómez was pitching. Cot Deal got the call for San Juan most of the time in 1952–53. Bracero stated that Deal was a fine outfielder and a good switch-hitter, but not quite as good a pitcher as Rubén.

It was around this time that Pedrín facilitated Gómez's signing a $15,000 deal with the New York Giants which included a bonus and a 1953 salary.[23] Giants scout Tom Sheehan traveled to Puerto Rico to sign Gómez. Al Campanis with the Brooklyn Dodgers had also attempted to sign Gómez, but was unsuccessful. Monte Irvin, a Giants outfielder, was in Puerto Rico on a business trip during early February 1953, and stated that "Gómez will be O.K. with the Giants."[24]

Number 22 was clicking on all cylinders when the league playoffs began. He shut out Ponce, 1–0, in game one of the semi-finals on a three-hitter in the 11-inning game. Buster Clarkson's single scored William Figueroa with the winning run.[25] Santurce faced San Juan in the finals.

Gómez won two games with his arm and another with his bat. Games two and five were complete game wins for Gómez by 9–6 and 15–5 scores, respectively. Gómez's bases-loaded triple in the second inning of game three provided Santurce with a 6–3 win.[26]

The clutch hitting continued in the 1953 Caribbean Series. Gómez opened the series, hosted by Havana, on February 20, 1953 against Panama's Chesterfield Smokers. Santurce reinforcement Víctor Pellot hit a 435-foot homer and Gómez clubbed another home run in their seven-inning, 15–6 win. Two nights later, Gómez's two-out, ninth inning hit drove in Junior Gilliam with the game-winning run in Santurce's 6–5 win over Havana.[27]

That hit was Gómez's most special memory in his Santurce career.

"Nothing can top that one," said Gómez. "It was the only time a [professional] team from Puerto Rico won the Caribbean Series in Cuba."

Santurce's 1953–54 season was a disappointing last place one, and Gómez suffered from a lack of run support in posting a 5–6 record.[28] Early that season, Gómez was notified of his selection to the 1953 Sporting News All-Rookie team, along with two former Santurce teammates, Brooklyn's Junior Gilliam and Milwaukee's Billy Bruton. Harvey Haddix and Ray Jablonski, two St. Louis Cardinals who performed for the arch rival San Juan Senators in 1952–53, were also named to that select squad.[29]

Gómez's status as Puerto Rico's only big league pitcher was a factor in his being chosen to reinforce Caguas for the 1954 Caribbean Series held at Escobar Stadium. And he came through a big league performance in Caguas' 3–2 win over Venezuela's Magallanes Navigators on February 20, 1954, by striking out 10 hitters, second only to Pantalones Santiago's existing record of 11 strikeouts in Caribbean Series play.[30] The win was preserved by fielding gems by third baseman, Víctor Pellot, and right fielder Canena Márquez. Mickey Owen, the Caguas player-manager, caught Gómez and later complimented him.

There was no bigger name in Puerto Rico baseball circles than Rubén Gómez after he won game three of the 1954 World Series on October 1, 1954 before 71,555 fans. The U.S. media noted that Gómez was more effective than were Sal Maglie or Johnny Antonelli in the first two wins by the New York Giants over Cleveland.[31] Rubén Gómez even got the backing of former Yankee pitcher Vernon "Lefty" Gómez:

"I am rooting for [Rubén] Gómez because a 'Gómez' has never lost a World Series Game." (Lefty Gómez had a 6–0 mark in World Series contests for the Yankees during the 1930s).[32]

Willie Mays (who joined Santurce two weeks after this World Series) drove in two

Rubén Gómez is a hero after his game-winning hit gives Santurce a win over Havana in the 1953 Caribbean Series. Pedrín Zorrilla is all smiles (courtesy of Diana Zorrilla).

runs in Gómez's 6–2 win. Gómez gave up a homer to Vic Wertz on a "hanging screwball" and experienced some sinus problems pitching in Cleveland's Municipal Stadium. Hoyt Wilhelm relieved Gómez in the eighth frame to preserve the win. Puerto Rico's governor, Luis Muñoz Marín, wired the following message to Gómez after that historic win:"I am certain that all Puerto Ricans share my rejoicing over your brilliant work on this first occasion in which Puerto Rico has been represented by a pitcher in a World Series Game."[33]

A huge multitude welcomed Gómez at the Isla Grande Airport upon his arrival in Puerto Rico. Island baseball fans had welcomed Luis Olmo at the same airport five years earlier after his stellar play in the 1949 World Series for Brooklyn which included the first World Series homer by a Puerto Rican player. The reception for Gómez featured more fans.

"I will never forget that," said Gómez. "Fans from all over Puerto Rico were at the airport."

Gómez pitched the league's first shutout on October 31, 1954 over Caguas.[34] It was around this time that Willie Mays went on a tear for Santurce. Rubén Gómez was a major reason for Mays wearing Santurce flannels. The Giants sent Mays to Santurce to help repay Pedrín for tipping them off to Gómez. Gómez encouraged Mays to play for Santurce,

Left to Right: Willie Mays, Pedrín Zorrilla, Rubén Gómez, 1954–55 (courtesy of Diana Zorrilla).

reminding him that he missed most of 1952 and 1953 due to the military."Once Willie made the decision to play in Puerto Rico, he made the adjustment quickly," says Gómez. "Willie was the best athlete I ever saw or played with."

Mays and Gómez were involved in a pre-game episode during the latter part of Santurce's regular season. Roberto Clemente was taking batting practice prior to a January 11, 1955 game, when he stepped out of the box and Gómez suddenly stepped in against Milton Ralat. But Ralat refused to throw to Gómez, and Gómez opted to sit on home plate. Mays was standing at the side of the batting cage and Ralat began lobbing pitches to him.

It was apparent that Mays wanted harder pitches and he lined one lob right at Ralat. Then Mays went to the mound in frustration with Gómez close behind.

Santurce skipper Herman Franks told Mays that Gómez was trying to protect him from an altercation with Ralat. Pedrín dismissed this episode as normal emotions and noted that it was business as usual come game time.[35]

Gómez had won nine straight games at the time of this pre-game discussion. When the regular season ended, Gómez had a 13–4 record including his 12–0 season-ending shutout of San Juan. That was his third win in five decisions against the Senators, and gave Santurce the city championship.[36] Gómez won his first league All-Star game when he started and pitched two scoreless innings for the combined San Juan-Santurce (North) squad versus the Caguas-Mayagüez-Ponce (South) team.[37]

The season was memorable for other reasons. Gómez's son, Rafael (a future class-mate of mine in elementary school), was born shortly after the winter season began. Gómez earned the respect and friendship of Santurce's second baseman, Ronnie Samford, who told me that Rubén and Teresa Gómez opened their home to him and that he (Sam-ford) went on numerous fishing outings with his likable teammate. Gómez's home, at the time, was in the Roosevelt urbanization of Hato Rey, not far from the future location of Hiram Bithorn Municipal Stadium.

A writer for *El Mundo*, R. Santiago Sosa, was impressed by Gómez's new 1955 Buick with license plate number 22, a gift from the Puerto Rican community living in New York City. Gómez told Sosa that 22 was his lucky number and showed Sosa elaborate fishing equipment used to catch fish in the 10- to 35-pound range. Gómez fished in the Escam-brón area near Sixto Escobar Stadium and had studied the ocean currents at Stop eight to the point where his bait (sardines, shrimp, worms and flies) got quick bites. When Gómez fished from the pier off the Escambrón Beach, it was common to see his close friend, Pepe Lucas, or another player sharing the moment.[38]

Post-season highlights included Gómez's two final series wins over Caguas. Gómez then pitched the Caribbean Series opener against Cuba's Almendares Blues on February 10, 1955 before a crowd of 34,000 in Caracas' University Stadium. The public address announcer stated that fans should pay no more than 30 cents for a Coca Cola and a beer instead of the 45 cents charged by the vendors at game time as they cheered and pelted the vendors with paper cups.[39]

Gómez's 6–2 win was a masterpiece since one of the runs allowed came on an error by first baseman, George Crowe, and Earl Rapp's triple. Gómez retired Almendares' last 10 hitters and ended the two-hour and ten-minute game with seven strikeouts.[40] Willie Miranda, Almendares' shortstop, told a Venezuelan sportswriter after the game that the "Santurce hitters are a threat, but the 'real deal' (cosa seria) was Rubén Gómez ... chico, what a pitcher, that Rubén Gómez!"[41]

Gómez was congratulated by Puerto Rico's governor at a La Fortaleza ceremony after Santurce returned home. Herman Franks, Willie Mays and other teammates looked on.

The next three winter seasons followed Gómez's big league campaigns with the 1955–1957 New York Giants. Baseball writers in New York and some Giants officials expressed concern about the wear and tear on Gómez's arm. But Gómez helped Santurce win three straight regular season pennants while pitching and also playing the outfield.

The sale of Roberto Clemente, Juan Pizarro and Ronnie Samford to Caguas in late December 1956 resulted in Gómez taking over Clemente's center field position down the

Rubén Gómez is congratulated by Puerto Rico's governor, Luis Muñoz Marín, during a ceremony honoring the 1955 Caribbean Series champions. Herman Franks and Willie Mays look on (courtesy of Diana Zorrilla).

stretch and in the league finals. When that sale was first announced prior to Santurce's twin-bill at Mayagüez on December 30, 1956, Gómez took off his Santurce uniform in protest.[42] Gómez's professionalism prevailed, and his clutch hitting and fielding down the stretch were instrumental in Santurce's pennant.

Rafael Bracero saw Gómez patrol the outfield in his (Bracero's) first trip to Escobar. He felt that Gómez's fielding skills were second to none.

"Rubén made basket catches from different angles," said Bracero. "He had a sense of rhythm and timing that you do not see anymore."

Gómez continued his fine pitching for the New York Giants in 1957. He pitched the first shutout for the San Francisco Giants after they moved to the West Coast.[43] That 8–0 win over the Los Angeles Dodgers and Don Drysdale at Seals Stadium on April 15, 1958 was special since Valmy Thomas called the pitches. Other current, former and future Santurce teammates (Willie Mays, Orlando Cepeda, Daryl Spencer and Willie Kirkland) were in the Giants line-up that day.[44] Cepeda later told me that he shared an apartment with Gómez in San Francisco and that Gómez was extremely helpful during his (Cepeda's) rookie season in the majors.

Cepeda and Gómez played pivotal roles in Santurce's last championship season of the 1950s. Gómez started 15 games for Santurce and completed all of them in compiling a 12–3 record.[45] That campaign included nine straight wins to open the season culminating with a 2–1 victory over San Juan on December 7, 1958.[46]

A semi-final series playoff incident between Gómez and Mayagüez's Joe Christopher resulted in severe damage to Gómez's red corvette. Santurce was on the brink of elimination when Gómez sped to Mayagüez in his corvette on January 25, 1959, prior to changing into his uniform and warming up before game five. Gómez had permission to drive to away games because he got sick riding on the team bus.

Gómez hit Mayagüez's first batter, Joe Christopher, on the head. This created some bad blood and Christopher (who continued in the game) went to the Mayagüez broadcast booth to help cool off the fans' emotions, according to Mayagüez broadcaster, Ismael Trabal. Gómez had a 4–0 lead in the eighth inning when Orlando Cepeda was drilled with oranges, bottles and empty beer cans when going after a foul ball. Cepeda could not make the catch and threw the ball into the stands. This created a bigger barrage. In the meantime, angry Mayagüez fans did all the damage they could to Gómez's corvette by breaking the windows and windshield as well as ruining its frame. Crew chief Frank Walsh forfeited the game to Santurce when the bombardment continued, but league President Carlos García de la Noceda fined Cepeda $200.[47]

Rubén Gómez won the seventh and decisive semi-final series game. The fining of Cepeda had a happy ending when Santurce fans made a collection before game four of the finals against Caguas to pay the $200 fine by the February 1, 1959 deadline. Gómez won game four to square the finals at two games each before Santurce won the next three contests in the best-of-nine series.[48]

Gómez won his sixth Caribbean Series game without a defeat when he beat the Almendares Blues in the series opener, 2–1.[49] He suffered his first Caribbean Series defeat four days later when the host Oriente ballclub from Venezuela defeated Santurce, 5–3.[50]

The 1960s: Gómez Ages Gracefully

A 32-year-old Rubén Gómez began his 13th season with Santurce in October 1959 and spent time on the disabled list (due to a trick right knee) for the first time in his Puerto Rico career. It may have been prophetic that this stint lasted 22 days between November 18 and December 10, 1959.[51] Gómez started 13 games and posted a winning ledger at 5–4.[52]

He was the property of the Philadelphia Phillies after the San Francisco Giants traded him and Valmy Thomas to the Phils for Jack Sanford prior to the 1959 big league season. That trade helped end the Giants-Crabbers' connection which began when Pedrín helped sign Gómez with the New York Giants.

Gómez could be feisty on the mound. In a mid–December 1959 game against Mayagüez, he gave up a homer to Ramón "Wito" Conde and then decked Conde in his next at-bat. Conde rushed to the mound, but cooler tempers prevailed and no one was hurt.[53] Gómez's best outing of the season was a 5–3 win over Caguas when he struck out 11 Criollos.[54] Caguas later defeated Santurce in the semi-finals.

The 1960–61 season was not fun due to Santurce's last place finish. Gómez started 16 games (one-fourth of the team's 64 contests) and had his first losing record (4–6) since 1953–54, when Santurce finished last.[55] Juan Pizarro was now the ace of Santurce's pitching staff. At 23, he was 10 years younger than Gómez and the Puerto Rico league's fastest pitcher.

Santurce rebounded to win the 1961–62 title, but Gómez was limited to 10 relief appearances.

"I could have pitched more, but Benson thought I was hurt," said Gómez. "He used me in the outfield, to pinch-hit and as a pinch-runner."

An interesting moment was when Orlando Cepeda opted not to return to his left field position after striking out in a late season game against Mayagüez. Home plate umpire Doug Harvey motioned for Benson to send in a replacement, and Gómez got the call.[56] Gómez was one of the last league players to do quadruple duty (pitch, pinch-hit, play a position or pinch-run).

Gómez befriended his Santurce teammate Bob Gibson and challenged him to lift a 1953 Pontiac off the ground. Gibson showed his strength by doing this and won a case of beer from Gómez.

"It took Gibson about three months to finish that case," said Gómez. "He really didn't drink much...had the best slider that I have ever seen."

A determined Gómez completed 12 of his 13 1962–63 regular season starts for Santurce skipper Ray Katt.[57] Gómez and Katt were teammates with the New York Giants from 1953 through 1957. Katt, a former catcher, was the same age as Gómez and a coach with the 1962 Cleveland Indians. Ray Katt put in a good word for Gómez, and Gómez's pitching talent enabled him to make that Cleveland team prior to his acquisition by the Minnesota Twins. Gómez started and won Santurce's first game against San Juan at the new Hiram Bithorn Municipal Stadium. Bob Turley opened for San Juan, but took the 6–1 loss on October 28, 1962.[58]

"I was disappointed in my performance," said Turley. "It wasn't like my [1953–54] season with San Juan when I led the league in strikeouts."

Gómez started Santurce's third semi-final series game against Caguas on January 28, 1963, but was not involved in the decision. This was a nostalgic game since it would be the last time that Gómez and Valmy Thomas would be batterymates in a 13-season winter league stretch and three big league seasons. Gómez left the game for a pinch-hitter in the bottom of the eighth. Little did he know that this game would last 19 innings, the longest in league history at the time, before Caguas prevailed, 5–3. *The San Juan Star* reported that Gómez was "throwing a great many change-ups."[59]

Preston Gómez used Gómez in relief throughout 1963–64 except for two spot starts. Gómez's summer stints were with Jacksonville and Portland in the St. Louis Cardinals chain at this time, and he relied on his smarts to get hitters out. He shared his knowledge with younger pitchers such as Mike Cuéllar. Cuéllar told me that his success as a big leaguer was due to Gómez's influence and patience in helping him develop a screwball. Juan Pizarro also benefited from Gómez's expertise in using the screwball.

The 1963–64 Crabbers did not make the playoffs, but Gómez was signed by one of the "vultures" to pitch for the Licey team in a special series comprising the top two Dominican and Venezuelan teams. "Vultures" were the Dominican and Venezuelan team officials and representatives who signed players from Puerto Rico teams as "mercenaries" for their post-season play. Gómez was given a start by Vern Benson against the Aguilas Cibaeñas in that series hosted by Santo Domingo on February 9, 1964, and pitched six plus innings in Licey's 8–4 win.[60] Licey had contracted Tony Oliva from the Arecibo Wolves and Mike de la Hoz of Santurce. Felipe Alou and Willie Stargell were the Aguilas top sluggers, and they picked up Cookie Rojas and Julio Navarro. The Valencia Industrialists featured Luis Aparicio and Luis Tiant and added Santurce's Elrod Hendricks. The Caracas Lions' top hitters were César Tovar and Vic Davalillo.

Rubén Gómez was 37 when the 1964–65 season began. There were some fans and players who wondered how much he had left. Bob Thurman was in Puerto Rico during November 1964 on a scouting assignment for the Cincinnati Reds when he took in a Santurce-Mayagüez game. Gómez hurled six strong innings in Santurce's 2–1 win before giving way to Jim Dickson in the seventh. Thurman complimented Gómez's performance: "That Rubén is a fine competitor," said Thurman. "He uses his head when he pitches."[61]

Jim Dickson marveled at Gómez's command of his pitches. "I would sit in the bullpen behind center field and chat with Rubén," said Dickson. "It was fascinating to see him throw that screwball ... away from left-handed hitters ... he was in good shape and didn't throw real hard."

Gómez was a stickler for conditioning who kept himself fit by running, playing golf and weight lifting. His master's degree in physical education was a plus. I first saw Gómez pitch during the 1964–65 season and was hooked by his positive demeanor with fans and fellow teammates.

Santurce's fans honored Gómez before their game against San Juan on December 23, 1964, by giving him a watch, household items, a rocking chair and other gifts. A *San Juan Star* writer stated that Gómez was a great teacher who "no longer pitches with his arm but with his heart and guts."[62]

Gómez proved this with four scoreless relief innings against San Juan in game six, the final one, of their semi-finals. He was warned twice for throwing at San Juan batters, but walked none and struck out three.[63] Pandemonium broke loose after Gómez got the last out to win it, 6–3.

Rubén Gómez did not see action in the finals against Mayagüez, but exhorted his teammates on to victory. No Caribbean Series was held.

A restless Gómez decided to pitch in Mexico. Many older and some younger professional ballplayers from Puerto Rico have ended or extended their summer careers in Mexico. The summer in Mexico plus the naming of Luis Olmo to manage the 1965–66 Crabbers were positive developments.

The snap was back in Gómez's slider and he pitched three shutouts for Santurce, including his first one in six seasons, a two-hitter against Arecibo on December 12, 1965.[64] Gómez blanked San Juan, 11–0, five days later.[65] A fine effort was an early season 3–2 win over Caguas and their ace, Ferguson Jenkins. Gómez singled off Jenkins and later scored on a three-run homer by Tany Pérez.[66] Gómez was Santurce's best pitcher with a 7–3 mark, nine complete games and a 1.92 E.R.A.[67] His scoreless inning in the league All-Star game helped the Latin Americans win it, 3–2.[68]

Life Continues at 39 and Beyond

Earl Weaver had no idea that Rubén Gómez would give him over 100 innings of work in his 20th winter season when Weaver managed the 1966–67 Crabbers. Nor could he imagine that Gómez exhibited the best control of his Puerto Rico career with 12 walks in 111 regular season innings,[69] not to mention a shutout in the semi-final as well as final series. Gómez showed leadership qualities as the team rep and the president of the Puerto Rico's Professional Baseball Players Association.

Gómez's 1966–67 season included a shutout of San Juan on January 5, 1967[70] followed by a scoreless ninth the next day against the Imports to preserve a 5–1 win for the Latin

Americans in the All-Star game. This contest was dedicated to Gómez, who received a plaque prior to the game.[71]

Gómez started game one of the semi-final series against the Arecibo Wolves and used 84 pitches in taming the Wolves, 5–0. Tito Stevens, sportswriter with *The San Juan Star*, noted that Gómez had not walked a batter in his last three regular season games plus this playoff win. Arecibo's only threat came in the eighth inning when Sandy Alomar, Sr. and Luis Isaac singled with none out. Gómez got Lucas Buyé to ground into a double play and Cookie Rojas to pop up to end the inning.[72]

Ten days later — on January 29, 1967 — Gómez turned the final series against Ponce around with a 7–0 win in game three, after Santurce had lost the first two games. The grim determination of Gómez was caught by the lens of David Acevedo, a photographer with *The San Juan Star*. Gómez struck out seven Lions and walked only one in going the route.[73]

Gómez's shutout inspired Santurce to sweep the next three games and claim the team's seventh league championship. He had earned another shot in the majors with the 1967 Phillies. Gómez made the Philadelphia team, and pitched in his tenth big league season prior to being released.

The 1967–68 season featured another solid performance by Gómez with a 5–4 record and 2.94 E.R.A. for the regular season champions.[74] Darrell Osteen, Juan Pizarro, Jim Hardin and Dave Leonhard comprised the starting rotation along with Gómez.

Gómez pitched in the All-Star game, and gave up a run in middle relief as the Imports took one from the Puerto Rico All-Stars, 3–1.[75] Darrell Osteen earned the win.

A week later, Gómez competed in a 36-hole golf tournament for baseball players at the Dorado Hilton, held on January 8–9, 1968. He carded a 153 to easily win this event over Santurce mates' Dave Johnson, Darrell Osteen, and Larry Haney; San Juan's Johnny Bench; and others.[76]

Santurce was favored going into the playoffs after winning the regular season. They advanced to the finals after knocking off Ponce in their five-game semi-finals. The 40-year-old Gómez's win in game four was his tenth and final semi-final series victory during his storied career.[77]

Gómez won game three against series-winning Caguas in the finals. His effort included an RBI double and scoring a run in Santurce's 6–3 win. He did not walk any and struck out four in six and two-thirds innings. This would be Gómez's eleventh and last final series win for the Crabbers.[78]

If Gómez surprised Earl Weaver with his pinpoint control and fluid post-season pitching, he startled new manager, Frank Robinson, with a 9–1 regular season mark and 2.05 E.R.A. in 1968–69.[79] Gómez earned the right-handed pitcher slot on the league's regular season All-Star team.[80]

Gómez continued serving as a mentor to the team's younger Puerto Rican and stateside players. Al Severinsen was throwing the ball well for the Baltimore Orioles in Clearwater, Florida, during the Instructional League, when they sent him to Santurce. Severinsen recalled that Rubén Gómez had a tutorial effect on him by explaining pitching thoughts and spending an exorbitant amount of time teaching and showing techniques.

"It was quite beneficial," said Severinsen. "If you made a mistake during a game, then they would work it out...."

Gómez started for the Native All-Stars in the league All-Star game and pitched a scoreless inning. Gómez's time with Severinsen paid dividends when the latter pitched two scoreless innings to save the game for the Imports, 2–1.[81]

Santurce's semi-final series with San Juan was a different matter. The Crabbers were heavy favorites after having won 49 regular season games and placing seven players on the league's final 10-player All-Star team. Gómez, Pizarro and Hendricks were joined on this select squad by George Scott, Leo Cárdenas, Paul Blair and Dave May. But San Juan took the first two semi-final series games, including a hard-fought 5–4 win in game two which Gómez lost in relief.[82]

Frank Robinson called upon Gómez to start game five with the series knotted at two wins apiece. Gómez gave up three runs in the fourth inning, but was otherwise impeccable when he was relieved by Severinsen in the seventh with San Juan holding a 3–2 lead. Severinsen remembers: "The fans' enthusiasm was the greatest thing. I came out of the bullpen and there were 10,000 people whistling and chanting 'Ese es tu Papá' (He is your Father/Master). I've been out of baseball a long, long time ... and had never seen anything so great happen in baseball."

The fact that San Juan won the series in seven games was academic to Severinsen almost 30 years later. He experienced a special moment when the Santurce faithful honored Gómez and the Crabbers with the chant "Ese es tu Papá," based on Gómez's long domination over San Juan.

1970s: The End of the Line

Gómez's final season in Santurce's starting rotation was the 1969–70 one when he was part of a quartet featuring Juan Pizarro, Dave Leonhard, Fred Beene and himself. He had two early season shutouts against Arecibo and the league's best team, the Ponce Lions. The second of these efforts was a 2–0 gem against Wayne Simpson, the loop's top pitcher and MVP.[83]

Roster changes were becoming more frequent by the early 1970s and Santurce used 14 pitchers and 18 position players throughout the season.[84] Teams still traveled by bus to the away games, but Gómez continued to use his own car for these games. The Mayagüez and Ponce teams would normally overnight in the San Juan area if they had a weekend series scheduled.

Dave Campbell was rooming with his Mayagüez teammate, Daryl Patterson, during one weekend series against Santurce.

"We checked into some little hotel near the Condado Beach," remembers Patterson. "Dave was going to have to face Rubén Gómez that night. He was laying there on the bed and all of a sudden said, 'I'm not going to take it, I'm going to charge the mound if he throws at me one more time.' Gómez didn't have large hands or size, but he was a magician with the ball. I've always told people you don't have to have large hands to make that ball do things, 'cause I've seen one of the best doing it."

Gómez started the All-Star game for the Native squad on Three Kings Day, 1970, and struck out Dave Campbell and Bernie Carbo, two of the league's best hitters, while allowing an infield hit in two scoreless frames. He did not figure in the decision, but his team posted a 6–1 win.[85]

Frank Robinson did not use Gómez in Santurce's semi-final series against Mayagüez, but started him in game one of the finals versus Ponce. Gómez was hit hard in the opening

Rubén Gómez showed Earl Weaver he could pitch very well in 1966–67 (courtesy of *The San Juan Star*).

frame, and replaced with Rogelio Moret in Ponce's 5–3 win. Number 22 made a three-inning relief appearance in game five at Bithorn, but was not involved in Ponce's 7–6, 10-inning win.[86]

Rubén Gómez pitched sporadically for Santurce during five more seasons, ending in 1975–76. He managed the Crabbers in 1971–72. His playing career ended after pitching eight games for the 1976–77 Bayamón Cowboys, formerly the San Juan Senators.[87]

Frank Robinson managed Gómez through 1974–75, and admired him due to his longevity, work ethic and the fact that he could still pitch. Gómez had hit Frank Robinson on the head during a big league game and hoped it was not taken personally. They ended up being good friends.

A nice moment of the 1970–71 season was when Gómez was carried off the field by his fellow Puerto Rican All-Stars after pitching two innings in the league All-Star game. Roberto Clemente, who respected Gómez from their days as Santurce teammates, opted to use Gómez in the fifth and sixth innings in the 4–1 win by the local stars. Gómez fanned his Santurce teammate, Tany Pérez, and gave up an unearned run.[88]

Gómez made a relief appearance in the 1971 Caribbean Series against the Hermosillo Orange Growers and took the loss when Hermosillo scored twice in the ninth.[89] That 7–5 loss would be Gómez's last Caribbean Series game. His career Caribbean Series record was six wins and two losses.[90]

Santurce returned to the Caribbean Series in 1973, but Gómez was no longer an integral part of the Crabbers' pitching staff. He pitched eight games in relief during the 1972–73 season while posting a 1–0 mark.[91] When the 1973–74 season opened, Gómez was on Santurce's inactive list. He got activated, but pitched sparingly through mid–December with his only win coming against San Juan. Thursday, December 20, 1973, was a night I will never forget. Frank Robinson sent Gómez to the mound against San Juan's Orlando Peña. Gómez was 46 at the time with Peña a mere 40.

It seemed like a pleasant dream. Gómez's tantalizing screwballs got the best of a San Juan line-up with Chris Chambliss, José Pagán and Rusty Torres. Mickey Rivers gave Gómez the only run he needed when he homered off Peña to open the bottom of the first inning. Rivers got three more hits in Santurce's 8–0 win. This would be Gómez's final regular season win for Santurce as well as his 33rd regular season shutout.[92]

"I think I felt stronger tonight than when I pitched against them last week," said Gómez. "The fans can keep the adrenaline flowing."[93]

There were 4,135 fans at Bithorn Stadium that night including myself and two older brothers. The crowd roared when Sergio "Cuchito" Ferrer struck out on a change-up. By the ninth inning, the chant "Ese es tu Papá" reverberated throughout Bithorn. I was in awe of Rubén Gómez that night and joined the fans in giving number 22 a standing ovation. Gómez earned his 51st regular season win and 17th shutout against San Juan.[94]

Santurce kept Gómez for two more seasons. Frank Robinson gave him one start in 1974–75 while Jack McKeon did likewise in 1975–76.[95] McKeon gave younger players a chance to shine in his earlier managing stint with Arecibo and continued this approach with Santurce. It became clear to Gómez that Santurce did not have him in their plans.

Gómez signed a contract with the 1976–77 Bayamón Cowboys, formerly the San Juan Senators. Bayamón mainly used Gómez against Santurce.

Dickie Thon was an 18-year-old youngster on Bayamón's practice squad when Gómez joined the team in their pre-season workouts. Thon's grandfather, Freddie, Sr., had played against Gómez in the late 1940s. Dickie Thon recalled that Gómez did not appear too happy at this stage of his career and that it had "something to do with Gómez not feeling appreciated by his former ballclub."

Gómez won one game for Bayamón, but called it quits when it became apparent that his 49-year-old right arm had enough mileage. Santurce paid homage to Gómez by having him throw out the first pitch prior to the league All-Star game at Bayamón's Juan Ramón Loubriel Stadium. Valmy Thomas caught the pitch while Pedrín Zorrilla was the symbolic hitter.[96]

There would be plenty of time for Gómez to work on his golf game after retiring from winter league competition. He rejoined Santurce in 1980–81 as a coach and enjoyed sharing these duties with former teammates Orlando Cepeda and Juan Pizarro. His 1981–82 Santurce managing stint did not last the whole season since Jack Aker took over at the halfway mark.

Rubén Gómez accomplished a lot in his baseball career from being the first Puerto Rican pitcher to start and win a World Series game, to winning 200 total regular season, All-Star, semi-final/final series, and Caribbean Series games with Santurce.[97] Gómez smiled when he told me that the Crabbers asked him to throw out the first pitch to open the 1990–91 season.

"They won the title that year for the first time in 18 years," said Gómez. "That tells me something."

Rubén Gómez showed "true grit" and determination throughout his Santurce career. He was a competitor in every sense of the word who kept focused on the task at hand.

4. From Caracas
to Caracas

*That [1954–55] Santurce ballclub was the greatest club I had ever been on
... it just jelled.*
— Bob Thurman, former Santurce outfielder/pitcher

Santurce's Caribbean Series trips to Caracas, Venezuela, in February 1955 and February 1959, followed league titles. Santurce won four straight regular season titles from 1954–55 through 1957–58, and finished second in 1958–59. Pedrín Zorrilla's close ties with the New York and San Francisco Giants resulted in Willie Mays, Steve Ridzik, Al Worthington, Jackie Brandt and Willie Kirkland wearing Santurce uniforms. League attendance faltered from the mid-to-late 1950s, and Pedrín was forced to sell his franchise.

1954–55: A "Dream Team" and "Dream Season"

The big "scoop" was Pedrín securing the services of National League MVP Willie Mays to patrol center field for Santurce. The Crabbers romped to the pennant, won the league finals and captured the Caribbean Series.

Guigo Otero Suro remembers how he and Pedrín got official permission from the New York Giants to use Willie Mays. It took a trip to New York and several meetings with Horace Stoneham and other Giants officials.

Chub Feeney, a nephew of Stoneham, was opposed to Mays playing for Santurce. Pedrín and Guigo felt that Mays might get hurt in the States during a barnstorming tour, and was less likely to suffer an injury in Puerto Rico.

One morning meeting dragged on in Stoneham's office until noon, when Stoneham took the group to his Riverside Apartment. Herman Franks, a Giants coach slated to manage Santurce, and Jack Schwarz, the organization's Director of Minor League Operations, were present. Stoneham served himself and the group some drinks. Later that afternoon, Stoneham took a phone call from a friend he had not seen for 25 years who had a layover at New York's Idlewild Airport. Stoneham then told Pedrín — whom he also called "Mr. Baseball": "I am on my way to the airport ... you can have Willie Mays."

New York Daily News columnist Jimmy Powers was concerned that Mays might get hurt playing winter ball and jeopardize his future. Powers felt that Mays' estimated $4,500 salary including expenses for the full winter season did not justify his Santurce stint. He added that Rubén Gómez should take the winter off after his stellar pitching for the 1954 Giants.[1]

Mays arrived at Isla Grande on October 16, 1954, accompanied by New York Giants scout Frank Forbes and writer Tom Meany. Pedrín, Herman Franks, and close to 1,000 fans met the party at 6:40 a.m.[2]

Tom Meany described the fans as half a welcoming committee and half a settling of wagers. He later wrote that there were bets that Mays would return to the States by November 1, and then by December 1.[3] Meany noted that Mays came to Puerto Rico to play ball as well as leave New York.

Santurce's other imports were Artie Wilson, Billy Klaus, George Crowe, Buster Clarkson, Sam Jones, Bob Thurman, Hal Jeffcoat and Pete Burnside. Burnside and Klaus were property of the Giants. Jeffcoat had pitched for the 1954 Chicago Cubs while Sam Jones was recently acquired by that franchise. Artie Wilson played for Seattle of the Pacific Coast League; Buster Clarkson's 1954 season was with Dallas in the Texas League; and George Crowe hit the long ball for the 1954 Toledo Mud Hens. Bob Thurman's 1954 season with Escogido, in the Dominican Summer League, had the most loop homers.[4]

An Escobar seating capacity crowd of 13,340 saw Mays make his Santurce debut against the San Juan Senators on October 17, 1954. Mays and Bob Thurman each hit three long batting practice homers.[5] San Juan was piloted by Harry Craft, the Kansas City Blues manager in the New York Yankees farm system. They had Yankee prospects Bob Cerv and Woody Held. Tom Meany threw out the first pitch. Mays struck out in his first two trips against Arnold Portocarrero, but then singled twice in Santurce's 9–8 loss.[6]

Some of Santurce's imports lived in the Gallardo Apartments across the street from Escobar Stadium. Tom Meany noted that Mays, George Crowe and Bill Greason (after joining Santurce) were three who did. Mays and Greason had most of their meals out until Mrs. Greason came to Puerto Rico.[7] Rice and chicken, local seafood and roast pig were Mays' favorite dishes. He enjoyed chatting with Herman Franks on road trips.

Mays hit his first league homer off Mayagüez's Tom Lasorda on November 7 several weeks after Lasorda had given Mays the "collar."[8] Lasorda briefly basked in the latter accomplishment.

"I teased him with the first pitch making it good enough to hit, but not good enough to overpower," said Lasorda. "Maybe I've discovered his weakness."[9]

A month into the season, Santurce was in fourth place with a 10–11 record, three games behind first place San Juan.[10] A turning point for Santurce was the wins over San Juan and Caguas the final week in November. Sam Jones blanked San Juan, 2–0, and struck out 15. Willie Mays was the hero the following night with a two-run homer in the 7–6 win over Caguas. Roberto Vargas had beaten Santurce three times when he only needed three more outs to protect his 6–5 lead. But Roberto Clemente singled and Mays cracked his seventh homer to give Santurce the win.[11]

Mays was in a good frame of mind since Horace Stoneman had signed him to a $25,000 contract for the 1955 big league season during an early winter season visit to Puerto Rico. Stoneham was impressed with Mays' new batting stance and first few homers for Santurce.

"Willie hit one to dead center, one to left center and one to right center," said

Herman Franks and Willie Mays outside the team bus on a 1954–55 road trip (courtesy of Diana Zorrilla).

Stoneham. "He wasn't pulling the ball to left, as he had been early in the [1954] National League season...."[12]

Roster changes were made by various league teams between early November and Christmas. Santurce released Artie Wilson and Billy Klaus with Klaus catching on with Caguas. The Crabbers signed infielders Ronnie Samford and Billy Gardner from the New York Giants organization. Elston Howard joined San Juan. Mayagüez dropped Don Zimmer, but Herman Franks convinced Pedrín to sign Zimmer. Hal Jeffcoat was inactivated so that Bill Greason would have a roster spot. Billy Gardner was let go due to a ruling prohibiting a major league club from having more than five players in winter ball. Shortstop Don Zimmer replaced Gardner on Santurce's roster.

"I was struggling with Mayagüez and they let me go," said Zimmer. "There was some kind of rule that if I left Puerto Rico, then any other club could bring me back to Puerto Rico to play ... went to Miami, and Herman Franks called me to play for Santurce ... got on an airplane to Puerto Rico."

Zimmer began hitting the ball and teamed with Ronnie Samford to give Santurce defensive strength up the middle. Ronnie Samford called it a "heck of a ballclub." Samford became known as the "White Sea" by Santurce fans for his good range and the fact that Santurce's former second baseman, Junior Gilliam, was the "Black Sea." Samford recalls being the first white continental (U.S.) player with Santurce to have a day in his honor.

"They passed around two five-gallon buckets," said Samford. "After the game I walked across the street with all those nickels and dimes...."

Pete Burnside, Zimmer's roommate at their Gallardo Apartment near Escobar, also has fond memories of that season.

"My first recollection of the Escobar clubhouse was a big picture, four feet by two feet, of Josh Gibson, with the caption: 'Bambino of the Caribbean,'" said Burnside. "Dick Seay, one of our coaches, would say a lot of things about the old-timers ... Orlando Cepeda was a kid running around the ballpark. I was a young kid with talent, but the older guys were the 'players'."

Burnside befriended Santurce pitcher, Ben Quintana, from a well-to-do family, who showed him around. He recalls the veteran Luis Olmo as someone who spoke English very well, a very dignified guy. Burnside paid special attention to the former Negro leaguers (Clarkson, Crowe, Greason, Thurman).

"My [undergraduate] thesis at Dartmouth was on the Negro leaguers," said Burnside. "They [Santurce's ex-Negro leaguers] couldn't have been nicer. George Crowe and Bob Thurman were class guys. Clarkson was in a class [at third base] with Ray Dandridge and Brooks Robinson ... some real team leaders in Crowe, Clarkson and Thurman ... it was wonderful."

Santurce's "big three" starters (Rubén Gómez, Sam Jones and Bill Greason) were tops in Burnside's book. He admired Gómez for sticking up for the Caribbean/Puerto Rican players. Jones was a sidearmer with a wicked curve ball, and the first African-American pitcher to hurl a big league no-hitter.[13] Greason was a consistent workhorse who got the job done.

Poto Paniagua followed Santurce closely throughout the season. He told me that if they had two or three additional pitchers, then there was no doubt in his mind they stacked up against any big league team.

Hal Jeffcoat, who pitched and played some outfield for Santurce, stated that it was an honor to play for the Crabbers. Jeffcoat belonged to the Chicago Cubs at the time.

"Puerto Rico's fans were great," said Jeffcoat. "They were almost as good as Cub fans and Brooklyn fans ... our bus would get stoned by the fans after defeating the home team. And what a team we had! Surely, history will prove that to be true."

Mays and Clemente, according to Burnside, were younger stars trying to outdo each other on the field in a friendly rivalry. Even backstop Valmy Thomas got into the act by using white tape around his fingers during the night games at Escobar and other league stadiums where the night lighting was not so good. The white tape enabled Santurce's pitchers to see Thomas' signs. This was a team which got closer together and developed a great chemistry as the season wore on.

Santurce opened up a game-and-a-half lead over Caguas and a four-game margin over San Juan by December 15.[14] They had won 15 of their last 18 games, including a December 9–10 home-and-away sweep of the Criollos. Roberto Vargas was shelled on December 9, in Santurce's 14–2 win by Rubén Gómez. Mays enjoyed a four-for-four night with two doubles and Clemente and Clarkson drilled long homers. Santurce pulled a fourth inning triple play. Víctor Pellot and Rance Pless were on second and first, respectively, when Willie Tasby smashed a line drive to Samford at second. Samford doubled off Pless by throwing to first, and Pepe Lucas threw it back to Samford to complete the triple

Pete Burnside, 1954–55 season (courtesy of Diana Zorrilla).

play![15] Sam Jones went the route the next night in Santurce's 8–2 win. Pepe Lucas and Bob Thurman homered. Some Santurce players then participated in the All-Star game.

The league's All-Star game was played in Mayagüez on December 12 with the San-turce-San Juan players as the "North" squad against the Caguas-Mayagüez-Ponce play-ers, or "South" team. Roberto Clemente hit two homers as the North won, 7–5. Willie

Left to Right: Santurce's "Murderers Row" in 1954–55, Willie Mays, Roberto Clemente, Buster Clarkson, Bob Thurman, George Crowe (courtesy of Diana Zorrilla).

Mays put the visitors on the board first with his inside-the-park homer in the initial stanza. Clemente's blasts were a solo shot off Roberto Vargas in the third inning and a two-run homer against Ponce's David Cole in the fifth. Rubén Gómez got the win.[16]

Luis Cabrera came into the picture two weeks later when he hurled a two-hit shutout over Caguas in game two of a twin-bill. This brought tears to many since it was Cabrerita's first league win in nearly three years.[17]

One concern for league officials was the low attendance despite the heroics of Cabrera, Mays and other league stars. Santurce's home attendance by season's end was down 7.5 percent from the 1953–54 season. Overall league attendance was down by 33 percent.[18]

Pedrín pinpointed two reasons: the advent of television and the island economy.[19] Other league owners and fans echoed Pedrín's sentiments on television as the culprit. Puerto Rico's economic expansion of the 1950s took a pause in fiscal year 1955 (July 1, 1954 — June 30, 1955) when a fairly high number of manufacturing plants closed their doors.

Santurce's romp to the pennant was a third reason. Fans in Mayagüez and Ponce lamented the lack of league parity. Pundits noted the higher number of imports [nine] per team was a reason for lower attendance and that more native players would bring the fans out.

Caguas won three of its four semi-final series games with San Juan while Santurce enjoyed a bye. Willie Mays, called "Sey Juey" (crab kid) by his older Santurce teammates, won the batting title and league MVP Award; Buster Clarkson was the RBI king; and, Roberto Clemente finished fourth with a .344 batting mark behind Mays, San Juan's Elston Howard, and Canena Márquez of Mayagüez in the batting chase.[20] Sam Jones (14–4), Rubén Gómez (13–4) and Bill Greason (8–2) were the league's best pitchers.[21]

Santurce hosted Caguas to begin the best-of-seven finals. Their only line-up change since Christmas 1954 was at catcher with Harry Chiti replacing Valmy Thomas. Pete Burnside was put on the inactive list to make room for Chiti. The Crabbers lined up with Zimmer at short, Clemente in left, Mays in center, Clarkson at third, Thurman in right, Crowe at first, Chiti catching, Samford at second and Rubén Gómez on the mound.

Caguas was crushed, 10–3, in game one, as Clemente went four-for-five with four RBI. Thurman hit a homer and Gómez went the distance.[22] Caguas evened the series the next night, 7–3, behind Chi Chi Olivo's pitching and homers by Charlie Neal, Bob Montag and Félix Mantilla. Paid attendance was 7,679, half of what a final series game at Escobar game used to draw.[23]

Santurce came back in game three to trounce Caguas, 14–0, with Bill Greason on the mound. Joey Jay started for Caguas, but left the game in pain after throwing two pitches. Don Zimmer's four hits and four RBI paced the 17-hit Santurce attack. A Caguas official later admitted that he hid Joey Jay in his own house for two days because of his concern for the pitcher's safety from angry Caguas fans.[24]

The Crabbers won game four, 13–1, on February 6, 1955. Rubén Gómez had a no-hitter going through seven innings, but settled for a three-hitter. Four of Santurce's 13 hits were home runs by Chiti, Clarkson, Mays and Thurman.[25] Sam Jones won the clincher, a 6–2 win on February 7, 1955 as Zimmer cracked his third series homer for the visiting Crabbers.[26]

The celebration began just after midnight when Tetelo Vargas grounded out to Ronnie Samford. Guigo Otero Suro exclaimed, "Se acabó!" (It's over). Willie Mays hugged Pedrín in the dugout area. Santurce players boarded the team bus after their showers and a brief celebration. Rubén Gómez and Sam Jones later joined Pedrín in his house to celebrate Santurce's title.[27]

Pete Burnside was thrilled to find out he would fly to Caracas for the 1955 Caribbean Series.

"Pedrín released me, but kept me at the same salary for the Caribbean Series," said Burnside. "As I remember, there were armed guards in the stadium with automatic weapons. We stayed at the Hotel Tamanaco on the hill in an upper class section."

Burnside was Santurce's batting practice pitcher for the six-game round-robin event which featured Cuba's Almendares Blues, Panama's Carta Vieja Yankees and the host Magallanes Navigators. Santurce would win five of the six series games en route to their third Caribbean Series title.

Dick Young wrote about the rabid enthusiasm in Caracas that would make "Brooklyn's Ebbets Field seem like a whimpering cry from a hospital nursery.... violent hatred for all umpires ... a sharp, if sometimes biased knowledge of baseball ... but above all, a burning desire to do things in big league style."[28]

Rubén Gómez got Santurce off to a splendid start when he held the Almendares

Blues in check for a 6–2 win on February 10, 1955 before 34,000 paid lunatics. This Santurce club was the first and only team from Puerto Rico to not sign reinforcements for a Caribbean Series. The Crabbers were too much for George "Red" Munger as Harry Chiti and Ronnie Samford drove in two runs apiece. Don Zimmer's seventh inning home run capped the scoring.[29]

Zimmer led off game two against Panama with another homer and Bill Greason later cracked a fifth inning home run in Santurce's 2–1 victory over Panama. Greason: "It was great ... one of the largest crowds I had ever pitched before. I remember the home run and winning, 2–1. There was a lot of excitement competing against Panama, Cuba and Venezuela."

Santurce faced the hosts in game three. Herman Franks had managed Magallanes the prior winter, and knew about the rabid Caracas fans and Magallanes' starting pitcher, Ramón Monzant, a New York Giants prospect. He remembered that Willie Mays had not had a series hit yet.

"Mays went 0-for-12 [including game three] and then he got hot," said Franks. "Zimmer hit a few home runs and we won it."

Carta Vieja upset Almendares, 3–2, in an 11-inning game on February 12, 1955, prior to the Santurce-Magallanes contest. That game was decided on a homer by New York Giants prospect Gip Dickens. Monzant and Sam Jones then went the distance in the 11-inning, 2 hour-and-twenty-five minute classic, won by Santurce, 4–2. It was two minutes past midnight local time when Roberto Clemente singled to open the Santurce half of the 11th. At precisely 12:03 a.m., Willie Mays broke his 0-for-12 slump with a home run on a 1–1 pitch.[30] Gui Gui Lucas, the Magallanes catcher, walked away as Mays circled the bases and leaped upon home plate.

Juan Vené, who covered this series, told me that the baseball fell halfway into the bleachers, after going over the 385-foot sign in left center. Vené and his fellow sportswriters got to chat with Mays.

"Mays hit it over 400 feet ... one of the highlights of Caribbean Series history," said Vené. "Mays was quite friendly with the press. He spoke some words in Spanish to us and identified himself with Puerto Rico."

Enriqueta Marcano Zorrilla was in the stands throughout that series. She also enjoyed dancing the "cha cha cha" with Santurce trainer, Pepo Talavera, after the games. Enriqueta remembers that Venezuela's fans did a "quiet sign" routine while Mays was in his hitting slump.

"When Mays stepped to the plate, you could hear a sh sh sh whisper throughout the stadium," said Enriqueta. "That changed."

Mays went four-for-five against Almendares in Santurce's come-from-behind win in game four. Rubén Gómez left the game with a fifth inning hand injury and a 5–0 deficit. Santurce trailed 6–0 when Mays' two-run triple in the home sixth scored Zimmer and Clemente. Clarkson's single made it 6–3. Mays scored in the eighth on a Bob Thurman double.

Almendares' Red Munger retired Chiti and Samford on grounders in the ninth. Alfonso Gerard pinch-hit for reliever Jorge "Garabato" Sackie, and singled to left. Zimmer hit a homer to left center field, to tie the game at 6. Clemente walked on four pitches, and Al Lyons came in from the pen to face Mays. The "Sey Juey" kid hit a single to right and Clemente never stopped running. Almendares right fielder Lee Walls bobbled the ball, but got it to second baseman Al Federoff, who threw it wide of the plate.[31]

Santurce clinched the series crown with a 11–3 thrashing of Carta Vieja on February 14, 1955. Bill Greason won his second game and Willie Mays got three of Santurce's 16 hits. Harry Chiti's three-run homer and Roberto Clemente's two triples were key blows.[32] Magallanes defeated Santurce in a meaningless final game of the series.

The Crabbers placed five players on the series All-Star team: Chiti at catcher, series MVP Zimmer at shortstop, center fielder Mays, Greason and Jones. Mays (.440) finished runner-up to Rocky Nelson (.471) of Almendares for the series batting title, but had the most hits (11) and RBI (9). Clemente scored the most runs (8).[33] Luis Muñoz Marín sent a congratulatory telegram to Pedrín Zorrilla: "I commend Puerto Rico's representative for their resounding triumph ... it exemplifies the fighting spirit of our people."[34]

Over 50,000 fans awaited the arrival of the plane from Caracas with the inscription: "Santurce, Campeón Séptima Serie del Caribe." (Santurce, Champion Seventh Caribbean Series). Enriqueta Marcano Zorrilla recalled that it was painted on the plane by Venezuelan workers. The silver bird landed at Isla Grande at 3:26 p.m. on Wednesday, February 16, 1955. Four minutes later, it came to a complete halt in front of the National Guard offices.[35] Monchile Concepción and Rubén Gómez deplaned first.

The first to speak was Pedrín: "We had the utmost confidence in our players ... the Americans as well as the native [Puerto Rican, U.S. Virgin Islands, Dominican] players gave it their all ... special thanks to those fans who took time off from work to be here ... those who could not be with us."[36]

Most eyes were riveted on the two trophies carried by Santurce equipment manager, Vicente Figueroa. One was the series cup and the other one a special trophy commemorating Santurce's third Caribbean Series title.

This was the highlight of Ronnie Samford's baseball career in terms of the festivities (a parade from the airport and a party at La Fortaleza with the governor) followed by more parties. Don Zimmer later told me that this was the greatest winter league ballclub ever assembled — a big league ballclub with an outstanding manager in Herman Franks. Franks felt the team's only shortcoming was its lack of pitching depth compared to major league teams. Hal Jeffcoat echoed Zimmer's sentiments when he told me that Franks was an excellent manager who had sound judgment and was fair.

Pedrín Zorrilla deserved much of the credit for Santurce's success, according to Jeffcoat: "Pedrín was one of the finest gentlemen I ever met ... he was fair, thoughtful, a real baseball fan ... credit to Puerto Rico and its people."

Willie Mays' positive attitude also rubbed off on his teammates. Branch Rickey, Jr. saw Mays warm up the Santurce batting practice pitcher during a regular season game in Caguas. Mays even threw a strike to second base on the final warm-up pitch.

"I've always maintained that you can learn more about a ballplayer by watching him two days in the winter leagues than you can by watching him for two weeks in the States," said Branch Rickey, Jr. "Down here, the fellow who puts out is the fellow who likes to play ... and the fellow who likes to play is the fellow who'll help your club."[37]

Bob Thurman's face lit up when we conversed about this Santurce team during an October 1992 weekend. Thurman: "That ballclub was the greatest ballclub I had ever been on. Then, too, we were just like a big family; everyone would do something for somebody else ... it just jelled 'cause we had the talent to play the game ... and it's really a happy situation when you can play with a bunch of good kids and win like that. With all those long ball hitters and guys catching balls over their heads ... nobody could beat us. I often thought that we could beat any major league club with the set-up we had."

The plane which brought the 1955 Caribbean Series champs home (courtesy of Diana Zorrilla).

Left to Right: Willie Mays, Dick Seay, Bob Thurman, 1954–55 (courtesy of Diana Zorrilla).

1955–56: Caguas Dethrones Santurce

Santurce led from start to finish in winning the regular season title, but were denied a Caribbean Series trip by Caguas. Herman Franks returned as the skipper. New Santurce faces were Steve Ridzik, Daryl Spencer, Bill White, Al Worthington, Orlando "Peruchín" Cepeda, José Pagán and Juan "Terín" Pizarro. League attendance was 394,173 paid fans, a 13 percent decrease from 1954–55.[38] The first league game was televised.

The New York Giants signed an agreement with the Escogido Lions in the new Dominican Winter League. Escogido had Felipe Alou and Ozzie Virgil, Sr., plus more Giants prospects, but could sign players from other big league teams like Harry Chiti of the Cubs. Some of Santurce's Dominican players (Pepe Lucas and Jorge Sackie) returned to their homeland to play. The new four-team circuit was not under the Caribbean Confederation comprising Cuba, Panama, Puerto Rico and Venezuela.

Pedrín Zorrilla received the Puerto Rico league winner's trophy from Julio Monagas, the island's Parks and Recreation Commissioner, prior to the season opener against Caguas on October 15, 1955. Santurce won it, 5–2, behind Rubén Gómez.[39]

The injury bug hit the Crabbers for the first time on October 24, when Don Zimmer fractured his wrist after being hit by a pitch. Zimmer made more news than the prior day's event (the first televised game in league history between Caguas and Ponce).[40]

Santurce's longest regular season game was a 16-inning affair at Ponce on October 30, 1955, a 3–2 Lions win. Mickey Owen, Ponce's player-manager, gave Ponce the early lead with an RBI single, but Orlando Cepeda's first league homer, a two-run shot, tied the

Orlando Cepeda crosses the plate after hitting his first league homer, October 30, 1955 (courtesy of Diana Zorrilla).

game. Rubén Gómez pitched six scoreless relief innings before Faye Throneberry's homer won it.[41]

Two of Santurce's best imports were pitcher Steve Ridzik and first baseman Bill White. Ridzik was 4–0 after defeating Ponce on November 4, 1955, on his way to a 14-win season. White hit his sixth and seventh homers of the season in that win over Ponce.[42] Orlando Cepeda recalled that White hustled all winter before earning the New York Giants first base job.

"Bill was there with his advice and goodwill," said Cepeda. "He was a gentleman."

Ridzik had pitched for Ponce in 1953–54 and was looking to catch on with a big league club when he joined Santurce. He was impressed with the Santurce environment and his teammates. Ridzik: "Clemente was not a one-dimension type guy [player] ... very capable.

We had Juan Pizarro, José Pagán, Cepeda just at an age [18] getting ready to break in. Rubén [Gómez] was there … Worthington, Greason. In my case, it was to get extra work I needed to develop my stuff and keep it going."

Ridzik's abode was the Gallardo Apartments, where teammates Daryl Spencer, Bill White, Al Worthington and Don Zimmer lived. He recalls that they invited Pedrín and Diana Zorrilla there for a Christmas party.

"Pedrín was very knowledgeable," said Ridzik. "He knew the game of baseball very well."

Former Santurce radio broadcaster and *The Sporting News* correspondent Pito Alvarez de la Vega wrote this about Ridzik:

> The strong right arm of Steve Ridzik is creating the major surprise of the Puerto Rican League campaign. The former Phillies and Cincinnati chucker …can claim much of the credit for Santurce's comfortable lead in the pennant race. With the season five weeks old, he boasted the spectacular record of seven victories without a defeat.[43]

Ridzik's showing was the key factor in his selection by the New York Giants in the minor league draft. He also started the league's All-Star game for the Imports, but was not involved in the decision.[44]

By the season's halfway point, Santurce was 25–11. All 25 wins were accounted for by Ridzik, Worthington, Gómez and Greason.[45] Santurce's fortunes changed when Worthington was shelved with a stomach ailment and Zimmer, who rejoined the team after his wrist injury, suffered an appendicitis attack on December 17, 1955.[46]

Carl Hubbell, in his capacity as the New York Giants minor league coordinator, arrived in Puerto Rico on January 9, 1956, to get a closer look at Gómez, Ridzik and Worthington. Hubbell had heard great things about Santurce rookie, Juan Pizarro, and hoped to see him pitch.[47] Pizarro never became the property of the Giants since Santurce's Luis Olmo was a Milwaukee Braves scout who signed him to a lucrative bonus.

While Hubbell was in Puerto Rico, the print and radio commentary focused on the league's attendance woes. One theme was that most of Puerto Rico's baseball owners were true sports aficionados who loved the game, but did not have the business instincts to make a go of it.[48] There were the usual comments on having fewer imports, the negative impact of television and the fact Santurce made a mockery of the pennant race.

It took Caguas and San Juan 10 days to play their semi-final series since heavy rains postponed six straight contests. Caguas won three of the four games to challenge Santurce for the title. Herman Franks showed his class, prior to the finals, by asking league officials to give the Manager of the Year award to Caguas pilot, Ben Geraghty, after both received 14 votes apiece from members of the island media.[49]

Caguas visited Santurce for a Sunday afternoon-night twin-bill to open the finals on February 5. Roberto Vargas won the opener, 6–5, over Al Worthington as Wes Covington and Ramón Maldonado homered. But Steve Ridzik won the second contest, 1–0, when Tom Lasorda walked Bill White in the 11th inning and gave up base hits to Roberto Clemente and Allie Clark.[50]

"It was always tough winning in the [Puerto Rico] winter league," said Ridzik. "You couldn't just walk in there and win … had to earn it."

Rubén Gómez's complete game (3–2) win the following day gave Santurce a short-lived series lead since Caguas swept the February 7 double-header, 10–8 and 10–2, behind

Bill White slides into second as Félix Mantilla of Caguas tries to tag him (courtesy of Diana Zorrilla).

the pitching of Taylor Phillips and Lasorda. The finals ended on February 8, when Roberto Vargas won his second series game, 8–3. Félix Mantilla hit two homers for Caguas and Bob Lennon, a late season acquisition, slugged two homers in a losing cause.[51]

1956–57: Changing of the Guard

The New York Giants sent their top U.S. prospects to Escogido in the Dominican Republic. Willard Brown made his final Santurce appearance. Sandy Koufax pitched for Caguas. Pedrín sold his team to Ramón Cuevas, who, in turn, sold Roberto Clemente, Juan Pizarro and Ronnie Samford to Caguas. Clemente won the batting title and set the all-time league standard with a 23-game consecutive hit streak. Santurce won a third straight regular season crown, but lost the final series to Mayagüez.

This was a season of transition and change. No All-Star game was scheduled. Four of the five clubs opened with new managers: Mayagüez (Mickey Owen), Ponce (Quincy Trouppe), San Juan (Ralph Houk) and Santurce (Monchile Concepción). Caguas' Ben Geraghty returned for his third year.

Bill Rigney, the New York Giants manager, was not happy with the big league performance of Rubén Gómez and Al Worthington. This resulted in the Giants sending their top prospects to Escogido. Among them were Pete Burnside, Bob Lennon and Willie Kirkland. The Giants even sent Leon Wagner to Caguas! Their less seasoned prospects went to other winter leagues; Willie McCovey signed with Vanytor of the Colombian League.[52]

Pedrín's friendship with Bill White was instrumental in White being the only New York Giants' import to return. There was still a Santurce-New York connection since Pedrín had signed Julio Navarro for the Giants in the "Class of 1955" along with Orlando Cepeda and José Pagán. Navarro was born in the offshore island of Vieques, Puerto Rico, but grew up in St. Croix, U.S. Virgin Islands, where he impressed Santurce coach Dick Seay and Alfonso Gerard in practice games against a combined San Juan-Santurce team.

"Pedrín signed me for a $300 bonus after a March 1955 tryout in Puerto Rico," said Navarro. "Cepeda and Pagán got $500 each. Pedrín gave us our start [in organized baseball] and we were grateful to him."

The loss of the Giants' imports was made up by others such as Earl Hersch of the Milwaukee Braves. Hersch: "They treated me like a long lost friend ... Mr. Z was there to help you with any problem you might have. His tales about the old times were always fun ... used to talk about Josh Gibson and Satchel Paige and the duels they used to have. Mr. Z always had a winner, so he knew something!"

Caguas' Sandy Koufax was the talk of the league after his one-hit shutout of Mayagüez on Halloween night. So was Juan Pizarro two nights later when he defeated Caguas, 2–1. Ronnie Samford, now with the Detroit organization, hit the game-winning homer in the bottom of the ninth.[53]

"Juan and I became good friends," said Hersch. "We were teammates at Wichita [Braves farmclub] for awhile. He had good stuff ... were comparing him to Koufax back then ... both had a lot of potential."

Hersch remembers facing Koufax in Puerto Rico on a Sunday afternoon.

"He had a good curve ball that day ... reached up and cocked his arm ... and threw so hard and so good...even terrific down there."

Santurce won 10 straight games in November to claim first place. One of them was a 20–3 pasting of Mickey Owen's Mayagüez club on November 10, 1956. The streak's final win came on November 16, 1956, when Willard Brown cracked two homers against the Ponce Lions. These were Brown's last league home runs. Santurce activated Brown to replace Bill White, who was called to the States for induction into the U.S. Army.[54]

"I had wedding plans that winter and Pedrín offered us his Manatí beach house for our honeymoon," said White. "The Army called me ... Pedrín's love of all persons, regardless of race or origin, made me appreciate him even more ... and he was one of the most important figures in my life."[55]

Santurce's pitching staff included former big leaguers Marion Fricano, Duke Markell and Charlie Gorin. All were minor leaguers at the time. Rubén Gómez was the only current big leaguer on the staff. Much of the attention was on 19-year-old Juan Pizarro.

Pizarro continued his fine pitching with back-to-back shutouts versus San Juan on December 4, and Ponce on December 9, 1956. Pizarro and Cepeda hit solo homers and Earl Hersch cracked a two-run shot in the latter game.[56]

Sandy Koufax's final Puerto Rico league game on December 16 was a 2–0 win over Santurce. Clemente got Santurce's only two hits off Koufax.[57] Caguas released Koufax due to a league ruling which precluded teams from having more than three imports with big league experience. Caguas owner Rafael Ramos Cobián, a theater mogul, announced Koufax's release.

Pedrín then sold his beloved Crabbers to Ramón Cuevas in a deal completed shortly after Christmas. A tearful Pedrín bid his players farewell before the game against Caguas on December 27, and exhorted them to play hard.[58] On December 30, Cuevas confirmed the sale of Roberto Clemente, Juan Pizarro and Ronnie Samford to Caguas for $30,000. Those proceeds were used to liquidate Santurce franchise debts. Monchile Concepción resigned as Santurce's manager the day after a December 30, 1956 twin-bill at Mayagüez, and was replaced by Santurce coach Ted Norbert.[59]

Caguas failed to make the playoffs despite their powerful line-up. The Criollos finished fourth after losing a tie-breaker with San Juan for third. San Juan then lost three straight semi-final series games with Mayagüez to set up a Santurce-Mayagüez final series.

Mickey Owen's club won four of the five games to earn a trip to Havana, Cuba, for the Caribbean Series. Herb Plews of the Washington Senators and Bill Harrell of the Cleveland Indians were Mayagüez's hitting stars along with Canena Márquez. Bob Smith and Pete Wojey pitched well.

1957–58: A Fourth Straight Pennant

League imports were reduced to four per team. No All-Star games were scheduled for the next two seasons. Bob Thurman returned for his 11th and last Santurce season to help the Crabbers win their fourth straight regular season title. Santurce's Bill Harrell won the league batting crown. Orlando Cepeda hit for power and average on his way to the big leagues. Caguas spoiled Santurce's fun by sweeping them in the finals.

Santurce had Monchile Concepción back in the fold as the manager. Santurce's four imports (Marion Fricano, Bill Greason, Bill Harrell and Bob Thurman) produced throughout the season and stayed injury-free.

Several team owners including Alfonso Valdés of Mayagüez and José M. Rivera of San Juan followed in Pedrín Zorrilla's footsteps by relinquishing their franchise ownership. The pessimists asserted that the growing popularity of horse racing would continue to take its toll since an estimated $500,000 weekly was being wagered at the new El Comandante Racetrack which had opened on January 11, 1957.[60]

Sunday baseball games at Escobar were scheduled for 10:30 a.m. to give the fans a chance to enjoy the ballgames and the afternoon horse races. One Sunday morning game on October 27, 1957, between San Juan and Santurce, drew 4,150 fans who saw the Crabbers' three-run rally in the ninth for a 9–7 win.[61]

San Juan responded to their new manager, Luis Olmo, by tying Caguas for second place and making the playoffs. Mickey Owen managed Mayagüez in their playoff quest. Ponce hired Pancho Coímbre as their skipper and replaced him with another legend, George Scales, when Coímbre resigned.

Caguas' Juan Pizarro's MVP season included 19 strikeouts in nine innings against Ponce on November 20, 1957.[62] Only Leon Day had recorded that many strikeouts in a league game, but his gem was a 13-inning game.[63]

There was more league parity since three-and-a-half games separated the five teams at the midway point of the season on December 4, 1957.[64] Santurce rebounded from their 16–17 record at the time to win 20 of their 31 "second half" games and claim the pennant.

One reason for Santurce's second half surge was the starting pitching of Rubén Gómez, Bill Greason, Marion Fricano and Julio Navarro who combined for all 36 Santurce wins.[65] Shortstop Bill Harrell won the batting crown while Orlando Cepeda tied Víctor Pellot for the league lead in homers and led the circuit in RBI.[66] Bob Thurman paced the league in triples and Mayagüez's Maury Wills topped the loop in stolen bases.[67] Harrell told me this Santurce team was a scrappy bunch which gave 110 percent, just like Maury Wills. Santurce decided to sign Harrell after his final series exploits for Mayagüez against the Crabbers the prior winter.

San Francisco Giants owner Horace Stoneham stated, during a trip to Puerto Rico, that Cepeda was ready for the big leagues. Stoneham was looking forward to spring training.[68]

Cepeda later told me that this winter season was important.

"It definitely prepared me for my rookie season with the Giants," said Cepeda. "There is no question about that."

Santurce faced Caguas, now managed by Ted Norbert, in the finals. Caguas defeated San Juan in the semi-finals by winning three of the four games.

Roberto Clemente was back in a Caguas uniform. Clemente dominated Caguas' four-game sweep of Santurce by hitting .529. Ronnie Samford got into the act early by hitting a two-run homer off Rubén Gómez at Caguas in the Criollos' 9–2 series opening win on January 30, 1958. Clemente hit a double and two singles off his friend and former teammate, Bill Greason, in game two, a 5–0 home win for Roberto Vargas.[69]

The series moved to Escobar on February 1. Pizarro struck out 15 Crabbers and hit a key double in a four-run eighth inning rally to lead the Criollos to a 7–4 win. Caguas put the icing on the cake with a 10–3 win on February 2, as Jerry Nelson went the route.[70] Caguas chose Valmy Thomas and Marion Fricano to reinforce them for the Caribbean Series.

1958–59: A Return Trip to Caracas

Pedrín Zorrilla returned as Santurce's general manager. The San Francisco Giants sent Jackie Brandt and Willie Kirkland to bolster Santurce. Monchile Concepción managed Santurce to a second place finish behind San Juan. Both clubs stopped televising their games to help attendance. The Crabbers bested Mayagüez in the semi-finals, and Caguas in the best-of-nine finals to earn a Caribbean Series trip to Caracas.

Maximum player salaries were cut from $1,000 to $800 per month. Imports who were married received a $250 monthly living allowance while "bachelor imports" were given a $200 monthly stipend.[71] Jackie Brandt and his wife liked their Puerto Rico living arrangements. A maid was paid $10 per week to do the shopping, cooking and help tend to the baby. There were no car expenses since Brandt lived in the Carmen Apartments, catty corner from Escobar. Pedrín invited Brandt to the racetrack and to have meals. Jackie Brandt recalled meeting Chi Chi Rodríguez at a Dorado golf course.

Jackie Brandt began the season on a tear. During the week of October 20–26, 1958, he had 13 hits in 21 at-bats and nine consecutive hits at one stretch. Brandt's four straight hits in a 14–2 win over Mayagüez were followed by five hits in a 14–4 drubbing of San Juan.[72] Brandt kept up his torrid hitting finishing second to Orlando Cepeda in the batting chase. Valmy Thomas and José Pagán were also stinging the ball for Santurce.

Horace Stoneham, San Francisco manager Bill Rigney, and scout Tom Sheehan sojourned to Puerto Rico on November 7, 1958, to find Brandt, Cepeda, Pagán, Thomas, Rubén Gómez and prospect Andrés Curet doing well. They kept tabs on their Escogido players in the Dominican Republic such as Felipe Alou, Juan Marichal, Willie McCovey and Bill White.

Santurce and San Juan kept the season interesting with their jockeying for first place. San Juan went one game up on January 2, 1959, when Gene Oliver's two-run ninth inning homer gave the Senators a 2–1 win.[73] The Senators maintained their lead and won the pennant by three games.

Santurce's playoff chances were weakened when Bill Greason came up with a sore arm and Pantalones Santiago had health problems. This left Gómez, Marion Fricano and Julio Navarro as the healthy starters.

The second place Crabbers faced fourth place Mayagüez in one semi-final series with San Juan and third place finisher Caguas going at it in the other series. Both series went the seven-game limits with Santurce and Caguas prevailing. Caguas took two of the first three final series games.

Rubén Gómez stopped Caguas in winning game four, 6–1. Cepeda cracked two homers and a double in game five on February 2, 1959, as Santurce won, 9–3, behind Marion Fricano. Cepeda's slugging continued in game six with three RBI on a homer and two hits. Santurce won that game, as well as the final game. Julio Navarro pitched the clincher and his friend, José Pagán, had a single, triple and homer in Santurce's fifth win.[74]

Pedrín signed Víctor Pellot and pitcher Lloyd Merritt from Caguas, as well as hurler Tite Arroyo and Nino Escalera from San Juan to reinforce the Crabbers. Santurce's Caribbean Series opponents were Cuba's Almendares Blues, the Azucareros from Panama, and Oriente representing Venezuela.

Santurce had Jackie Brandt, Bob Lennon and Escalera in the outfield. Willie Kirkland left before season's end, but Lennon replaced him. Pellot played third with Cepeda at first. Pagán covered short and Tony Alomar played second. Valmy Thomas caught while Gómez, Navarro and Fricano were joined in the rotation by Arroyo and Merritt.

The Crabbers defeated Almendares, 2–1, on February 10, 1959. Jackie Brandt's triple off Orlando Peña tied the game in the bottom of the ninth, and Bob Lennon's single won it.[75] Rubén Gómez pitched a masterpiece.

Oriente brought Santurce down to earth with a four-run rally in the last of the ninth on February 11, to earn a 6–5 win. Tite Arroyo gave way to Pete Wojey in the ninth with the score 5–3 in Santurce's favor. Norm Cash's bases-loaded single tied the game, and Cash scored the game-winner. Marion Fricano pitched Santurce to a game three win over Panama, 9–3, as Cepeda, Pellot and Valmy Thomas got three hits apiece.[76]

Almendares' Orlando Peña shut out Santurce, 1–0, in game four as Rocky Nelson drove in Angel Scull with the game's only run, a first-inning single off Lloyd Merritt. Santurce lost their next game to Oriente, 5–3, when Rubén Gómez fell victim to some shoddy fielding. Ramón Monzant saved the win for Babe Birrer. The Crabbers finished the series in third place, with a 3–3 mark, after Julio Navarro shut out the Azucareros, 1–0.[77]

Almendares was first followed by Oriente. Tom Lasorda pitched for the series champs. "That was a great team with Bob Allison, Tony Taylor, Camilo Pascual, Art Fowler and Mike Cuéllar," said Lasorda. "Dick Brown caught ... Sandy Amoros and Willy Miranda were on that team." Tony Taylor noted that Pascual was a reinforcement from the Cienfuegos Elephants. Cuéllar had fond memories of the series including his game-five win in relief of Lasorda against Panama. Miguel de la Hoz, a reserve infielder for Almendares, later told me how tough it was to crack the starting line-up in the four-team Cuban League.

Santurce's franchise went through a lot between the mid– and late–1950s with a change in ownership, several managerial changes, and a pause, followed by a continuation in the working agreement with the New York/San Francisco Giants. It was the end of the Santurce line for Willard Brown, Bob Thurman and Bill Greason. Pedrín Zorrilla moved on to other endeavors including two terms in Puerto Rico's House of Representatives, where he represented many Santurce constituents.

Pedrín remained "El Cangrejo Mayor" and "Mr. Baseball" to many, including Poto Paniagua. Paniagua: "Pedrín will always be 'El Cangrejo Mayor.' His title of 'Mr. Baseball' was well-deserved due to the esteem and respect that major league baseball executives had for Pedrín."

5. Escobar Gives Way to Bithorn

Escobar had more atmosphere ... Bithorn had more seating and better parking.
     — Craig Anderson, former Santurce pitcher

Santurce and San Juan used Sixto Escobar as their home stadium through the 1961–62 season before moving to Hiram Bithorn Municipal Stadium. Baseball became more of a business for Santurce and the other league teams. The Crabbers won the 1961–62 and 1964–65 crowns, and became the only franchise in league history to win an InterAmerican Series when they copped the 1962 event at Escobar.

Santurce from a Personal Standpoint

My family moved to Santurce in 1960 from the Isla Verde sector of Carolina, so that dad could be closer to his Stop 22 office on Europa Street. Dad was an Economist with the Puerto Rico Economic Development Administration, a.k.a. FOMENTO. His first Puerto Rico Winter League memories were of Roberto Clemente wearing a Santurce uniform at Escobar in October 1956, soon after our family left the port of Baltimore on a cargo ship destined for Puerto Rico. The ship also carried wood to rebuild homes and businesses that were ruined by a recent hurricane.

In January 1961, mom took a job near Stop 17 in Santurce with the new Puerto Rico Commerce Department as a Special Assistant to the first Secretary of Commerce. I was six at the time and remember that most of our family activity for the next six years (work-related, school, or a meal at a restaurant) took place in Santurce. There might be lunch at Santurce's El Nilo Restaurant, one of dad's favorite eating spots, an evening meal at Miramar's Cathay Chinese Restaurant. A special treat during the mid–1960s was when dad took me to a Santurce baseball game at Bithorn Stadium.

The early to mid–1960s may have been Santurce's final "glory" years from a residential and business standpoint. Our home on Estrella Street was not too far from Santurce's

"Plaza del Mercado" (Farmers Market), nor that far from the Condado section with its high-rises and beaches. Downtown Santurce had at least 10 movie theaters, a variety of department stores, government buildings, banks, and other businesses.

Miguel "Tato" Gaud, a co-worker of mine from 1980–1984, was born, raised, and still lives in Santurce. Gaud is familiar with the Barrio Obrero and Villa Palmeras sectors of Santurce, having moved to his present Villa Palmeras house in 1963. This section of Santurce had a strong working class in the late 1950s and early 1960s, and plenty of rabid Santurce Crabber baseball fans.

"Santurce's 'Golden Era' really ended in the 1960s," said Gaud. "Most of the generation that grew up in Santurce back then, left Santurce."

1959–60: End of Crabbers-Giants Link

The Crabbers dealt Julio Navarro and José Pagán to Caguas for Juan Pizarro. Proceeds from the league All-Star contest went to the new Players Association. Bob Thurman finished his Puerto Rico career with Ponce while Pete Burnside did likewise with Mayagüez. Ray Murray was replaced as Santurce's manager by Luis Olmo. Orlando Cepeda had a banner season. Santurce finished fourth, but lost to Caguas in the semi-finals.

Caguas made two huge deals prior to the season by trading Roberto Clemente to San Juan and Juan Pizarro to Santurce. The 22-year-old Pizarro and $10,000 in cash went to Santurce for Julio Navarro and José Pagán.[1] This deal was made subject to the approval of the Milwaukee Braves and the San Francisco Giants, the team Pagán began with in 1959. Navarro was in the Giants' minor league system. Both big league teams approved the trade.

Pizarro was glad to be back with the Santurce Crabbers, the team he had followed since his childhood in the Villa Palmeras section of Santurce. Harry Rexach, a long-time Santurce fan and friend of Pedrín and Diana Zorrilla, took an interest in Pizarro when "Terín" was a teenager. Pizarro pitched for Rexach's amateur Santurce ballclub, prior to signing with Pedrín's professional team.

Santurce's new manager, Ray Murray, had managed San Francisco's Corpus Christi farm club in 1959. Four imports were allowed on Puerto Rico league rosters. Santurce contracted outfielder Al Nagel and hurler Charlie Gorin from the Amarillo and Austin clubs in the Texas League; Chuck Churn of the Los Angeles Dodgers and Chris Nicolosi of Spokane in the PCL.[2]

Santurce did not jell under Ray Murray. San Francisco was grooming Willie McCovey to be their everyday first baseman for 1960 and wanted Cepeda to play left field for Santurce. Murray's insertion of Cepeda in left field was not appreciated, nor was Santurce's losing record. Murray was fired on December 1, 1959, and replaced with Luis Olmo. The firing of Murray ended the Santurce-San Francisco link. Jack Schwarz, secretary of the Giants' farm system and scouting department, stated: "Ray isn't the first manager fired by Santurce, nor is this the first time we've [Giants] been annoyed with the situation down there … we let it be known that we'd prefer to have Cepeda play left field."[3]

Olmo was given a three-year deal, worth a reported $6,000 per season. He was very popular and highly thought of in league circles.

Ponce Lions signed Bob Thurman that winter, but were fined $100 for using Thurman before his contract had been officially submitted to the league office.[4] Thurman hit three homers with Ponce to finish his Puerto Rico career with 120 round trippers, the most in league history.[5]

Pete Burnside pitched very well for Mayagüez. The season's best pitching duel was between him and Santurce's Charlie Gorin toward season's end. Burnside allowed two hits and whiffed 15 Crabbers en route to an 11-inning, 1–0 win. Joe Christopher's homer won the game.[6]

Rubén Gómez and Pantalones Santiago were Santurce's player reps. Santiago and his manager, Luis Olmo, shared a love for horse racing. There were times that season when Olmo would have Pantalones make the trek to the El Comandante Racetrack and place a "cuadro" (bet) on Olmo's behalf, if Pantalones was not the scheduled pitcher that day.[7]

The new Players Association sponsored the January 1960 league All-Star game and raised some $6,400. Santurce and San Juan players were the North team who won the 11-inning contest, 6–5, against the South squad comprising Caguas, Mayagüez and Ponce. Roberto Clemente and Dave Ricketts of San Juan and Santurce's Al Nagel each got two hits for the winners. Julio Gotay hit a homer for the South team. The pre-game 95-meter dash was won by Santurce's Félix Juan Maldonado with a time of 9.9 seconds.[8]

The Crabbers gave Caguas a scare in the semi-finals by winning the first two games. Juan Pizarro won game one, 3–2, on January 20, 1960 with help from Valmy Thomas who hit a two-run homer. Pantalones Santiago won game two, 2–1. Caguas posted three straight wins at Escobar behind the hurling of George Brunet, Julio Navarro and Bob Giggie, and the hitting of Félix Mantilla and Tommy Davis. Earl Wilson wrapped it up on January 25, with a 3–1 win. Orlando Cepeda ruined the shutout with a home run.[9]

"I hit a lot of post-season home runs in Puerto Rico," said Cepeda. "I was coming into my own in the majors, and loved to play in front of the Puerto Rico fans."

Caguas defeated San Juan in the finals and picked up Cepeda, Pizarro and Pantalones Santiago for the 1960 Caribbean Series in Panama. Pizarro defeated the host Marlboro Smokers, 4–3, in Caguas' series opener on February 10, 1960. Cepeda hit a two-run homer against the Smokers three days later. Santiago pitched against the series champs, Cuba's Cienfuegos Elephants, on February 14, when Camilo Pascual twirled a 4–0, one-hit shutout for Cienfuegos.[10]

1960–61: Cepeda and Pizarro Reinforce San Juan

League imports were increased and a salary cap was set. The 64-game season was divided into two halves, with the winners facing off in the finals. Elrod Hendricks made his Santurce debut. Santurce finished the first half in last place, but tied for second in the next half. San Juan won the league finals and participated in the new InterAmerican Series.

Mayagüez and Ponce were allowed seven imports with San Juan and Santurce's allotment set at six imports. Caguas, the defending champs, had a quota of five imports. A league salary cap of $800 per month for imports went into effect. Imports were limited to two years of big league time.

Winds of change affected the Cuban and Dominican Winter Leagues. Neither used U.S. players that winter due to their political situations.

Ford Frick, the commissioner of baseball, was invited by San Juan owner, Bob Leith, to throw out the first pitch at Escobar's season opener. Frick suggested that the 1961

Caribbean Series be switched from Cuba to another country since "it would not be wise for Puerto Rico's players to play in Havana." The ban on stateside players performing in Cuba would be extended to Puerto Rico's big leaguers unless diplomatic relations improved between the U.S. and Cuba.[11]

The Caribbean Confederation selected Venezuela to host an InterAmerican Series in February 1961. Two teams represented the host country plus the winners from Panama and Puerto Rico. This event lasted from 1961 through 1964. Cuba discontinued its winter league at the end of the 1960–61 season and did not participate in the InterAmerican Series.

Santurce's fans had high hopes following Juan Pizarro's 9–3 home-opener win over San Juan, but they missed Orlando Cepeda during the first half since he was touring Japan as a member of the San Francisco Giants. San Juan's Roberto Clemente opted to rest during the season's first half.

The Crabbers won only 12 of their 32 first half games.[12] Joe Hicks, Gene Oliver and Cliff Cook provided some punch, but could not make up for the absence of Cepeda. Carl Mathias, Mark Freeman and Juan Pizarro did most of the mound work. Pizarro and his teammates showed some emotion after Gene Oliver was drilled on the shoulder by a pitch from Ponce's Tom Cheney. This November 27, 1960 bench-clearing episode had a happy ending for Santurce when Oliver retaliated in his next at-bat with a game-winning homer off Cheney.[13]

Santurce welcomed Orlando Cepeda with open arms in mid–December 1960. Cepeda got 12 hits in his first 23 at-bats. This included his perfect four-for-four game against Caguas on December 22, 1960, and a grand slam in Santurce's 18–3 win. Juan Pizarro also homered.[14]

The league All-Star game was held on Christmas Day. Tingo Daviú, a member of Santurce's first 1939–40 team, threw out the first pitch. Pre-game events included the home run hitting contest won by Orlando Cepeda and an egg-tossing contest between pairs of fans and players. The Imports won the game, 6–1, behind the hitting of San Juan's Ronnie Samford and Jerry Adair. Juan Pizarro started for the native All-Stars.[15]

Elrod Hendricks, a native of St. Thomas, broke in with Santurce. Hendricks roomed with San Juan infielder Horace Clarke, a native of St. Croix. They stayed in San Juan's YMCA, not too far from Escobar Stadium. Hendricks and Clarke were the best of friends, but they, too, got caught up in the excitement of the San Juan-Santurce rivalry.

San Juan's fans went to town on January 15, 1961, when their team (with Clemente in the line-up) swept a twin-bill from Santurce, 2–1 and 6–2. This sweep solidified San Juan's second-half hold on first place. Jim Archer, with relief help from Jack Fisher and Luis "Tite" Arroyo, won game one. Mack Jones' 10th inning grand slam gave Arroyo the game two win.[16]

It had been a rough season for Santurce skipper Luis Olmo. He needed 10 days in a hospital to recover from an ulcer attack that he experienced on the last day of the regular season.

San Juan manager Luman Harris selected Orlando Cepeda and Juan Pizarro to reinforce San Juan for the 1961 InterAmerican Series. Rules allowed only two reinforcements per team.[17] San Juan owner Bob Leith picked up Juan Pizarro at his Santurce home en route to the airport.

The Senators arrived in Caracas on February 10, 1961, for their opener against Rapiños of Venezuela's Occidental League. Pizarro pitched well, but singles by Luis Aparicio and

Camilo Carreón produced the margin of victory in Rapiños' 4–3 win. Four days later, Pizarro defeated Panama's Cervecería Balboa Brewers, 7–6, with relief help from Tite Arroyo. Clemente and Cepeda were the big guns with three hits apiece. Bob Gibson pitched Valencia to a 1–0 win over San Juan on February 15, 1961. This created a tie-breaker between both Venezuelan clubs which was settled the next night by Valencia's 2–1, 10-inning win by José "Carrao" Bracho.[18]

1961–62: An InterAmerican Series Title

Sixto Escobar Stadium had its last season of professional baseball. Luis Olmo managed the expansion Arecibo Wolves and the six teams played 80-game schedules. Vern Benson was hired to manage Santurce and led the Crabbers to the league and Inter-American Series titles. Orlando Cepeda's 19 homers set a then single-season mark for Puerto Rican and U.S. Virgin Islands players. Bob Gibson pitched superbly for Santurce in the league playoffs and InterAmerican Series.

Hiram Cuevas' first season as Santurce's full owner was a success.

"We won it all," Cuevas said. "[I] thought it would be easy the rest of the way."

The hiring of Vern Benson as Santurce's manager was a wise choice in light of his familiarity with winter ball. Benson's Caribbean Series stints were as a third baseman with the 1951–52 champion Havana Reds and at shortstop for the 1953–54 Pastora Milkers. He was familiar with player turnover, the lack of pitching depth and other winter challenges.

Benson, a coach with the 1961–64 St. Louis Cardinals, witnessed Caribbean Series history when his Havana teammate, Tommy Fine, pitched a no-hitter against Venezuela in 1952. Benson knew that a winner in the Caribbean had to have four solid starters, good defense, above average power and adequate team speed. He recommended that Bob Gibson and Craig Anderson of the St. Louis pitching staff join the Crabbers. Anderson had pitched for Benson with Tulsa after his graduation from Lehigh University.

"They gave me a five-day tryout at Tulsa," said Anderson. "Benson was the manager and kept me … won the 1960 Pan-American title against Mexico City. Then I went to Portland under Benson in 1961 and onto St. Louis. Benson went to St. Louis right after me."

Anderson would be selected in the expansion draft by the 1962 New York Mets. He told me that Bob Gibson was an "in-between" pitcher at that point just getting ready to become a great hurler.

"When we went to Puerto Rico, we congregated together," said Anderson. "Heck, I started playing bridge with Bob and his wife … even did so on the plane coming home after the season was over. Pizarro, Gibson, Al Schroll and myself were the four starters … honored to be in that crowd."

Anderson's Santurce debut was a 10–4 win over Mayagüez on October 21, 1961.[19]

Juan Pizarro was in fine form. Al Schroll, a member of the 1961 Minnesota Twins, was a reliable fourth starter and pinch-hitter. Orlando Cepeda, Martín Beltrán, Cliff Cook and Elrod Hendricks provided the power.

The Arecibo Wolves, managed by hometown hero Luis Olmo, were a pleasant surprise on their way to a playoff berth. Luis Rodríguez Olmo Stadium, named after their skipper, was a hitter's paradise for Tommie Aaron, Ed Charles, Lee Maye, Octavio "Cookie" Rojas and Bob Uecker. Arecibo could use 10 imports, two more than the other clubs.

Elrod Hendricks gets a handshake from Vern Benson, rounding third after hitting a homer, 1961–62 (courtesy of *The San Juan Star*).

Arecibo hosted the league All-Star game. In pre-game events, Orlando Cepeda hit three homers in the home run hitting contest to once again win this event. The Imports then edged the players from Puerto Rico and the U.S. Virgin Islands, 3–2, in 10 innings.[20]

Santurce was in first place most of December 1961 and early January 1962. Benson wanted more production out of the second base position shared by Antonio Alomar and

Sammy Hernández. The termination of the Dominican Winter League on December 3, 1961, due to political instability, gave Benson the chance to insert Julian Javier at second base. Benson traveled to the Dominican Republic to get Javier. Javier's fielding solidified the defense, but he did not finish out the season.

Ed Bauta left the Crabbers with a sore arm, but Orlando Peña was signed by Santurce after his release by San Juan. Peña saved one of Santurce's late-season wins in game two of a January 9, 1962 twin-bill against San Juan. Orlando Cepeda's 19th homer helped Santurce win the first game for Juan Pizarro. A colorful argument ensued in that contest when Cepeda was called safe at home. San Juan catcher Joe Montalvo let home plate umpire Paul Pryor have it.[21]

The Crabbers were no-hit by Caguas' Julio Navarro in a seven-inning first game of a January 14, 1962 twi-night double-header. Navarro did not allow a hit in seven frames, but Al Schroll kept Caguas in check on two hits. Santurce won it in the home eighth when Sammy Hernández drew a one-out walk and was sacrificed to second by Félix Juan Maldonado. Schroll's grounder was fielded cleanly by shortstop José Pagán, but the errant throw went past Frank Howard as Hernández scored.[22] Orlando Cepeda stated that Navarro's pinpoint control along with a good fastball and slider did the trick. This no-hitter was the only one at Escobar from 1938–39 through the 1961–62 seasons.[23]

Juan Pizarro etched his name into league record books when he struck out seven straight Ponce Lions the night before Navarro's gem. This tied a mark set in the league's early days by Satchel Paige, Roy Partlow and Berthum Hunter.[24] Pizarro led the league in strikeouts for a fifth straight time with 154 while teammate Bob Gibson was runner-up with 142 strikeouts.[25]

The semi-finals began at Escobar against Caguas on January 24, 1962. Julio Navarro pitched the series opener for the Criollos and gave up seven runs in three innings, as Santurce won, 10–0. Bob Gibson fanned 13 and allowed three hits. Martín Beltrán, a St. Louis prospect, cracked a homer and a double as did Orlando Cepeda.[26]

Earl Wilson blanked Santurce, 8–0, the next night and struck out 12. Frank Howard had a perfect night with four hits.[27]

"You learned to hit in old Sixto Escobar Stadium facing Bob Gibson, Juan Pizarro, Bob Bolín, Tite Arroyo," said Howard. "They were tough."

The series shifted to Caguas for the next three games. Caguas player-manager Jim Rivera hit a two-run homer in game three to propel Caguas to a 5–4 win. Al Schroll's pinch-hit in game four was the difference in Santurce's 5–4 victory.[28] Bob Gibson won game five, 8–1. Gibson fanned seven to give him 20 series strikeouts and Cepeda hit his second series homer.[29]

Caguas tied the series in game six (the opener of a January 29 twin-bill) at Escobar, when Earl Wilson won a seven-inning contest, 6–2. The finale, a nine-inning classic, had Luis Tiant facing Juan Pizarro. Martín Beltrán's sixth inning homer scored the game's only run.[30] Tiant: "That was my first winter season in Puerto Rico. The league was very strong and had many good pitchers including Pizarro. We gave it our best, but Beltrán got hold of my fastball. Ay [oh], Martín Beltrán!"

Santurce advanced to the finals and a January 31 date with Mayagüez at Escobar. The *San Juan Star* sports headline that morning was 'We'll Win in 5,' Claims, Pérez, The Indian Chief.[31] Craig Anderson told me that headline served to motivate him and his teammates.

Anderson posted a 3–1 win before 4,429 fans. His third-inning hit drove in Al Cruz

Bob Gibson smiles after blanking Mayagüez in game two of the 1961–62 finals (courtesy of *The San Juan Star*).

Rodríguez. A homer by Leo Cárdenas provided an insurance run. The play of the night was a game-ending catch by center fielder Félix Juan Maldonado on Charlie Lau's long fly ball.[32] Bob Gibson twirled a two-hit shutout and struck out 14 the next night. Cárdenas scored the game's only run when Joel Horlen balked with Gibson at the plate.[33]

Pizarro continued his mastery of Mayagüez with a 3–1 win in game three. Valmy Thomas drove in two runs while Pizarro's hit knocked in Elrod Hendricks with an insurance run.

"That season was special," said Hendricks. "I was in my second season and Valmy Thomas did most of the catching … learned a lot from him."

Orlando Cepeda's two-run homer off Bob Dustal on February 3, gave Santurce a 5–4 win and a sweep.

"We were losing, 4–3, when I hit it out," said Cepeda. "I hit some 70 homers including the [1961] National League and winter league seasons plus the playoffs."

Santurce was reinforced for the nine-game InterAmerican Series by Arecibo second baseman Cookie Rojas, and two San Juan players, third baseman Miguel de la Hoz and center fielder Tony González. Orlando Peña and Leo Cárdenas were the two other Cubans on Santurce's roster.

Mayagüez, reinforced by Luis Tiant and Tite Arroyo, was Puerto Rico's other series entry. Venezuela sent the Caracas Lions to Puerto Rico. The Marlboro Smokers represented the Panama-Nicaragua circuit, and had just defeated Nicaragua's Boer Indians to earn a series berth. The Smokers could use 10 imports; all other clubs were limited to eight imports.

Eddie Napoleon was a Panama "native" by virtue of having been raised in the Panama Canal Zone. Napoleon's mother had come down to Panama as a child since her dad worked on the Panama Canal in the early days.

Napoleon's baseball career spanned the 1950s and 1960s. He had hit a three-run homer off Pizarro in the 1960 Caribbean Series hosted by Panama.

"Back then it was like having four major league All-Star teams competing against each other in a round-robin tournament," said Napoleon. "There was no weak club … Panama would be the weakest … wonderful to play against Cepeda and the rest."

Ticket prices for Escobar's final event ranged from 75 cents for the bleacher seats to $4 for the box seats.[34] Bob Gibson won Santurce's February 6, 1962 opener over Marlboro, 5–4, with relief help from Orlando Peña in the ninth. The winning run scored when Diego Seguí hit de la Hoz with a bases-loaded pitch in the seventh inning.[35]

Juan Pizarro and Bo Belinsky took the mound the next evening. Santurce hit Belinsky hard and the southpaw would suffer a hand injury after slamming the dugout's water cooler after the fourth inning. The greatest catch in InterAmerican Series history took place three innings later when César Tovar hit a long blast between Félix Juan Maldonado in left and Tony González in center. González climbed the wire fence with his spikes caught in the mesh and snagged the ball. Pizarro went the route and fanned 15 in the 10–1 win.[36]

Miguel de la Hoz's two-run homer in the ninth pulled game three out, 3–2, over Mayagüez. Orlando Peña got the win after relieving Craig Anderson in the eighth.[37] Peña came back the next night in long relief to earn the 5–3 win over Marlboro, aided by Cookie Rojas' two-run double.[38]

Bob Gibson won his second series game on February 10, and hit a three-run homer in a 5–2 win over Caracas. Leo Cárdenas and Tony González hit solo homers and Craig Anderson saved the game in the ninth.[39] Santurce's only loss was a 12–8 slugfest with Mayagüez in game six. Luis Tiant and Wito Conde hit homers for Mayagüez, while de la Hoz cracked two home runs, including a grand slam off Tiant. Tite Arroyo got the save.[40]

Santurce clinched the series crown on February 13, after Craig Anderson shut out Marlboro, 2–0, and Orlando Peña hurled a 12-inning complete game win over Caracas. Martín Beltrán's 12th-inning homer off Sherman Jones in the nightcap gave the Crabbers a 2–1 win and the series title. Beltrán was 0-for-29 in the series prior to that homer.[41]

Escobar's final professional baseball game was played on Valentine's Day 1962. Bob Gibson faced Mayagüez, but did not figure in the decision, a 5–4 Santurce win. Miguel de la Hoz was the hero when he hit a Tiant fastball over the left field fence in the 11th inning.

"I liked the way the ball carried at Escobar," said de la Hoz. "There was a favorable ocean breeze toward left field."

Sportswriters chose five Santurce players to fill the 10 All-Star slots: Series MVP Orlando Peña, Juan Pizarro, de la Hoz, series batting champ Tony González and Orlando Cepeda. A trio of Caracas infielders (Jim Frey, César Tovar and Ted Obregón) were named. Mayagüez catcher, Charlie Lau, and Marlboro left fielder, Al Pinkston, were also chosen.[42]

Craig Anderson remembers Hiram Cuevas hosting a big party.

"I made $1,000 a month in Puerto Rico," said Anderson. "Hiram paid for the round trip airfare and let us go home to New York first class. Bob Gibson went home to Nebraska … I didn't have a winter home … visited my family in D.C. and Benton, Illinois, where my wife, Judy, is from."

1962–63: Hiram Bithorn Stadium and Sam McDowell

Hiram Bithorn Municipal Stadium was inaugurated to open the 70-game season. Santurce had Cleveland Indians coach, Ray Katt, as their skipper. Cleveland sent Sam McDowell and other prospects to Santurce. Orlando Cepeda did not play. Santurce's José

"Kindo" Geigel was the league Rookie of the Year. Santurce lost the semi-final series to Caguas. Juan Pizarro reinforced Mayagüez in the InterAmerican Series and twirled a no-hitter.

Bithorn Stadium, with a seating capacity for 20,000 fans, opened for play on October 24, 1962, in the Hato Rey section of San Juan. Its new $100,000 Banco Popular scoreboard was the talk of the town. By season's end, Bithorn Stadium helped with increasing the regular season attendance to the 579,099 level, a 43.4 percent increase over the 1961–62 figure.[43]

Sam McDowell was a flame-thrower who needed more seasoning. Frank Funk and Dave Tyriver of Cleveland joined McDowell on Santurce's pitching staff, as did Juan Pizarro, Rubén Gómez and Kindo Geigel.

"Cleveland simply told me that I was going to play in Puerto Rico," said McDowell. "It was just as much fun, but not near the level of major leagues in that you don't have much depth."

McDowell, a native of Pittsburgh, told me that Puerto Rico was another world to him at the time with a different language and culture. He lived on the beach with his wife and baby until a hurricane hit. Santurce then found another apartment for the McDowells.

McDowell's first Puerto Rico win came against San Juan, 3–1, on November 6, 1962.[44] No wonder he found Puerto Rico's fans to be very friendly, admiring and enthusiastic!

Perhaps the most fun McDowell had came on certain road trips when he recalls leaving the team bus and running out in the fields and picking up some pineapples. This provided vitamin C and comic relief on the trips from Santurce to Arecibo, Mayagüez or Ponce.

Santurce signed Craig Anderson the second half of the season to shore up their pitching. Anderson had pitched for the 1962 New York Mets.

"The Mets sent me to the Instructional League after the 1962 [big league] season," said Anderson. "Then I spent a month with Santurce."

The Crabbers had speed with Félix Juan Maldonado, Hiraldo "Chico" Ruíz and José Tartabull. They competed in the 100-yard dash prior to the league All-Star game with Joe Gaines, Joe Christopher and Julio Gotay. Gaines won the sprint event, but Ruíz and Tartabull were one-two in circling the bases. The hitting star of the January 10, 1963 All-Star game was Santurce's Miguel de la Hoz with four hits including a homer in the Imports' 4–1 win.[45] Three Santurce players were later named to the league All-Star team: Chico Ruíz at shortstop, José Tartabull in center field and pitcher Juan Pizarro.[46]

Santurce played Caguas in one semi-final series. Caguas won the 14-innning opener on January 26, 1963, 1–0. Juan Pizarro and John Tsitouris pitched a scoreless duel through 12 innings. Craig Anderson relieved Pizarro in the 13th inning, followed by Sam McDowell to face Tom McCraw in the 14th. McCraw's single scored Howie Goss with the only run.[47]

Santurce took game two when Valmy Thomas' two-run homer by plus run-scoring doubles by Félix Juan Maldonado and Martín Beltrán gave Santurce a 5–3 win. Kindo Geigel pitched four scoreless relief innings to earn the victory.[48]

Former heavyweight boxing champ Joe Louis attended game three at Bithorn Stadium on January 28. Jim Rivera's 19th inning triple off Dave Tyriver scored Nate Oliver with the winning run. Dave Wickersham hurled 10 relief innings as Caguas won it, 5–3. The 19-inning contest was the longest in league history up to that point.[49]

Caguas won game four, 6–0, behind Earl Wilson. Sam McDowell gave way to Craig

Anderson in the eighth. Santurce was without Anderson's friend, second baseman Sammy Hernández, who had broken a bone in his left hand.[50]

"Sammy Hernández spoke English perfectly and had a regular job outside of baseball," said Anderson. "After pitching at Bithorn in the playoffs, I felt Escobar Stadium had more atmosphere.... Bithorn had more seating and better parking."

Juan Pizarro's 9–2 win in game five kept Santurce's hopes alive. Martín Beltrán's bases-loaded triple in an eight-run second inning rally paved the way for that win.[51] The series moved to Caguas for game six.

Craig Anderson enjoyed a 5–1 lead after Elrod Hendricks' two-run homer in the top of the sixth. Valmy Thomas was then hit by a John Tsitouris pitch and said something to the pitcher on his way to first. Tsitouris threw a new baseball at Thomas and a fight ensued. Ray Katt separated the pair, but was seriously hurt in the fracas, according to Sam McDowell.

"Ray Katt tore his heel because of that fight with the opposition," said McDowell. "He lost his job as he was to manage the Cleveland Indians in 1963, but couldn't because he was on crutches for six months."

Tsitouris and Thomas were allowed to remain in the game (delayed by 15 minutes) due to its importance. Anderson was relieved by Kindo Geigel in the sixth, who gave up a three-run, pinch-hit homer by Herminio Cortés in Caguas' 8–5 win. Julio Navarro saved the game.[52]

Mayagüez defeated Caguas prior to the InterAmerican Series in Panama. The Indians signed Juan Pizarro as a reinforcement and he pitched the only no-hitter in series history on February 8, 1963. Pizarro fanned 10 and walked four in no-hitting Valencia, the Venezuelan champions, 5–0. Wito Conde's first inning backhand catch of a line drive by Angel Scull was the play of the game. Panama's Chiriqui-Bocas Farmers defeated Nicaragua's Boer Indians in a tie-breaker to win it.[53]

1963–64: A Kansas City/Cuban Connection

Pedro "Preston" Gómez managed Santurce. Orlando Cepeda had a fine season as did Roberto Clemente of San Juan. Some of Santurce's imports were from the Kansas City A's, but this was not due to a working agreement. Cepeda and Pizarro reinforced San Juan in the final InterAmerican Series.

José Tartabull returned to Santurce and encouraged his Kansas City A's teammates (Aurelio Monteagudo, Diego Seguí and Orlando Peña) to join him. Chico Ruíz and Miguel de la Hoz returned, and Harry Watts filled the second base slot. Pitcher Phil Ortega of the Dodgers joined Santurce.

Preston Gómez was a native of Cuba as were most of Santurce's imports. He had managed Caguas earlier in the decade, and was a disciplinarian who treated his players in a professional manner, according to José Tartabull.

The regular season belonged to Caguas. Santurce was two games behind second-place Ponce and one game in back of third-place San Juan on January 2, 1964, after defeating San Juan, 7–3. That win by Juan Pizarro clinched the city championship.[54] San Juan put a damper on Santurce's playoff hopes with a 4–1 victory on January 3, 1964 when Roberto Clemente's two-run double in the seventh broke a 1–1 tie.[55]

The league's All-Star game on January 6, 1964 had the Latin American squad play the

Orlando Cepeda hits a line drive, 1963–64 (courtesy of *The San Juan Star*).

U.S. imports. Ticket prices were set at $1.50 for box seats, $1 for general admission and 50 cents for bleacher seats. Clemente and Cepeda hit third and fourth for the Latin Americans, who also had Félix Juan Maldonado and Miguel de la Hoz in their starting line-up.[56]

Cepeda hit three opposite field homers during the pre-game home run contest to win this event. The Latin American stars used a 14-hit attack in defeating the U.S. players, 7–2. Starter Juan Pizarro got the win while Santurce teammates Diego Seguí and Orlando Peña pitched in relief.[57]

Pizarro came back on one day's rest to shut out Mayagüez, 4–0. Chico Ruíz scored Santurce's first run. Tartabull's third inning triple plated another. Cepeda hit a Phil Niekro knuckler over the left field bleachers in the sixth and Harry Watts knocked in de la Hoz with the last run. Santurce was one game back of fourth place Mayagüez with three games left.[58]

Santurce traveled to Ponce for a January 11–12, 1964 weekend series. Ponce's Sonny Siebert won the single game on January 11, 3–2, despite a Cepeda homer. A depleted Santurce pitching staff used Seguí, Ortega, Monteagudo and Rubén Gómez in that game.[59]

Pizarro kept Santurce's playoff hopes alive with a 4–3 win in game one of the January 12 double-header. Two ninth inning errors by Santurce gave Ponce a 4–3 win in game two. Chico Ruíz and Cepeda hit second game homers. José Tartabull felt that Santurce hustled and gave it their best.

Cepeda and Pizarro reinforced league champion, San Juan, in the final InterAmerican Series, hosted by Managua, Nicaragua. The local Cinco Estrellas ballclub upset San Juan, 4–3, on February 9, 1964, to clinch the title. San Juan tied Panama's Marlboro Smokers with 3-3 records, two games behind Cinco Estrellas. Nicaragua's other entry, Oriental, won one game.[60] San Juan pitcher, José "Palillo" Santiago, and shortstop, Marv Staehle, couldn't believe that a team with Clemente and Cepeda would fall short.

1964–65: Another Santurce Title

Santurce won its second title in four years. Lou Johnson won the batting crown and Marv Staehle earned the team MVP award with his hustle and fine play. Jim Dickson shined in relief for Santurce. Preston Gómez managed Santurce to a semi-finals win over San Juan and to the championship against Mayagüez. Tany Pérez was one Santurce catalyst in the playoffs.

Hiram Bithorn Stadium sparkled to the fans, but created headaches for Hiram Cuevas and San Juan's owner, Tuto Saavedra. The city of San Juan rented this stadium to the Crabbers and Senators with a rental fee based on eight to ten percent of ticket sales. An additional 16.5 percent excise tax was applied to each ticket sold, making the total tax bite 25 to 26 percent for both clubs. Parking fees and stadium concessions were also controlled by the city of San Juan.[61]

Hiram Cuevas wanted a winner to make up for a fifth place finish and a drop in attendance the year before. His staff ace, Juan Pizarro, had won 19 games for the 1964 Chicago White Sox to break Hiram Bithorn's single-season big league standard for a Puerto Rico-born pitcher — of 18 wins set with the 1943 Chicago Cubs. Bob Short, the White Sox GM, had offered Pizarro $5,000 not to pitch in Puerto Rico.

"Terín would have none of that," said Cuevas. "He accepted my offer of $1,300 per month to pitch because he loved the Santurce fans."

Several years later, Cuevas rewarded Pizarro with a 20-year contract: 10 years to finish his Santurce playing career, and another 10 years to retain him as a pitching coach.

The Crabbers signed George Brunet, a portsider with the Los Angeles Angels, and Phil Ortega of the Dodgers to join Pizarro and Rubén Gómez in the rotation. Manly Johnston, off an excellent season with Lynchburg in the Southern Association, was a "find." The signing of reliever Jim Dickson, a teammate of Tany Pérez with San Diego in the 1964 PCL, paid dividends when he led the league in saves and relief wins.

"I began the 1964 [big league] season with Cincinnati and was sent to San Diego a month into the season," said Dickson. "We won the PCL pennant. Danny Ozark, Spokane's manager, made the contact with Puerto Rico."

Dickson earned plaudits from Santurce fans on October 29, 1964, when he relieved Phil Ortega in the fourth inning and allowed one run in a 5–4 win over San Juan. Dickson got his third win when he relieved Ortega the following week in a 4–2 win over Caguas. Santurce was in first place.[62]

An amusing experience for Dickson was when he and Ortega had a meal in Arecibo after an away game. They were late getting to the team bus and found it had left without them.

"We walked along a highway where sugar cane was growing," said Dickson. "Oh, what we did!" From then on, Dickson got to the bus on time, and endured the bus driver's (Almodovar) fast driving throughout the island and the mountain curves. These were the curves that Rubén Gómez handled in his sports car.

Other early season excitement included a fight between Lou Johnson and Mayagüez hurler Joe Sparma in game two of a twin-bill. The third inning had ended when Sparma and Johnson traded insults before going at it. The fight was broken up, but Sparma went after Johnson from the visitor's dugout and put a headlock on him. Santurce catcher Jesse Gonder put a headlock on Sparma to keep him at bay.[63]

Fred Talbot replaced Phil Ortega in the Santurce rotation in mid–November 1964. This solidified the rotation.

"Talbot developed his curve in Puerto Rico and used it in tight games," said Hiram Cuevas. "Lou Johnson gave 110 percent ... just one heck of a player. I went to the States and liked him [with Spokane] in AAA."

Santurce activated Cepeda, but he only played a few games before re-injuring his right knee. Cepeda flew to New York City on November 30, 1964, to have torn cartilage surgically removed.

"I played hurt most of my baseball career," said Cepeda. "In my first [1964–65] game with Santurce I stepped into a hole ... felt pain in the right knee."

Preston Gómez traveled to Miami in December 1964 and Joe Morgan briefly assumed the role of manager. Morgan, an All-Star third baseman for the 1964 Jacksonville Suns of the International League, played his final three big league games for the 1964 St. Louis Cardinals. He typified Santurce's winning spirit by playing first, third and the outfield. Santurce fans dubbed the 34-year-old Morgan "The Pirate" due to his calm, yet confident swagger and demeanor.

Marv Staehle, Santurce's 22-year-old second baseman, brought a winning attitude from having played for the 1963–64 league champion San Juan Senators, and from recent pennant race games with the 1964 Chicago White Sox. Jim Beauchamp, a first baseman, also produced for Santurce.

Santurce's native players included Martín Beltrán, Kindo Geigel and Félix Juan Maldonado. Geigel was a Class A pitcher in the Los Angeles Angels system who enjoyed bantering with Joe Morgan. When Santurce had their annual Christmas dinner for players and families, Morgan asked Geigel, "How do you like to pitch, Kindo? Do you like to start or come in relief?"

Geigel responded: "Any time you say, skipper. I just want to pitch."[64]

Geigel had been one of the island's top amateur pitchers with the Rio Piedras Goya team of the AA Superior Amateur Baseball Circuit. Arturito Miranda, Santurce's regular shortstop, and Sixto "Tuta" García, the team's backup catcher, were two Rio Piedras teammates who signed with Santurce.

Four Santurce position players were selected by fans to start in the January 6, 1965 All-Star game; Tany Pérez and Félix Juan Maldonado started for Caguas manager Luis Olmo's Latin American squad; Lou Johnson and Marv Staehle for Preston Gómez's North American team.[65] Rain and the soggy turf resulted in the postponement of this contest until January 11. Jesse Gonder and San Juan second baseman, Don Buford, teamed to win the pre-game wheelbarrow race. Gonder tied Caguas' Woody Huyke in the catcher's contest,

Preston Gómez observes the action, 1964–65 season (courtesy of *The San Juan Star*).

by hurling a baseball into a barrel near second base. Mayagüez's Jim Northrup won the home run hitting contest over Tany Pérez and Arecibo's Johnny Briggs.[66]

A shortage of players required the North American squad to use three Santurce players (infielders Arturito Miranda and José Martínez, and reserve catcher, José Cruz) and Ponce's Horace Clarke. George Brunet and Juan Pizarro started this contest. José Martínez's two-run homer off José Pagán in the 11th gave the North Americans a 5–3 win. Pagán pitched the last two innings since the Latin Americans ran out of pitchers. Roberto Clemente had a pinch-hit single for the Latin Americans.[67]

Santurce made history two days before the All-Star contest when Dennis McLain pitched Mayagüez to a 4–2 win. All Santurce hitters were retired on fly balls, popups, strikeouts or a fielder's choice not involving Mayagüez first baseman, Fred Hopke.[68] Hopke had no putouts or assists in that January 9, 1965 game, a "first" in league history.

Santurce clinched the regular season crown on January 12, when they bested Ponce, 5–4. Lou Johnson's three-run homer scored Kindo Geigel, the winning pitcher, and Marv Staehle in the third, while Félix Juan Maldonado had a two-run double in eighth. Jim Dickson got the final out.[69]

San Juan qualified for the final playoff spot and played Santurce in the semi-finals. Roberto Clemente was limited to managing San Juan, since he had a thigh injury which required surgery. Santurce won game one, 2–1, behind Juan Pizarro. Jesse Gonder's sacrifice fly and a wild pitch by Palillo Santiago with Joe Morgan on third accounted for the Santurce runs.[70]

"Terín was the league's best pitcher at that time," said Palillo Santiago. "He dominated certain teams … San Juan was one of them."

Tommie Sisk shut out the Crabbers the following night, 9–0, to even the series.[71] Sisk told me that officials from the Dominican Republic offered him a lot of cash ($1,500) to pitch in a post-season tournament with teams from Venezuela. But he did the honorable thing for San Juan and his Pittsburgh teammate, Roberto Clemente, by pitching against Santurce.

Santurce took game three, 4–2, behind Fred Talbot and Jim Dickson. Marv Staehle was the spark plug with two singles and two runs. Staehle had been named Santurce's MVP and the second baseman on the final All-Star team. Lou Johnson was named to this team in center field.[72]

Juan Pizarro won game four of the semi-final series, 3–2, on January 24. San Juan's Joe Hoerner blanked Santurce, 1–0, the following night and Canenita Allen scored a run on George Brunet's wild pitch.[73] Santurce advanced to the finals after Tany Pérez' 400-foot homer to dead center in the top of the 10th gave them a 6–3 win in game six on January 26. San Juan scored a trio of runs in the home fifth when Duke Carmel hit a two-run homer followed by a Cocó Laboy blast. Lou Johnson and Jesse Gonder had hit homers for Santurce.[74]

Bob Priddy gave up the winning homer to Pérez. Priddy and other San Juan and Santurce players stayed at Bithorn for several hours to discuss the game. Priddy noted that when he came in the eighth inning he told Clemente that he only had two good innings left after having pitched seven innings two days earlier. Marv Staehle asked Pérez if he had tried to hit a homer.

"No, man, I was just trying to meet the ball," said Pérez. "I knew Priddy had to come in with the fastball."

Priddy agreed, stating that his curve wasn't breaking and he didn't want to risk the

Juan "Terín" Pizarro, the league's best pitcher in the mid–1960s (courtesy of *The San Juan Star*).

slider, so he shook off both signs from McNertney. Duke Carmel joked that he would have caught the ball if he hadn't run out of room. Pérez stated there wasn't any wind blowing in, as often happened at Bithorn. Carmel put it best: "We gave you guys a battle. All the games were close and the fans couldn't ask for more."

Jerry McNertney, San Juan's catcher and Staehle's roommate, said good-bye. He would fix up his T-Bird and make it to New Mexico for rabbit hunting while Staehle was still playing baseball.

"Don't worry," Staehle said. "I'll be five or six days behind you. It won't take long to win this other series."[75]

Staehle was a prophet as Santurce defeated Mayagüez in a six-game final series. The Crabbers won the opener, 5–4, as Staehle scored the game-winner in the home ninth on a hit by Jesse Gonder.[76] Santurce tied it by scoring three in the eighth, capped by an alert Félix Juan Maldonado scoring from second base on a fielder's choice. Fred Talbot went the route and drove in a run with a triple.

Juan Pizarro pitched a three-hit shutout in game two. His seventh inning hit off Joe Sparma drove in the game's first run. Tany Pérez's two-run single and Martín Beltrán's RBI hit accounted for the other runs.[77]

Santurce won one of the three contests (game four) played in Mayagüez. Marv Staehle got a prolonged standing ovation in game three when he made the best play of the series by snagging a Wito Conde line drive in the first inning. The liner was well to Staehle's left, but he dove headfirst and rolled over twice after catching the ball before flipping it to the mound.[78]

Game four was a Sunday afternoon contest on January 31. Dennis McLain blanked Santurce through three innings, but Santurce broke the ice on a fourth inning RBI double by Tany Pérez. Santurce went on to earn a 5–0 win behind Manly Johnston and Jim Dickson.[79]

Game five took one hour and 33 minutes to play, as Jack Hamilton blanked Santurce, 2–0.[80] Fred Talbot allowed two unearned runs.

Juan Pizarro continued his mastery of Mayagüez by winning game six, 6–1, at Bithorn before 12,412 fans on February 2. The game featured more bad blood between Joe Sparma and Lou Johnson in the fifth inning. Marv Staehle scored the game's first run after he, Lou Johnson and Tany Pérez hit first inning singles. Julio Gotay's third inning homer tied the game. Arturito Miranda's sacrifice fly plated a Santurce run in the next frame. The Crabbers rallied in the fifth after Sparma hit Johnson. Tany Pérez's RBI double and Jesse Gonder's RBI single gave Santurce a cushion before they scored twice in the eighth.[81]

"All Terín needed to do against Mayagüez was to throw his glove on the mound," said Ismael Trabal. "There was a stretch in the 1960s that we could do nothing against him."

Staehle was so confident that Pizarro would win game six that he made reservations to leave Puerto Rico early Wednesday (February 4) morning.

"We did win it," said Staehle. "Juan told me, 'I'm going to pour you on that plane.' We went out after the final game and celebrated. That was really special."

1965–66: A Long Season

Santurce's fortunes crumbled and they finished last. A combined Santurce/San Juan squad played a pre-season exhibition series against a squad of Cuban players. Luis Olmo managed Santurce for the final time. Tany Pérez was the only Santurce player named to the league's All-Star team. Rubén Gómez and William de Jesús were the team's best pitchers.

San Juan and Santurce players from the U.S. mainland, the U.S. Virgin Islands and Puerto Rico played a three-game series against professional players from Cuba. The Cubans won the first two games behind shutouts by Pedro Ramos and Camilo Pascual. San Juan/Santurce salvaged the finale, as Elrod Hendricks hit the only series homer in game three.[82]

Luis Olmo signed as Santurce's manager after managing Caguas in 1964–65. It would be Olmo's last tour of duty with Santurce, the team he first managed during World War II.

"We got off to a slow start," said Olmo. "It was a long season."

A headline in *The Sporting News*, "Champion Crabbers Start Like a Tortoise, Jolt Fans," said it all. The Crabbers opened the season at home against Mayagüez and 9,214 fans expected a win by Juan Pizarro. Mayagüez's four eighth inning runs gave John Hiller a 5–1 win on October 21, 1965. Santurce's pitchers would allow 45 runs in the next three games.[83]

Puerto Rico's correspondent for *The Sporting News*, Miguel J. Frau, wrote another piece under the heading: Placid Olmo Hits Roof; Crabbers Scrape Bottom. Santurce had started the season with 10 straight losses, an all-time league record to begin a campaign. It got so bad that Olmo had a policeman remove an agitator from Bithorn Stadium.[84]

One of the few highlights for Santurce was their twin-bill sweep of Arecibo by 3–0 and 3–1 scores on December 12, 1965. Rubén Gómez and William de Jesús each threw a two-hitter in their wins. Tany Pérez hit a two-run homer to win game two.[85]

Elrod Hendricks became a close friend and roommate of William de Jesús. Hendricks told me that de Jesús was most instrumental in his path to the big leagues. It was de Jesús who recommended that Jim Rivera, Jalisco's manager in Mexico's summer league, sign Hendricks to a contract. Other Santurce players who plied their trade in Mexico included Kindo Geigel with Jalisco and Rubén Gómez with Poza Rica.

One Santurce import, pitcher Bill Wilson, played for the North Americans in the league All-Star game on January 6, 1966. Santurce's four players on the Latin American squad were Rubén Gómez, Tany Pérez, Angel Luis Alcaraz and Félix Juan Maldonado. Maldonado stole home in the sixth inning to give the Latin American team a 3–2 win.[86] Tany Pérez was later named as the final All-Star team first baseman.[87]

Hiram Cuevas had experienced success with two league titles, but also went through two seasons without making the playoffs. Cuevas devised strategies to bring Santurce another title. Prior to his passing, Cuevas told me that his best promotional tool as an owner was having a winner. He focused on the 1961–62 and 1964–65 champions when we reminisced about his teams between the early and mid–1960s.

6. Baltimore Comes to Town

We did not bring our dress clothes to Ponce for game six (of the 1966–67 Final Series) … we expected to win.
— Paul Blair, former Santurce outfielder

A Baltimore-Santurce axis emerged in the fall of 1966 when Hiram Cuevas signed Earl Weaver to manage the 1966–67 Crabbers. This opened the door for the Crabbers' working agreement with the Orioles. Cuevas met Harry Dalton (Baltimore's Director of Player Development) when he signed Weaver.

"We had a good chemistry and developed a good friendship," said Cuevas. "Every Baltimore player under Dalton had first refusal to play in Puerto Rico and my friendship with Harry never interfered with the business aspects."

Hato Rey, a New Home

Our family moved to Hato Rey on October 14, 1966, about the time the 1966–67 season began. We now lived in a 15-story building near Hato Rey's "Golden Mile" of banks and other financial institutions. FOMENTO had moved its offices to Hato Rey. Dad walked to his office, while mom's consulting and university work took her to various parts of San Juan including the University of Puerto Rico's main campus in Rio Piedras.

I completed grades 6–12 between 1966 and 1973 at Robinson School in the Condado. One of my sixth grade classmates was Rafael Gómez, the son of Rubén and Teresa Gómez. Rafael was the best baseball player in our class, and it was fun to be on his team during our after school pick-up games. Some special moments were when Rubén Gómez joined us in these games before taking his son home. Rubén pitched for both teams, and I can still hear his encouraging words. He was in great physical shape and very nimble.

Bithorn Stadium was a 10-minute bus ride from Hato Rey's "Golden Mile." The rides to and from the ballpark were fun with plenty of chatter by baseball and non-baseball fans alike. A new shopping mall, Plaza Las Americas, opened across the avenue from

103

Bithorn Stadium in the late 1960s. This mall with its movie theaters, food courts, shops, and other amenities did not bode well for Santurce's businesses.

1966–67: A New Beginning with Baltimore

This season featured a league MVP performance by Tany Pérez. The Crabbers' eight pitchers came through for Earl Weaver. Santurce tied Ponce for first place, but lost a tie-breaker to determine the regular season champion. Santurce swept Arecibo in the semi-final series before besting Ponce in the finals.

Paul Blair was one hero of Baltimore's sweep of Los Angeles in the 1966 World Series. The 22-year-old Blair and several Baltimore prospects — backstop Larry Haney and outfielder Dave May — joined Santurce for the Crabbers' 28th season in 1966–67.

The Santurce faithful were excited about the team's prospects. Many still had vivid memories of the most talented big league center fielder to wear the Crabber uniform — Willie Mays. And Blair, like Mays a dozen years earlier, had come to Puerto Rico after a four-game World Series sweep. Santurce fans expected immediate dividends.

It did not take long for Santurce's loyal followers to give Weaver the sobriquet "Mickey Rooney." Weaver was quite feisty, namely when he stood up for his players during arguments with the U.S. and Puerto Rican umpires. Crabber fans, like all Puerto Rico Winter League fans, were enthusiastic and demonstrative. They really took to Weaver's style, and appreciated his passion for the game.

Larry Haney had played for Weaver in Elmira and Rochester, two Baltimore farm teams. Haney: "This was Earl's first chance to manage good league ballplayers ... he wasn't intimidated. He managed his type of ballgame and gained the respect of Pizarro, Gómez, and Pérez ... Earl was a quality manager wherever he managed and the players had to adjust to his style of play."

Santurce stayed relatively injury free and stable in terms of roster changes. The only major line-up/roster change took place before mid-season when third baseman Steve Demeter, hitting .184,[1] was replaced in the line-up by Orlando Cepeda. This allowed league MVP Tany Pérez to play third base and strengthened Santurce's line-up. Santurce had Dave May in right field and Gilberto Torres in left field. Félix Juan Maldonado was the fourth outfielder. Angel Luis Alcaraz and Arturito Miranda formed the keystone combo at second and shortstop. Elrod Hendricks was the team's top slugger off the bench and a reserve catcher.

This team won because of stellar pitching. Their hurlers' regular season earned run average was 1.93. The four starters — Dick Hughes (1.79), Darrell Osteen (1.83), Juan Pizarro (2.08), and Rubén Gómez (2.11) — had low ERA's. All started 15 or more games in the 71-game season.[2] When Weaver called upon his bullpen, Ted Davidson (1.72), William de Jesús (1.76), or Kindo Geigel (2.45), came through.[3] De Jesús and Geigel got a few spot starts; Osteen and Pizarro were also used in relief.

The only team that could match Santurce in terms of pitching was Ponce, with a rotation of Nelson Briles, Steve Carlton, John Boozer, and Pedro Ramos. Ponce shut out the opposition 16 times, the most of any team.[4] They finished the season in a dead heat with Santurce at 45–25, but won a one-game tie-breaker in Ponce to earn the regular season title.[5] Ponce benefited from their contacts and links with the New York Yankees and St. Louis Cardinals. Ponce skipper Tite Arroyo had pitched for St. Louis in the mid–1950s

Earl Weaver, Santurce's manager, with hands on his hips, 1966–67 (courtesy of Rai García).

and for the Yankees in the early 1960s. This helped secure pitchers such as Briles, Carlton, Ramos, and Dooley Womack, and position players Roger Repoz and Roy White. Horace Clarke of the Yankees was Ponce's shortstop.

The regular season had some exciting moments including November 6, 1966 when Larry Haney tagged out two Ponce players at home on the same play.[6] Paul Blair was the catalyst of an unusual triple steal against San Juan with the bases loaded. San Juan's Jorge Rubio was on the mound on December 14, when Blair broke for home in the third inning and made it. Tany Pérez and Angel Luis Alcaraz also got credit for stealing third and second base. But Santurce achieved notoriety of a different sort when Arecibo's Luis de León pitched the league's only perfect game against the Crabbers in a 1–0 Arecibo win on November 20, 1966.[7]

It was a warm Sunday afternoon at Bithorn Stadium when the Wolves and Crabbers faced off at 4:20 p.m. in a seven-inning second game of a twin-bill. The 1-hour, 36-minute game was over before 6 p.m. when Paul Blair slapped a grounder to Eddie Olivares at third.

"No one really knew it was a perfect game until the very end," said third base umpire Kermit Schmidt. "By the seventh inning, we were aware of it."

Santurce had 11 players participate in the league's All-Star game on January 1, 1967.[8] Blair, Haney and May were joined on the U.S. players squad by Davidson and Osteen while Cepeda, Tany Pérez, Pizarro, Gómez, Félix Juan Maldonado and Gilberto Torres formed

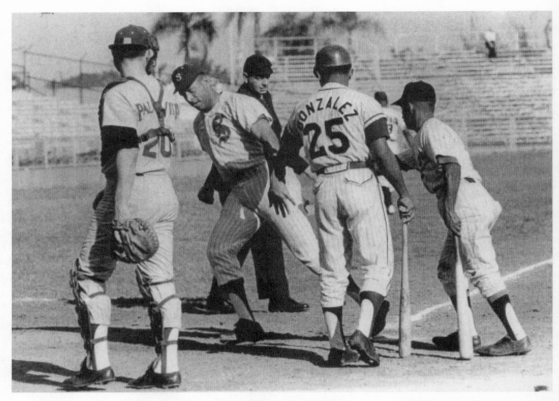

Orlando Cepeda is congratulated by San Juan's Tony González after homering in the January 1, 1967, All-Star game (courtesy of *The San Juan Star*).

part of the Latin American squad. Osteen and Pizarro started for their respective teams. It was Pizarro who earned the win with three scoreless innings in the 5–1 victory. Orlando Cepeda hit the game's only homer.[9]

Rafael Pont Flores had a unique perspective of the January 18, 1967 tie-breaker between Ponce and Santurce. Pont Flores went to the game with league umpire Alfred "Art" Frantz. He noted that the "suicidal drivers on the Rio Piedras to Caguas road passed Frantz like baseballs thrown at his head."[10] Frantz had been a New York City cab driver, so this did not faze him. This is an excerpt of what Pont Flores wrote after Ponce's 3–2 win over Santurce to win the regular season title: "The fans went wild when the 'Durango Kid' [Nelson Briles] was introduced as the starting pitcher. [Horace] Clarke's two-run single brought the fans to life ... they screamed, danced, hugged, and a loud siren came to life. When Repoz caught the final out, hundreds of frustrated athletes ran onto the field...."[11]

Pont Flores, in paraphrasing Casey Stengel, duly noted that the post-season would be the key measuring stick. All that Ponce accomplished — they had won their first regular season title in 20 years — would go for naught unless the post-season was a success.

The "real season" began on January 19, 1967 when Santurce hosted third place Arecibo in the best-of-seven semi-finals. Rubén Gómez shut out the Wolves, 5–0, in game one. Santurce swept the Wolves after William de Jesús, who pitched for all six league teams in his Puerto Rico career, won game four at Luis Rodríguez Olmo Stadium with the help of an Angel Luis Alcaraz homer.[12] Olmo Stadium was a pitcher's park since the dimensions at that time were 419 feet down the right field line, 402 feet to center and 435 feet down the left field line. Only 18 regular season homers were hit in Arecibo during thirty-five 1966–67 games.[13]

Ponce hosted the first game of the best-of-seven finals on January 27, 1967, following their triumph over Caguas in the other semi-finals. Steve Carlton went the route in Ponce's 11–2 win. Roger Repoz, Roy White and Carlton hit home runs. Ponce blanked Santurce, 4–0, in game two.[14] Santurce was facing "do or die" when the series moved to Bithorn for the next three contests. The Crabbers had already used six of their eight pitchers in the first two games. Ted Davidson and Rubén Gómez had not seen action.

According to Gómez, Earl Weaver considered bringing down one of Baltimore's pitching prospects for the post-season, since he was concerned about Gómez's age — 39 — at the time. But Gómez was confident. Weaver called Gómez at home the day of third final series game to tell him he would start that night.

An overflow crowd of 20,001 rabid fans jammed Bithorn on January 29. Gómez' mound rival was spitball-throwing John Boozer. Paul Blair and ex-Caguas pitcher Grant Jackson later told me that Boozer cheated in terms of throwing this illegal pitch. Blair tried to hit the "dry side" of the horsehide when facing Boozer. Rubén Gómez's screwball was so effective that switch-hitting second baseman Roy White batted right-handed against Gómez instead of left-handed. Gómez had a five-hit shutout as Santurce won 7–0.[15]

Santurce knotted the series at two games when Dick Hughes atoned for his showing in game one with a one-hitter before 18,269 fans. Horace Clarke got Ponce's only hit. The Crabbers bested Steve Carlton in game five at Bithorn when the future Hall of Famer threw a wild pickoff throw to first base which opened the floodgates in Santurce's 5–2 win.[16] A number of Santurce players including Paul Blair did not want to overnight in Ponce after game six on February 1, 1967. They did not pack their suitcases for the road trip, assuming they would win game six and return home on the bus for a victory celebration.

"We did not bring our dress clothes to Ponce for game six," said Blair. "We expected to win."

Ponce's Nelson Briles had not pitched since game three of their semi-final series in Caguas on January 21.[17] According to some Santurce players, Ponce team owner Yuyo González promised Briles $1,000 if he would defeat Santurce and force a final game. A final game would not be held, thanks to homers by Dave May and Paul Blair. Blair's three-run shot in the ninth frame provided Santurce's margin of victory, 6–3. Ted Davidson held Ponce at bay in the bottom of the ninth to give Juan Pizarro the win. For Davidson, that game and the winter season were special.

"The Ponce fans were upset," noted Davidson. "Our fans had some kind of a motorcade in front of us." Davidson was not part of the Baltimore connection and was "recruited" to play for Santurce by Cincinnati teammate Tany Pérez during the summer of 1966. Pérez knew that Davidson could give Santurce an edge, based on his winter experience in Venezuela when he played on the same Caracas team with Pete Rose in 1964–65. Davidson had pitched for the Licey franchise in the Dominican Winter League, where he had started a game against Juan Marichal. His vita included post-season pitching in the Dominican Republic.

"Hiram [Cuevas] was making his annual swing to the States and was going to be in Cincinnati the day after Tony (Pérez's U.S. nickname) asked me if I wanted to go down there and I told him, yeah, I'd love to play," recalled Davidson. "Hiram signed me the next day."

Dick Hughes has nothing but pleasant memories. He enjoyed the rivalry with Ponce since they had two St. Louis Cardinals pitchers — Nelson Briles and Steve Carlton — who would be his teammates for the 1967 World Champions. Hughes liked playing card games with Earl Weaver and several other players on the long bus trips. On Weaver: "He was a pepperpot, a demanding type manager … different from anyone I played ball with before or after … a banty rooster."

An unsung hero was Santurce trainer Nick Acosta. Nick impressed Earl Weaver, and was later offered a job as Baltimore's "second trainer." But he opted to continue his year-round work in Puerto Rico.

Some 30 years later, Earl Weaver informed me that he just liked being involved in baseball year round at the time he managed Santurce. Weaver: "The [1966–67] championship was just like winning any other championship including the World Series. Puerto Rico's baseball fans were outstanding and similar to those who follow the Yankees or Mets."

1967–68: Earl Weaver Returns

Santurce won the regular season title in Weaver's second season. The season had a sad note after the passing of Monchile Concepción and a season-ending injury to Paul Blair. Orlando Cepeda was a catalyst in Santurce's march to the finals including a semi-final series win over Ponce. Caguas dethroned Santurce in the finals.

Earl Weaver returned to Santurce's helm and earned Manager of the Year laurels. Paul Blair and Dave May returned. Orioles' second baseman Dave Johnson and hurlers Jim Hardin and Dave Leonhard came down. But it was a bittersweet season. Monchile Concepción, a member of the Crabbers' first team in 1939–40 and their former coach and manager, passed away at age 62 on December 6, 1967.[18] Paul Blair tore the ligaments in his right ankle 20 days later in a game against San Juan and was lost for the season and playoffs. Blair returned to Baltimore to undergo surgery.[19]

Santurce was still the team to beat. Tany Pérez, the team MVP, had another solid season. Orlando Cepeda, the 1967 National League MVP, put on Crabber flannels just before Thanksgiving. Santurce's home attendance —144,707, or about 4,130 per game — was about 1,000 more per game than the prior season.[20] Santurce topped fourth place Ponce in five games during the semi-finals. Ponce won the opener, but Pizarro, Jim Hardin, Gómez, and Darrell Osteen took charge in the next four contests while Elrod Hendricks and Orlando Cepeda hit key homers.[21]

Caguas bested Santurce in six games to claim the league championship. Ted Savage drove in all three runs in his team's 3–1 opening game win. It was Savage who robbed Cepeda of a three-run homer in the final game played on a rainy night, which turned into a 17–2 rout.[22]

"I remember the beer that was thrown in my face at Bithorn," recalled Savage. "Those Santurce fans were not pleased."

Johnny Briggs took away another three-run homer from Cepeda to frustrate the Crabber faithful. The agony was compounded by a two-hour rain delay. Julio Navarro was the winning pitcher and relief ace Tom Timmerman pitched the final three frames.

Dick Hughes had an outstanding 1966–67 season for Santurce (courtesy of *The San Juan Star*).

"It meant a lot," said Navarro. "They [Santurce] were the defending champions and a very strong team. We, too, had a fine team with the league's best reliever, Tom Timmerman, plus Grant Jackson, Tom Burgmeier, Cleon Jones, José Pagán, Guillermo Montañez...."

1968–69: Frank Robinson Joins Santurce

Frank Robinson lobbied for the Santurce managing job and was hired by Hiram Cuevas. Jim Palmer pitched the first no-hitter in Santurce's history and resurrected his pitching career. Santurce posted the best regular season record in their history, but were eliminated by San Juan in a seven-game semi-final series.

Baltimore named Earl Weaver as their manager during the 1968 season. When Weaver decided he could not manage Santurce for a third season, Frank Robinson lobbied for this job. Frank Robinson was 33 at the time, and making $115,000 per season with the Orioles.[23] He asked Weaver to put in a good word for him with Hiram Cuevas. This was done during a long distance Weaver-Cuevas telephone call from New York to Puerto Rico.

Weaver's recommendation was the crucial one prior to the meeting held between Cuevas and Frank Robinson when the Orioles returned home from their road trip. Hiram Cuevas lunched with Frank Robinson at the Baltimore Hilton where they agreed to everything except salary. Prior to their meeting, Cuevas had Weaver tell Frank Robinson what he made as Santurce's manager.

"We cut a napkin in half and each of us was to put down a 'fair' dollar figure," said Cuevas. "I put $1,800, but Frank left it blank — he was willing to take whatever I offered. I gave him $2,000 [per month] and we became good friends."

Frank Robinson had major league managing aspirations and was willing to sacrifice his off-seasons to gain the necessary experience. Some of his Baltimore teammates — Paul Blair, Elrod Hendricks, Dave Leonhard and Dave May — played for Robinson that first winter. So would Jim Palmer, coming off two injury-plagued seasons, and ex-Baltimore hurler Wally Bunker, selected by Kansas City in the big league expansion draft. Robinson told reporters that he would feel his way that first season, but he understood that the players tended to be a little looser in winter ball as compared to the big leagues.

Hiram Cuevas signed George Scott and Joe Foy of the Boston Red Sox to play the corners as well as big league shortstop Leo Cárdenas. Julio Gotay was acquired to play second base. Félix Juan Maldonado was a fixture in the outfield. Frank Robinson had the firepower to win 49 games — more than any Crabber team in its history, including the 1954–55 dream team.[24]

San Juan's skipper, Sparky Anderson, told me that Santurce was "loaded." Anderson knew they had the best club with Scott, Gotay, Cárdenas, Foy, Hendrick, Blair, Palmer, Pizarro, Gómez.

Julio Gotay recalls that the team's imports and native players would spend time and have meals together. Gotay told me that Robinson really liked the rice and beans.

"Frank was the best winter league manager I ever had," said Gotay. "He knew his baseball and how to treat the players ... had a lot of tact."

Robinson remembered that season with its 49 wins and a 15-game winning streak, by stating: "It was a tremendous ballclub, they played very well, and the thing I really liked was the effort they put in."

Jim Palmer turned in the team's best pitching performance during game two of a Sunday afternoon double-header, December 22, 1968, before 1,843 fans in Mayagüez. Palmer pitched the first no-hitter in Santurce history, albeit a seven-inning contest,[25] after Rubén Gómez won the first contest. Ozzie Virgil, Palmer's mound opponent, was pressed into duty, but only lasted one-third of an inning as Santurce scored the game's only four runs. The 1-hour, 25-minute game sailed along after the top of the first inning. Santurce trainer Nick Acosta is still proud of Palmer's progress that winter in overcoming a career-threatening inflamed right rotator cuff.

"We gave him first class treatment in Puerto Rico," said Acosta. "He recovered and became a Cy Young winner. Jim listened to me and followed all my tips. That was a plus."

Palmer made excellent progress that winter after starting the season on Santurce's inactive list. According to Hiram Cuevas, Harry Dalton offered to cover Palmer's Puerto Rico salary while he remained on the inactive list, but Santurce covered his salary once he was activated. During the 1960s, a typical monthly salary for a talented Santurce import such as Paul Blair was $1,000, with perhaps another $350 for living expenses. Cuevas preferred to keep salaries low.

Four Santurce players — Blair, Cárdenas, May, and Scott — started for the Imports in the January 1, 1969 All-Star game. Joe Foy, Wally Bunker and Al Severinsen were selected to this team. Rubén Gómez, Juan Pizarro, Elrod Hendricks, and Félix Juan Maldonado played for the Native Stars.[26]

Al Severinsen called this a "great blend of players from the big leagues to top local talent." Severinsen savored the whole Puerto Rico experience from eating tripas (pig intestines) in Mayagüez to empanadillas and pastelillos on the one-lane road trips to Ponce.

A team official took Severinsen to the El Flamingo Restaurant on his first night in Puerto Rico. Severinsen found out that the word for pork chops was chuletas and ordered a few. The next night, he was back by himself and the same waitress took his order.

"I said chuletas and then she said something else," said Severinsen.

"Then I said 'si, si'" [yes, yes] to her other questions ... and she brings out many plates — a whole table full of food! Elrod Hendricks walks in, and sees that sight; he asks me, 'Did you order for us?'"

Santurce's only disappointment was losing the semi-finals to San Juan. Their fate was sealed in game seven when José Cardenal cracked two homers off Jim Palmer in San Juan's 12–2 win.[27] There were 21,014 fans at Bithorn who were equally divided between the two rivals. Wally Bunker relieved Palmer in the fourth inning after Cardenal's second homer. Miguel Cuéllar won both his starts for San Juan. Sparky Anderson told me that Cuéllar was all business in this series after a so-so regular season.

1969–70: Fred Beene's No-Hitter

The heated rivalry with San Juan continued and the fans came out. Fred Beene pitched Santurce's second no-hitter. Frank Robinson made a pinch-hitting appearance in the league's All-Star game. Santurce topped Mayagüez in the semi-finals, prior to losing to Ponce in the finals.

Hiram Cuevas and company regrouped with the hopes of producing another winner. Santurce had drawn over 110,000 fans to their home games the prior season, and this enthusiasm continued in 1969–70 when the Crabbers drew nearly 120,000 fans to once again lead the league in attendance.[28] Santurce struggled a bit on the field, but finished third.

The Santurce and San Juan fans were out for each other's blood. A case in point was November 28, 1969 when Miguel Cuéllar made the headlines. Santurce's Merv Rettenmund, a Cuéllar teammate with Baltimore, remembers: "We beat him [Cuéllar] bad. The fans were all over him. He was a superstar in the big leagues ... some fan came down and threw beer all over him. Some San Juan players beat him to a pulp. We felt bad for him, but he got into it."

Cuéllar's exit was in the eighth inning when the fan, jumping on the top of the dugout, threw the cup into the hurler's face. Several San Juan players jumped into the stands to exchange blows with the fan, who was eventually escorted onto the field by detectives and park police, finally taken away from Bithorn Stadium.

George Scott, Santurce's first baseman, told the *Sporting News* correspondent that "those [1969] Mets proved that Baltimore isn't invincible ... the Mets World Series victory should open the eyes of other teams in the American League who have the idea the Orioles were unbeatable."[29]

Frank Robinson managing from the third base coaching box, 1969–70 season (courtesy of Rai García).

Santurce made headlines on December 20, 1969, when they played Arecibo at Lionel Roberts Stadium in St. Thomas, U.S. Virgin Islands. It was designed to be a special homecoming day for St. Thomas native Elrod Hendricks. Hendricks had already enjoyed a "Day" in his honor shortly after the 1969 Baltimore–New York Mets World Series, when St. Thomas schools and government offices were closed. This would be Santurce's only regular season game away from Puerto Rico.[30]

Frank Robinson made a pinch-hitting appearance in the January 6, 1970 league All-Star game. He singled after a ninth inning walk to Ponce manager Jim Fregosi. San Juan's Thurman Munson drew another walk to load the bases, but Jackie Hernández, José Cardenal and Danny Thompson were retired to preserve the Natives' 6–1 win over the Imports. George Scott drove in the Imports' only run, while José Pagán accounted for the game-winner, a homer hit off Fred Beene. Elrod Hendricks won the pre-game home-run hitting contest over Tany Pérez.[31]

Hendricks, Tany Pérez, and George Scott were the team's top three sluggers. Dave May and Merv Rettenmund also hit the long ball.

Santurce's best hurler was Baltimore prospect Fred "Habichuelita" Beene. "Habichuela" is Spanish for bean, and the Santurce fans fell in love with the gritty 5'8" Texan who enjoyed the Puerto Rican rice and beans and the black bean soup. This love grew after Beene pitched the second no-hitter in Santurce history. Beene's masterpiece was a nine-inning one.

January 17, 1970 was a typical Puerto Rico afternoon with 80 degree weather made comfortable by the trade winds. Fred Beene took the Bithorn Stadium mound at 3 p.m. Atlantic Standard Time to face switch-hitter Jimmy Rosario of the Arecibo Wolves. Rosario and right fielder José Silva (batting fifth in the Arecibo line-up) were the only Wolves to reach base via walks. Only 685 fans attended the 1-hour, 41-minute game which ended when Beene retired shortstop Jack Heidemann.[32] Beene: "It was a Sunday game and they [Arecibo] were in last place. I remember facing [first baseman] Elmo Plaskett. It was my first and only no-hitter in baseball and the one thing I remember is that I threw the same number of pitches Don Larsen threw in his perfect game [97]."

Merv Rettenmund usually wintered in Venezuela, but opted to play for Santurce in 1969–70 since Frank Robinson was managing. He had first come out of AA ball to play in Venezuela. By the end of the 1969–70 season, his fifth winter baseball season, he changed his entire batting stance. Rettenmund had been mired in a season-long hitting slump for Santurce, but got some timely hits including a key homer in the final game of the Santurce-Mayagüez semi-final series to help the Crabbers earn the right to face Ponce in the finals.

Santurce wanted Frank Robinson to be eligible for the semi-finals and finals, but Major League Baseball Commissioner Bowie Kuhn turned this proposal down soon after arriving in Puerto Rico for a short vacation. League President Guigo Otero Suro and San Juan Mayor Carlos Romero Barceló, a Santurce fan, felt that Robinson's playing would boost post-season attendance. Kuhn denied the request by citing the rule which prohibited winter league clubs from offering employment to any non-native with four or more years of big league experience.[33]

The final series format had Santurce visit Ponce for the first two games, followed by three games at Bithorn Stadium, and games six and seven at Ponce's Paquito Montaner Stadium, if necessary. Both teams split the first two games. Fred Beene's five-hit shutout in game two tied the series.[34]

Ponce won two of the next three games to take a three games-to-two lead going into game six at Montaner Stadium. A record crowd of 12,008 was on hand to roar their approval in Ponce when Vern Geishert took the mound for the Lions. Frank Robinson counted on his ace, Fred Beene, to knot the series one more time. Ponce had a solid line-up with Bernie Carbo, Sandy Alomar, Sr., Pat Corrales, Luis Meléndez, and Jim Hicks.

The February 2, 1970 game was a 12-inning thriller won by Ponce, 3–2, when pinch-hitter Wito Conde drove in the winning run on a base hit.[35] Beene trudged off the mound with his head held high. This outing earned him the adulation of the Ponce fans and mayor. After Beene had showered and gotten on Santurce's bus, Ponce's mayor made it on that bus to personally invite Beene to reinforce Ponce for the 1970 Caribbean Series against the champions from the Dominican Republic (Licey) and Venezuela (Magallanes). But Beene politely declined.

"I had a bad finger and was tired," stated Beene. "I really didn't want to go [to the Caribbean Series], but appreciated being asked."

Tany Pérez reinforced Ponce in Caracas, Venezuela, and hit their first Caribbean Series homer.[36] Magallanes won this event.

Guigo Otero Suro deserves a lot of credit for renewing the Caribbean Series with his dedication and hard work. Guigo also set the wheels in motion for the inclusion of Mexico starting with the 1971 Caribbean Series.

1970–71: Reggie Jackson Hits 20 Homers

Roberto Clemente managed San Juan which created added interest in their regular and post-season games with Santurce. Clemente and Frank Robinson were selected to manage the Native and Import All-Star teams, respectively. Santurce and San Juan squared off in a semi-final series won by the Crabbers, who went on to defeat Caguas in the finals. The Licey Tigers of the Dominican Republic won the 1971 Caribbean Series.

Fred Beene was named Santurce's Opening Night pitcher by Frank Robinson to face San Juan. Roberto Clemente, San Juan's skipper, went with lefty Ken Brett. There was almost no game as hordes of fans crashed the gate and created utter chaos. A power outage at Bithorn Stadium did not help matters. While the official paid attendance was listed at 19,979, or about full capacity, those who were there thought at least 25,000 souls were sitting or standing inside Bithorn Stadium.

"We played San Juan and Clemente was managing [them]," said Beene. "I blew my arm that night in the third inning pitching to Ken Singleton. Boy, I tore a tendon. Couldn't throw a lick anymore that winter, but stayed there about six weeks. That's when Roger [Rogelio] Moret came alive and Reggie hit 20 homers."

Oakland A's owner Charles Finley suggested that the 24-year-old Reggie Jackson play winter ball after a sub-par 1970 season. Baltimore's Harry Dalton got the green light from Finley to contact Jackson. Hiram Cuevas was ecstatic: "When I first brought him down, Reggie thought he'd hit more for average, but it wasn't until later in the season that he started hitting homers. He wanted to improve in all aspects of the game, hitting, running, sliding ... got a salary of some $2,000 a month and stayed the whole season."

Jackson began the winter season much like he ended the 1970 big league season — in a slump. He struck out 14 times the first week alone.[37] Santurce coach Germán Rivera began pitching morning batting practice to Jackson, who once got so disgusted that he threw his bat into the Bithorn Stadium stands.

Reggie Jackson, on-deck circle, 1970–71 season (courtesy of Rai García).

But, Rivera says, "Reggie told me he had to do his part. He realized the Puerto Rico fans expected a lot from him, and came out of his slump."

Credit eyeglasses with an assist. Jackson was fitted for glasses on a week-long trip to the States around Thanksgiving. By mid–December 1970, Jackson was on a homer binge which included five in four games.[38] Frank Robinson had also worked with Jackson on his hitting and was impressed.

"He's just not striking out anymore," Robinson said. "He's made up his mind just to make contact and with his power, the results have been something else."

Santurce's outfield included Baltimore prospects Don Baylor and Roger Freed. Freed had the hot bat during the first half of the season and was leading the league in RBI when he injured his right arm. Freed: "In fact, Reggie told me when I was hitting third and he was hitting fourth, that [Roger], you don't leave anybody on base for me to pick up."

Catcher John "Buck" Martínez was a gamer. Elrod Hendricks played first base much of that winter. Santurce's double-play duo was veteran Julio Gotay and young shortstop Milton Ramírez. Tany Pérez joined the team later in the season and played third base. An eclectic pitching staff included Dave Leonhard, Rogelio Moret, Juan Pizarro, Rubén Gómez, Joe Decker, Mike Kekich, Darrell Osteen and Bob Chlupsa.

The All-Star game had San Juan-Santurce overtones when Robinson and Clemente managed the Imports and Natives, respectively, on January 6, 1971. Milton Ramírez's hit

Tany Pérez drives off in a 1971 Buick Riviera, a gift from Santurce's appreciative fans (courtesy of *The San Juan Star*).

began the game-winning rally in the second.[39] Ramírez also cracked a double off his Santurce teammate, Joe Decker, in the Natives' 4–1 win. Tany Pérez scored the Imports' only run. Santurce's fans honored Tany Pérez with a special night on January 12. One of his gifts was a 1971 Buick Riviera.

Santurce and San Juan hooked up for real in the semi-finals. Clemente counted on

Ken Singleton, Dave Cash, Manny Sanguillén and Cocó Laboy for offense. Ken Brett and Jim Colborn were his best available starters, since Jim Lonborg and Bill Denehy had left the Island early. Al Oliver and Fred Patek also exited from San Juan.

Ken Brett noted that the San Juan-Santurce rivalry from the fans' point of view was much more intense as compared to how many imported players saw it. Most of San Juan's imports were doing their jobs in the hopes of improving aspects of their game, but not as caught up in the rivalry. Clemente felt there was some intensity missing and activated himself for the semi-final series. In Brett's words, "Clemente was so mad at the way we were playing that he decided to show us how to play and the people went crazy."

Clemente's clutch, two-run pinch-hit single helped San Juan win game three, 7–4, on January 22, 1971.[40] The next night's game was rained out. Prior to game four, Reggie Jackson received a trophy for the most league home runs from a representative of the Puerto Rico Savings & Loan Association.[41] Santurce then knotted the series thanks to three RBI from Baylor and the pitching of Joe Decker. Baylor, Jackson and Tany Pérez had first inning singles off Ken Brett to jump start the Crabbers to their 5–2 win. Clemente inserted infielder Mako Oliveras to pinch-hit for Brett in the seventh inning with Cocó Laboy and Luis Alvarado on base. Oliveras grounded out to a cascade of boos. San Juan's fans wanted Clemente to hit.

When the line-up cards were made for game five, Clemente penciled his own name in the third slot to play right field. The drama began early when San Juan outfielder José "Polilla" (termite) Ortíz was called out for leaving third base too soon on a fly ball. Baylor drove in the game's first run, but San Juan tied it in their half of the fourth. The game's pivotal play ensued in that frame with Clemente on third and Sanguillén on first. Ken Singleton's fly ball was caught by Reggie Jackson and his throw nailed Clemente at the plate. Javier "Terín" Andino drove in the game-winner in the bottom of the fifth to give Pizarro the win. Jim Colborn was the hard-luck loser. Rafael Pont Flores called this game a night with plenty of heart attacks.[42] Santurce won game six thanks to Dave Leonhard's superb pitching and hitting. Leonhard drove in the game's first two runs with a bases loaded single. This sent lefty Angel "Papo" Davila to the showers. San Juan's fans did not agree with using an untested pitcher in such an important game. They took their frustrations out on Clemente when Palillo Santiago relieved Davila. Leonhard went the distance and became the toast of the town after fanning pinch-hitter José Manuel Morales to end the game.

"Half of Bithorn was rooting for each team," says Leonhard. "There would be chanting back and forth. It made for a more enjoyable, electric atmosphere, to play ball, in my opinion."

Hiram Cuevas went on the radio airwaves to dedicate the Santurce win to the team's fans. Frank Robinson praised the team's effort and his coaches, Germán Rivera and Pochy Oliver. Santurce then came back from a three games-to-one deficit to defeat Caguas in the seven-game finals.

Mike Kekich hurled a 4–1 win over Caguas on February 1, 1971. Reggie Jackson's two-run homer off Julio Navarro in the first inning gave Kekich all the runs he needed. Arsenio "Pinolo" Rodríguez drove in the other runs with a double and home run and robbed José Pagán of a home run. Kekich told reporters he had relied on his curve ball half the time.[43] He dedicated the win to Maritza de Jesús, an eight-year-old child from a broken home who spent the Christmas holidays with the Kekich family in Puerto Rico.[44]

Santurce forced a seventh game by winning game six, 3–2. Reggie Jackson scored the first of Santurce's three sixth inning runs on a wild pitch by Jim Rooker. An RBI double by Buck Martínez was followed by Milton Ramírez's RBI single. Bob Chlupsa saved the game for Joe Decker.[45]

Game seven was a cliffhanger that ended with Santurce on top, 5–4. Hiram Cuevas called it one of the most spectacular wins in team history. Bob Chlupsa won it in relief when William de Jesús got Angel Muñiz to fly out to Don Baylor. Caguas skipper Napoleón Reyes credited Chlupsa and Pinolo Rodríguez for being two of Santurce's key heroes.[46]

Milton Ramírez remembers celebrating that win at a pub owned by former Caguas pitcher Roberto Vargas. Ramírez: "I lived at Borinquen Towers where the pub was located," said Ramírez. "During the season some of the Puerto Rican players would meet at a Stop 22 restaurant/bar and later share some moments with Frank [Robinson] and the imported players at Rudy's 10th Inning Lounge near Loíza Street." (Rudy's was owned by former league pitcher Rudy Hernández, the first Dominican-born hurler to pitch in the majors.)

Ramírez told me that he had used Frank Robinson's bats when he noticed Robinson hit some long homers in batting practice.

"Frank's bats were sent to Puerto Rico and I was impressed by his power when he hit," said Ramírez. "Frank helped me a lot and let me use his bats."

The Crabbers had one day of rest prior to the Caribbean Series slated for Bithorn Stadium. Milton Ramírez noted that the Santurce pitchers were tired after the tough Caguas series. They picked up Sandy Alomar, Sr. and several other reinforcements.

Tany Pérez's eleventh inning single drove in Alomar in a 5–4 win over the Hermosillo Orange Growers on opening night.[47] Celerino Sánchez had tied the game in the final inning with a two-run homer. Hermosillo, managed by Maury Wills, had scored its other runs on two Zoilo Versalles homers. Rubén Gómez and William de Jesús preserved the win for Bob Chlupsa.

Santurce's downslide began the next day, a Sunday, before some 13,500 fans. I was there and saw Reggie Jackson's towering two-run homer, his only one of the series, against Venezuela's LaGuaira Sharks, who prevailed, 6–5. Santurce then faced the Licey Tigers of the Dominican Republic. Licey edged Santurce, 5–4, on their way to a 6–0 mark.

My recollection of the series' final game includes Federico "Chi Chi" Olivo being summoned from the bullpen by Licey player-manager Manny Mota. Santurce had scored two ninth inning runs to cut the Licey lead to 6–4, but Olivo struck out Reggie Jackson and Elrod Hendricks before Terín Andino skied to left.

Mota recalled that Dominican President Joaquín Balaguer had held a reception for the Licey players prior to leaving for Puerto Rico. Mota: "We had a moral obligation with the Dominican Republic to win. Santurce had a trabuco [powerhouse], but we had momentum. Our fan support in Puerto Rico was strong. The players gave 100 percent after I told them we wouldn't win individually, but collectively … should represent our flag with pride and dignity."

Former Santurce player Jim Beauchamp noted that Licey went on a mission to win. First baseman Beauchamp was one of four Licey players including Mota, Ted Martínez and Chris Zachary named to the All-Series team. Mota was the series MVP. Mike Kekich and Milton Ramírez were the Santurce players on the select squad. LaGuaira's José Herrera and Pat Kelly, and Hermosillo's catcher, Sergio "Bazooka" Robles, and third baseman, Celerino Sánchez, rounded out the select squad. Licey players earned $535 apiece as their winning share.[48] Low attendance during the last two nights brought the share down.

1971–72: Rogelio Moret Wins 14

Rubén Gómez was tapped to manage Santurce. Dave Leonhard told his side of the story on an article that he authored for a Baltimore newspaper. Don Baylor won the league batting title and Rogelio Moret was the league's best starter. Santurce qualified for the playoffs, but lost to Ponce in the semi-finals. Ponce contracted Don Baylor to reinforce them for the 1972 Caribbean Series held in Santo Domingo.

Baltimore went on a 1971 post-World Series tour of Japan. Frank Robinson could not manage Santurce and Rubén Gómez got the nod. Dave Leonhard, Fred Beene and Bob Chlupsa were back along with Don Baylor and Buck Martínez. Terry Crowley from Baltimore's Rochester AAA club played first base. Jerry DaVanon, a Baltimore prospect, played some shortstop while Milton Ramírez was moved to second. Atlanta's Dusty Baker played the outfield. Rogelio Moret became the staff ace.

Dave Leonhard found himself in the middle of a storm with Puerto Rico's fans when the season began. He had prepared an article published in the *Baltimore Sun* in January 1971 which complimented Puerto Rico and the quality of its professional baseball. Leonhard was a graduate of Baltimore's Johns Hopkins University who wrote that a good sacrifice bunt in Puerto Rico is more appreciated than a base hit in the States. Several of his positive comments were left out of an October 14, 1971 excerpt prepared by a sportswriter with one of Puerto Rico's newspapers. Some amusing anecdotes were taken out of context.

What Leonhard found amusing was the time the Santurce team bus was roach-infested and some roaches took his sandwich off the luggage rack. Then there was the time at Caguas when Santurce second baseman Julio Gotay referred to several Caguas players as witches after they made a cross of chicken bone at his position. Gotay refused to go out until the cross was removed. Elrod Hendricks went out to pick up the cross and handed it to Frank Robinson. A Caguas player smacked Hendricks on the head with the swing of his bat and Robinson was later thrown out of the game.

"Blood was everywhere," Leonhard says, "the cross had worked."

Leonhard received hate letters from fans in Puerto Rico prior to the 1971–72 season. He could have traveled to Japan with the Orioles, but decided to come to Puerto Rico to straighten everything out.

"The first time I was introduced [the home opener] they booed me for about 10 minutes," recalls Leonhard. "They threw stuff at me in the bullpen. Their faces were contorted with hatred and I got kind of scared ... got a police escort that night."

This episode had a peaceful ending when Leonhard wrote his side of the story for *The San Juan Star*. Leonhard did not pitch in Puerto Rico for money, citing that Baltimore players had made over $50,000 in World Series earnings between 1969 and 1971.[49] He admitted laughing at the Bithorn Stadium grounds crew for mopping and sponging the infield once, but later suggested that the Baltimore ground crew do it during the rainy 1971 season. Leonhard's version concluded with the goodwill he felt toward Puerto Rico, its players, coaches, Rubén Gómez, team officials, grounds crew.... Gómez made it clear that Leonhard had his backing: "Why, I've even seen roaches and other nasty bugs scurrying across the ice in Canada," joked Gómez, in downplaying the roach episode on the team bus.

Gómez was selected to manage the Natives in the All-Star game. The contest ended in a 3–3 tie after being called when 12 innings were completed. Milton Ramírez had a fine game with three hits. An old-timers contest preceded the regular game. Víctor Pellot and Valmy Thomas were the hitting stars.[50]

Santurce finished the regular season in third place behind San Juan and Ponce. Individual honors included Don Baylor winning the batting title and Rogelio Moret copping top pitcher laurels with his 14–1 record.[51] The playoffs were another matter.

Chris Zachary, a veteran of winter ball, and Daryl Patterson, another seasoned hurler, were two reasons why Ponce stopped Santurce in the semis. Patterson remembers: "I defeated Santurce twice, once in relief and once as a starter. I didn't have problems with Baylor and Baker. "Corrales knew exactly how to pitch them ... move in and out and would make you throw the ball there."

Ponce handled Santurce's line-up which included Orlando Cepeda for this series. Only Juan Pizarro's shutout kept them from sweeping Santurce. The Lions roared past San Juan prior to flying to Santo Domingo and representing Puerto Rico in the Caribbean Series.

Don Baylor reinforced the Lions. His grand slam against Venezuela's Aragua Tigers propelled Ponce to its fourth straight series win, and helped them clinch the title. Baylor was rewarded with a berth on the All-Star team along with Aragua's player-manager, second baseman Rod Carew, and shortstop Dave Concepción. Other All-Stars were series MVP Carlos May and Pat Corrales of Ponce, Celerino Sánchez of Mexico's Guasave Cotton Pickers and César Cedeño of the Aguilas Cibaeñas of the Dominican Republic.[52]

Baylor's main goal was not to get tired toward the end of the season. "I haven't changed my style or stance any," noted Baylor. "The only thing I have been working on is trying to be more selective at the plate. I played left field and center field as well as first and third. I've also batted everywhere from leadoff to fifth in the line-up."[53]

1972–73: Santurce's Ninth League Title

Santurce had a new look with some Los Angeles Dodgers players when Frank Robinson returned to manage them. The passing of Roberto Clemente in a tragic aviation accident put a damper on the final part of the regular season, the playoffs and Caribbean Series. Santurce's first-place regular season finish was followed by playoff wins over Arecibo and Ponce. The Crabbers once again fell short in the Caribbean Series.

Don Baylor returned to Santurce after his first full season with the 1972 Orioles. But the Baltimore-Santurce era was coming to an end. Fred Beene, now with the New York Yankees, signed with Caguas for 1972–73. Frank Robinson had been traded to the Dodgers prior to the 1972 season. When he returned for his fourth season at Santurce's helm, the Crabbers had a different look. Third baseman Ron Cey, outfielder Willie Crawford and hurler Mike Strahler were three Dodger prospects who joined Santurce. Juan Beníquez had been acquired from Arecibo. Jerry DaVanon returned to Santurce as did Dave Leonhard. An interesting twist was Doyle Alexander's presence in Santurce's starting rotation. Alexander, a member of the 1972 Orioles, had been involved in the Orioles-Dodgers trade which sent Frank Robinson to Los Angeles.

Juan Pizarro and Rogelio Moret joined Alexander and Strahler in the rotation. Lloyd Allen was inserted in the rotation later on. The bullpen comprised Ramón "Mon" Hernández, Bob Reynolds and Dave Leonhard.

A balanced offensive attack featured the power of Elrod Hendricks, Beníquez, Cey and Crawford. Tany Pérez also provided punch when he put on the Santurce uniform for the final month of the season. Baylor and DaVanon stole 14 bases apiece as the speed merchants.[54]

"We had a great team that could score a lot of runs," said DaVanon. "When you win, not too many things go wrong."

DaVanon told me that the fans were great and most fun when Santurce played San Juan before full houses. DaVanon, his wife and daughter lived in an Isla Verde condo next to the ocean. It had a pool and tennis court.

The DaVanons loved Puerto Rico, its people and the weather.

Santurce's march to the pennant and post season play was tempered by the sudden passing of Roberto Clemente. Pre-game ceremonies at the January 6, 1973, league All-Star game were conducted in Clemente's memory.[55] Mike Schmidt was the game's MVP with three RBI in the 4–2 win by the Imports. He received the Monchile Concepción trophy, named after the long-time Santurce player, coach and manager.[56]

Santurce players had voted not to play a scheduled game several days after the December 31, 1972 plane crash which claimed Clemente's life. But Elrod Hendricks recalls that Hiram Cuevas wanted Santurce to play. "That's when I started thinking and doing some soul searching," says Hendricks. 'Where is the heart?'" Hendricks asked himself. "Here is an island where the world of baseball has lost one of its best players. We lost a great human being, someone who meant a lot to baseball, Puerto Rico and the world."

Santurce bested Arecibo, four games to one, in the semi-finals, behind Juan Pizarro's two shutouts.[57] The Crabbers then faced Ponce in a final series for the third time in the last seven seasons. Santurce avenged the 1970 final series setback by winning four of the six games.

Doyle Alexander pitched 19 final series innings without allowing an earned run. Pizarro pitched another shutout, his third straight in post season play. Moret and Lloyd Allen came through with wins. Jim Magnuson and Chris Zachary accounted for the only wins by the defending Caribbean Series champs. [58]

Santurce's ninth title came before a packed house of 20,473 fans at Bithorn Stadium on January 29, 1973. Lloyd Allen squeezed home Ron Cey with Santurce's second and decisive run after Cey had driven in their first run with a second inning single. A two-run homer by Willie Crawford in the next frame and a two-run double by Tany Pérez in the fourth inning sent Chris Zachary to the showers and Santurce on the way to an 8–1 win.[59]

The Licey Tigers managed by Tom Lasorda were ready for all comers in Venezuela when the 16th Caribbean Series opened. This series, dedicated to Roberto Clemente's memory, was disappointing to Santurce players, officials and fans. Licey won its second Caribbean Series title in three years. Santurce tied the host Caracas Lions for second. Mexico's Ciudad Obregón Yaquis finished last.

Those who came through for Santurce in the Caribbean Series were Tany Pérez with a home run and .353 mark; Don Baylor, who hit .357; Elrod Hendricks with a home run; and Doyle Alexander with two wins and a 1.38 earned run average.[60]

Licey's line-up comprising Manny Mota, Jesús (Jay) Alou, Bobby Valentine, Steve Yeager, Von Joshua and Steve Garvey hammered the ball. Licey's pitchers — Pedro Borbón, Bruce Ellingsen, Lerrin LaGrow, Dick Tidrow and Charlie Hough — came through. Tom Lasorda was their manager since Licey had a close working agreement with the Dodgers.

"That was a great ballclub and a good experience for me," says Lasorda. "I managed Licey some five seasons and enjoyed working with our owner, Monchin Pichardo."

Ron Cey remembers this about Lasorda and that Caribbean Series: "Tom Lasorda would talk to me the whole game while I was playing third base. He was coaching from the third base coaching box telling jokes and trying to distract me the entire game. We had a good laugh."

Frank Robinson was not laughing. Twenty years later, he expressed his disappointment about the 1973 Caribbean Series during a conversation we had in his Baltimore Camden Yards office. Robinson knew Santurce had the talent to win it with reinforcements such as Cheo Cruz and Angel Mangual. Robinson smiled when I reminded him that two Caribbean Series trips in his first four seasons as Santurce's manager were something to be proud of.

7. The Dry Spell Begins

I had heard that Frank Robinson was a bit tough on his players ... if you played hard for him, he liked you.
— Gary Allenson, former Santurce catcher.

Santurce was unable to win a league title between 1973–74 and 1981–82. Frank Robinson put his Santurce managing experience to good use in 1975 when he became the first African-American manager in big league history. The San Juan-Santurce City Championship became a "Metropolitan Series" when San Juan moved to Bayamón for the 1974–75 season. Orlando Cepeda, Rubén Gómez and Juan Pizarro had all retired by January 1977. Poto Paniagua purchased the Santurce Baseball Club from Hiram Cuevas.

A Transition Period

The mid–1970s to early 1980s was a transition period for Puerto Rico, Santurce and the winter league. Puerto Rico attracted U.S. pharmaceutical companies to pick up the slack for the downturn in the Island's petrochemical industry. The refineries were devastated, and Puerto Rico went through deep recessions in the mid–1970s and early 1980s.

Puerto Rico's motorists, like their U.S. counterparts, paid more at the pump, but enjoyed the opening of a new expressway linking San Juan to Ponce in about 90 minutes, about half the time it used to take. Work proceeded on the Minillas Tunnel, near my old Santurce home. Completion of this Tunnel made it quicker to travel between Santurce and other parts of San Juan to and from the San Juan International Airport.

All six of the league's baseball teams curtailed use of team buses to transport players to away games. The native players drove to the games from their homes while the imports used rental cars to move around. This had some bearing on team camaraderie, since players tended to go their separate ways after the games.

1973–74 and 1974–75:
Frank Robinson Prepares to Make History

Frank Robinson managed Santurce for a fifth and sixth time prior to becoming a player-manager for the 1975 Cleveland Indians. Robinson's six seasons at Santurce's helm were a key factor in his becoming major league baseball's first African-American manager. The 1973–74 and 1974–75 Crabbers finished in fifth place and were plagued by bad defense and inconsistent pitching. George Hendrick, Mickey Rivers and Robin Yount were three of the team's top hitters, but could not compensate for the club's other deficiencies. The designated hitter (DH) rule went into effect in the league beginning in the 1973–74 season.

Gil Flores, a reserve outfielder for Santurce in 1973–74, had a good perspective of Frank Robinson's managerial style. Flores got little playing time since George Hendrick, Mickey Rivers and Angel "Cookie" Mangual were the regulars. Flores was a talented boxer in his early teens who turned to baseball at age 16. Tite Arroyo wanted to sign Flores for the Yankees, but Germán Rivera got his signature for Baltimore.

"I began my league career with Santurce in 1973," said Flores. "Frank Robinson was very strict with the players and wanted things done his way. If not, they would pay the price. Frank had great outfielders with Santurce in the early 1970s (Don Baylor, Reggie Jackson, Rich Coggins) and then you had Mickey Rivers and George Hendrick. The best players seemed to come to Santurce and by this time, Frank had managed many big leaguers. Santurce later traded me [in 1974–75] to Ponce, but I did get the chance to observe Frank in action and to share some time with Orlando Cepeda, one of my heroes."

Frank Robinson felt Santurce would repeat in 1973–74, based on a pre-season conversation with Tito Stevens of *The San Juan Star*. Robinson liked his pitching staff with Mike Strahler, Ed Farmer, Dave Sells, Rogelio Moret, Juan Pizarro, Mon Hernández, Bob Reynolds and Lloyd Allen. Mickey Rivers had stolen 47 bases for Salt Lake City and had hit .349 with California the last month of the 1973 big league season.[1] Ron Cash starred for the Toledo Mud Hens and was counted on for speed and infield defense. Home runs were expected from Dave Kingman of San Francisco and George Hendrick of Cleveland's Indians. Juan Beníquez had shone with AAA Pawtucket.[2]

Santurce started on a bad note when eventual league and Caribbean Series champion Caguas inflicted a 21–2 defeat on them.[3] The Crabbers held on to fourth place much of the season thanks to the hitting of Hendrick, the league's batting champ; the hitting and running of Rivers; and, timely slugging by Elrod Hendricks. Their Achilles tendon was infield defense.

Connie Lepore, a sportswriter with *The San Juan Star*, wrote that Santurce's infield had more holes than a slice of Swiss cheese.[4] Dave Kingman was sent packing after he made too many errors at third base and often struck out with men in scoring position. Ron Cash had fielding lapses at second and Juan Beníquez was an erratic shortstop and so veteran players such as Angel Luis Alcaraz and Arturito Miranda got playing time. Manuel "Nolín" Ruíz filled in at second, short, or third.

Juan Pizarro hurled a one-hit shutout against Arecibo on November 6, 1973, with the last out recorded by Dave Sells.[5] A bloop single by former Crabber, Rich Coggins, in the fourth inning kept Pizarro and Sells from pitching a no-hitter. Arecibo later defeated Santurce in a one-game playoff for fourth place.

Santurce fans enjoyed their team's November 11 sweep of San Juan, propelled by two long homers by Dave Kingman in game one.[6] Santurce reverted to their inconsistent play five days later when they committed six errors, including two by Kingman, in losing a 13–11 game to their arch rivals.[7] By Thanksgiving, Santurce was averaging four errors per game and in trouble.

Frank Robinson juggled his line-up in December and inserted Gil Flores as a leadoff hitter a time or two. Flores tripled home the winning run off Balor Moore in a December 1 game versus San Juan and scored an insurance run on Arturito Miranda's suicide squeeze. Moore was coming off his perfect game against Ponce on November 25, 1973 — the only one thrown in the league's first 60 years.[8] Some other Santurce highlights included Elrod Hendricks' two-homer, six-RBI game against Arecibo and Charlie Sands' six RBI against Caguas in a mid–December game.[9]

Mickey Rivers proved he was the league's fastest runner by winning the 100-meter dash prior to the League All-Star game on January 6, 1974. Rivers later ignited a rally for the winning Imports with a base hit, followed by a Mike Schmidt hit and a two-run double by Danny Walton, the game's MVP.[10]

The 1974–75 season was similar to 1973–74, as Santurce's inconsistent play resulted in a fifth place finish. Orlando Cepeda played his final season for Santurce as their DH before calling it a career. Juan Pizarro returned for his 18th season with Santurce and 20th in the league after spending part of the 1974 season with Cordoba in the Mexican Pacific Summer League and Pittsburgh later that summer. Rubén Gómez began his 27th season with Santurce. Elrod Hendricks marveled at the work ethic, stamina and ability of these veterans.

"We're talking about professionals," said Hendricks. "They knew how to win, how to play the game. Contrary to what some fans may have believed, these guys played their hearts out for them ... loved to play and wanted to come home and do well. I think the fans expected them to hit homers or pitch shutouts all the time."

Frank Robinson's sixth season at Santurce's helm was special since he had played against this veteran trio in the National League during the late 1950s. Robinson told me that he enjoyed managing Cepeda, Gómez and Pizarro at the end of their Puerto Rico careers.

Cleveland offered their 1975 managing job to Robinson during the 1974–75 winter season. Robinson was 39 years old and toward the end of his big league playing career. He had come a long way since making his Santurce managing debut. When Robinson and I conversed in his Baltimore office in June 1992, he made it clear that the Santurce managing experience of working with league veterans from Puerto Rico, coupled with the top local and imported players, was invaluable to him, prior to getting a chance to manage in the majors.

Santurce's 1974–75 imports, for the most part, did not produce. Mickey Rivers contributed, but left prior to season's end. Robin Yount made his debut seven weeks into the season and played well at shortstop.

"I was injured the last month of the 1974 big league season and needed some extra work," said Yount. "It was very helpful having Frank Robinson as a manager and teammates like Ellie Hendricks, Sandy Alomar, Sr. and Cepeda. Sandy was my double-play partner and really great to play with. Cepeda was a hero of mine since I grew up in California as a fan of the San Francisco Giants. I still like the 'arroz con pollo' [rice and chicken] that we ate back then."

Santurce coach Germán Rivera noted that Yount would participate in two practices prior to evening home games at Bithorn Stadium and asked him (Rivera) and Robinson for advice.

"Robin Yount came here to play," said Rivera. "He deserved success due to his hard work."

Rivera assisted Frank Robinson in translating his thoughts from English to Spanish for the benefit of Santurce's Puerto Rican players who might not be fluent in English. Santurce's other coach during part of the 1960s and 1970s was Reinaldo "Pochy" Oliver, who had a good working relationship with Robinson and the players and also did some translating.

"That was one of our duties," said Oliver. "If a manager from the States needed help in communicating with the ballplayers, we were there to provide it."

Sandy Alomar, Sr. joined Santurce with outfielder Polilla Ortíz in the trade which sent Gil Flores and Cookie Mangual to Ponce. Alomar, Sr. was the New York Yankees regular second baseman at this time.

When it came time for the league All-Star game to be played on January 6, 1975, Santurce had Sandy Alomar, Sr., Elrod Hendricks, Pinolo Rodríguez and Rogelio Moret on the Native squad and pitcher Dyar Miller with the Imports. Hendricks scored the game's only run after he doubled off Dyar Miller and Arecibo's Luis Isaac drove him in with a single.[11]

The "new" Bayamón Cowboys won the league title and went on to win the Caribbean Series in their brand new Loubriel Stadium. Bayamón reinforced itself with a slew of Caguas players.

1975–76 to 1977–78: A Pair of Jacks Step In

Jack McKeon took over Santurce's managing reins for 1975–76 and 1976–77, and was followed by Jack Krol in 1977–78. The league went with a 60-game schedule in 1975–76 after having a 70-game season in place for 13 years. Santurce had a new owner by the end of 1976 when Poto Paniagua purchased the team from Hiram Cuevas. Paniagua put Santurce in a trust for several years after being named Puerto Rico's Secretary of State following the 1976 Island elections.

Santurce was no longer a pre-season favorite. Rubén Gómez and Juan Pizarro were finishing their playing careers. Rogelio Moret showed some signs of greatness for the 1975 Boston Red Sox in their run to the World Series. Moret and New York City-born Gilberto Rondón were McKeon's most reliable starters, with Glenn Abbott and Pizarro contributing down the stretch. McKeon got enough out of his pitchers to make the playoffs.

Elrod Hendricks was the team leader and its best clutch hitter. Hendricks and Charlie Spikes were the only power hitters on the 1975–76 team. Juan Beníquez became the everyday center fielder on his way to later winning a 1977 Gold Glove with the Texas Rangers. Sandy Alomar, Sr. provided veteran leadership at second base and earned a record sixth league stolen base title.[12] Jim Wolhford and Rod Gilbreath also provided some speed. Nolín Ruíz continued to be a good utility player. Gerardo "Gerry" Rodríguez was a fine defensive catcher used against left-handed pitching.

Jack McKeon knew the nuances of winter ball from having managed Arecibo in 1971–72 and 1972–73, prior to managing the Kansas City Royals. Arecibo had become a

Robin Yount went all out in 1974-75 (courtesy of *El Nuevo Día*).

competitive club under McKeon with a good nucleus of native players and Kansas City prospects such as Mark Littell, Gary Lance and Tom Poquette. McKeon gave younger native players a chance to shine because they represented the league's future. Ed Figueroa and Fernando González were two such players with Arecibo in 1972–73, when Arecibo qualified for the playoffs for the first time in six seasons.

Sandy Alomar, Sr., calls for time, 1974-75 (courtesy of *El Nuevo Día*).

"I had a good rapport with the fans and the Puerto Rican players," said McKeon. "That's why it was so special coming back to the Island to manage and later on, to check on the local talent.

Santurce's rivalry with Bayamón was still a heated one, but more of a regional one due to the fact they were not sharing Bithorn Stadium. Bayamón won the league playoffs with sluggers including Rusty Torres, Darrell Evans, Art Howe, Leon Roberts and Dan Driessen. Ken Griffey, Sr. contributed early on, but was injured. All these players, with the exception of Griffey, Sr., played in the league All-Star game at Loubriel Stadium on January 6, 1976. Elrod Hendricks won the pre-game home run contest by belting four homers in his ten swings.[13] Hendricks, Beníquez and starting pitcher Gilberto Rondón were Santurce's only native players. Rod Gilbreath and Ron Jackson represented Santurce for the Imports in their 7–5 win.

Bob Feller threw the ceremonial first pitch to Hank Aaron, who benefited from Nick Acosta's skills in loosening his neck muscles in the training room prior to the game. These moments would not have been possible without the work of Angel Colón, long-time official of the Puerto Rico Professional Baseball Player's Association, the entity which coordinates the league All-Star game.

Santurce edged Ponce by two games for the final playoff slot after regular season play resumed. "We knew from the beginning that we would have to get the job done with our pitching and they came through," said McKeon. "With a couple of hitters we would have been right up there."[14]

Ponce skipper Ken Boyer lamented the fact that so many of his imported pitchers had gone home.

"We also lost catcher Marc Hill and first baseman Keith Hernández," said Boyer. "We had a couple of games booted away and in a 60-game schedule, you can't afford to give away anything. A bad start can kill you too."[15]

League umpire Durwood Merrill, who went on to a long career as an American League arbiter recalled that Boyer, McKeon, Caguas' Jim Bunning and Frank Robinson the year before all wanted to get noticed in their pursuit of big league managing jobs. Merrill told me this made for colorful arguments in regular season and post-season games.

Santurce took Caguas to a seventh game in their semi-final series. It was a hard-fought series, but Caguas had too much firepower with Sixto Lezcano, Jerry Morales, Cheo Cruz, Guillermo Montañez and Jesús "Bombo" Rivera. Their pitching depth was impressive with Ed Figueroa, Craig Swan, Dan Warthen, Ed "Volanta" Rodríguez and Wayne Simpson. Simpson came through with the game seven win.

Jim Bunning had managed Simpson in the Dominican Republic and had confidence in the right-hander. Both Simpson and Bunning alerted me that they enjoyed the competition in Puerto Rico. Bunning had pitched for Cuba's Marianao Tigers in the 1957 Caribbean Series and knew about winter post-season play.

Bayamón recaptured the league title by besting Caguas in a best-of-nine final series. Their manager, José Pagán, surprised some pundits by asking Juan Pizarro to reinforce the Cowboys in the 1976 Caribbean Series hosted by Santo Domingo. Some eight years later, Pizarro and I conversed at Santurce's Parque Central, a municipal facility for working out where Pizarro was employed. Pizarro recalled shutting out Venezuela's Aragua Tigers on his 39th birthday.

"That was some 20 years after my rookie season with Santurce," said Pizarro. "I used my experience in winning that game for Puerto Rico. It was nice to finish my Caribbean Series career as a winner."

Juan Pizarro came back for his last (1976–77) season with Santurce. Rubén Gómez was on Bayamón's roster. Santurce had a new de facto general manager, Carlos Pieve, assisting Hiram Cuevas. Pieve had resigned his GM post with Arecibo in January 1976, after serving in this capacity during four seasons. He was reunited with Jack McKeon in Santurce. Santurce finished fourth for the second straight season. Pieve, in his book *Los Genios de la Insufiencia* (*The Geniuses of Insufficiency*), relates that he became friendly with Hiram Cuevas after socializing with him following the league meetings organized by Guigo Otero Suro. Cuevas and Pieve were avid domino players who spent long hours playing this game together.

Pieve's job offer did not carry an official title, and it came with a pay cut from his Arecibo salary. Cuevas operated on a tight budget and told Pieve: "On my team, there is only one person in charge — me."[16] Pieve's responsibilities also included serving as a scout for the California Angels, an arrangement made due to Cuevas' friendship with California executive Harry Dalton. Pieve did not sign any Puerto Rican players for California, but did find out that Julio Cruz — a player in the low minors with California then — was of Puerto Rican heritage and could play in Puerto Rico as a native.[17]

The fun began when Pieve assembled Santurce's 1976–77 club. He made a trip to New York and Yankee Stadium to check out Paul Hartzell, who started for the Angels. Hartzell was shelled for 15 hits in seven innings, but Pieve liked his poise and control. Pieve phoned Cuevas from a Yankee Stadium pay phone to put in a plug for Hartzell. Cuevas took the advice with the admonition to sign Hartzell the next day for a "lesser amount" since he would be in a humble frame of mind after being hit so hard by the first place Yankees.[18]

Then there was a trip made by Cuevas and Pieve that included a stop in Richmond, Virginia, to scout pitchers Rick Camp and Frank La Corte. Cuevas opted to move from their first base box seats to the section behind the screen facing home plate when Camp came in to relieve. Moments later, a great deal of laughter broke out near the screen. Cuevas had fallen asleep and began snoring. The home plate ump was laughing. Richmond and Santurce infielder Nolín Ruíz alerted Pieve through signs to check out this scene. Pieve discovered that Cuevas had narcolepsy and could fall asleep at a moment's notice under strange circumstances. Now he understood why his domino partner suddenly dozed off.

Santurce's 1976–77 squad featured home run power with Danny Walton, Tony Solaita from American Samoa and Ismael Oquendo. Walton became the second player in Santurce history to hit three homers in one game, a feat first accomplished by Dave May in 1968–69.[19] Danny Walton had become friendly with Pieve when he slugged homers for Arecibo earlier in the decade, not to mention a slugfest with Joe "King" Román, a heavyweight boxer from Puerto Rico who once fought George Foreman for the world title in Tokyo, Japan.

Walton was living at Santurce's La Rada Hotel one winter and on Arecibo's inactive list due to the presence of Frank Ortenzio. When Ortenzio hurt his knee in a slide one night, Pieve looked for Walton early the next morning and was shocked to find the 200-pounder trading blows with Román, a man about the same size as the ballplayer. Walton, upon hearing that Pieve would activate him, decided to go one more round with Román. He joked that Román could not lick a stamp and went on to hit a homer for Arecibo that same night.[20]

Luis Isaac was a former Arecibo catcher who shared the catching duties with Elrod Hendricks, Ron Pruitt and Orlando Sánchez in 1976–77. Isaac was Arecibo's player-manager in 1975–76 and had a keen mind for baseball strategy. The Crabbers' double-play combo of Sandy Alomar Sr. and Nolín Ruíz plus Beníquez in center gave them solid defense up the middle. Danny Walton and Wayne Gross, covered first and third base, respectively, by season's end. Santurce had lost Tony Solaita at first base, and used Mike Cubbage and Tommy Sandt at third, prior to acquiring Gross. Luis "Puchi" Delgado, Ron Pruitt and Orlando Isales were counted on for outfield duty. Ismael Oquendo could DH, play first or in the outfield.

Santurce's moundsmen on the active roster by mid–January 1977 included Jackson Todd, Tom Bruno and Gerald Pirtle to supplement Moret, Rondón, Pizarro, Mon Hernández and Esteban Texidor.[21] Todd and Bruno had pitched for Arecibo and were established winter league vets. Each of them were dominant minor league pitchers who had brief big league careers. Todd had a 1974 no-hitter to his credit for the Victoria Toros of the Texas League while Bruno pitched a no-hitter that summer for the Jacksonville Suns in the Southern League.[22]

"I was a dominant pitcher in the minors and pitched well in Puerto Rico," said

Bruno. "If I had pitched as well in the majors as in Puerto Rico, my big league career would have been a good one."

Bruno was a tough-luck pitcher in winter ball in terms of run support as evidenced when his Ponce mound opponent, José "Witito" Martínez, no-hit the Crabbers in Ponce a week before Christmas Day 1976.[23] Bruno's memories of holiday season time in Puerto Rico included attending parties with team trainer Nick Acosta. They mingled with hard-working people who might have a modest existence, but who treated Bruno very nicely.

Bruno and company were no match for the 1976–77 Caguas Criollos who won their semi-final series in six games. Caguas had won two-thirds of their regular season games with a team batting average of .307, the highest in league history.[24] The Criollos had placed six players in the starting line-up for the Native All-Stars: Jerry Morales, Félix Millán, Sixto Lezcano, Cheo Cruz, José Manuel Morales and Julio César González, and three more starters among the Imports — John Wockenfuss, Kurt Bevaqua and Tony Scott.[25]

A pre-game ceremony honored Pedrín Zorrilla, Rubén Gómez and Valmy Thomas. Zorrilla was the symbolic hitter when Gómez's first pitch fell in Thomas' mitt. Santurce's Danny Walton won the pre-game home run hitting contest and $100 prior to the 8–7 win by the Native squad at Loubriel.[26]

Jack Krol, a third base coach with the St. Louis Cardinals, took over the Santurce managing reins in 1977–78. Krol's minor league managing career with the Cardinals included stints with the Cedar Rapids Cardinals, Arkansas Travelers and Tulsa Oilers.[27] Hiram Cuevas, Santurce's GM, assembled this ballclub during the time the franchise was still in a trust set up by Poto Paniagua. Cuevas' prognosis was shared with Eric Bishop of *The San Juan Star* prior to the season opener. The emphasis was on pitching and defense, since last year's club "depended too heavily on power hitters who were hot and cold."

Jack Krol alerted Bishop that "we will be short on power and we're going to have to scrape for our runs."[28] Krol was on target by season's end as Santurce only hit 28 team homers.[29]

Juan Pizarro was a Santurce coach, thanks to a unique long-term contract. Elrod Hendricks played his final season with Santurce.

Hendricks and Luis Isaac platooned at catcher. Krol, who had previously managed Arecibo three years earlier, had Ismael Oquendo at first, Sandy Alomar Sr. at second, Nolín Ruíz covering short and Jamie Quirk playing third. Gary Woods, Juan Beníquez, Puchi Delgado and Dell Alston covered the outfield; Delgado and Alston split the DH duties.

Tom Bruno returned as the ace of Santurce's starters. Bob Galasso, Ed Farmer and Ken Reynolds rounded out the rotation. Balor Moore and Esteban Texidor gave Krol a lefty-righty duo out of the pen. Larry Andersen pitched for the Crabbers. Moore, a.k.a. "Sr. Juego Perfecto" (Mr. Perfect Game) in Puerto Rico, told me that San Juan and Santurce were the teams he preferred to pitch for due to the city's amenities and comforts.

Jamie Quirk remembers his season with Santurce after a summer with the Milwaukee Brewers.

"At that time in my big league career, I needed experience to play against quality players and went down to get 200 at-bats," said Quirk. "Caguas had a big league club and a new stadium. Bithorn and Bayamón's [Loubriel] were nice stadiums. The others were A ball type stadiums. I started off bad and the fans were a little hard; weren't hesitant to boo you, whistle at you … because of the way I was playing, I deserved it."

Quirk played fine defense, which earned him a spot at third base for the Imports in the League All-Star game. Quirk made several good defensive plays and drove in a run as the Imports won, 8–3. Dell Alston, Gary Woods and Tom Bruno joined Quirk with the Imports while Juan Beníquez and Luis Isaac suited up for the Native All-Stars. Roger Freed, now with Ponce, was the game's MVP. Jack McKeon, the winning manager, had returned to manage Arecibo.[30]

Santurce held a two-game edge over fifth place Mayagüez at the time of the brief (January 6–8, 1978) All-Star break.[31] The Crabbers won two of their final seven games while Mayagüez, who were in last place much of the season, took six of their last seven contests to finish fourth.

Elrod Hendricks had this to say about Santurce's fans, when we talked about his last winter season: "They were the greatest. Even in my worst years, I considered I was blessed. They never booed me and knew I played my heart out. I could have stayed home after making it to the big leagues. After playing in the World Series, I could have waited to play until December … they appreciated me."

Carlos Pieve was Mayagüez's GM and the "Tribe" made a major pre-season trade when they dealt Héctor Cruz and Fernando González to Caguas in exchange for Bombo Rivera, José Manuel Morales, Guillermo Hernández, Orlando Gómez and two other prospects.[32] José Manuel Morales, the Mayagüez DH, later told me how special that season was. Mayaguez had Ron LeFlore leading off, followed by Jim Dwyer, Kurt Bevaqua, Morales, Bombo Rivera, Raúl "Boogie" Colón, Ramón Avilés, Ed Romero and Buck Martínez.

"It was a long, tiring season," said Martínez. "We put it together and won the playoffs."

Ramón Avilés — a native of Manatí, Pedrín Zorrilla's hometown — and I conversed about that season prior to a 1992 Batavia-Elmira minor league game in Elmira, New York. He told me that he thought about that Mayagüez line-up during the Batavia to Elmira bus trip. His eyes sparkled when he recited some Mayagüez accomplishments: qualifying for the playoffs; upsetting the defending champion Criollos in the semi-finals; defeating Bayamón in the finals; and, winning the Caribbean Series!

Mayagüez reinforced themselves with Santurce's Tom Bruno; Dennis Kinney of Ponce; Caguas' Volanta Rodríguez; and, Rick Sweet, Henry Cruz and Iván de Jesús of Arecibo. Kinney won two games and saved another, and Bruno won the series-clincher, a 9–3 win over Mexico's Culiacán Tomato Growers.[33]

1978–79 to 1979–80: Frank and Pedrín Return

Poto Paniagua brought Frank Robinson back to manage his 1978–79 and 1979–80 Crabbers. A special position was created for Pedrín so he could work with Santurce in the 1979–80 season. Pedrín was honored in a special tribute on June 9, 1979. A 25th anniversary celebration commemorating the 1954–55 Santurce dream team was put together by Paniagua, Zorrilla and others.

Diana Zorrilla played this ceremony on tape for my wife and I at her house more than 18 years after the event, during our visit to Puerto Rico. It was clear that Pedrín meant the world to many of those in attendance.

The ceremony honoring Pedrín took place at Escobar Stadium on a warm and sunny June day. There were speeches by dignitaries including Governor Carlos Romero Barceló.

Poto Paniagua unveiled Santurce's new logo and officially welcomed Pedrín back. Luis Mayoral read a prepared statement by Major League Baseball Commissioner Bowie Kuhn. Guigo Otero Suro said some kind words. Valmy Thomas thanked Pedrín on behalf of the former Santurce ballplayers before catching a plane to St. Thomas.

Mario A. Rodríguez, writing for *El Mundo,* wrote:

> Pedrín was a native of Manatí, but all indications are that his first 'pampers' were put on in the best known and most popular barrio of Puerto Rico (Cangrejo) ... there can be Santurce with or without the plena music, but never without Pedrín.[34]

Santurce's pitching imports included Larry Andersen, Tom Bruno, Dave Ford, Andy Replogle, Randy Stein and Tim Stoddard. Paul Dade, Rob Ellis, Ron Pruitt, Billy Smith and Gorman Thomas were position players who reinforced Santurce.

Gorman Thomas, a power hitter with the Milwaukee Brewers, was a disappointment. Rob Ellis, now in the Cleveland organization, was Santurce's top hitter. Ron Pruitt, who Frank Robinson had managed at Cleveland, could play the outfield, third base, DH or catch. Billy Smith, a second baseman/shortstop with Baltimore, contributed when second baseman Julio Cruz opted to cut his season short.

Frank Robinson made good use of his native players. Luis Isaac provided leadership behind the plate. First baseman Ismael Oquendo hit the long ball. Nolín Ruíz and Julián Pérez performed well on the left side of the infield. Luis Delgado and Juan Beníquez were outfielders who hustled. Rogelio Moret, Gilberto Rondón and Esteban Texidor pitched well.

A potential labor dispute was solved just before the season when player reps including José Manuel Morales, Fernando González, Ellie Rodríguez and Héctor Cruz signed a compromise allowing up to 20 Puerto Rican players per team, up from 17 in the prior accord.[35] The new agreement allowed teams to have a 28-player roster, factoring in eight imports. If a native big leaguer opted not to play, his team could substitute him with a player from the States.

The league All-Star game produced dramatic moments thanks to two Crabbers. Ismael Oquendo tied the game at three with a two-run homer in the home ninth after a Gil Flores double. But the Imports scored four in the eleventh on a Rob Ellis grand slam with Mickey Hatcher, Mark Wagner and Hosken Powell on base. Oquendo, who won the pre-game home run contest, hit his second homer in the home eleventh to cut the lead to 7–6, the final score. He became Santurce's third player to hit two All-Star game homers, following Josh Gibson in 1942 and Roberto Clemente in 1955.[36]

Frank Robinson activated himself during the latter part of the regular season and appeared in four regular season games. Tany Pérez joined the club at season's end and hit a clutch three-run homer in the season's final game against Bayamón to clinch third place for the Crabbers and drop Bayamón out of playoff contention.[37] Santurce faced second place Mayagüez in the semi-finals. Tany Pérez and Tim Johnson (who took Billy Smith's place) performed admirably in the five-game series.

Mayagüez had better post-season pitching with a one-two duo of Jack Morris and Sheldon Burnside, plus stronger hitting. Lance Parrish was behind the plate when Morris defeated Santurce in game five, 8–5, to send Mayagüez to the finals against Caguas. Morris scattered 11 hits over seven innings, including Tany Pérez' two-run homer.[38]

Ismael Trabal recalled that Morris was an aggressive hurler who got ahead of Santurce's hitters. Trabal noted that Dennis Martínez came through for Caguas when they won the final series against Mayagüez.

Tany Pérez, Larry Andersen, Tim Stoddard and Sheldon Burnside reinforced Caguas in the Caribbean Series hosted by Puerto Rico. Pérez continued his torrid hitting when he hit .458 to place third in the Caribbean Series batting chase behind Jerry White of the winners, Venezuela's Magallanes Navigators, and Mike Easler of Mexico's Navojoa representative. Sheldon Burnside shut out the Aguilas Cibaeñas of the Dominican Republic in game three and was helped by a Tany Pérez RBI.[39]

The 1979–80 season was full of tradition, sentimental value and wins for the Crabbers. Poto Paniagua took full control of all operational aspects since he was no longer Puerto Rico's secretary of state. Paniagua: "The first person I contracted was Pedrín Zorrilla. I sought Pedrín because I knew him well from the time of my childhood as a friend of my father and we had a deep respect for Pedrín. Everyone in the baseball world loved Pedrín."

Paniagua gave Pedrín the title of Executive Vice-President and brought him back into the Santurce family as a special counselor. There would be no need to deal with Hiram Cuevas.

"We worked very closely together," said Paniagua. "I learned so much from him over the next two seasons and have a lot to be thankful for. Pedrín's title in U.S. baseball circles was still 'Mr. Baseball' ... well deserved ... he was the 'Cangrejo Mayor' (the top Crabber) and always will be."

Willard Brown, Bob Thurman, Buster Clarkson, Bill Greason, Dick Seay and other Old-Timers visited Puerto Rico in mid–December 1979 to take part in events commemorating the 25th anniversary of the special 1954–55 season. A Santurce-San Juan Old Timers game was held prior to the regularly scheduled game between Arecibo and Santurce on December 16, 1979. Buster Clarkson managed the Santurce squad.

Luis Mayoral conversed with Willard Brown after the game. A woman in her 40s got an autograph from Brown and told him that she lived next to the house on Refugio Street where the Santurce players lived in the late 1940s and early 1950s. Brown told Mayoral that "Puerto Rico was where I was treated best." Mayoral and Brown walked side by side to the Bithorn Stadium clubhouse. Brown, in a spontaneous gesture, gave Mayoral his cap and then took his uniform off.

"The game was over," recalled Mayoral.[40]

Santurce's 1979–80 season continued that afternoon with a win over Arecibo. Gilberto Rondón started and won with relief help from Joaquín Quintana and a save by Tim Stoddard.[41] Gary Allenson was Santurce's everyday catcher and enjoyed working with the league's top pitching staff.

"We all got along well," said Allenson. "I caught Bill Caudill, Larry Andersen, Stoddard, Len Barker and Wayne Garland ... pitchers from different organizations. Wayne Garland was trying to resurrect his career. I played American Legion ball against Caudill; with Santurce he threw 96–97 miles per hour. Tony [Tany] Pérez, he came to us some weeks into the season ... Lenny Randle played second; Beníquez was there."

Poto Paniagua secured hard throwing imports and versatile position players with speed and power. Paniagua caught up with Gary Alexander in Boston during the summer of 1979.[42] That's where he noticed Gary Allenson, Boston's hustling rookie catcher. Lenny Randle, coming off an injury-plagued season with the Yankees, was signed, as was Bob Molinaro.

Tany Pérez smoked the ball as a DH after he was activated and Ismael Oquendo hit for power. Kevin Bell and Nolín Ruíz contributed in the infield; Sandy Alomar, Sr. played

Buster Clarkson managed the Santurce "Old Timers" on December 16, 1979. Pancho Coímbre (signaling) and Angel Colón watch the action (courtesy of Angel Colón).

a utility role. Lenny Randle and Bob Molinaro were imports who stole bases, scored and drove in runs. Randle and outfielder Juan Beníquez received plaudits for their defensive gems in the league All-Star game.[43] Gilberto Rondón (the starter and winning pitcher in the league All-Star game) and Rogelio Moret had banner seasons as starters, and were joined in the rotation by Barker, Garland and Caudill. The bullpen was in good hands with Andersen, Stoddard, Joaquín Quintana and Carlos Díaz. Frank Robinson's final season at Santurce's helm produced a first place regular season finish.

"We had a good season, but the league was a bit stronger when I first managed Santurce," said Robinson. "There were more restrictions in terms of the number of imports allowed and they had to have four years' big league experience or less and so many at-bats and innings pitched."

"I liked Frank, and it was us and Bayamón as the two best teams," said Gary Allenson. "I had heard that Frank was a bit tough on his players — players that didn't have the ability he had, but I didn't see it. He was a real good manager, I thought, who motivated his players. If you played hard for him, he liked you."

Bayamón finished second to Santurce and faced the Crabbers in the finals after edging Mayagüez in a seven-game semi-final series. Santurce defeated Arecibo in five games. Ron Pruitt, Mike Vail and Roy White were on Santurce's post-season roster after joining the club at the end of the regular season. White had completed his career with the New York Yankees, and Paniagua (a Yankee fan since 1941) expected production from him.

Bayamón had their own ammunition with Dave Bergman, Denny Walling and Dickie Thon. They picked up Vern Ruhle for the stretch drive to solidify their mound corps, and surprised Santurce by winning the finals in five games. Ruhle pitched the fifth and final game.

"It was a great year with the big city [Bayamón and Santurce] teams in contention to see who was going to come in first or second," said Ruhle. "We ended up in the finals, and in the fifth game, Frank Robinson decided to start Wayne Garland, a right-hander with a sore arm, so Art Howe, our manager, had all his left-handed hitters in the line-up because we had a platoon situation. And Robinson pulled Garland out in the second inning and brought in a lefty ... Howe chose to pinch-hit his right-handed hitters in the second and third innings. He did that and we won the game. I pitched a complete game. It was an interesting rivalry...and seeing how the maneuvering was going on between Frank and Art Howe."

Tany Pérez, Roy White and Gary Allenson played well against Bayamón, but no Santurce players were selected to reinforce Bayamón for the 1980 Caribbean Series. The Licey Tigers won their fourth series title by outplaying Bayamón, the Caracas Lions and the Hermosillo Orange Growers.[44] Vern Ruhle pitched his heart out in blanking Licey for nine innings in his only series start before the champions pulled it out in extra innings against Doug Corbett, a reinforcement from Mayagüez.

1980–81 to 1981–82: Good-bye to Pedrín and Rubén

Pedrín gave Poto Paniagua one more year of hard work, dedication and wisdom before his passing on April 9, 1981. All of Puerto Rico and old-time baseball aficionados and officials throughout the U.S. and the Caribbean mourned Pedrín's passing. Cookie Rojas managed Santurce to a fifth place finish in 1980–81. Rubén Gómez was Santurce's skipper for half of the 1981–82 season before giving way to Jack Aker. The Crabbers finished second, but lost to Ponce in the semis.

Santurce's 1980–81 team was better on paper than the 1979–80 edition. Paniagua purchased Iván de Jesús and Fernando González from Arecibo for a good chunk of cash. Willie Mays Aikens signed a lucrative contract with Santurce. He had slugged four homers in the 1980 World Series for the Kansas City Royals[45] and was considered Santurce's most dangerous slugger since Reggie Jackson. Rudy Law joined Santurce and finished runner-up to Dickie Thon of Bayamón in hitting and second in steals to Ponce's Rickey Henderson.[46] Catcher Terry Kennedy came to Santurce with solid credentials. Gene Garber, Fred Martínez and Bob Owchinko were three imported pitchers.

Rubén Gómez threw out the ceremonial first pitch. Gómez was now a Santurce coach along with Orlando Cepeda and Juan Pizarro. Pedrín was on cloud nine that night as was Poto Paniagua. Then reality set in.

Terry Kennedy left Santurce after the St. Louis Cardinals announced that they had traded him to the San Diego Padres. Outfielder Dave Henderson played about half a season. Kevin Bell did not produce at the plate nor at third. Julio Cruz left the club with about a month left in the season. Benny Ayala slumped.

The most damaging blow was an injury suffered by closer Lee Smith which led to

Santurce's clubhouse, 1980–81. *Front, L to R:* Angel Colón, Iván de Jesús, Felipe Maldonado. *Standing, L to R:* unidentified, Willie Aikens, Luis R. Mayoral, Nick Acosta (courtesy of Angel Colón).

his departure. Smith led the league in appearances[47] and showed the form which later made him major league baseball's career leader in saves. Jaime Cocanower pitched well in middle relief, but Smith's exit left the club without a closer.

Gary Allenson and Orlando Sánchez helped fill the void left by Terry Kennedy's departure.

"I came down a little late 'cause I had just gotten married," said Allenson. "They were really struggling. You had eight American guys [imports] and everybody understood English on the club except the young ones who would work out, sit out, but didn't play ... with the money that Paniagua was paying (Aikens was making about $10,000 a month) and we weren't winning."

Allenson recalled the daily team meetings which could last 50 minutes with the first 45 minutes in Spanish: "I had to sit around for the first 45 minutes without knowing what was being said, and the last five minutes, they interpreted it. It was a little bit of a tough year. We just never got it going."

Santurce played better over the Christmas holidays. By January 4, 1981 they had a one-game lead over third place Caguas and a two-game margin over Arecibo and Mayagüez.[48] But Santurce lost six of their final seven games to finish fifth.

Gary Allenson was part of Puerto Rico baseball history on January 3, 1981, when Rickey Henderson stole his 42nd base of the season. That eclipsed Carlos Bernier's old standard of 41 set 31 years earlier.[49] Allenson maintains that he threw Henderson out: "Rickey was out, no question about it," said Allenson. "He could have moonwalked into third."

Henderson had stolen third with Gil Flores at the plate after the close call at second. Flores would take extra pitches so that Henderson could have a better chance to steal bases. Lost in the excitement of Henderson's stolen base mark was Allenson's first homer of the season and three RBIs to propel Santurce to victory over Ponce.[50]

Willie Aikens was one of eight Santurce players named to the Metro squad for the league All-Star game. The Metro team comprised players from Bayamón, Caguas and Santurce, who played an Island squad of Arecibo, Mayagüez and Ponce players on Three Kings Day, 1981. Arecibo's Candy Maldonado took game MVP laurels with two homers in becoming the fifth person to accomplish that feat. Aikens won the pre-game home run hitting contest.[51]

The 30-member Puerto Rico Sportswriters Association voted Aikens as the first baseman on the league All-Star team chosen at season's end. The other All-Stars were Luis Aguayo and Dickie Thon of Bayamón at second and short; Caguas' Cal Ripken at third and Junior Ortíz at catcher; Rickey Henderson and Candy Maldonado in the outfield with Mayagüez's Rusty Torres; José Manuel Morales of Mayagüez at DH; and, pitcher Dave Smith of Bayamón.[52]

Santurce had high hopes entering the 1981–82 season, a campaign dedicated to the memory of Pedrín Zorrilla. Luis Mayoral wrote an eloquent article in *The San Juan Star* titled "Pedrín Zorrilla had the common touch." Mayoral, Orlando Cepeda, and many others paid their respects to Pedrín at a Santurce funeral home the night after his passing.

Orlando Cepeda had a number of things to say about Pedrín:

> He was a father to all ballplayers. When my father died, Don Pedro [Pedrín] looked after me and today I recall that he bought me the first glove I used as a professional player. Even before my father's death he was helping me ... bought my brother's ring when he graduated from the university ... without him, it would have been very difficult for players like José Pagán, Julio Navarro, Juan Pizarro, Roberto Clemente, and myself to become stars in the majors. I owe much to Don Pedro.[53]

Cepeda later told me that Pedrín took care of Luis Raúl Cabrera's needs until Cabrerita's death. Cabrerita had a tough life after his playing career ended, but Pedrín stood by his ballplayers, regardless of their socioeconomic status and life's challenges.

Only five teams were in the fold due to Arecibo's 1981–82 suspension. Carlos Lezcano was an Arecibo player selected by Santurce via a special draft. Lezcano had spent parts of the 1980 and 1981 National League seasons with the Chicago Cubs, the last big league team which Pedrín scouted for.

"I had the pleasure of getting to know Pedrín when I played with the Cubs," said Lezcano. "We got to share some moments when I visited his Santurce home ... it was special talking to the person who started the Santurce franchise, a league powerhouse for many years."

Lezcano recalled being the league's Rookie of the Year in 1977–78 following his graduation from Florida State University. He now joined a veteran ballclub with Iván de Jesús, Jerry Morales, Guillermo Montañez, Juan Beníquez and Ellie Rodríguez.

"They were all true professionals," said Lezcano. "I knew de Jesús and [Jerry] Morales well from playing with the Cubs."

Poto Paniagua changed the team chemistry by purchasing Ed Figueroa, Jerry Morales and Guillermo Montañez from Caguas. He brought back Rudy Law and signed Pat Tabler. Bud Anderson was the team's best starter while Carlos Díaz also contributed. Rogelio Moret and Gilberto Rondón had spent the summer of 1981 in Mexico with Union Laguna and Yucatán, respectively.

It had been 10 years since Rubén Gómez last managed Santurce. He still remembered Moret's 14–1 record in 1971–72. That's why Moret got the nod to pitch the season opener on October 30, 1981. Tany Pérez threw out the first pitch, before Mayagüez clubbed four homers off Moret to send him to the showers. Santurce rallied to win the game, 7–6, and won the next night at Caguas on a shutout by Guillermo Hernández.[54]

Rubén Gómez told Carlos Galarza of *The San Juan Star*: "If we had a team like this one in 1971, we would have gone somewhere."[55]

Santurce went on a tear during the season's first three weeks and posted a league-leading 14–6 record at the one-third mark.[56] One win was a 20–18 slugfest over Caguas to set a league record for most runs scored in a nine-inning game.[57]

Rubén Gómez then witnessed a reversal of fortune in which Santurce lost 10 of their next 12 games, including a nine-game losing streak. Gómez resigned and Jack Aker replaced him. The Crabbers turned it around and finished second. They released Joe Cowley and Bob Blyth and signed Charlie Leibrandt, a 25-year lefty with the Cincinnati Reds. Leibrandt pitched out of the pen and as a starter in getting ready for the post-season. He enjoyed his brief stint with Santurce.

"It was a working vacation," said Leibrandt. "I was able to work on my pitches and enjoy plenty of free time."

Only four teams could play on a given night or day, leaving one club with a day off. This gave players more off-days to play golf, shop or lay out on the beach. It had been 21 years since the league went with a five-team format.

Santurce played their first-ever "home game" at Bayamón on December 21, 1981, to determine fan interest. It proved successful when 14,333 fans paid to see Santurce play Bayamón.[58] The opportunity to win a new car that day did not hurt attendance. Santurce's win made Paniagua smile.

"Every Santurce win always gives me a great deal of satisfaction," said Paniagua. "When we play well and bring the fans to the ballpark, it enhances the league. Baseball becomes alive, the fans comment about it and the tradition continues."

Caguas got into the act several days later when they hosted Santurce in the Juncos ballpark, as a way of thanking the Juncos fans for their support. That baseball town is held in high esteem by many island fans since Roberto Clemente played for the Juncos Mules prior to signing with Santurce.

Mayagüez hosted the league All-Star game for only the second time and fans witnessed a no-hitter courtesy of five Metro team pitchers including Carlos Díaz of the Crabbers. Miguel Torres, Juan Agosto, Francisco Javier Oliveras and José Alvarez were the other hurlers. Dickie Thon was the game's MVP with a homer and a stolen base. Cal Ripken, Jr. won the pre-game home run hitting contest.[59]

Santurce faced Ponce in the semi-finals. Bud Anderson won game one, but Ponce tied the series the next night when John Butcher won a 1–0 decision over Charlie Leibrandt on a Ramón Avilés sacrifice fly.[60]

I witnessed the pivotal game of this series, game three, at Bithorn on January 22, 1982. Reggie Patterson, a late-season pick-up for Santurce, was nursing a 1–0 lead in the top of the ninth when Georgie Cruz hit one out to tie it. The fans on the Ponce side were buzzing and that buzz changed to rabid shouting a few moments later when Charles "Chili" Davis hit a grand slam off Guillermo Hernández to give Ponce a 5–1 win. It was a turning point since Ponce went on to win that series in six games and then edged Bayamón in seven games for the title.

The passing of Pedrín Zorrilla overshadowed on-the-field activity during this nine-season dry spell. Rafael Bracero, Santurce's broadcaster during 1980–81 and 1981–82, real-ized that he was in the presence of someone covered with honesty and dignity from head to toe.

"I had the fortune of knowing Pedrín during his final year in baseball and he was a kind and caring person," said Bracero. "That's when I realized why he had been so suc-cessful in terms of signing and bringing the best African-American ball players to Puerto Rico. You had to be special to sign and develop a closeness with Willard Brown and the other players. They needed someone like Pedrín to be a father figure to them ... and were welcomed by Pedrín and Diana as part of an extended family. I have kept my ties with Pedrín's widow, Diana, because the Zorrillas are an integral part of Puerto Rico's history."

8. The Dry Spell Continues

I still have that [MVP] trophy in my room. It's something they can never take away from you.
    — Jerry Willard, former Santurce catcher.

Santurce continued its quest for the elusive league title. The Crabbers from 1982–83 through 1989–90 showcased future island stars such as Sandy Alomar, Jr. and Rubén Sierra, and the solid play of veterans Juan Beníquez, Iván de Jesús and Tany Pérez. Rick Mahler, Otis Nixon and John Wetteland were three of many imports who plied their trade with Santurce.

"El Tapón de Bayamón" (The Bayamón Traffic Jam)

Bayamón was Puerto Rico's fastest growing municipality in the 1970s with its share of older urbanizations as well as newer ones. The 1980 U.S. Census of Population revealed that Bayamón's 195,965 residents made it Puerto Rico's second most populated municipality behind San Juan.[1] Bayamón is part of the heavily populated San Juan Metropolitan Statistical Area (MSA), and to some degree, a bedroom community of San Juan. Parts of it resemble U.S. suburbs. During the late 1970s, I worked closely with socio-economic data pertaining to the island's 78 municipalities as an economist for Puerto Rico's Municipal Services Administration; as a city planner with Carolina; and, as the San Juan Area Agency on Aging Planning Coordinator.

"El Tapón de Bayamón" refers to the constant traffic on old Highway 2 to and from this municipality. Bayamón's nickname had been "La Ciudad del Chicharrón" (The City of Pork Rinds) due to the many food vendors stationed along Highway 2 who sold chunks of pork rinds. Between 1980 and 1984 I commuted from my apartment on Del Parque Street in Santurce to an office in Guaynabo, also in the San Juan MSA. The incoming early morning traffic from Bayamón to San Juan as well as the late afternoon traffic in the other direction were a way of life. Bayamón holds sentimental value since dad, who was in the Navy and assigned to the Office of Strategic Services in World War II, is buried in the National Military Cemetery located in Bayamón's Hato Tejas section.

1982–83: Bayamón Becomes Santurce's Home

The Santurce brass moved the home games to Bayamón. A record number of home fans saw Tany Pérez's final season with Santurce. Santurce claimed first place at the end of the regular season with a tie-breaker win over Ponce. The season's "Cinderella Team," the Arecibo Wolves, ended Santurce's post-season hopes in the best-of-seven semi-finals.

Bayamón's Juan Ramón Loubriel Stadium, with a seating capacity of about 16,500, served as Santurce's home field. Poto Paniagua was rewarded when 200,414 paid fans made their way to 31 home games at Loubriel,[2] including a first place tie-breaker with Ponce. "Puerto Rico's team" weighed in with "big catches" according to the October 24, 1982 winter league preview in *The San Juan Star*.

Santurce had two Cuban legends on their roster, 40-year-old Tany Pérez and 41-year-old Luis Tiant. Tiant knew Santurce general manager José "Ronquito" García from his days pitching in Mexico. Pérez was a Santurce icon. Pérez: "It was really a farewell tour of sorts to say good-bye to all those wonderful fans for the last time."

"Poto Paniagua ... was great ... he gave me the opportunity to play for Santurce as a veteran and I wanted to do something for him and the Santurce franchise. Puerto Rico had helped me a lot and I owe a debt to the island and its fine people."

Chris Bando from the Cleveland organization was Santurce's catcher. The infield included Guillermo Montañez, Glenn Gulliver, Iván de Jesús and Manuel "Nolín" Ruíz. Fernando González could play the infield or outfield. Juan Beníquez, Jerry Morales and Sixto Lezcano were a big league outfield. Tany Pérez was the full-time DH. Otto Vélez and Orlando Sánchez provided depth. Sánchez also caught some as did veteran backstop Ellie Rodríguez.

The Crabbers counted on former Yankee hurler Ed Figueroa, the first Puerto Rico-born hurler to win 20 big league games in one season.[3] Ken Dayley, coming off a AAA season for Richmond, also started. White Sox prospect Reggie Patterson and Tiant — who hurled his last big league innings for the 1982 California Angels — rounded out the rotation. Brian Kelly and Carlos Díaz joined the team during the season and started a few games. José Alvarez, Guillermo Hernández, Mark Brown and Mark Smith were the relievers.

Roster changes included the addition of Pat Tabler to play third base. Tabler called Tany Pérez the "most influential guy on the team" for his leadership abilities. Luis Tiant was another veteran who Tabler looked up to. He once asked Tiant how he could still pitch so well past the age of 40. Tiant responded that he ate a daily rattlesnake concoction, a powdery thing that if sprinkled on food, could prolong one's career. But Tabler took one sniff of it, licked it and tasted it before throwing it away.

Santurce experienced some highs and lows, including being no-hit by Bayamón's Andy Hawkins in their sixth regular season game on November 2, 1982. It was the first no-hitter at Loubriel Stadium.[4] Hawkins, who walked four Crabbers, relied on an overpowering fastball and changeup.

Tany Pérez Day was held at Loubriel on December 12, 1982.[5] Pérez, his wife Pituka, and his teammates enjoyed the gift giving and other amenities. Luis Tiant with relief help from Guillermo Hernández defeated Bayamón.

Juan Beníquez, "El Clipper Cangrejero" (courtesy of Angel Colón).

In mid–December, Santurce traded 14-year vet Rogelio Moret to Caguas for a player to be named later.[6] Moret, Beníquez and Pérez had been the only Santurce players who had played on the championship team 10 years ago.

Ken Dayley received the nod to start in the league All-Star game for the Metro (Bayamón, Caguas and Santurce) squad. Dayley pitched well in the 3–2 Metro win over the Island (Arecibo, Mayagüez and Ponce) team. Iván de Jesús of the Crabbers got the game-winning hit.[7]

Santurce and Ponce finished the regular season tied for first place and the Crabbers edged the Lions, 7–6, in a tie-breaker, on January 17, 1983, to claim first place behind the hurling of Ed Figueroa and Dayley.[8] Tany Pérez earned a standing ovation in his last regular season game with Santurce. His three RBI helped the Crabbers prevail.

Oddsmakers had their bets skewed in Santurce's favor when they took on Arecibo at Loubriel Stadium to open the semi-finals. Fireworks began in game one, a Santurce win, when Arecibo's Keith Creel hit Sixto Lezcano with a pitch that fractured his hand. Lezcano charged the mound and some punches were thrown. A visibly shaken Creel would become an important factor in the series. Sixto Lezcano was lost for its duration.

Game two went to Santurce behind Ken Dayley.[9] Arecibo's Carlos Lezcano, a second cousin of Sixto, recalls general manager Carlos Pieve meeting with the team just before game three at Loubriel. Cash incentives were offered to all Arecibo players if they could bounce back to defeat Santurce. This was a practice used by most, if not all, league teams come playoff time. Game three pitcher Kevin Hagen noted the Pieve offer was a "safe" one of $500 per player since it was quite unlikely Arecibo could pull the series out. Hagen pitched six plus innings in a winning effort.

Game four at Arecibo's Luis Rodríguez Olmo Stadium quickly turned into a rout for the home team. When the smoke cleared, the scoreboard read Visitors-2 and Arecibo-15. Arecibo starter René Quiñónes retired 14 straight Santurce hitters at one point.[10] Carlos Pieve later chronicled that Quiñónes would come off the mound after each inning and stare into the Santurce dugout before spitting in their direction.[11] It got so bad that Jack Aker inserted Fernando González as his fourth and final pitcher.

Arecibo continued to win by shelling Ed Figueroa in game five. Figueroa was relieved in the seventh inning after allowing seven runs in Arecibo's 9–5 win. The series ended on January 25, 1983, when Arecibo again scored nine times to defeat Santurce by a 9–6 score.[12] Glenn Walker's three-run homer was the difference. Keith Creel, Gary Lance and Kevin Hagen kept the Crabbers in check while Ken Dayley, Luis Tiant and Carlos Díaz did their best in a losing effort. Carlos Lezcano's two homers against his former team paid dividends, as Arecibo went to, and won, the final series for the first time, and then went on to win the 1983 Caribbean Series.[13] Lezcano remembers the tears of joy mixed with laughter.

"A number of us [Candy Maldonado, Onix Concepción, René Quiñónes] had been with Arecibo during the tough times," said Lezcano. "It was something else to win it all."

1983–84: Jerry Willard, League MVP

Another managerial change was made. Two of Santurce's best imports of the decade, Rick Mahler and Jerry Willard, had outstanding seasons. Willard was the league MVP and home run king while Mahler became the last hurler to win 10 games in a league season. John Shelby was named MVP of the league's All-Star game. Santurce lost another semifinal series; this time, to Ponce.

Ray Miller, Baltimore's pitching coach, was hired as Santurce's manager. This was not the beginning of a formal working agreement between the Crabbers and Orioles. Miller had managed Caguas in the early 1980s when Ronquito García was Caguas' GM and Dennis Martínez, Mike Boddicker and Cal Ripken, Jr. played for the Criollos.

Santurce's ticket prices were $3.50 for box seats, $2.50 for reserved seating and $1 for grandstand seats. Blue Cross and Puerto Rico government employees got discounts. Season ticket holders paid $105 for box seats or $75 for the reserved ones.[14] Loubriel Stadium had a dining area in the right field section overlooking the field.

Several Baltimore players or prospects suited up for Santurce. They included John Shelby, fresh from Baltimore's 1983 World Series win; Julián González, a pitcher, and outfielder Mike Young.

The big plus for Santurce was catcher Jerry Willard, a Cleveland prospect. Willard clubbed 18 homers to tie Buster Clarkson for the fourth highest single-season total in team history. Only Willard Brown (27), Reggie Jackson (20) and Orlando Cepeda (19) had hit more.[15] Jerry Willard had also hit the most homers by a catcher in league and team history, besting Josh Gibson's standard of 13 set 42 seasons earlier.[16] By season's end, Willard won the league MVP trophy.[17]

"I still have that trophy in my room," said Willard. "It's something they can never take away from you … you accomplished something."

Willard liked the tone set by manager Ray Miller, who knew winter ball and how to get the most out of a pitching staff. Team owner Poto Paniagua was very nice to him and it was a treat to mingle with veterans such as Beníquez, Jerry Morales and Otto Vélez.

"In my early years with Santurce [1983–84, 1984–85] there were more vets," recalls Willard. "Later [1987–88] we had younger, more AA caliber players. The Puerto Rican heroes were going into a transition period."

Two prominent Santurce starters were Rick Mahler and Bob Walk from the Atlanta Braves. This was Mahler's sixth season of winter ball, having pitched in Venezuela and the Dominican Republic. It proved to be his most enjoyable winter with 10 wins and plenty of time on the island golf courses, not to mention the modern amenities and U.S. currency. That winter turned Mahler's career around and he became a better big league pitcher. Mahler's 10 wins are a landmark; no other league pitcher since has won in double-digits nor surpassed his 113 innings pitched.[18] Santurce fans called Mahler "El Incansable" (he never tires).

Bob Walk was in a different boat. His days with Atlanta were numbered and he could search for a big league job in the spring of 1984 after scouts had seen him pitch in Puerto Rico. It was a real plus having Miller as his manager. Some years later, Walk was glad to see his team, the Pittsburgh Pirates, hire Miller as their pitching coach. Walk: "I had already dealt with him [Miller] in Puerto Rico and knew what to expect."

Ray Miller had managed Caguas to the 1980–81 league title and knew how to handle the delicate balance between winning and preserving some fresh arms down the stretch.

"Every now and then you had to take one on the chin," said Miller. "I had to do this in Caguas and Santurce to rest my pitching staffs." Miller faced some obstacles including Ed Figueroa's retirement on November 29, 1983 due to injuries after he had only made one start and two relief appearances. There was no dominant closer so Miller relied on the arms of Bud Anderson and Mark Brown part of the season, and John Pacella for the duration. José Alvarez and Nate Snell were contracted later in the season to shore up the bullpen. Santurce traded Fernando González to Arecibo for seldom-used lefty reliever Carlos Cabassa. Santurce officials recalled Cabassa's clutch pitching against them in the 1983 semi-finals.

It was to Miller's credit that Santurce finished third. Miller managed the Metro team in the league All-Star game held on January 6, 1984. Santurce's John Shelby received the Monchile Concepción trophy as the game's MVP. His triple drove in Caguas' Junior Ortíz with the winning run in the 4-1 win over the Island squad. Juan Beníquez accounted for the winner's first run with a long homer. Santurce infielders Ed Jurak and Steve Lubratich also were on the Metro team.[19]

Santurce's semi-finals began at Ponce on January 19, 1984. Rick Mahler was in good form in game one. His complete game and Mike Young's two-run homer gave Santurce a 3–2 win. Ponce won the next three games, including a 16-inning marathon in game three where Nicaraguan David Green had the game-winning hit in Ponce's 2–1 win.[20]

Santurce won a 10-inning thriller in game five. José Alvarez started game six and pitched a complete game win. Joe Carter's two-run homer with two outs in the ninth kept Alvarez from a shutout in Santurce's 5–2 win.[21] When Ponce took the field prior to the start of game seven, most of the 8,590 lunatics on hand cheered them on. Ponce manufactured two first inning runs against Bob Walk. Ray Miller lifted Walk in the second frame after Ponce tallied two more. John Pacella and Rick Mahler — pitching on only one day of rest — shut down Ponce, but Santurce fell short, 5–3.[22]

The season had ended for the Crabbers with the exception of first baseman/DH Orlando Sánchez. Sánchez reinforced the Mayagüez Indians in the 1984 Caribbean Series, held at Bithorn Stadium.

1984–85: A San Juan–Santurce Final

Sandy Alomar, Jr. and Rubén Sierra — the league's Rookie of the Year — made their Santurce debuts. Solid performances by speedster Otis Nixon, home run king Jerry Willard and batting champ Orlando Sánchez kept Santurce in the hunt. Santurce hurler Zane Smith won the league All-Star game. Santurce defeated Caguas in the semi-finals, but lost a dramatic seven-game final series to archrival San Juan.

Santurce geared up for another season as "Puerto Rico's Team." They were ready to take off with the corporate logo of Eastern Airlines on the back of their uniforms as was the case in 1982–83. (The 1983–84 Santurce uniforms had the Paloviejo Rum logo on the players' backs.) Santurce's archrivals were now the San Juan Metros in a marketing move designed to attract a broader fan base. San Juan's new owner, Ernesto Díaz González, had done Santurce's radio broadcasts between the mid–1960s and early 1970s. Luis Mayoral, a dynamic executive with Eastern Airlines for some time, was San Juan's GM.

Poto Paniagua noted that his franchise is an important "anchor" for all league teams, much like the Yankees, Red Sox and Dodgers. Paniagua: "Santurce brings the most fans to the ballparks. When they do well, it's a good sign for the league."

Paniagua hired Frank Verdi as his manager. Verdi was a two-time winner in league circles having managed the 1971-72 Ponce Lions to the Caribbean Series crown and the 1983–84 Mayagüez Indians to a Caribbean Series berth. No manager in league history had managed three different franchises to the promised land. Paniagua felt that Verdi could do this.

Frank Verdi was up to it. He gave José "Cheo" Cruz the Ponce right field job on an everyday basis when he took over in 1970–71 and strongly believed in giving the younger players a chance to win jobs over certain veterans. Rubén "El Indio" Sierra had turned 19 shortly before his rookie season with Santurce and Sandy Alomar, Jr. was just an

Sandy Alomar, Jr., got his start with Santurce (courtesy of *El Nuevo Día*).

18-year-old kid when he put on the Santurce uniform. Verdi inserted Sierra into the starting line-up while Alomar backed up Jerry Willard.

"Sierra could run, hit, throw and hit with power," said Verdi. "I wasn't trying to rush him in to play too soon, so he wouldn't get discouraged ... Alomar had a good arm, catching ability, and was a big, hungry kid."

Santurce veterans such as Jerry Morales, Guillermo Montañez and Otto Vélez received limited playing time with Verdi. Juan Beníquez and Iván de Jesús were among the regulars. Verdi gave playing time to 20 position players and 16 pitchers throughout the regular season,[23] as frequent roster turnover was common in the league by the mid–1980s. Some imports did not produce, as happened with second baseman Paul Runge from Atlanta and shortstop Dave Owen with the Cubs. Mike Young left, but John Shelby filled this void. Jerry Willard and Otis Nixon stayed, played and produced.

Otis Nixon was another in a long line of speedy Santurce outfielders. Nixon challenged Vince Coleman for the league stolen base title and enjoyed playing with Beníquez and Sierra.

"Actually, I was trying to catch him [Coleman] ... was young then, and didn't play that much in the majors," said Nixon. "I wanted to get more at-bats, work on my fielding, the whole nine yards ... I enjoyed it. Beníquez was established [but] Sierra was a raw, talented kid with a strong arm and quick bat and we all knew he was going to be a star. He didn't have the muscles he had later."

Rubén Sierra won league Rookie of the Year laurels.[24]

"If I hadn't produced, I wouldn't have played," said Sierra. "My nickname [El Indio] was given to me since birth in honor of our island's Indian heritage ... and El Indio Araucano."

Sandy Alomar, Jr. saw action in 15 games, but remembers his baptism of fire as a special experience thanks to the support from veterans Beníquez and Iván de Jesús. Alomar: "Frank Verdi was of great assistance that first season. My father coached that [Santurce] team and was always there."

Santurce's best pitcher was lefty Zane Smith, who had been a September 1984 call-up by the Atlanta Braves.

"I had pitched for Richmond most of the [1984] season," said Smith. "Atlanta wanted me to continue pitching and to get better."

Smith got better. He was the winning hurler in the league All-Star game, a 2-1 Metro triumph over the Island stars. Jerry Willard was Smith's battery mate in this game. The game was dedicated to ex-Santurce reliever Guillermo Hernández, the 1984 American League Cy Young and MVP winner.[25]

Santurce clinched third place the last day of the regular season with a double-header sweep of Arecibo. Jerry Willard put himself in the record books with a two-run homer off Arecibo's Vida Blue. This gave the Crabbers a 5–4 win and Willard his second straight league home run title.[26]

Paniagua and Verdi were both upbeat when Santurce visited Caguas on January 17, 1985, to begin their semi-final series. They were even happier after Zane Smith won the opener, 9–3.[27] Verdi opted to use Sierra as his DH to take advantage of John Shelby's speed and arm in right. Beníquez was in center and Otis Nixon played left. Jerry Willard hit clean-up. Santurce's infield included league batting champion Orlando Sánchez at first, Victor Rodríguez at second, Julio César González at third and Iván de Jesús at short. Kelly Paris took over at third base from game two on.

Caguas copped games two and three, but Santurce won three in a row and faced San Juan in the finals. A big plus for the Crabbers was Dennis Martínez who joined the team late in the season and defeated his former Caguas team in game four. Santurce put on their hitting shoes in games five and six to overpower Caguas, 10–6 and 9–7.[28]

Dennis Martínez started game one of the finals against San Juan on January 24, 1985, and pitched scoreless ball for six frames before tiring in the seventh. Santurce won the game, 4–2, and Rich Carlucci got credit for the win. Jerry Willard put the icing on the cake with a long homer.[29]

Zane Smith gave Santurce another strong outing in game two with seven plus scoreless innings. But he got no run support. San Juan's "Skeeter" Barnes hit a sacrifice fly off reliever Tom Henke in the home eighth for the game's only run. Santurce's John Pacella and Jeff Dedmon combined for a three-hit shutout in the only "breather" of the series, a 6–0 Santurce win in game three.[30]

San Juan tied the series at two games apiece when Luis Aguayo drilled a bases-loaded single in the bottom of the ninth to give San Juan a 2–1 victory. The next night it was John Shelby's turn to be the hero with his game-ending homer in the bottom of the tenth to leave San Juan on the field. Tom Henke won the contest in relief of Dennis Martínez.[31]

Some seven years after this series, Henke would tell me that he recalled the chanting, music and swaying of the San Juan-Santurce fans more than the actual game developments. Henke called it "a lot of fun."

Otis Nixon compared that San Juan-Santurce series to the World Series atmosphere he had as a member of the Atlanta Braves. Nixon: "That was a big thing. Once you get those two teams [San Juan-Santurce], that's more excitement than anything ... like a World Series ... so much going on, screaming, fighting."

Bithorn Stadium was rocking with 11,041 fans on January 29, 1985. Otis Nixon scored the game's first run in the third after he doubled and John Shelby singled him home. But two miscues by Kelly Paris at third base gave San Juan a couple of unearned runs in their half of the inning. Santurce tied the game in the sixth on a double by Iván de Jesús and Orlando Sánchez's RBI single. Verdi had used Ulises "Candy" Sierra, Brad "The Animal" Lesley and Jeff Dedmon, before he brought in Rich Carlucci to face Benito Santiago in the ninth.

The 19-year-old Santiago belted a 2–2 pitch over the left field fence to win game six.[32]

"I really didn't play much that season or have a long winter league career," said Santiago." But that homer will always stay in my heart."

A disappointed Frank Verdi would remember this dramatic clout a decade later, but put the onus on Kelly Paris' two errors.

"If he [Paris] makes those plays, we win," said Verdi. "That was my third [managing] title right there."

Loubriel was filled to capacity with 16,280 fans for game seven. Santurce had waited 12 years for this moment; it had been 21 dry seasons for San Juan. Zane Smith took the mound and matched scoreless frames with Brian Kelly into the fourth until Chico Walker's RBI single opened the scoring for San Juan. Luis Aguayo's fourth-inning double gave San Juan an insurance run. Gary Redus scored the Metros' third run on a fifth inning double by Adalberto Peña.

Tony Fossas stifled a Santurce rally in the eighth, but gave up a hit to Iván de Jesús to open the ninth inning. Kelly Paris got on when second baseman Luis Aguayo muffed a grounder. But Fossas struck out Nelson Pedraza and got Otis Nixon to ground into a game-ending double-play.[33]

"That was something else," said Fossas. "Mako [Oliveras] had confidence in me to get the job done. We did it!"

It was back to the drawing board for Santurce. This one really hurt because they had come so close.

1985–86: The Round-Robin

An 18-game round-robin tournament with the top four teams replaced the best-of-seven semi-finals. The first and second-place teams advanced to the finals. Guigo Otero Suro became league president. Santurce fired Frank Verdi and replaced him with Sandy Alomar, Sr. Devon White and Mitch "Wild Thing" Williams got seasoning. Santurce made it to the round-robin.

"Crabbers' nets reap blend of youth, experience" was *The San Juan Star* headline.[34] Some 15 players on the Santurce roster were in the 19–23 age bracket and Frank Verdi liked this. But a smattering of veterans — Beníquez, de Jesús and Sixto Lezcano — dotted Santurce's roster. Some of the reasons for the optimism included three California Angels prospects — Devon White, a native of Kingston, Jamaica, in the outfield; third baseman Jack Howell; and, second baseman Mark McLemore. Howell provided punch from the left side of the plate and consistency at third base during the season and round-robin. McLemore left early and Luis Aguayo and José "Chico" Lind then filled in at second base.

Devon White had played AA and AAA ball in 1985 with Midland and Edmonton, respectively, before a September call-up with California. He had observed Rod Carew, Reggie Jackson and Juan Beníquez go about their duties and learned from them.

"Beníquez helped in adjusting to what my role was on the [Angels] team," said White. "Consistency with the bat and hitting for average is basically what I want with Santurce. I was contacted by the Dominican league and Venezuela, but everybody I talked to told me Puerto Rico was the best place to play winter ball right now."[35]

Verdi put White's name in left field with Beníquez in center. Sierra was the right fielder with Sixto and Carlos Lezcano both contributing part-time duty. Santurce faltered the first month, losing 14 of their first 21 games. Frank Verdi was fired. Sandy Alomar, Sr., a Santurce coach, took over. His Santurce managing debut was a successful, come-from-behind 8–4 win in Ponce on November 20, 1985, with his son, Sandy, Jr., catching the game and working with Reggie Ritter, Mitch Williams and Brad Havens.[36]

Santurce responded to Sandy Alomar, Sr., and finished third. There was a threat of a possible players strike which put the four-team round-robin tournament in jeopardy. A strike was averted with concessions including two off-days during the 18-game round-robin event. Guigo Otero Suro also had to contend with covering the players' medical plan payments.[37] The round-robin competition resulted in Mayagüez and San Juan finishing one-two to move on to the finals. Santurce did not get off to a good start on January 4, 1986, when Mitch Williams was hit hard by Mayagüez in the Crabbers' 12–3 loss.[38] Some consolation for Santurce fans was the naming of Iván de Jesús, Rubén Sierra, Juan Beníquez and Brad Havens to the league's All-Star team, announced by Eduardo Valero, president of the Puerto Rico Sportswriters Association, a day earlier.[39]

Santurce's fate was sealed in the round-robin competition when they were trounced by Mayagüez, 13–0, on January 22, 1986. That loss, coupled with San Juan's win over Caguas, sent the Crabbers home. Mayagüez defeated San Juan in the finals and they contracted Candy Sierra for the Caribbean Series.

1986–87: Los Angeles and Santurce Hook Up

Santurce set up a working agreement with the Los Angeles Dodgers which provided the Crabbers with a manager, a pitching coach and some top prospects. Kevin Kennedy got valuable managing experience, but some Los Angeles prospects did not produce. Chris Gwynn, the brother of former San Juan/Bayamón star, Tony Gwynn, played well, as did U.S. Virgin Islander Jerry Browne, voted the league Rookie of the Year.

Santurce's management signed a working agreement with the Los Angeles Dodgers. This three-year project included the signing of Kevin Kennedy, then a manager in the Dodgers farm system; pitching coach Dave Wallace; and, trainer Mike Lopriore. Paniagua told me that this agreement was complicated by the fact that Los Angeles also sent some of their best prospects to the Licey Tigers in the Dominican Republic. This meant that Santurce did not always get the Dodgers' top prospects. Paniagua made it clear that some imports during this period could still come from other big league organizations.

The young Dodgers prospects who wore Santurce flannels were position players Chris Gwynn, Tracy Woodson, Mike Devereaux, Jack Fimple, Larry See and pitchers Jeff Edwards, Bob Hamilton and Steve Shirley. Fimple, See and Shirley had completed seasons at the Dodgers AAA team in Albuquerque of the Pacific Coast League. The other five had spent 1986 with San Antonio in the Texas League.[40] There were mixed results for Santurce.

Edwards, Hamilton and Shirley did adequate mound work. Devereaux only played 12 games and See was released after playing in 18 games.[41] Fimple was Santurce's first-string catcher, and backed up by Sandy Alomar, Jr. Tracy Woodson led the league in RBI, and was selected to the league's All-Star team.[42] Chris Gwynn produced and enjoyed himself.

"It was nice and important to play in Puerto Rico," said Gwynn. "That league was loaded! You learned as you were having fun … so it didn't seem like work. I lived in Dorado [a resort area] where the living conditions were great."

Santurce did not qualify for the round-robin tournament, finishing fifth. Juan Beníquez, Iván de Jesús, Orlando Sánchez and Rubén Sierra had below average seasons. Chico Lind emerged as a talented second baseman. Another bright spot was St. Croix, U.S. Virgin Islands native Jerry Browne, a versatile player and the league Rookie of the Year.[43]

"I had played a few games with Texas in September [1986]," said Browne. "It was important for me to play well in Puerto Rico and I did."

Kevin Kennedy called this a great experience with good young players and the veterans.

"Having [Sixto] Lezcano, Beníquez and de Jesús … with the young prospects was not a tough job, but a good job," said Kennedy. "The agreement was to supply the manager, pitching coach and a trainer, but Nick Acosta was still there."

1987–88: Close, but no Cigar

Santurce finished the regular season in first place. Their versatility was exemplified by blue collar players such as Juan Beníquez, Orlando Sánchez and Mike Sharperson who played different positions. Santurce shortstop Jay Bell had a fine round-robin tournament to help Santurce qualify for the finals. The Crabbers came up short as Mayagüez pulled out the final series, four games to three.

Kevin Kennedy stated that coming over from rookie ball in the U.S. and going to Puerto Rico the prior winter was like going from rookie ball to the big leagues. Kennedy became used to the "produce or pack" mentality and the fact that winning — not developing players — was paramount in Puerto Rico. Santurce won the regular season title in Kennedy's second season at the helm. As a result, Kennedy was voted Manager of the Year.[44] Kennedy also managed the Metro team to a 1–0 win over the Island All-Stars in a game dedicated to Angel Colón, long-time Puerto Rico Professional Baseball Players Association official.[45] This 54-game regular season was followed by a 12-game round-robin tournament and the league finals. Kennedy: "I think the round-robin gave the fans a chance to see more players. But as a manager, when you win a pennant, you like to go to the finals. In the case with us, we sent some of our pitchers home...and battled Mayagüez in a seven-game series. Unfortunately, we lost. They had Bobby Bonilla; we had Rubén Sierra ... a lot of fun."

Jerry Willard was back to catch after playing some games for Oakland in 1987. Sandy Alomar, Jr. platooned with the lefty-hitting Willard. Juan Beníquez and Mike Sharperson could play just about anywhere. Chico Lind and Jay Bell anchored the middle defense. Rubén Sierra was a regular for the fourth straight season. George Hinshaw hit with power when he joined the team. Iván de Jesús, Sixto Lezcano and Orlando Sánchez contributed as role players.

What carried Santurce in the regular season and round-robin series was its pitching. Their regular season team E.R.A. of 2.99 was the league's lowest and the Crabbers had six different pitchers registering saves, including eight earned by Dodgers prospect Mike Hartley and Mike Pérez's six saves.[46] Bill Krueger, Jeff Kaiser, Reggie Ritter, Ron Mathis and Candy Sierra were the five main starters.

Bill Krueger was a 29-year-old lefty who had been acquired by the Dodgers from Oakland. He had pitched in Venezuela and the Dominican Republic, but stated that Puerto Rico's league was better on all counts, including the food, living conditions and ballparks. Puerto Rico's fans were a bit more temperamental than those in Venezuela and the Dominican Republic, but perhaps not as fanatical.

Krueger told me that Sandy Alomar, Jr. was an excellent game caller. He praised Santurce's pitching coach, Dave Wallace, as one of the best ones he ever had, adding that the Dodgers system has great coaching. Kevin Kennedy was easy to play for and knew the game.

That winter was special to Krueger since he and his fiancée, Jo, shared many fun times such as sightseeing in Puerto Rico, going to St. Thomas and enjoying the beach. Santurce helped with the rental car expenses, but Krueger had to cover his Isla Verde apartment's rent and other cost-of-living expenses.

Most of Santurce's starters including late-season acquisition Ed Wojna had spent some time in the majors. Wojna considered himself to be a "AAA-plus-plus" pitcher, based on brief stints in the majors and then back to AAA with the pattern repeating itself.

Orlando Sánchez exemplified another Santurce perspective from a player without a set position or big league affiliation. Sánchez is on a long list of Puerto Rico's ballplayers to ply their trade in Mexico after stateside minor league and big league careers. He hit .384 for Puebla in 1985, followed by .402 and .417 marks in 1986 and 1987,[47] and wanted to prove that he could make it back to the "show" again.

Iván de Jesús, 1987–88 (courtesy of Angel Colón).

Mike Devereaux and Mike Sharperson were two future Dodgers who benefited from the work ethic displayed by Sánchez and the other Santurce vets — Beníquez, de Jesús and Sixto Lezcano.

"I had played for Mayagüez the prior [1986–87] winter and gotten to be good friends with teammate Bobby Bonilla ... we talked a lot about the majors," said Sharperson. "With Santurce I got to see how the veterans accepted their roles and helped the younger players. This helped me make it back to the majors with the 1988 Dodgers where we won the World Series."

Devereaux was called up by the Dodgers in the latter part of 1988. "Beníquez was one guy who worked with me," said Devereaux. "I came back the following season to work on my game. Later on I played in a [Puerto Rico] golf benefit. The baseball and the golf were a lot of fun."

Mayagüez and Santurce finished one-two to set up the final series match-up. Jay Bell, a league All-Star, was a factor in Santurce's success. His three-run homer off Ponce's Doug Jones in game eight of the round-robin was the difference in Santurce's 5–2 win.

"I'm getting some good pitches and I'm just on a roll," said Bell.[48] Bell made some errors in early round-robin games, but atoned for them with his hitting. That winter was a plus for Bell's major league career.

"The field conditions forced me to improve my defense," said Bell. "It rained too much and the maintenance was not the best. There were a few too many round-robin/finals games, but it was a great experience. Puerto Rico was a comfortable place to live and a super place to play."

The finals began the next night at Mayagüez's Isidoro García Stadium. John Cangelosi, Kevin Romine, Luis Raúl Quiñónes, Bobby Bonilla, Tom Howard and Tom Pagnozzi were part of Mayagüez's line-up. Mayagüez had talented native hurlers such as José Guzmán, Luis "Mambo" de Léon and Juan Agosto. Jeff Brantley complemented Agosto in the Mayagüez bullpen.

Mayagüez took the opener, 8–0, but Santurce retaliated by winning the next two games. Jay Bell hit a pivotal two-run homer in game two, a 6–3 Santurce win.[49] Tracy Woodson, a late-season addition, overcame a bout with food poisoning to score both runs in the Crabbers' 2–1 win in game three, with the second run coming on a homer off Luis "Mambo" de Léon.[50]

Mayagüez won three of the next four games to claim their third league title of the decade. Santurce wasted seven shutout innings by Ed Wojna in game five to come within one win of the elusive title.

"I felt a twinge in the seventh inning and it became a dull throb," said Wojna. "Coming back from an arm injury there was no reason to stay in the game with Mike [Pérez] in the bullpen."[51]

Wojna's remarks summed up the reality facing Santurce and other league teams by the mid to late 1980s. Many big league teams, with some exceptions, were reluctant to send their top pitching prospects to winter ball. The Dodgers still believed in the virtues of winter ball and continued to send position players and a highly touted pitcher to Santurce.

1988–89: A Severe Power Outage

The three-year working agreement with the Dodgers concluded. Santurce pitching coach Dave Wallace benefited from working with a diverse group of hurlers, but the team's lack of offense did them in as they finished last. Kevin Kennedy managed the Metro All-Stars to a win.

Dave Wallace started his third and final season as Santurce's pitching coach. He knew exactly where Ed Wojna was coming from since he (Wallace) had spent nine years as a AAA pitcher with some brief big league stints in the 1970s. Wallace was a roving pitching instructor in the Dodgers minor league system by 1988 who believed winter ball kept players sharp. That coincided with the Dodgers philosophy. The Santurce job allowed Wallace to work with his own pitching staff on a regular basis, much like he would do in the 1990s as the Dodgers pitching coach under Tom Lasorda and Bill Russell.

Dennis Burtt, Mike Hartley and John Wetteland were three pitchers in the Dodgers chain who pitched for Santurce. Burtt was an older AAA+ type hurler. Hartley used that winter to prep for his first relief appearances with the Dodgers. Wetteland, the baby of the group at 22, was a hard-throwing starting pitcher out of AA ball.

"We had an agreement to send some players there, so Kevin Kennedy and I went there for three years," said Wallace. "Juan Pizarro showed me the ropes in Puerto Rico and was very helpful ... knew the Puerto Rican players. I have probably more time in winter baseball than many ... four-five years as a coach and two-three years as a player in the Dominican Republic, time in Venezuela and three years in Puerto Rico."

The Santurce stints definitely helped the progress of Devereaux, Sharperson and Wetteland, according to Wallace. It also paid cultural dividends in terms of helping Kennedy learn the Spanish language. Wallace:"It lends credibility when you go over there and learn the language and live the culture. The players sense you're trying...."

Santurce finished the season in the cellar. Sandy Alomar, Jr. did not play and eventually joined his father the following winter when Sandy Alomar, Sr. got the Ponce managing job. Santurce's lack of production was evidenced by their league-low 189 runs and 23 team homers in the 60-game season.[52] This put a lot of pressure on a hot-and-cold pitching staff which accounted for one complete game.[53]

Dennis Burtt was Santurce's most consistent and durable starter. Mike Hartley converted on save opportunities. John Wetteland got important experience prior to his big league debut on May 31, 1989.[54] His Puerto Rico outings were monitored in terms of pitch counts. Jaime Navarro, a Milwaukee Brewers prospect, pitched well in a starting role.

Outfielder Dwight Smith and shortstop Ed Romero were the two Santurce players to start for the Metro squad in the league All-Star contest. Kevin Kennedy managed the Metro players to a win for the second straight year. San Juan's Lonnie Smith was the hero and game MVP with a two-run homer in the first inning scoring Dwight Smith ahead of him.[55]

Mayagüez later won their fourth league title of the decade. Ken Caminiti, Steve Finley, Chris Hoiles, Al Newman, John Cangelosi and Tom Pagnozzi were some of the top guns. Their three "Jeffs"— Brantley, Fassero and Gray — shut down the opposition out of the bullpen.

1989–90: Ray Miller Does His Best

Hurricane Hugo was in the news. Much of the San Juan metropolitan area and the U.S. Virgin Islands were hit hard by this hurricane. The winter season was shortened to 50 games from 60 contests, but more round-robin games, 18 as opposed to 12, were added

Hard throwing John Wetteland, 1988–89 (courtesy of *El Nuevo Día*).

to the mix. Santurce hired Pittsburgh's pitching coach, Ray Miller, for a second time. The team's inconsistent play resulted in a fifth-place finish.

Miller observed that much had changed in Puerto Rico since he first managed Caguas in 1980–81 in terms of more cable TV stations, other entertainment options and the security factor. He told me that there was a big decline attendance wise between his first (1983–84) Santurce managing stint and the second one six years later. This was verified by league records which revealed that only 254,047 fans paid to see league games in 1989–90, a 51.8 percent decrease from the 527,219 paid fans in 1983–84.[56]

Miller used his baseball acumen and 19 pitchers in the 50-game season. Rick Reed gave Miller the most league innings, and pitched three of the team's five complete games.[57]

Catcher Terry McGriff, first baseman Mark Ryal, outfielder Albert Hall, and backup catcher Angel Morris produced. Charlie Hayes was sent packing with his .184 batting average.[58] Chico Lind played well at times; Iván de Jesús performed admirably. Shortstop Rey Quiñónes was a big enigma.

Gabrielle Paese, a sportswriter with *The San Juan Star*, conversed with Ray Miller a few days before the end of the regular season. Quiñónes had been traded by Seattle to Pittsburgh in the summer of 1989. Pittsburgh released Quiñónes before the end of the big league season. Miller then had to contend with Quiñónes' inconsistent defense and lack of a work ethic.

"We've played 45 games," stated Miller. "Rey's missed 14 of them. I think that's a good enough reason to drop him."[59]

Another problem for Santurce was that Rubén Sierra, did not suit up in 1989–90. Some of the younger island stars with the other franchises did play. League batting champ Edgar Martínez, Carlos Baerga and Héctor Villanueva performed for San Juan. First-place Ponce had the Alomar brothers, Sandy, Jr. and Roberto, and Joey Cora. Juan González emerged as a bonafide power hitter with Caguas after the Criollos acquired him in a trade with Ponce for Roberto Alomar. Bernie Williams was a terrific New York Yankee prospect playing for Arecibo. Mayagüez' Roberto Hernández was throwing bullets.

It did not help matters when eventual league champion San Juan signed imported pitchers Dennis Burtt and Mike Hartley from the Dodgers. After San Juan put away Caguas, five games to three in the best-of-nine finals, the Metros secured Joey Cora and Juan González to reinforce them in the ill-fated 1990 Caribbean Series hosted by Miami. The Escogido Lions of the Dominican Republic won that event, which was plagued by low attendance.[60]

The attendance problems affecting the Puerto Rico Winter League were not unique to that island. Mexico, Venezuela and the Dominican Republic had their share of attendance problems as well.

When I conversed with Ray Miller in the visitor's clubhouse at Philadelphia's Veteran Stadium prior to a Pittsburgh-Philadelphia game in mid–September 1991, he reiterated his concern about the status of winter ball throughout the Caribbean. Miller, as did others, saw the reluctance of big league organizations to send their top prospects to the Caribbean. This reality was compounded by the high-salaried native players not playing in front of the home fans.

9. A New Decade

The Caribbean Series was more thrilling than my big league playoffs or a major league All-Star Game. Representing Puerto Rico is the ultimate ... tremendous source of pride.
— Dickie Thon, former Santurce DH/infielder

Santurce began the 1990s by winning the 1990–91 league title to end an 18-year drought, or "sequía," and duplicated that feat two years later. They won the 1993 Caribbean Series thanks to Dickie Thon's heroics. Their informal working agreement with the Atlanta Braves in the early 1990s preceded the informal Santurce-Houston Astros link from the mid to late 1990s, when Frankie Thon — a Houston scout — was Santurce's General Manager.

Baseball/Economic Updates

The U.S. economy was in a 1990–1991 recession, and Puerto Rico followed suit. I visited Puerto Rico in October 1991, some six years after leaving the island, to cover the first Puerto Rico Professional Baseball Hall of Fame Induction Ceremony in Ponce. It was an honor to meet and share moments with Bob Thurman, one of the inductees, and to once again touch base with Orlando Cepeda, Juan Pizarro and Víctor Pellot. Some baseball fans, sportscasters and officials told me that Puerto Rico's Winter League was in a recession of its own, and heading for a depression.

Things looked better during my January 1993 visit to Puerto Rico. Juan "Igor" González and Dickie Thon were two big leaguers wearing Santurce uniforms. Other teams also benefited from this trend. League attendance exploded during the 1994–95 season after the 1994 big league strike. Big league native players and imports opted to play that whole winter instead of a month or two. Artificial surface was installed in Caguas, Ponce and Bithorn Stadium between the 1993–94 and 1996–97 seasons. More corporate sponsors and stadium billboards were secured by league teams.

The island's economic front went through a period of change as a result of FOMENTO ceasing to function at the end of 1997. Some of its functions and staff were transferred to the Puerto Rico Industrial Development Corporation, but FOMENTO no longer had an administrator nor its name. FOMENTO's "936 Program" offering tax incentives to U.S. corporations was eliminated by the U.S. Congress in 1996.[1] FOMENTO had helped build the island's infrastructure, develop manufacturing and the tourism industry; modernize the food distribution system, and, organize the Casals Music Festival.[2]

1990–91: A Championship at Last

Santurce won their first title in 18 years, but it was an uphill struggle with injuries, player turnover and some fan apathy during the regular season. They qualified for the four-team round-robin tournament and finished second. Santurce bested Mayagüez in the best-of-nine league finals before traveling to Miami, Florida, for the Caribbean Series.

The Crabbers had returned to Bithorn Stadium to share this facility with the San Juan ballclub and their rivalry was still very intense. Just ask Santurce fan Luis Maldonado, who became a Santurce fan due to his godfather. Luis' father and one brother have been life-long San Juan fans, while Luis' oldest brother has always followed Santurce. Luis' father, Dr. Norman Maldonado, and his three sons went to a San Juan — Santurce game in 1991 and sat in the box of the San Juan owners.

"The San Juan owner learned that my oldest brother and I were rooting for Santurce and he was not pleased by it," said Luis Maldonado. "I remember the game very fondly ... interrupted because of rain and during the rain delay we talked about Santurce beating San Juan ... I can still see the steam rising from the head of the San Juan owner — he was gracious enough NOT to ask us to leave."

Santurce's roster covered the gamut from vets such as the 40-year-old Juan Beníquez, 37-year-old Iván de Jesús and 34-year-old Orlando Sánchez, to prospects including Mark Lemke, Eric Anthony and Andy Tomberlin. Junior Ortíz was behind the plate and caught a good nucleus of native pitchers — Jaime Navarro, Candy Sierra, Luis Aquino and John Burgos.

Luis Aquino had pitched for Mayagüez in the 1980s and told me that it was important for a contender to have reliable native pitchers due to the extensive turnover of the imported hurlers.

"With Mayagüez we had Juan Agosto, José Guzmán, Jesús Hernaíz and Mambo de León," said Aquino. "Our 1990–91 Santurce club had two solid native starters — Jaime Navarro and Candy Sierra — plus lefty reliever John Burgos, and myself, a right-hander who could come in middle relief, save a game or even start, if needed."

Santurce manager Mike Cubbage contended with the normal turnover coupled with a rash of early season injuries that left the Crabbers decimated. Santurce used 25 position players and 15 pitchers during the course of their 58 regular season games.[3] By early December 1990, Cubbage was quite discouraged and "resigned." Mako Oliveras, a Santurce coach and San Juan's former manager, took over with the team sporting a 17–17 mark.

"We did what was humanly possible ... Cubbage had his hands tied — we have a hospital here," said Oliveras. "I have to go to church and light some candles next to [GM] Carlitos Ríos."[4]

Santurce owner, Poto Paniagua, saw a positive side.

"I see an awakening and have faith that he [Mako] will have some success like he had with San Juan in the past."

Santurce played better baseball under Mako and qualified for the 18-game round-robin tournament. Paniagua lamented the season-ending injury to Mark Lemke when he left Puerto Rico with a .347 batting average. Lemke told me that the Santurce stint was very helpful after injuring an ankle in the States. He enjoyed the camaraderie on the Santurce club and would have stayed for the whole season if he had remained injury-free.

Casey Candaele replaced Lemke; Edwin Alicea came via a trade with Arecibo; and Scott Leius arrived to play shortstop. Alicea and Candaele were sparkplugs. First/third baseman Leo Gómez provided power.

"The important thing was that we won as a team," said Gómez. "I had also played in a few games for Baltimore at the end of the 1990 big league season and wanted to be in top shape when spring training began."

San Juan won the regular season pennant, but were losing ground for the second and final round-robin spot when they faced Santurce on January 13, 1991. Jack Lazorko, who joined Santurce at the end of the regular season, pitched a two-hit shutout against the Metros to give Santurce a 1–0 win and breathing room in their quest to qualify for the league finals. San Juan's line-up of Luis Alicea, Lenny Harris, Lenny Webster, Héctor Villanueva, Edgar Martínez, Joel Chimelis, Carlos Baerga, Barry Jones and Rubén Escalera posted a double by Alicea and a single by Villanueva.[5]

"I knew Mako Oliveras from the California organization," said Lazorko. "I had been pitching for the Sun City Rays in the Senior League along with Fergie Jenkins and Rollie Fingers when the league folded right before Christmas ... was in great shape with a 7–0 record ...had pitched with Calgary that summer and wanted to keep pitching. Mako wanted me so I flew down the day after Christmas in time to make the round-robin roster."

Lazorko stated that the 1991 round-robin and final series were "awesome" with a World Series atmosphere in the finals. He had pitched for the 1984–85 Ponce Lions and had prior round-robin and final series experience with the 1986–87 league champion, the Caguas Criollos, managed by Tim Foli. Lazorko made the rounds throughout the Caribbean Confederation, having pitched for the Aguilas Cibaeñas in the Dominican Republic, Magallanes in Venezuela, and Los Mochis in Mexico.

"I had been a teammate of José Cruz in Ponce and with Barry Bonds on that Magallanes club," said Lazorko. "We had Ellis Burks and Bernie Williams with Caguas, and Pete O'Brien and Aurelio Rodríguez with Los Mochis in Mexico."

Pitching depth was a concern when David West left Puerto Rico with good memories after the round-robin series. His departure affected the pitching staff. Both West and his Santurce catcher Junior Ortíz would soon begin spring training with the 1991 World Champions, the Minnesota Twins.

"I would like to arrive rested for spring training," said West. "Junior Ortíz is a great defensive catcher and a big help...."[6]

Most of Puerto Rico's sportswriters and baseball officials felt Mayagüez would defeat Santurce in the finals, since the "Tribe" had just defeated Santurce six straight times during the round-robin after winning eight of 12 regular season games. But Carlos Pieve predicted a Santurce win. Pieve felt that Casey Candaele was a mirror image of Wayne Tolleson, who had helped the 1982–83 Arecibo Wolves win the league title. Iván de Jesús had a few "bullets" left, as did Pedro García with Arecibo. Juan Beníquez was a class veteran much like Orlando Alvarez had been for the Wolves. The addition of Tony Fossas to Santurce's mound corps gave them someone like Arecibo's Gary Lance — a pitcher with a lot of heart. Mako Oliveras, along with Arecibo's Ron Clark, was a winner, according to Pieve.[7]

Santurce won five of the eight final series games. They were close games including the last one played at Bithorn on January 30, 1991 before a packed house. The Crabbers started Chris Beasley, who joined them for the post-season. Mayagüez countered with Don Heinkel.[8]

Edwin Alicea and Casey Candaele got Santurce on the board in the third with back-to-back homers. A Pedro Muñoz RBI hit in the sixth followed by Chad Kreuter's seventh inning homer tied the game at 2. Santurce won it in the home 11th when Junior Ortíz doubled and scored on Edwin Alicea's single. Alicea told reporters that his hit came on a forkball by Mayagüez reliever Daniel Boone.[9]

Tony Fossas, who earned the win by retiring the only hitter he faced, told me he was happy for the team, Mako, and GM Carlos Ríos.

"I saved game seven of the 1985 finals against Santurce," said Fossas. "Then I won the last game of the 1991 series ... came down to help Santurce as a favor to my brother in Christ, Carlos Ríos. It was special."

Juan Beníquez was crying tears of joy.

"I wanted this championship ... thank God and the fans," said Beníquez. "It was great the first time [1973] and even greater now! It's what all players want — to retire with a championship."[10]

Jack Lazorko recalls Tany Pérez and Ed Figueroa joined in the celebration. Mako Oliveras had already won two crowns as San Juan's manager, but noted that "this one has a more sentimental flavor since it gives the title to the Crabber faithful who waited 18 years."[11]

Santurce's Caribbean Series reinforcements included Carlos Baerga, Rubén Escalera, Lenny Harris and Héctor Villanueva of San Juan; three Mayagüez pitchers — Mambo de León, Don Heinkel and Roberto Hernández — plus first baseman Rod Brewer; and, Caguas hurler Omar Olivares.[12]

This Caribbean Series was hosted by Miami, Florida, and included preliminary games prior to a best-of-three series between the top two squads. The Licey Tigers won their sixth Caribbean Series crown by sweeping the Lara Cardinals from Venezuela in the finals. Mexico's Tijuana Colts and the Crabbers did not advance.

The Crabbers were no match for Licey in their series opener, an 8–2 loss.[13] Licey skipper John Roseboro had a line-up with Gerónimo Berroa, Francisco Cabrera, Andujar Cedeño and Henry Rodríguez along with pitchers Juan Guzmán, Mélido Pérez and closer Rod Beck. Santurce lost two games to Lara, which had Derek Bell and Luis Sojo. Santurce's only win in the prelims came against Tijuana when Omar Olivares went the route in a 6–1 win. Vinny Castilla was one of Tijuana's young stars.[14]

1991–92: Turk Wendell Takes a Bow

It was the year of Steve "Turk" Wendell, a colorful right-hander who captivated Santurce and league fans with his antics. Several Atlanta prospects had mixed results for the Crabbers, while other Braves never made it to Puerto Rico. Iván de Jesús retired. Santurce finished fourth to qualify for the round-robin, but did not make the finals. Eric Fox and José Meléndez helped Mayagüez win the 1992 Caribbean Series.

Jack Lazorko blanked San Juan in the 1991 round-robin series (courtesy of *El Nuevo Día*).

Five youngsters from the Atlanta Braves parent club or farm clubs — Brian Hunter, Ryan Klesko, Keith Mitchell, David Nied and Mark Wohlers — were slated to reinforce Santurce. Hunter, Mitchell and Wohlers bailed out at the last minute, citing that "they needed time off after the 1991 World Series and would not report."[15] This set the tone for musical chairs which saw 25 position players and 20 pitchers wear the Santurce uniform.[16] The season was dedicated to the memory of Esteban Texidor, a former Santurce pitcher and Puerto Rico Players Association official.

Santurce fan Luis Maldonado was in heaven at this time. He began following the Crabbers in the mid to late 1970s. By the early 1980s he had become an Atlanta Braves fan, so he was thrilled that Santurce's agreement with Atlanta resulted in some of their prospects playing for the Crabbers.

"This was a great connection, yet another reason to follow the Santurce franchise," said Luis. "I remember watching Turk Wendell — what a strange guy. When he got traded to Chicago, it was bittersweet ... remember Klesko, Nied with Santurce...."

Turk Wendell had been acquired by the Chicago Cubs from the Atlanta Braves toward the end of the 1991 National League season. Wendell spent most of the summer at Greenville, the AA level, before moving up to AAA Richmond prior to the trade. He then had a successful season with Santurce, starting with a 1–0 shutout of San Juan on November 3, 1991.[17] Wendell's mound antics in Puerto Rico had Santurce fans calling the team's office to find out when his next start would come.

Eric Edwards of *The San Juan Star* did an in-depth feature on Wendell and his pitching rituals. Wendell drew three crosses on the dirt; prayed before he pitched; waved to the center fielder before his first pitch; and, leapt over third base when going toward, or leaving the mound. He chewed black licorice; brushed his teeth between innings; and, wore no socks.

"I'm superstitious ... If I find something that works for me I stay with it no matter how crazy it may seem," said Wendell. "Sometimes I would rather not be, but that's the way I am."[18]

Wendell got his nickname in Dalton, Massachusetts, as a three year old, after jumping face first from a window into a mound of snow made by his grandfather. He repeated these jumps before stepping inside the house when his grandfather stated "that was something only a Turk would do."[19]

Wendell got hitters out with a change-up and his 85–89 mile-per-hour fastball. Mako Oliveras felt that Wendell's high leg kick and rapid delivery were his strong points. Wendell received the Juan Pizarro Award at season's end as the league's Most Outstanding Pitcher and was named as the right-handed pitcher on the All-Star team.[20]

Santurce had two other talented pitching imports, Kyle Abbott and David Nied. Abbott had pitched for Mako Oliveras at Edmonton in 1991 and liked his skipper and Santurce's pitching coach, Juan Pizarro.

"Puerto Rico was great, but I was traded to the Phillies that winter and they [Phillies] told me to come home," said Abbott. "Pizarro was a fine pitching coach and I could relate to him."

David Nied was placed on a 50-inning limit by the Atlanta Braves. He would travel to away games in a rental car shared with Ryan Klesko and Turk Wendell. Nied particularly liked Puerto Rico's geography ranging from flat areas to majestic mountains and told me that he hated to leave the island when the Braves asked him to do so.

Three other imports — Eric Fox, Scott Hemond and Gerald Williams — produced.

Turk Wendell, 1991–92 (courtesy of *The San Juan Star*).

Fox, from the Oakland A's organization, played well. Williams, a New York Yankee outfield prospect, was named to the league's All-Star team at season's end, as was Hemond at third base. Hemond also played shortstop, left field, or catcher, and reminded historian Héctor Barea of versatile imports from an earlier era.[21]

But Santurce sent Troy Afenir home after hitting only .051 in 15 games. Ryan Klesko left Santurce with a .171 batting mark.[22]

"There is no question that Afenir was the worst hitter the league had seen in some years," said Barea. "Afenir brought back memories of Harry Chappas who could not hit with Caguas."

Santurce's pitching kept them in the playoff hunt. Nied shut out San Juan, 5–0, in his last start on December 14, 1991, to keep Santurce in contention.[23] Wendell blanked Mayagüez four days later[24] before pitching in the league All-Star game on December 21.

It was all Santurce in the All-Star game, a 4–0 triumph by the Metro stars over the Island squad. Scott Hemond scored twice for the Metro team while Eric Fox and Gerald Williams tallied the other Metro runs.[25]

The round-robin was not pleasant after Santurce lost their first four games, including the opener to San Juan. Scott Hemond suddenly left the team during the round-robin event prompting team Poto Paniagua to state that "Hemond just didn't want to play."[26]

My first round-robin experience included a visit to the Santurce clubhouse prior to their opening game against San Juan. I caught up with Turk Wendell playing cards with Junior Ortíz and several other teammates. Wendell, who loved Puerto Rico and its people, was disappointed in not being able to start the round-robin opener. He ambled toward the left field stands before game time to hold a baby and chat with Santurce fans. Denny Neagle was sharp in besting Santurce that night. San Juan qualified for the finals, but lost that best-of-nine series to Mayagüez.

Eric Fox stayed and reinforced Mayagüez for the Caribbean Series with Santurce infielder-outfielder Edwin Alicea and pitcher José Meléndez. Meléndez won game three of the series, 4–3, against the Escogido Lions from the Dominican Republic, despite allowing homers to Junior Félix and Gerónimo Berroa.[27] Fox hit .320 in the 1992 Caribbean Series, including the tie-breaker win against Venezuela's Zulia Eagles.[28]

"It's still kind of strange playing for a team you played against all year long, but I can see why this team [Mayagüez] did so well," said Fox. "They have great chemistry."[29]

1992–93: Dickie and Igor Shine

Santurce's chemistry enabled them to win their eleventh league title and their first Caribbean Series since 1955, discounting the 1962 InterAmerican Series crown. Dickie Thon and Juan "Igor" González shined during the latter part of the regular season and post-season. A combination of fine pitching and the hitting of Dickie Thon and Héctor Villanueva propelled Santurce to the 1993 Caribbean Series title.

There were only five league teams and a 48-game season due to the folding of the Bayamón (formerly Caguas) franchise. Santurce picked up several Bayamón/Caguas players including Juan "Igor" González and hurler Francisco Javier Oliveras. The Crabbers also acquired Héctor Villanueva via a late-season trade with San Juan for Carlos Delgado.

Santurce featured the league's best pitching staff with a 1.63 team E.R.A.[30] José Lebrón, Francisco Javier Oliveras, Greg Harris, Nap Robinson and Scott Bailes were effective

Juan "Igor" González responds to Rafael Bracero's question after receiving the MVP award for 1992–93 (photograph by the author).

starters. A real plus was middle and short relief with Mike Cook, Darryl Scott, Wil Fraser and Billy Brewer. José Alberro did the job as a spot starter and in relief.

José Lebrón started for the Metro squad against the Island team in the league All-Star game, but did not figure in the decision. Neither did Alberro, Cook and Scott who pitched in relief.[31]

The next day, December 7, 1992, marked Juan "Igor" González's season debut against the San Juan Metros and one of their aces, Dennis "Oil Can" Boyd. Homers were hard to come by until Igor donned the Santurce uniform. Some fans and sportscasters including Rafael Bracero told me that the ball used in Puerto Rico during the 1992–93 season was made in China and did not travel as far as those baseballs made in Haiti. Juan "Igor" González hit seven rockets in only 66 official at-bats to win the league's home run title.[32]

"Igor was the league's savior," said Mako Oliveras. "He turned our team and the league around. This team had a different attitude with him in the line-up."

Santurce swept the individual honors with González winning the league MVP award.[33] I was at Bithorn Stadium the evening the awards were presented and captured the moment when sportscaster Rafael Bracero interviewed Juan "Igor" González. Oliveras was the Manager of the Year; José Lebrón won the Pitcher of the Year honor; and, Francisco "Terín" Meléndez was the Comeback Player of the Year. The six Crabbers on the league All-Star team were Héctor Villanueva (1B), Germán "Deportivo" Rivera (3B), Darrell Sherman and Gerald Williams (OF), Juan "Igor" González (DH) and José Lebrón (Starter).[34]

The Crabbers advanced to the league finals against San Juan after a round-robin series which required a tie-breaker between Mayagüez and Santurce to determine San Juan's opponent. Santurce took that game, 4–2, when Edwin Alicea, filling in for Igor, lined an RBI double to put Santurce ahead for good.

Santurce's positive attitude came through when I witnessed a Santurce-San Juan round-robin game which took six hours and 50 minutes to play due to several rain delays. I came away seeing Santurce's camaraderie and good team chemistry with Dickie Thon, Deportivo Rivera and Francisco Javier Oliveras joking with the team's younger players. Juan "Igor" González and Thon both expressed concern about the condition of the Bithorn playing field when I sat between them in the Santurce dugout during a rain delay.

Eric Fox joined Santurce for the round-robin, replacing the departed Darrell Sherman. Fox played for Oakland in the 1992 American League Championship Series, prior to taking the winter off to teach, lift weights and use the Stairmaster in California.

"Mako knew me from the PCL when I played for Tacoma in 1991," said Fox. "It was a big thrill winning the 1992 Caribbean Series [for Mayagüez] and I looked forward to playing in one with Santurce."

Fox's wish came through when Santurce bested San Juan in five of their six final series games to earn the plane tickets to Mazatlán, Mexico. No one was happier than Dickie Thon: "I had always been a San Juan fan as a kid," said Thon. "My grandfather [Freddie, Sr.] had played for them and so did I. But they traded me and later, when I was with the Phillies, I called San Juan to let them know about my interest in playing for them … they said they did not need me."

Santurce acquired Thon through a trade with Arecibo and he wanted to have a good final series. His two-run single in game one of the finals was the difference in Santurce's 4–2 win. Eric Edwards started his write-up of game two: Dickie Thon 2, San Juan 0, after Thon's homer down the left field line in the home 11th off Rafy Montalvo gave Santurce a 1–0 win.

"I know he [Montalvo] likes to come inside," said Thon. "I was looking for a pitch I could drive and he gave me one."[35]

Juan "Igor" González was the hero in game three with a three-run homer in Santurce's 4–0 win. San Juan won game four, 2–0, but Santurce won games five and six. Francisco Javier Oliveras shut out the Metros, 3–0, in game five for his second series win. Then Wil Fraser and Mike Cook combined for a four-hit shutout to win game six, 4–0, before a standing room only crowd of 23,709.[36]

"It really was a great moment for me and the team," said Thon. "There was such an incredible chemistry on this club all year. I'm so happy things turned out as they did."

Igor González was also happy.

"This was my first baseball title at any level of competition," said González. "I celebrated that championship to the hilt."

Santurce went to Mazatlán sans González, due to other commitments. The Crabbers used Edwin Alicea, San Juan's Rubén Escalera and Mayagüez's José Valentín as a "left field by committee trio." Tony Barron of San Juan was inserted in right field since Gerald Williams did not make the trip. Santurce bolstered its pitching staff with Kevin Brown of Mayagüez and San Juan's Orlando Lind, Rafy Montalvo and David Rosario. Edwin Correa and José Alvarez were signed to pitch in Mazatlán.

The pitching reinforcements paid dividends as Kevin Brown won twice, including game two against the host Mazatlán Deer and a tie-breaker against the Aguilas Cibaeñas from the Dominican Republic. Orlando Lind, with help from Brown and Darryl Scott, defeated Mazatlán in game five. Mike Cook won games one and four in relief against Venezuela's Zulia Eagles.[37] Santurce's toughest foe was the Aguilas Cibaeñas, who beat them twice.

"They had Moisés Alou, Andujar Cedeño, Tony Peña, Alex Arias, Félix Fermín, Luis Polonia, Henry Rodríguez...." said Dickie Thon. "We were not as strong as them on paper."

Juan Vené, writing for New York's *El Diario*, recalls that the tie-breaker started at 7:03 p.m. local time on February 9, 1993. Mazatlán had been scheduled to face Zulia in the series finale, but Mako Oliveras and Miguel Diloné—the Aguilas Cibaeñas manager—along with their coaches and a player representative, decided that the tie-breaker be played first.[38]

Dickie Thon emerged as the Caribbean Series hero when his two-run homer in the sixth inning off José Musset broke a 5–5 deadlock to lead Santurce to a 9–5 win. Kevin Brown came through with five plus scoreless relief innings before Darryl Scott got the final out for the save.[39]

"I hit a fastball off Musset," said Thon. "The Caribbean Series was more thrilling than my big league playoffs or a major league All-Star Game. Representing Puerto Rico is the ultimate ... tremendous source of pride."

Héctor Villanueva was named the series MVP and thanked Nick Acosta, the team trainer, for getting him ready to play. Villanueva (1B) was one of five Crabbers named to the series All-Star team including José "Chepito" Muñoz (2B), Edwin Alicea (LF), Dickie Thon (DH) and Mike Cook (RHP). The Dominican Republic placed three: catcher Tony Peña, third baseman Andujar Cedeño and center fielder Moisés Alou. Shortstop Cristobal Colón from Venezuela and Ernie Johnson, a Mazatlán lefty, rounded out this team.[40]

Tony Peña waited four more years before being on a Caribbean Series winner. He reiterated what Dickie Thon had said—that the most important role in these events was to represent his country with dignity and pride. Santurce's celebration was short-lived for some. Dickie Thon flew back to Houston to rejoin his wife and children. José Alvarez, who joined Santurce for their final series against San Juan, remembers a celebration in their Mazatlán hotel that night, prior to his flying home to Tampa.

"I pitched three scoreless innings in one of our losses to the Dominican Republic and another scoreless inning against Venezuela," said Alvarez. "I think we felt that we gave a couple of games away [to the Aguilas Cibaeñas]. I'm glad that we won that extra game."

1993–94 and 1994–95: San Juan Comes Back

The "new" San Juan Senators earned back-to-back league titles in 1993–94 and 1994–95. Santurce qualified for the 1993–94 round-robin event and made it to the finals against San Juan, but the Senators won the best-of-nine series. The Crabbers failed to make the playoffs in 1994–95. San Juan's "Dream Team" won six straight games in the 1995 Caribbean Series.

Frankie Thon had a unique perspective of San Juan and Santurce's fortunes these two seasons. He started the 1993–94 campaign as San Juan's GM and filled the same slot for Santurce in 1994–95. Thon did a fine job with San Juan in 1993–94, but resigned on December 15, 1993.[41] Thon's GM duties included payroll matters, solving problems pertaining to living accommodations, and making airport trips to pick up the imports.

Santurce finished fourth in 1993–94 and counted on Rubén Sierra and Leo Gómez. Juan "Igor" González joined the team later in the season. Deportivo Rivera signed with San Juan. Francisco Javier Oliveras, Wil Fraser and Mike Cook returned to the mound and performed quite well.

Francisco Javier Oliveras started for the Santurce-San Juan Metro squad against the Island team in the December 26, 1993 All-Star game. Five Santurce position players saw action—catcher Junior Ortíz, second baseman Luis López, and the outfield trio of Juan "Igor" González, Rubén Sierra and Gerald Williams. The Island team won the contest, 8–2, as Ponce's Roberto Alomar, Mayagüez's Iván Rodríguez and Arecibo's Candy Maldonado had RBI.[42]

A home run hitting contest and an Old-Timers game were held prior to the main event. José "Cheo" Cruz won the Old Timers home run event while Carlos Lezcano drove in the only run in their four-inning contest. Juan Pizarro, Juan Beníquez, Palillo Santiago and Mako Oliveras played in it.[43]

Puerto Rico's league was on much more solid footing thanks to the return of the native big leaguers. Mako Oliveras and San Juan's skipper, Luis "Torito" Meléndez, alluded to this when I conversed with them.

San Juan and Santurce posted 8–4 records in the round-robin.[44] The Senators cracked 20 homers in their 12 contests, propelled by five from Carlos Delgado, and three each by league MVP Carmelo Martínez and his cousin Edgar Martínez. Juan "Igor" González and Rubén Sierra—who had been named to the league's final All-Star team along with Santurce's Iván Calderon—cracked four homers apiece for Santurce, while Héctor Villanueva and Gerald Williams both hit three home runs.[45]

San Juan won the final series, five games to two. Home runs by Carlos Delgado and Carmelo Martínez coupled with Frank González's three-hit shutout in game seven, gave San Juan its fifth and final win.[46]

José Alberro was the only Crabber to reinforce San Juan in the Caribbean Series hosted by Venezuela, and won by the Licey Tigers for the seventh time. Alberro relieved in three games.

"It was an honor to represent Puerto Rico," said Alberro. "I reinforced the San Juan 'Dream Team' in the 1995 Caribbean Series after pitching for Arecibo that season."

The 1994–95 season was a success for the league with 729,809 tickets sold.[47] Caguas was back in the league with newly installed astro turf on their field. Juan "Igor" González and Francisco Javier Oliveras returned to Caguas, leaving a void in Santurce.

The 54-game season did not begin well for Santurce when they lost nine of their first ten games en route to their fifth place finish. Frankie Thon had warned Santurce's outfield trio of Carl Everett, Troy O'Leary and Gerald Williams that he would have to "fire them" if they didn't produce.

"Between them they were hitting about .175 and had two home runs," said Thon. "I had to do something, get some new guys in there. This is a performance league, not a development league. You have to win."[48]

That trio hit .158 prior to their release.[49] Rubén Sierra performed well in right field once he was activated while Derek Bell, Johnny Monell and Terrell Lowery were the other outfielders. Santurce used 26 position players and 19 pitchers.[50] Some who produced were Cuban shortstop Rey Ordoñez, Leo Gómez, Junior Ortíz, starter Ryan Karp and reliever Troy Percival. Héctor Villanueva hit for power. Dickie Thon cracked a few hits before retiring.

Dickie Thon drills a single, 1994–95 (courtesy of *El Nuevo Día*).

One highlight took place on November 9, 1994 when Mako Oliveras received the Pedrín Zorrilla Award/plaque from Diana Zorrilla prior to a game with Ponce.[51] This award honors former and current players, officials and managers for contributions to Puerto Rico's league and/or the majors.

"This is very touching," said Oliveras. "I am quite honored and surprised."

The longest regular season game in league history, a 25-inning one between Caguas and Mayagüez, was suspended after 16 innings on November 23, 1994, and concluded on December 10. This broke the record set by Bayamón and Santurce on December 26, 1975, when they played a 21-inning game, the longest regular season game in terms of innings played in one day.[52]

Santurce played better baseball after the All-Star break from December 24–26, 1994, but did not qualify for the round-robin. Rubén Sierra was the only Crabber to reinforce San Juan in the Caribbean Series. This "Dream Team" featured Sierra, Bernie Williams and Juan "Igor" González in the outfield; an infield of Carlos Delgado behind the plate, Carmelo Martínez at first, second baseman Roberto Alomar; shortstop Rey Sánchez; and, third baseman Carlos Baerga; and DH Edgar Martínez.

The Dream Team won all six games against Venezuela's Caracas Lions; Mexico's Hermosillo Orange Growers; and, the Azucareros del Este from the Dominican Republic. Sierra's bat came alive in game five against Caracas when he scored Puerto Rico's first run, and later hit a homer following a two-run shot by Juan "Igor" González.[53] This series was dedicated to Luis Olmo.

"It means a lot to me," said Olmo. "It's an honor which I accept with pride and appreciation on behalf of my family."[54]

1995–96 to 1998–99: The Astros Touch Base

The round-robin event was discontinued and the league went back to the standard semi-final and final series approach favored by many fans, players and officials. Bithorn Stadium had a new "carpet" for the 1996–97 season. League attendance in terms of tickets sold surpassed the one million mark for the first time in 1995–96; a new record of 1,149,870 tickets sold was set in 1996–97.[55]

José "Cheo" Cruz was hired as Santurce's manager in 1995–96. This paved the way for an informal working agreement with the Houston Astros which resulted in some Astros prospects reinforcing Santurce. Frankie Thon, the GM, was a Houston scout who facilitated the paperwork.

Santurce finished third in 1995–96 and lost to Arecibo, the eventual champions, in the semi-finals.[56] José "Cheito" Cruz, Jr. made his Santurce debut. Darryl Strawberry joined the Crabbers for a brief stint as did Dennis "Oil Can" Boyd. Leo Gómez, Orlando Merced, Melvin Nieves and Eduardo Pérez (the son of Tany Pérez) wore Santurce flannels. Shortstop Rey Ordoñez, an excellent fielder, emerged as Santurce's best hitter for average in challenging San Juan's Roberto Alomar for the hitting title.

Roberto Alomar stole the show that season with his aggressive base running, hitting and defense. His presence added an extra dimension to the San Juan-Santurce rivalry, a heated one.

San Juan signed Dwight Gooden to a contract while Santurce did likewise with Darryl Strawberry. Neither stayed for very long. The New York Yankees requested that Gooden

Top: Rey Ordoñez had two fine seasons for Santurce (courtesy of *The San Juan Star*). *Bottom:* San Juan's Roberto Alomar gets back to first as Héctor Villanueva applies the tag (courtesy of *The San Juan Star*).

leave Puerto Rico after making only three starts. Gooden had already left the island when Strawberry, who made a big league comeback with the 1995 Yankees, hit two homers in his Santurce debut against San Juan on November 18, 1995.[57] He followed this effort with two more homers at Caguas the next night![58]

"Major league teams tend to protect their pitchers more," said Frankie Thon. "The Yankees made it clear that that they want Strawberry to get as many at-bats as possible … if he wants to leave, there's nothing we can do to stop him either."

And leave he did when the Yankees did not exercise their option to sign Strawberry to a $1.8 million contract for 1996.[59] Strawberry flew back to the States. He eventually played for the 1996 Yankees.

Santurce slumped a bit after Strawberry's departure, but held on to third. A special moment for the Old-Timers took place prior to a December 20, 1995 Santurce-Mayagüez game when Cefo Conde threw out the first pitch. The 1995–96 season was dedicated to Conde,[60] a pioneer who pitched many a game against Santurce.

The Island squad won the Three Kings Day All-Star game over the Metro team. Santurce's Melvin Nieves scored the first run for the Metro squad, but Arecibo's Bernie Williams paced the Island squad to a 6–2 win.[61]

Santurce's Rey Ordóñez was leading the league in batting at the time, but went hitless in his final regular season game on January 8, 1996. Roberto Alomar clinched the batting crown against Ponce three days later.[62]

The Crabbers' best regular and post-season hurler was Bronswell Patrick, an Astros farmhand. Patrick was undefeated in the regular season and blanked Arecibo, 2–0, in game one of the semi-finals.[63] But Santurce's pitching depth was questionable after several imports had left Puerto Rico. David Nied and Dennis "Oil Can" Boyd were then signed late in the season.

Boyd started game six of the semi-final series and was hit hard in the first inning. Santurce came back to make it a close game through seven innings before Arecibo broke it wide open with eight runs in the eighth and three more in the ninth to win it, 16–4.[64]

Leo Gómez and Caguas' Iván "Pudge" Rodríguez were among those who reinforced Arecibo in the Caribbean Series hosted by Santo Domingo. Gómez was the hitting star with his series-leading three homers and nine RBI, and finished third with a .458 batting mark.[68] Mexico's Culiacán Tomato Growers won the series over the favored Aguilas Cibaeñas from the host country and Arecibo. Venezuela's Magallanes Navigators also fielded a strong team.

Santurce's 1996–97 cast had a Houston flavor with manager Matt Galante, an Astros coach; pitching coach Vern Ruhle, the Astros 1996 roving minor league pitching instructor; and, prospects Dennis Colón, Mike Grzanich, Chris Holt, Brian Hunter, Russ Johnson, James Mouton and Bronswell Patrick. José Cruz, Jr., Leo Gómez and Eduardo Pérez returned. Santurce tied Mayagüez for first place, but lost to San Juan in the semi-finals.

Poto Paniagua emphasized that the Santurce-Houston link was not a formal agreement. Paniagua:

"We have their Caribbean scout [Frankie Thon] and can bring in a pitching coach — Vern Ruhle — to work with Terín Pizarro, and are able to choose their prospects first. But that is a courtship and not a marriage, OK, because you have to be very careful with these agreements."

Paniagua emphasized that the big league team should not insist that he sign imports who played positions that were already capably filled by local talent. He reiterated that

Darryl Strawberry, 1995–96 (courtesy of *The San Juan Star*).

Dennis "Oil Can" Boyd, 1995–96 semi-finals (courtesy of *The San Juan Star*).

in winter ball it is crucial to build a team around the native players and it serves no purpose to bring in a "name player" if he is not needed.

"Neither the Dodgers nor the Astros contributed one cent to our operation," said Paniagua. "That does not interest me ... prefer to keep our organization's autonomy and not receive orders from another entity. It's hard enough dealing with the realities of organized baseball...."

Those realities included pitchers Chris Holt and Bronswell Patrick going home early. Santurce signed Mike Grzanich and Tom Martin of the Astros organization, and Brian Maxcy, formerly with Detroit.

Grzanich spent the 1996 minor league season with the AA Jackson Generals when Vern Ruhle asked him if he might be interested in winter ball. Grzanich was interested, provided there was a roster spot open.

"It came about at the end of the Arizona Fall League," said Grzanich. "They asked me if I wanted to come down and join Santurce and I said, sure, and talked to Frankie [Thon] ... he set up a place for me to live, gave us an idea of who to talk to, things like that. It was a real easy transition... Isla Verde was beautiful. A bunch of the guys wanted to go home around Christmas time, and Houston was the first team asked if they wanted to bring any more players over."

Grzanich's first start came against San Juan in late December 1996. He also started a semi-final series game versus the Senators when Roberto Alomar, Carlos Baerga and Juan "Igor" González were in their line-up.

"It was real exciting for me and I was pretty nervous in my first outing and hadn't pitched against talent like that," said Grzanich. "But I enjoyed it and enjoyed the enthusiasm. The crowds were magnificent. Whenever anything happened, it was just a roar through the crowd. When they scored runs, their fans would chant at our fans ... a huge rivalry."

Brian Maxcy found out through his agent that Santurce needed pitching help. The agent contacted Frankie Thon and the arrangements were made. Maxcy had been a teammate of Santurce's Melvin Nieves with Detroit. His first Santurce win came against Mayagüez on December 20, 1996, in a 13–3 slugfest. A Friday night crowd of 10,722 saw José Cruz, Jr. drive in seven runs with a bases-loaded double and a grand slam.[66]

"It was a real pleasure to play with Cruz, Jr.," said Maxcy. "He plays hard."

José Cruz, Jr. stole two bases and scored the only run for the Metro All-Stars in the Three Kings Day All-Star game. Russ Johnson's double drove in Cruz, but the Island squad — Arecibo, Mayagüez and Ponce — won their fifth straight contest, 7–1.[67]

Santurce was no match for San Juan in the semi-finals. The Senators outscored the Crabbers, 39–8, in their four-game sweep. Average attendance was about 10,000 per game.[68]

The 1997–98 season was dedicated to the memory of Roberto Clemente and the number 21 became permanently retired for all six ballclubs.[69] A 62-game schedule was set with Santurce playing Caguas and San Juan 16 times. The Crabbers, who finished last, only played 10 games apiece against Arecibo, Mayagüez and Ponce. Pete Mackanin, a coach with the Montreal Expos, managed Santurce, but was replaced by GM Frankie Thon in December 1997. Houston prospect Scott Elarton pitched the third no-hitter in team history. Rubén Sierra was Santurce's best hitter. He worked hard in the pre-season.

November 19, 1997 was the 504th anniversary of Puerto Rico's "discovery" by Christopher Columbus on his second voyage to the New World. My wife and I enjoyed a San Juan-Santurce game that afternoon along with another 11,421 fans at Bithorn Stadium.

Frankie Thon and Poto Paniagua shared some time with me prior to that 3 p.m. holiday game. Thon noted that the crop of Houston prospects was not as plentiful as the 1996–97 one. Two catchers — Ramón Castro and Pedro López — were Houston prospects

Rubén Sierra prior to the 1997–98 season (courtesy of *The San Juan Star*).

from Puerto Rico on Santurce's roster. Their Astros pitching prospects included Scott Elarton and Trever Miller.

Thon told me that the league salary limit for big leaguers was $5,000 per month. League rookies were paid $900 per month while second year native players could earn about $1,250 monthly, based on the three-year labor agreement in place. Imports could be reimbursed for certain expenses as long as their combined salary and expenses did not exceed $5,000.

An import might phone Frankie Thon at midnight or at 1 a.m. to solve a problem. There might be times when Thon's wife assisted him in areas pertaining to players' apartments and living arrangements. Brian Maxcy was one Santurce import whom she assisted.

The Santurce Crabbers officially retire #21, the number worn by Roberto Clemente for Santurce in the mid–1950s, in a ceremony at Hiram Bithorn Stadium on October 31, 1997. *L to R:* Rubén Sierra — the last Crabber to wear #21, Vera Clemente — Roberto Clemente's widow, and Luis Roberto Clemente — one of the Clemente's three sons (courtesy of Yuyo Ruíz and included in his 1998 book — *The Last Hours of Roberto Clemente*).

Brian Maxcy chatted with me outside the Santurce clubhouse. He had shoulder surgery a few months earlier and was looking forward to some good outings with the hopes of getting noticed by big league scouts. Maxcy, a native of Amory, Mississippi, lived in Isla Verde and drove to the games in his rental car.

"It's totally different than small town Mississippi," said Maxcy. "I like to drive to the away games in Ponce and Mayagüez by myself, put my headphones on, and listen to a couple of CD's."

Scott Elarton won his first game that afternoon in defeating San Juan, 8–1. Outfielders Raúl Ibañez and Rubén Sierra were the big guns. Sierra looked fit and determined. The younger Ibañez was a Seattle Mariner farmhand. Santurce's Chris Stynes, a Cincinnati prospect, hustled.

There must have been over 50 business signs adorning Bithorn's outfield fence from banks to distilled spirits to high tech companies. Banco Popular de Puerto Rico — the island's top local bank in terms of assets — was prominently displayed on the Santurce uniforms.

Vern Ruhle, who became Houston's pitching coach in 1997, spoke with me prior to a Santurce-Caguas game the next evening at Bithorn. He told me the Santurce-Houston link had paid dividends for Chris Holt and Billy Wagner.

"It turned out to be a very successful venture as many of the players had some of their better years in the major leagues," said Ruhle. "We think it has a lot of bearing in their future and is a launching pad for many players to get into the major leagues."

Ruhle used Scott Elarton to illustrate another point. Elarton had pitched well in Puerto Rico during the 1997–98 season, and Ruhle could stand up for him in spring training if a decision was to be made.

"I can say that I had him in Puerto Rico and he performed in such-and-such a way against some major league hitters ... as opposed to say that all he's ever faced are AA and AAA guys," said Ruhle. "But now he has some quotation marks as to how he's been able to face major league hitters; there's a settling thing — a feeling of confidence that comes from being able to say I'm not out of my environment and know what I'm able to do."

Elarton pitched a no-hitter against Caguas on December 14, 1997, in his final Santurce start. That gem came in game one of a twin bill and preceded Brian Maxcy's win in the nightcap.[70] Elarton threw 110 pitches, and allowed two walks — one to Carmelo Martínez in the second, and the other to Willie Greene in the fourth.[71] There was not much else to cheer about as Santurce finished last while San Juan won the regular season crown under Mako Oliveras. Poto Paniagua replaced skipper Pete Mackanin with Frankie Thon, and the Crabbers played better baseball for a spell. Thon had told me that "this is a league to win ballgames and not develop players" for the GM and manager.

Rubén Sierra took the winner, Caguas' Carmelo Martínez, to the wire in the pre-game home run hitting contest prior to the January 13, 1998 league All-Star game. The contest was played after the regular season due to a rainout. Carmelo Martínez then went 3 for 3 with a homer and three RBI in the Metro's 13–3 win over the Island All-Stars.[72] Martínez was the league's only remaining active player who had been signed by Pedrín Zorrilla. Pedrín had signed Carmelo Martínez for the Chicago Cubs.

Mayagüez defeated San Juan in the league finals to win their seventh league title in the past 15 seasons.[73] The Mayagüez franchise was in good shape on-and-off the field, but San Juan was not.

The big news in February 1998 was San Juan's future move to Carolina, the municipality where Roberto Clemente was born and raised. San Juan had not done well at the box office in 1997–98 in averaging about 1,000 fans per home game.[74] Five of their big leaguers — Roberto Alomar, Carlos Baerga, Juan "Igor" González, Edgar Martínez and Bernie Williams — did not play in 1997–98. The team's ownership was unhappy with the municipality of San Juan for not providing a special parking area for season ticket holders and did not like the fact that city workers were painting the inside of Bithorn Stadium during the season and leaving materials and equipment in various sections.[75]

A 15-year agreement was signed with Carolina to play in an $18 million stadium with a seating capacity of 16,000, starting in late 1999.[76] The stadium was named after Roberto Clemente, with the new team known as the Carolina Giants. Artificial turf would be installed as well as parking for 3,500 cars.[77]

The City Championship Series ended in January 1999, when San Juan completed its final season at Bithorn, before moving to Carolina. Luis Maldonado, an executive with George Washington University Hospital in Washington, D.C., told me that the San Juan-Santurce rivalry and the fact they played in the same stadium helped keep the winter league going and the fans coming to those games season after season.

"My father always makes it a point to tell me how San Juan is doing and never misses an opportunity to rub it in that San Juan is doing better, or that they beat Santurce," said Maldonado. "He never calls me to tell me that Santurce is doing well ... when I go to the island, I make sure to look at the boxscores and to look at players who are on the roster that year. I try to go to games, but it is difficult ...."

Luis Maldonado's face lit up when we discussed Santurce and Puerto Rico's Winter League in the 1990s after having lunch near his D.C. office. His comments concerning the San Juan-Santurce rivalry were appropriate in light of San Juan's move to Carolina. One can only wonder if his father, Dr. Norman Maldonado, and other San Juan fans will follow the Carolina Giants with the same passion that they displayed for their beloved Senators.

10. Thanks for the Memories

I look back at it and they are great memories. A no-hitter doesn't happen very often.
— Scott Elarton, former Santurce pitcher.

During a four-week period from May 9 to June 6, 1998, I touched base with a number of former and current Santurce players, managers and coaches in New Orleans, Louisiana, and Jackson, Mississippi, as well as Houston and Arlington, Texas. These "joyrides" and trips enabled me to finalize the research for this book and more importantly, put the Santurce franchise in its proper perspective as the Puerto Rico Winter League's best known ballclub.

Tradewinds Near New Orleans

My wife and I made the two hour and forty minute drive from Florence, Mississippi, to the "Shrine on Airline" a.k.a. Zephyr Field just outside of New Orleans in Metairie, Louisiana. Our May 9, 1998 trip was a scenic one down the "Causeway" going toward New Orleans. The busy Airline Highway led to Zephyr Field, home of Houston's AAA franchise, the New Orleans Zephyrs.

Scott Elarton, one of the tallest pitchers to ever wear the Santurce uniform at nearly 6'8", conversed with me in a cubicle of the Zephyrs administrative offices. Elarton would start the evening's game against the Fresno Grizzlies, but alerted me that he was not superstitious in terms of conversing prior to a start. He has fond memories of his December 14, 1997 no-hitter against Caguas. Elarton:

> About the fifth or sixth inning, I knew I had a no-hitter going. At that time, I never thought it would happen ... eight of the [Caguas] guys were in the big leagues. By the eighth inning, nobody was talking about it — they were superstitious, not wanting to jinx it. After the eighth, there was a buzz around the whole stadium. The pressure starts building ... as soon as I got out of the dugout, the fans stood up and

were clapping. With every strike the crowd went nuts. The first hitter in the ninth hit a ball to the warning track, but it was caught. Then I struck out the next two hitters to end the game and to end my season down there. I look back at it and they are great memories. A no-hitter doesn't happen very often.

Elarton's six-week contract with Santurce precluded him from pitching any more games. His starts were monitored by pitch counts except for the no-hitter where he threw 110 pitches. Elarton had pitched a combined 187 innings between the AA Jackson Generals and the AAA Zephyrs in 1997.[1] He noticed subtle differences between the level of play in Puerto Rico and AA/AAA. There was no doubt that AAA hitters had more experience than AA hitters. But most Puerto Rico Winter League hitters had seen everything that could happen.

"Going down there [Puerto Rico] ... to those hitters, I didn't have anything special," said Elarton. "They had seen guys throw curve balls, change-ups and fastballs. That aspect of the competition was what I'd notice most. It wasn't like the Instructional League or the Arizona Fall League in terms of development of talent. If guys aren't getting the job done, they bring in new players ... very competitive."

Living in Puerto Rico was an adjustment for Elarton, who grew up in Lamar, Colorado, or as he put it — "in the middle of nowhere." Puerto Rico's crowded highways at all times of day threw him for a loop, but he enjoyed the whole experience. Elarton told me that the biggest plus of his Santurce stint was boosting his confidence in terms of getting big league hitters out.

"The first couple of times I faced Caguas, I was kind of scared — 'Pudge' Rodríguez, Carmelo Martínez, Felipe Crespo — just a real tough line-up. Once I did go out and have success against that team, it really boosted my confidence that I could go to the big leagues and have some success."

That evening was the second time in six months that I had seen Elarton pitch, since I saw him defeat San Juan on November 19, 1997. Other parallels and contrasts were the tradewinds that made for a pleasant experience at Zephyr Field, as they did at Hiram Bithorn Stadium, plus Boudreaux — the Zephyrs mascot — and a Santurce cheerleader.

Fans at Zephyr Field enjoy refreshing evening tradewinds — at least in May — courtesy of Lake Ponchartrain, just as Santurce fans are able to stay cooler thanks to Atlantic Ocean tradewinds. But there is a huge difference between a cute mascot and a massive, 400-pound cheerleader. I met Santurce's cheerleader, Víctor Martínez Andrades, who also sold lottery tickets prior to the ballgame. Víctor put forth much effort in sliding on the top of the dugout and leading the cheers.

One Zephyr who worked hard in Puerto Rico was infielder Russ Johnson. I was familiar with his hustle and talent, having seen him play for the Jackson Generals in the summer of 1996. Johnson hit .310 for the Generals[2] before playing for Santurce in 1996–97.

"Houston told me that they wanted me to play winter ball with Santurce," said Johnson. "So I went over there and played and it was a great experience for me. You get a lot of the big name guys that play there and then you got your AAA prospects that are real talented. It's in-between the big leagues and AAA."

Johnson was Roberto Alomar's double play partner for the Metro team in the league All-Star game, and recalled several other teammates such as Juan González and Quinton McCracken. He was tired by season's end, and that was one reason why he did not return the following winter.

"I played almost every day for 30 days in spring training after winter ball," said

Santurce's cheerleader, 1997–98 (courtesy of Donna T. Van Hyning).

Johnson. "The 140 minor league games ... instructional ball for a month, winter ball for three months, home for two weeks, and then into spring training. It was wearing down on me mentally and physically."

Two Catchers from Vega Baja in Jackson

Vega Baja, Puerto Rico, is the hometown of Guigo Otero Suro, Juan "Igor" González and Iván "Pudge" Rodríguez. Pedro López and Ramón Castro can be added to that list. I conversed with López and Castro at Smith-Wills Stadium in Jackson, Mississippi, on May 15, 1998.

Pedro López had shared Santurce's catching duties with Ramón Castro in 1997–98, but was not considered a prospect due to his 10 years in minor league baseball. He had originally been signed by the San Diego Padres in 1988, prior to stints in the Milwaukee Brewers and Houston systems. His second season with Santurce —1996–97— featured the influx of Houston prospects including Russ Johnson and pitchers Chris Holt, Bronswell Patrick, Mark Small, among others.

"That was a plus ... they knew each other," said López. "One of the challenges in winter ball is that you have a fairly short season with ballplayers from different organizations. It can take time for things to jell. But Frankie Thon put together a good group

José "Cheito" Cruz, Jr., in action for the 1995–96 Crabbers (courtesy of *The San Juan Star*).

of imports, and that made it easier for us, the native players, to have them as teammates. It benefited all of us since we finished the regular season in first place."

López told me that Vega Baja has good baseball leagues from the toddlers to Little League to the Roberto Clemente League. Perhaps López's biggest legacy will be his positive attitude and willingness to help others in his hometown and fellow players in the states, including Ramón Castro.

An 18-year-old Ramón Castro was a number one pick of the Astros in the 1994 draft. Castro noted that he and Scott Elarton signed with Houston in 1994 and were Gulf Coast Rookie League teammates.

"We got along and he liked my catching style," said Castro. "We work well together."

Castro later caught Elarton's no-hitter for Santurce. He told me that Elarton relied on his fastball the first five innings, before throwing more curves and change-ups from the sixth inning on. Castro benefited from being Pudge Rodríguez's back-up with Caguas in 1995–96, prior to joining Santurce in 1997–98. He made the most of his opportunity in 1997–98.

My conversations with Pedro López and Ramón Castro brought back some memories of Guigo Otero Suro, who had worked so hard on behalf of the Puerto Rico Winter League. Guigo would be proud of these two catchers from Vega Baja.

The Eighth Wonder of the World

Houston's Astrodome, capacity 54,370, is quite a contrast to Smith-Wills Stadium, capacity 5,200.[3] I found myself on the Astrodome's artificial surface on Saturday, May 16, 1998, after a road trip. The 72 degree "room temperature" inside the Astrodome was 20 degrees cooler than it was outside. It was the first time I had been inside a domed baseball stadium.

I saw Vern Ruhle, Houston's pitching coach, who was working with several Astros pitchers. Another familiar face appeared on the scene, and it was Houston's first base coach, José "Cheo" Cruz, Sr., who had managed the 1995–96 Crabbers.

Cruz told me that Orlando Merced, Darryl Strawberry and Héctor Villanueva were the big guns for that Santurce team and Strawberry's early departure hurt the club's offense. Cruz' son, José "Cheito" Cruz, Jr., played for him that winter despite the fact that Caguas had drafted Cruz, Jr. Caguas and Santurce made a deal which allowed Cruz, Jr. to begin his Puerto Rico career with Santurce.

"Cheito wanted to play for me," said Cruz, Sr. "I was very pleased because it was his first season in Puerto Rico ... gave him a chance to play, and then he did a great job the following season."

Houston's hitting coach, Tom McCraw, was perched on the back of the home dugout when I conversed with him a few minutes later. The Astrodome dugouts do not have a top and it felt strange sitting in a dugout without a "roof." McCraw told me that if one went to Puerto Rico and did well in the Winter League, then he had a real good chance of sticking in the big leagues.

McCraw, a native of Malvern, Arkansas, had played for Caguas in 1962–63 prior to beginning his 13-year big league playing career with the 1963 Chicago White Sox. He later wore the San Juan uniform as a teammate of Roberto Clemente.

"Clemente was a great, great ballplayer and a greater human being," said McCraw.

"He respected the game, carried himself well … one of the greatest players to ever play the game…."

One of McCraw's best friends with the Chicago White Sox between 1963 and 1966 was Juan Pizarro. McCraw had faced Pizarro, Sam McDowell and other Santurce pitchers during the 1962–63 regular season and semi-final series.

"Once you met a player, played with him or against him in Puerto Rico, and had a drink or dinner with him, you could establish friendships in an atmosphere that is a little more relaxed," said McCraw. "Some of the guys I played with/against in Puerto Rico have been my friends all through and probably until the day I die. It's really special."

McCraw has a special fondness for Juan Pizarro since Pizarro and White Sox outfielder Floyd Robinson — a fellow Arkansan — let him stay with them in Chicago when he first came up as a rookie.

"Terín just took me under his wing and told me where to go and where not to go in Chicago, which is very important," said Robinson. "Terín is a special friend … will always be a special friend. I went to Puerto Rico in 1997 and saw him for the first time in a long time and it was great — just like I saw him yesterday. That was the kind of friendship we had. And he was an outstanding pitcher with a lot of nerve and a lot of courage."

Jack Howell was playing catch with his 13-year-old son when I finished conversing with McCraw. Howell struggled a bit as a rookie with the 1985 California Angels before joining Santurce for the 1985–86 season. His wife and his baby son accompanied him to Puerto Rico.

"That's the first time when you really go away to play against guys who have some time in the big leagues or were prospective players becoming major league ballplayers," said Howell. "It's the first time when you really had a chance, in somewhat of a more relaxed atmosphere — not the pressure of your [stateside] team — but the pressure of just playing in Winter League baseball, to really see how you compare with the real good talents. So I think it's very important. I had some success and played with some big league players and I think that gave me a boost — because I did really well there — that I could play in the big leagues."

Trever Miller then conversed with me in the Houston dugout. Miller had pitched for Santurce in 1997–98 after a AAA season at New Orleans. He had been traded to the Astros by the Detroit Tigers prior to the 1997 season in a deal which brought Brad Ausmus, José Lima, C.J. Nitkowski and Daryle Ward to Houston.[4]

I had first noticed Miller warming up with his fellow Houston pitchers at about 4 p.m. that afternoon. Mike Hampton — who pitched for San Juan in 1993–94 — and several other hurlers including ex-Crabbers Mike Grzanich and Billy Wagner, and José Lima — a native of the Dominican Republic — knew who the "Cangrejeros" were.

Trever Miller got to Puerto Rico when Pete Mackanin was on the verge of being let go as Santurce's manager. Frankie Thon was Miller's manager with Santurce.

"We weren't winning games and there was a lot of pressure on him," said Miller. "He took it upon himself to take the managing job instead of putting the pressure or blame on someone else, so I respect him for that … I like Frankie, he's a stand-up guy."

Miller took the team bus on the Puerto Rico trips to Mayagüez and Ponce. Miller's wife and son were in Puerto Rico, and his wife, who was pregnant at the time, could use the rental car in case of an emergency. He knew some Spanish, so that made the overall experience more enjoyable.

Miller's month on Santurce's active roster proved fruitful since his arm stayed strong and he went into spring training very sharp. Vern Ruhle did a great job with Miller in terms of mechanics.

"The reason I didn't make the club in 1997 out of spring training was the Astros didn't know who I was," said Miller. "They never really had seen me throw — so they sent me to AAA. Vern Ruhle wasn't there and Larry Dierker wasn't in AAA, obviously, so they hadn't seen me throw. By going to Puerto Rico with Vern Ruhle being the pitching coach ... he got to see me throw nearly 30 innings, and get an idea on what I could do. And then going into spring training, they knew what I could do, so I was able to make the Houston team."

Trever Miller went to the outfield to shag flies and I chatted with Darrell Simon, an Astros Media Relations official, before conversing with outfielder Derek Bell, who had played against Santurce in the 1991 Caribbean Series, and for the Crabbers in 1994–95.

"We ran into a buzz saw with that Dominican [Licey] team in the 1991 Caribbean Series," said Bell, who was wintering in Venezuela at that time. "I was on the verge of making it to the big leagues and I got a chance to play against guys like Juan Guzmán who I later played with in Toronto, Henry Rodríguez and Sammy Sosa. When I played for Santurce, we played against Iván Rodríguez, Roberto Alomar and Bernie Williams. It was a great experience playing against those guys ... had to concentrate on being a good hitter if I wanted to stay there cause if you didn't hit, you were gone."

Bell was injured during the 1994 big league strike season, and needed some at-bats to get back in playing shape. He found the San Juan-Santurce rivalry exciting and fun with the crowd always in the game. San Juan's Roberto Alomar had been his Toronto teammate and that made the San Juan-Santurce games even more fun.

Houston's Assistant GM, Tim Purpura, was next. Tim loves Puerto Rico and its ballparks. He called it a great environment since a lot of the fields are turf fields, just like the Astrodome.

"It's like winter ball and it's not like winter ball 'cause you're in the U.S.," said Purpura. "It's a great set-up ... the biggest impetus was when Matt Galante went down there as the Santurce manager. That's when we really started to look seriously at it ... before that, with Frankie Thon — a very talented guy covering Puerto Rico and South Florida — and the relations we had with him being one of our scouts, it's a real fertile area to send players to."

Houston also has close ties with the Magallanes Navigators in Venezuela. According to Tim Purpura, a lot of behind-the-scenes work goes into sending a prospect to winter ball. Tim stated that the player has to be interested and willing to play for Santurce. Two examples might be Lance Berkman, who played with the Jackson Generals in 1998; and, Daryle Ward, on the New Orleans Zephyrs roster most of that season and with Houston for a portion of it. Tim Purpura:

> What we'll do with both Lance and Daryle is to take a look at their number of at-bats and physically, how are they, have they had any injuries? Have they had the time that we want them to have — both of them are playing left field — to see if it would be advantageous for them to go down there? If all those factors are in place, then we go to the player and say: 'This is something we would really want you to do. Are you interested in going for the whole season? If not, for a half?' So I think, those are questions that probably won't come until early August, when we start talking about winter ball and that type of thing. But they are certainly two guys that I can see interest being expressed by the Santurce club to come down there....

Innings pitched are closely monitored by the big league organization in terms of whether or not to send a pitcher down to winter ball. Scott Elarton and Trever Miller pitched 53 and 26 innings, respectively, for Santurce in 1997–98, following the 1997 minor league season.[5] Elarton pitched 240 innings between AA/AAA and winter ball; Miller threw 193 combined AAA/winter ball frames.[6]

"That's why we wait until late August to see how the inning total is," said Purpura. "And our theory is to get 175–200 innings pitched in the course of a regular season — we look at how many they had in spring training and then we project how many would be a minimum for them to pitch in the winter. We try to keep them 225–250 total for the year ... depends on the guy, his medical history, does he have shoulder/elbow problems ... that type of thing. That's what goes into those decisions." Purpura further states:

> Our Venezuelan connection is very strong. We have a lot of players that we signed from Venezuela and bring to the States. This year [1998–99], the manager of Magallanes will be Alfredo Pedrique, our AAA coach. César Cedeño — who works for us — is going to be a coach, too. We really have got our hands in a couple of different pots which is great, because you get more guys winter ball jobs, and it's not just the job, it's the opportunity for them to play and get the extra innings and the extra at-bats that you really need to progress and get over the hump. The winter ball experience, whether it's in Puerto Rico, Venezuela, the Dominican, or the Arizona Fall League or the Hawaii Winter League, is a great opportunity for players to get those extra at-bats, those extra innings, to perfect themselves.

Tim Purpura recalled a trip to Puerto Rico during the 1997–98 season. He was in the Condado section of Santurce one evening and there was a traffic jam. A sign then appeared out of nowhere — Where are you, Matt Galante?

Matt Galante sat next to me in the Houston dugout at 5:40 p.m. when batting practice ended. He enjoyed his 1996–97 managing stint with Santurce, and planned to return until he came up with a neck problem which could have required surgery. Galante didn't want to start the 1997–98 season as a manager and leave, so opted for neck therapy. His neck improved, but he was missed by Santurce fans.

The 1996–97 Crabbers managed by Galante were the talk of the league with the Houston prospects who produced. Matt Galante:

> We had Chris Holt trying to make the jump from AAA to the big leagues ... he really helped the ballclub and that got him a jump into the big leagues last year [1997]. Billy Wagner worked on his curve ball a lot more, slider a lot more, so when he came into the big leagues, he was a more effective closer. It certainly helped him a tremendous amount. We had James Mouton and Brian Hunter in center field, and Russ Johnson — who we wanted to get a good look at shortstop. He played well ... moved him to third base for the long term. We came in first place, but Leo Gómez went to Japan to play; James Mouton broke his wrist. Two of our starters had tired arms and couldn't pitch. So, unfortunately, we went into the San Juan semi-final series a little short-handed. We played them very well during the season ... wish we had the opportunity to play them with the full squad.

Galante, a New Yorker, found that Puerto Rico's Winter League had better hitting than AAA ball. The level of pitching in Puerto Rico was not up to par with the hitting. He had seen what San Juan's Roberto Alomar, Juan González and company had done to his depleted pitching staff in the semi-finals. Galante was walking in the Plaza Las Americas Mall across the avenue from Bithorn Stadium when fans stopped to chat with him.

Santurce's fans could relate to the enthusiastic Galante, who is quite expressive when he speaks.

"They understood what was going on…that we didn't have our full team," said Galante. "They know the game well and they let you know if things were going right and you know what, that's not too bad…they have their eye on the game."

Billy Wagner was one of those missing arms in Santurce's post-season. Wagner was done for the day in terms of stretching, taking some cuts and shagging flies in the Astrodome. He is low-key and soft-spoken, but is one of the hardest throwing big league relievers of the late 1990s. Wagner is a former Jackson General, circa 1995, who pitched for the AAA Tucson Toros in 1996, before making his big league debut for the Astros that summer.[7]

He signed a six-week contract with Santurce for 1996–97, and got extra work on his pitches. Wagner told me that it paid off in terms of getting a few starts and then focusing on his bullpen work. Facing hitters such as Roberto Alomar and Carlos Baerga helped Wagner in terms of getting big league hitters out. The food was great as was the hospitality. Living arrangements at Isla Verde's Coral Beach Condominium were fine, and he made the adjustment to the heavy traffic.

My final Astrodome conversation took place with Moisés Alou, a native of the Dominican Republic, who has participated in several Caribbean Series events, including the 1993 one in Mazatlán, Mexico, won by Santurce. Alou recalls the tie-breaker:

"José Lima started that game for us. He had pitched two innings in the earlier game [game six] against Santurce. I don't think that was the best move by our manager; perhaps our other starters were unavailable … if he started another pitcher, we would have had a better chance."

Moisés Alou had cracked three hits in the tie-breaker for the Aguilas Cibaeñas, including a two-run homer off Santurce starter Francisco Javier Oliveras, but Santurce rallied en route to their 9–5 win.[8] The Caribbean Series and representing the Dominican Republic is a source of pride for Moisés Alou, the son of Felipe Alou. Moisés Alou: "When we get together, we usually talk baseball and fishing. He talks about his seasons with the Escogido Lions … and would like to see me play with that club some day. I think winter ball is great for the position players who are on their way up to the majors or have been in the big leagues for one or two seasons. But pitchers are another matter. This year we have Ramón García from Venezuela and José Cabrera of the Dominican Republic who were supposed to contribute. They were injured in winter ball and are unable to pitch right now…. A pitcher who has a big league job could pitch a month, but not the whole winter season … may end up with career-threatening injuries."

The Houston-Atlanta game that evening had electricity due to an Astrodome record regular season paid attendance figure of 51,526. That total surpassed the 50,908 that watched Sandy Koufax and the Los Angeles Dodgers beat the Astros, 5–2, on June 22, 1966.[9] I enjoyed the pitching duel between Houston's Shane Reynolds and Atlanta's Greg Maddux and seeing the crowd erupt after Craig Biggio's game-winning homer in the bottom of the ninth. It seemed fitting that Houston played Atlanta due to the connection between them and the Santurce franchise during the 1990s.

There were other Santurce connections in the news in the next five weeks. Baseball history was made on May 17, 1998, when David Wells of the New York Yankees hurled a perfect game against Minnesota.[10] Jorge Posada, used by Santurce as a DH in the 1997–98 season, caught that gem while Wells' mound opponent, LaTroy Hawkins, had pitched for

Santurce in 1997–98. Rubén Sierra was released by the Chicago White Sox in May 1998[11] before signing a contract with the New York Mets organization in June. Lee Smith, the all-time big league saves leader, was signed by Houston to a minor league contract and assigned to New Orleans.[12]

Scott Elarton made his big league debut for Houston on June 20, 1998.[13]

The Ballpark in Arlington

One more trip was in store. I was in Fort Worth, Texas, on a business trip, from June 4–11, 1998, and made it to The Ballpark in Arlington on June 6, to attend a San Diego Padres-Texas Rangers game. The taxi got me to the stadium at 2 p.m. and I walked over the commemorative spots outside the ballpark depicting honors earned by Texas players and managers between 1972 and 1997. Juan Beníquez had his name engraved for the 1977 Gold Glove he earned as a Texas Ranger.

The Ballpark in Arlington is a 49,166-seat open-air ballpark, which opened for play on April 1, 1994.[14] It is part of a 1.4 million square foot complex including a baseball museum, a four-story office building, and a 12-acre lake. The field and weather were perfect on that Saturday afternoon.

James Heath, a Texas Rangers employee, gave me the credential at 3 p.m. and I made my way to the playing field. Tony Gwynn and several other San Diego Padres were getting ready to take "early" batting practice. I walked up to Gwynn and asked if we could converse later that afternoon about his two seasons with Bayamón/San Juan and the rivalry with Santurce. Gwynn nodded his head affirmatively. It was quite a thrill to see Gwynn, an eight-time National League batting champion at the time, take some swings.

Shortly before 4 p.m. I saw Eddie Napoleon, Texas' first base coach seated in the Texas dugout. Napoleon's minor league playing career began at Dothan, Alabama, in 1956, and ended at Gastonia, North Carolina in 1970.[15]

We talked about winter ball for a few minutes, including Napoleon's seasons with the Chesterfield and Marlboro Smokers in Panama. Napoleon brought up the final play of the 1956–57 season when a bad call at first base cost Chesterfield a win against the Carta Vieja Yankees, and a chance to tie the Cerveza Balboa Brewers for first place.

"That [bad] call cost us a chance for the 1957 Caribbean Series in Cuba," said Napoleon. "But winter ball was a lot of fun … Humberto Robinson pitched for us back then; Héctor López played for Cerveza Balboa."

Napoleon later played in the Caribbean and InterAmerican Series. He and Héctor López were two of Marlboro's best hitters in 1961–62, the season they qualified for the 1962 InterAmerican Series at Escobar Stadium. I felt a special bond with Napoleon because he left Baltimore when he was two weeks old for Panama's Canal Zone in 1937, and had graduated from high school there.[16] My family moved to Puerto Rico on a cargo ship leaving Baltimore in 1956 when I was two years old, and I graduated from high school there.

The Texas Rangers clubhouse was comfortable and neat. Roberto Kelly, who is a native of Panama City, Panama, was the first player I saw. He had just been activated after a stint on the disabled list. Mark McLemore, the Texas second baseman, took a look at the Texas line-up posted in one corner and broke into a smile when he saw Kelly's name as the leadoff hitter followed by him.

McLemore had a better season with Mayagüez in 1986–87 than with Santurce in 1985–86. He found Mayagüez to be "nice and laid back," as contrasted with the busier San Juan area. Dorado Beach was where he lived when playing for Santurce. Chuck Finley was his Mayagüez roommate, and they lived near the Mayagüez ballpark. Bobby Bonilla was another Mayagüez teammate while Rubén Sierra, Juan Beníquez and Devon White were on his Santurce club.

"It gave me more experience playing with some guys who were prospects ... a lot of Puerto Ricans with big league experience," said McLemore. "Those guys helped out a lot, too."

Santurce-born Luis Alicea recalled that San Juan had traded him to Santurce toward the end of his winterball career, but an injury precluded him from wearing the Santurce uniform.

"My grandfather always talked about Satchel Paige being the best pitcher in Puerto Rico's league," said Alicea. "I played for Arecibo and San Juan, but never did get to play with Santurce."

I said hello to Juan González and Iván "Pudge" Rodríguez in the Texas clubhouse before going to the other clubhouse. Both were in excellent physical condition and having great seasons.

Joe Macko, the visiting clubhouse manager, had a storied minor league career, including the 1953 Texas League season when he played against Willard Brown and Buster Clarkson.

"They were outstanding players...those guys could run, they could field, and I mean, they could hit," said Macko. "We hated to see both those guys come up ... they had a great following of fans in Dallas to watch those guys play — both players were very exciting."

Tony Gwynn conversed with me in the visiting team's dugout some 20 minutes later. What most impressed me about Gwynn was his enthusiasm. He vividly remembered the 1982–83 and 1983–84 Puerto Rico Winter League seasons. Tony Gwynn:

> When I started, we played at the same park, Loubriel Stadium. Both teams played there and the next year we played at Bithorn and they played at the 'old place' [Loubriel]. And it was like the Yankees-Red Sox kind of thing. It seemed like the more established guys played for Santurce and the younger guys played for Bayamón and San Juan. I had fun and liked it because it was always the biggest crowd of the year whenever those two teams got together and they were usually some interesting games. When I was at Bayamón, I got to play against Luis Tiant, Ed Figueroa ... guys that I had watched growing up...had a ball down there and learned a lot about the game going down there. Those were two of the best off-seasons that I have ever had.

I brought up Dickie Thon's name since he had been my favorite league player between the late 1970s and mid–1980s and was Gwynn's teammate in 1982–83 and 1983–84. Gwynn:

> Dickie Thon and Orlando Isales were two guys that really taught me what it was like to play ball in Puerto Rico because as an 'American guy,' I think the native players sometimes felt like you just came over there to work on your game — you didn't take it seriously. Dickie and Orlando sat me down one day and were telling me how much pride people take in the game when Santurce and Bayamón get together. It's more than just a game; it's more like a Civil War type of thing. So they really helped me a lot. And like I said, when I went to winter ball, I didn't just go down there to work on my game. I went down there to try to get better and to help my team win.

Luis Tiant, ex–Boston Red Sox hurler, 1982–83 season. Tony Gwynn faced Tiant and Ed Figueroa in Puerto Rico (courtesy of *El Nuevo Día*).

> Unfortunately we didn't have the pitching that we needed to compete with everybody....

San Juan had a great 1983–84 line-up with Gwynn, Thon, Luis Aguayo, Carmelo Martínez, Kevin McReynolds, Ismael Oquendo *et al.* which led the league in homers with 77[17], but finished fifth due to weak pitching. I can still see Gwynn at the plate hitting line drives at Loubriel and Bithorn Stadiums, prior to winning the 1984 National League batting title, his first one. Don Mattingly played for Caguas in 1983–84, and went on to win the 1984 American League batting crown. Gwynn:

> The Padres sent me down there to work on pulling the ball. And it's so funny, because I'm an 'inside-out' hitter and Mattingly was an 'inside-out' hitter. And the next year, we were in the big leagues winning batting titles ... he pulled the ball and I pulled the ball a lot better than I did that winter in winter ball, and so, yeah, I think was very instrumental ... not only were you working on your game, working at your craft ... having success in Puerto Rico gave you the kind of confidence you needed here to do what you do. The teams were so good down there that Sandy Alomar, Jr., Carlos Baerga, Luis López, Benito Santiago—they didn't get a chance to play because the teams were so stacked. But it gave you enough confidence that you could do it up here.

Eduardo Figueroa, the former New York Yankee pitcher, wearing Santurce pinstripes, 1982–83 (courtesy of Angel Colón).

Tony Gwynn was quite expressive when we conversed, and used his hands to make or reinforce a point. Gwynn:

> In a sense, it's just like playing major league baseball ... there were so many guys down there that had so much experience, it enabled you to learn about what it was going to take to be successful at this level ... anytime somebody asks me about winter ball, and they say they're going to Puerto Rico, I say 'GO.' You're going to learn

a lot about the game because they're so many people there who have knowledge about what it takes to be successful here, that if you go down there and do your due diligence ... there's no question that you'll come back a much better player.

Gwynn loved his Puerto Rico living arrangements. He lived in a house near the ninth hole of a Dorado golf course. Carmelo Martínez, his Bayamón/San Juan and San Diego teammate, was from the town of Dorado and recommended a restaurant that Gwynn really liked. The only problem Gwynn encountered was the night in Caguas when some-one broke into his rental car and stole the toll coins that he used to pay the tolls to and from the ballpark.

Tony Gwynn returned to San Juan for a second winter because he thought it would make him a better player. When I brought up the fact that his brother, Chris, had played for Santurce in 1986–87, Tony Gwynn smiled and alluded to Chris Gwynn and the San Juan-Santurce rivalry.

> As a matter of fact, he [Chris] was just down on Monday and we were talking about some of the young players the Padres had drafted and we were just talking about Puerto Rico because I played for Bayamón/San Juan and he played for Santurce. It's a good thing we weren't over there at the same time playing against each other ... we would have got caught up in that 'culture thing.' It was a heated rivalry ... we were just talking about how great it was the other day.

Scott Bailes and John Wetteland were on the agenda. Luis Mayoral introduced me to Bailes at 6:10 p.m. after he had shagged flies during batting practice and signed auto-graphs for fans. Bailes sat next to me in the Texas dugout after posing for pictures with two young kids.

Scott Bailes' two tours of duty with Santurce were four seasons apart — in 1992–93 and 1996–97. He lives in Springfield, Missouri, but has moved around a bit since his selection by Pittsburgh in the fourth round of the June 1982 draft.[18] Bailes was subse-quently acquired by the Cleveland organization as the "player to be named later" in a trade for infielder Johnnie Lemaster on July 3, 1985.[19] Bailes:

> I went from AA [Nashua] in 1985 to winter ball in Venezuela. In 1986 I made the Cleveland team and played seven years of major league baseball with them and Cal-ifornia. The Angels didn't pick up my option and I couldn't find a job for 1993, so my agent said, 'Would you mind going to winter ball?' And the first team that offered me a job was Santurce. So the winter of 1992–93, I played down there with Mako [Oliveras], who was one of our coaches in California ... so I got to be good friends with him. I speak a little Spanish — we practiced with each other in the bullpen all year, and then he was managing Santurce, and called me down... pitched well and ended up having a sore back....

Bailes left Puerto Rico the first week in January, prior to being signed as free agent by Kansas City shortly before spring training of 1993. Kansas City released him in early April 1993, but Toronto signed him as a free agent on April 25, 1993, and he pitched for the Syracuse Chiefs, before voluntarily retiring at age 30.[20] The only pitching Bailes did for the next three to four years was in a 30-and-over league circa late 1996. Bailes:

> I went out to Arizona in this 1996 National 30-and-over Tournament and pitched in two games. A [Texas] scout saw me pitch and said 'you're throwing better than you did your first seven years in the major leagues. Would you be interested?' I said no, I have a new business at home, my kids are older and I'm happy with what I've

been doing ... And I remember that night — was awake all night and thinking if I could still pitch — never heard of anybody gone four years... I just didn't pitch for over three years; didn't even play catch. And so I told him — it was a guy with the Texas Rangers — are you serious? And he says '— yeah, what do you think you need to do?'

Bailes told the scout that he needed to go over to winter ball to test his stuff and see how his arm would respond. The Texas organization found out that Santurce had an opening for a pitcher, and that they needed him "pronto." It was December 20, 1996, a day after Bailes signed a free agent contract with the Texas Rangers. Bailes:

> I called my [Santurce] General Manager, Frankie Thon, and I said my kids, Christmas. And he says 'Scott, we need you ... need a pitcher right now.' I said, OK, if we're going to try this, let's go do it. We told our kids that Santa Claus came a little early ... I went down there the next morning and pitched really well ... pitched in a lot of games, enjoyed winter ball and my time in Puerto Rico — in Isla Verde — like I always do. It's a wonderful place for players to go and visit and play. It's the best league for winter ball without a doubt as far as the cities, the stadiums, the accommodations. From there I got invited to spring training after almost four years out of baseball. They asked me if I wouldn't mind going to AAA for a couple of months; I said no, I need to get some innings....

There were Houston-New Orleans links in Bailes' second Santurce stint. Houston's Billy Wagner left Santurce after his six-week contract expired which opened up a roster spot for a left-handed reliever. Bailes, upon noticing my New Orleans Zephyrs carrying bag, noted that his 1997 Oklahoma team was New Orleans' opponent in the first game ever played at Zephyr Field.

Bailes had some kind words for Poto Paniagua and the Santurce franchise.

"Santurce is just a great organization," said Bailes. "You hear a lot of stories about winter ball — bad travel arrangements, bad accommodations, guys not getting paid ... but it's never happened in Santurce. The owner, Sr. Paniagua — I've met him — is a wonderful man who loves the game of baseball. So when I talk to young guys who ask about the one place to go and play ... [tell them] if you can get to Puerto Rico, especially Santurce, it's the only place to play. The first time, I couldn't get a big league job after seven years, and the second time, they took me back for my comeback," said Bailes. "I think I'm going to go back when I turn 40."

He credits Santurce for saving his big league career, coming up to Texas during the second half of 1997, and having the best second half of his big league career. Texas re-signed him for 1998.

John Wetteland was the last ex–Santurce player I conversed with, after he saved Texas' 3–0 win. Prior to the game, I had dinner in the press lounge with Josué Pérez, who works alongside Luis Mayoral in broadcasting the Texas Rangers game in Spanish via radio. It was 10:25 p.m. when I approached Wetteland in front of his locker. Wetteland, like Scott Bailes, had pitched in Venezuela and for Santurce. Just as we began our conversation, Luis Mayoral passed by and gave Wetteland a sign implying that I was OK.

"Every winter league is helpful for young pitchers because they can work on some things, especially against quality ballplayers that you're going to find in Latin America," said Wetteland. "It's no secret that they are very talented hitters ... so it gives you the opportunity to work against some of the best around and hone your skills."

Wetteland smiled during our conversation. It brought back good memories for him although he was itching to begin his post-game workout. Wetteland: "It was a wonderful time and the people and the climate were good. You realize that you're there to work, not just have fun ... the fans were great 'cause they were really into it ... all the flag-waving, dancing between innings ... something to watch as a player, 'cause you don't see that here in the States. Those kind of things made it fun coming to work."

John Wetteland proceeded to work out and I said good-bye to John Blake, the Texas Rangers Vice-President for Public Relations, on my way out of the clubhouse. It was almost midnight when I returned to my Fort Worth hotel.

On June 11, 1998, I read that the American and National League clubs had approved the sale of the Texas Rangers to Thomas O. Hicks for $250 million.[21] Major league baseball is a business — big business.

I posed several questions to Luis Mayoral concerning Santurce prior to my visit to Texas. One concerned Santurce's importance to Puerto Rico's Winter League. Mayoral called Santurce a legendary franchise which symbolizes to Puerto Rico what the New York Yankees are to big league baseball. The "end" of the City Champ series following the 1998–99 winter season was another item.

Mayoral has assisted San Juan/Carolina franchise owner Benjamín Rivera with some blueprints for the new Roberto Clemente Stadium in Carolina. He (Mayoral) affirms that times have changed and that the City Champ series, like other things, have gone by the wayside. San Juan municipal officials apparently did not have a sense nor feel for baseball history, as evidenced by the need for the San Juan baseball club to find another home outside of Hiram Bithorn Stadium. Pedrín Zorrilla, on the other hand, was a "sincere public servant" from Mayoral's perspective and an exceptional human being who loved and knew a lot about baseball.

Postscript

The 1998–99 City Championship began on November 6, 1998, and came to a close on December 29, 1998, when Santurce played San Juan for the final time. It ended the baseball tradition with both teams sharing Sixto Escobar and Hiram Bithorn Stadiums. Santurce played its 60th league season in 1998–99, and finished second before bowing out in the semi-final series.

The Crabbers' web site — http://www.santurcebaseballclub.com — made its debut on November 7, 1998. The "Hogar Cangrejero" or "Crabbers Home" provides a wealth of information, and enables Internet users to hear radio broadcasts of home and away games.

Puerto Rico hosted the February 2–7, 1999 Caribbean Series,[22] dedicated to Rubén Gómez. "El Divino Loco" had come a long way since his childhood in southeastern Puerto Rico when he saw Satchel Paige pitch for the 1939–40 Guayama Witches. Paige and Gómez were Santurce teammates for a brief time during Gomez' rookie 1947–48 season. Rubén Gómez was also the co-recipient of the 1998 Pedrín Zorrilla Award, and received the plaque from Diana Zorrilla in December 1998.

Orlando Cepeda was voted into Cooperstown, via a Veterans Committee vote, on March 2, 1999. Cepeda had also come full circle from the time he saw his dad play for Santurce in 1945–46, until his own retirement as a Santurce Crabber following the 1974–75 season. Robin Yount, Cepeda's 1974–75 teammate, made it to Cooperstown on the first ballot in 1999.

Santurce School mural and school children, November 1997 (photograph by the author).

Final Thoughts

Manuel Junco, a good friend of mine and of my mother's, is one of the persons I know who still feels strongly about certain traditions of Puerto Rico and Santurce. Manuel told me that being a "Cangrejero" is an anachronism, a nostalgic illusion at this point in time — something that has been torn asunder or cut off like some trees to make way for new development. So Manuel tends to reflect on, or sympathize with, certain sentimental memories — memories of his childhood in Miramar when being a "Cangrejero" was something more tangible.

At one time, a "Cangrejero" was one who identified himself or herself with Santurce's barrios or sectors as well as certain landmarks or special places. Manuel cited a few words from a popular song: "De Barrio Obrero a la 15 un paso es ... cantando bajito y me iba a pie." (It is only a step from Barrio Obrero to Stop 15 ... singing in a low voice and going on foot). Manuel went on to add:

> One would identify with the Escambrón area, the Isla Grande Airport, several beaches, the beautiful public school buildings, the aroma of coffee from the Yaucono plant, the Plaza del Mercado, or Farmer's Market, the movie theaters, Loiza Street, the Condado Lagoon, empty lots where baseball games were played, the legend of the San Jerónimo Dog, the Corona Brewery, Radio Station WKAQ ... a sense that Santurce was passed down by generations and belonged to everyone ... but today it appears that it is 'tierra de nadie' (belongs to no one).

Santurce was part of my environment for one generation — from 1960 to 1985. I cherish the memories of going to school there, frequenting its movie theaters and restaurants, playing Little League and sandlot baseball on its fields and concrete, living on Estrella and Del Parque streets and going to Crabbers' games.

I walked, took a taxi, rode the bus, and/or got rides through various sections of Santurce, including my old neighborhoods, during the November 1997 trip to Puerto Rico. One ride was courtesy of Enriqueta Marcano Zorrilla. She picked us up at Diana Zorrilla's house in Santurce, and a few blocks away we saw a flag of Puerto Rico and a good-looking crab painted on a mural in a Santurce public school. Enriqueta stopped her car so that I could get out and take a photo of the Puerto Rico flag and the crab.

Three Santurce school children happened to be on the court near the mural and asked to be included in my snapshots. I took three photos, had a brief chat with them, and waved good-bye.

Appendices: Puerto Rico's Santurce Crabbers Statistics

1. Team Standings: Wins-Losses, 1939–1999

1938-39

Guayama*	27–12
Humacao	23–19
San Juan	22–19
Ponce	20–20
Caguas§	16–24
Mayagüez	12–26

1939-40

Guayama*	39–17
San Juan	38–18
Ponce	33–23
Santurce	26–29
Caguas	23–33
Humacao	22–33
Aguadilla	21–34
Mayagüez	20–35

1940-41

Caguas*	27–15
Guayama	24–18
San Juan	22–20
Santurce	21–21
Aguadilla	19–22
Humacao	19–22
Ponce	19–23
Mayagüez	16–26

1941-42

Ponce†	30–13
Guayama	29–15
San Juan	24–20
Aguadilla	21–22
Caguas	21–23
Santurce	21–23
Mayagüez	19–25
Humacao/Arecibo	10–34

1942-43

Ponce*	19–16
Santurce	18–17
San Juan	17–19
Mayagüez	17–19

1943-44

Ponce†	37–7
Santurce	22–22
Mayagüez	18–26
San Juan	11–33

1944-45

Ponce†	28–11

League playoff champion. †Declared winners by winning both halves. §Caguas was renamed Bayamón–Rio Piedras in 1991-92.

San Juan	22–20
Santurce	19–22
Mayagüez	11–27

1945-46

Mayagüez	24–16
San Juan*	23–18
Ponce	21–20
Santurce	13–27

1946-47

Ponce*	38–22
Caguas	35–25
San Juan	31–25
Santurce	25–30
Aguadilla	24–36
Mayagüez	22–37

1947-48

Mayagüez	39–21
Caguas*	33–26
Santurce	33–27
San Juan	26–34
Aguadilla	24–35
Ponce	24–36

1948-49

Mayagüez*	51–29
Ponce	47–33
Santurce	47–33
Caguas	41–39
Aguadilla	32–48
San Juan	22–58

1949-50

Caguas*	47–31
Ponce	45–35
Santurce	45–35
Mayagüez	38–39
San Juan	35–44
Aguadilla	26–52

1950-51

Caguas	57–20
Santurce*	48–30
Ponce	43–35
San Juan	34–44
Aguadilla	25–51
Mayagüez	24–51

1951-52

San Juan*	43–29
Caguas	42–30

Santurce	41–31
Ponce	34–36
Mayagüez	18–52

1952-53

San Juan	45–27
Santurce*	42–30
Ponce	36–36
Mayagüez	31–41
Caguas	26–46

1953-54

Caguas*	46–34
San Juan	42–38
Mayagüez	41–39
Ponce	39–41
Santurce	32–48

1954-55

Santurce*	47–25
Caguas	42–30
San Juan	38–34
Mayagüez	27–45
Ponce	26–46

1955-56

Santurce	43–29
Caguas*	38–34
San Juan	36–36
Mayagüez	35–37
Ponce	28–44

1956-57

Santurce	43–29
Mayagüez*	41–31
San Juan	40–33
Caguas	39–34
Ponce	18–54

1957-58

Santurce	36–28
Caguas*	33–31
San Juan	33–31
Ponce	30–34
Mayagüez	28–36

1958-59

San Juan	38–24
Santurce*	36–27
Caguas	30–33
Mayagüez	28–36
Ponce	26–38

1959-60

San Juan	41–23
Caguas*	39–24
Mayagüez	35–28
Santurce	25–37
Ponce	17–45

1960-61

San Juan*	39–25
Mayagüez	33–31
Caguas	30–34
Ponce	29–35
Santurce	29–35

1961-62

Mayagüez	45–35
Caguas	43–37
Santurce*	42–38
Arecibo	42–39
San Juan	41–40
Ponce	28–52

1962-63

Mayagüez*	42–28
Caguas	41–29
Santurce	36–34
Arecibo	35–35
San Juan	30–40
Ponce	26–44

1963-64

Caguas	41–29
Ponce	36–34
San Juan*	35–35
Mayagüez	34–36
Santurce	33–37
Arecibo	31–39

1964-65

Santurce*	41–28
Arecibo	38–32
Mayagüez	36–34
San Juan	34–36
Caguas	32–37
Ponce	28–42

1965-66

Mayagüez*	42–28
Ponce	38–33
Caguas	37–34
Arecibo	34–36
San Juan	31–39
Santurce	29–41

League playoff champion.

1966-67

Ponce	46–25
Santurce*	45–26
Arecibo	34–36
Caguas	33–37
San Juan	29–40
Mayagüez	23–46

1967-68

Santurce	47–22
Caguas*	43–27
San Juan	36–34
Ponce	34–36
Arecibo	28–41
Mayagüez	21–49

1968-69

Santurce	49–20
Ponce*	43–25
Caguas	37–33
San Juan	36–34
Mayagüez	23–45
Arecibo	19–50

1969-70

Ponce*	44–25
Mayagüez	42–28
Santurce	35–33
Caguas	34–35
San Juan	33–36
Arecibo	19–50

1970-71

Caguas	41–29
San Juan	37–30
Santurce*	37–32
Ponce	34–33
Arecibo	32–37
Mayagüez	25–45

1971-72

San Juan	39–30
Ponce*	37–32
Santurce	34–33
Caguas	34–35
Mayagüez	32–37
Arecibo	28–37

1972-73

Santurce*	45–25
Caguas	38–32
Ponce	38–33
Arecibo	37–34
San Juan	33–37
Mayagüez	20–50

1973-74

Ponce	42–28
Caguas*	39–31
San Juan	36–34
Arecibo	35–36
Santurce	34–37
Mayagüez	25–45

1974-75

Caguas	43–27
Ponce	40–30
Bayamón*	37–33
Arecibo	33–37
Santurce	30–40
Mayagüez	27–43

1975-76

Caguas	35–25
Bayamón*	34–26
Mayagüez	33–27
Santurce	28–32
Ponce	26–34
Arecibo	24–36

1976-77

Caguas*	40–20
Ponce	38–22
Bayamón	34–26
Santurce	32–27
Mayagüez	19–41
Arecibo	16–43

1977-78

Caguas	37–23
Arecibo	36–24
Bayamón	31–29
Mayagüez*	29–31
Santurce	27–33
Ponce	20–40

1978-79

Ponce	33–27
Mayagüez	32–28
Santurce	31–29
Caguas*	29–31
Bayamón	28–32
Arecibo	27–33

1979-80

Santurce	36–24

Bayamón*	33–26
Mayagüez	29–31
Arecibo	28–32
Ponce	27–33
Caguas	26–33

1980-81

Bayamón	39–21
Mayagüez	31–30
Arecibo	30–31
Caguas*	29–31
Santurce	28–32
Ponce	24–36

1981-82

Caguas	37–23
Santurce	33–27
Ponce*	28–32
Bayamón	27–34
Mayagüez	26–35

1982-83

Santurce	35–26
Ponce	34–27
Bayamón	32–28
Arecibo*	28–32
Caguas	26–34
Mayagüez	26–34

1983-84

Mayagüez*	38–22
Ponce	32–29
Santurce	31–30
Arecibo	30–30
San Juan	26–34
Caguas	24–36

1984-85

Mayagüez	38–22
Caguas	33–27
Santurce	32–28
San Juan*	30–29
Ponce	25–35
Arecibo	21–38

1985-86

Caguas	33–21
Mayagüez*	31–22
Santurce	31–23
San Juan	26–28
Ponce	24–29
Arecibo	16–38

*League playoff champion.

1986-87

Ponce	34–19
Caguas*	31–23
Mayagüez	26–26
San Juan	25–28
Santurce	23–30
Arecibo	20–33

1987-88

Santurce	31–21
Mayagüez*	29–25
Ponce	27–27
San Juan	25–26
Caguas	24–30
Arecibo	23–30

1988-89

San Juan	35–25
Mayagüez*	33–26
Arecibo	31–27
Caguas	29–29
Ponce	25–34
Santurce	24–36

1989-90

Ponce	31–19
Caguas	28–22
San Juan*	27–23
Mayagüez	23–27
Santurce	22–28
Arecibo	19–31

1990-91

San Juan	33–25

Caguas	31–28
Santurce*	30–28
Mayagüez	31–29
Arecibo	29–30
Ponce	23–37

1991-92

San Juan	29–21
Mayagüez*	28–22
Ponce	27–23
Santurce	24–26
Arecibo	23–27
Bayamón§	19–31

1992-93

Santurce*	29–18
Mayagüez	26–20
San Juan	20–22
Ponce	22–26
Arecibo	14–25

1993-94

San Juan*	35–13
Arecibo	25–23
Mayagüez	25–23
Santurce	21–27
Ponce	14–34

1994-95

Mayagüez	33–21
San Juan*	32–22
Arecibo	28–26
Ponce	26–28

Santurce	22–32
Caguas	21–33

1995-96

Mayagüez	28–21
Arecibo*	27–22
Santurce	26–24
San Juan	26–25
Ponce	25–26
Caguas	18–32

1996-97

Santurce	28–22
Mayagüez*	28–22
Caguas	27–23
San Juan	26–25
Arecibo	25–26
Ponce	17–33

1997-98

San Juan	40–22
Mayagüez*	34–27
Caguas	30–32
Ponce	30–32
Arecibo	26–35
Santurce	25–37

1998-99

Ponce	29–18
Santurce	26–22
Mayagüez*	26–24
Arecibo	23–26
Caguas	21–28
San Juan	21–28

League playoff champion. §Caguas was renamed Bayamón–Rio Piedras in 1991-92.

2. Santurce's Post-Season Series: Results/Standings, 1940–1999

Season	Semi-Final Series Results*	Season	Semi-Final Series Results*
1948-49	Santurce (3) Ponce (2)	1962-63	Santurce (2) Caguas (4)
1949-50	Santurce (2) Mayagüez (4)	1964-65	Santurce (4) San Juan (2)
1950-51	Santurce (4) Ponce (1)	1966-67	Santurce (4) Arecibo (0)
1951-52	Santurce (3) Caguas (0)	1967-68	Santurce (4) Ponce (1)
1952-53	Santurce (3) Ponce (0)	1968-69	Santurce (3) San Juan (4)
1958-59	Santurce (4) Mayagüez (3)	1969-70	Santurce (4) Mayagüez (2)
1959-60	Santurce (2) Caguas (4)	1970-71	Santurce (4) San Juan (2)
1961-62	Santurce (4) Caguas (3)	1971-72	Santurce (1) Ponce (4)

Played in the post-season only.

Season	Semi-Final Series Results*	Season	Semi-Final Series Results*
1972-73	Santurce (4) Arecibo (1)	1982-83	Santurce (2) Arecibo (4)
1975-76	Santurce (3) Caguas (4)	1983-84	Santurce (3) Ponce (4)
1976-77	Santurce (2) Caguas (4)	1984-85	Santurce (4) Caguas (2)
1978-79	Santurce (1) Mayagüez (4)	1995-96	Santurce (2) Arecibo (4)
1979-80	Santurce (4) Arecibo (1)	1996-97	Santurce (0) San Juan (4)
1981-82	Santurce (2) Ponce (4)	1998-99	Santurce (0) Mayagüez (4)

Season	Final Series Results*	Season	Final Series Results*
1940-41	Santurce (3) Caguas (4)	1964-65	Santurce (4) Mayagüez (2)
1942-43	Santurce (1) Ponce (4)	1966-67	Santurce (4) Ponce (2)
1948-49	Santurce (2) Mayagüez (4)	1967-68	Santurce (2) Caguas (4)
1950-51	Santurce (4) Caguas (3)	1969-70	Santurce (2) Ponce (4)
1951-52	Santurce (2) San Juan (4)	1970-71	Santurce (4) Caguas (3)
1952-53	Santurce (4) San Juan (2)	1972-73	Santurce (4) Ponce (2)
1954-55	Santurce (4) Caguas (1)	1979-80	Santurce (1) Bayamón (4)
1955-56	Santurce (2) Caguas (4)	1984-85	Santurce (3) San Juan (4)
1956-57	Santurce (1) Mayagüez (4)	1987-88	Santurce (3) Mayagüez (4)
1957-58	Santurce (0) Caguas (4)	1990-91	Santurce (5) Mayagüez (3)
1958-59	Santurce (5) Caguas (2)	1992-93	Santurce (5) San Juan (1)
1961-62	Santurce (4) Mayagüez (0)	1993-94	Santurce (2) San Juan (5)

Season	Round-Robin Series		Season	Round-Robin Series	
1985-86	Mayagüez	12–6	1991-92	San Juan	8–2
	San Juan	10–8		Mayagüez	6–5
	Santurce	8–10		Santurce	5–7
	Caguas	6–12		Ponce	3–8
1987-88	Mayagüez	9–3	1992-93	San Juan	7–5
	Santurce	8–4		Santurce	7–6[T]
	Ponce	4–8		Mayagüez	6–7
	San Juan	3–9		Ponce	5–7
1990-91	Mayagüez	14–4	1993-94	San Juan	8–4
	Santurce	9–9		Santurce	8–4
	Caguas	7–11		Arecibo	5–7
	San Juan	6–12		Mayagüez	3–9

Year	Caribbean Series		Year	Caribbean Series	
1951	Santurce (Puerto Rico)	5–1		Chesterfield (Panama)	2–4
	Havana (Cuba)	4–2		Caracas (Venezuela)	1–5
	Magallanes (Venezuela)	2–4	1955	Santurce (Puerto Rico)	5–1
	Spur Cola (Panama)	1–5		Magallanes (Venezuela)	4–2
1953	Santurce (Puerto Rico)	6–0		Almendares (Cuba)	2–4
	Havana (Cuba)	3–3		Carta Vieja (Panama)	1–5

*The games won by each team during the semi-final and final series are in parentheses.
[T]Santurce defeated Mayagüez in a one-game tie-breaker to advance the finals.

Year	Caribbean Series		Year	Caribbean Series	
1959	Almendares (Cuba)	5–1		Santurce (Puerto Rico)	3–3
	Oriente (Venezuela)	4–2		Obregón (Mexico)	1–5
	Santurce (Puerto Rico)	3–3	1991	Licey (Dominican)	5–0*
	Cocle (Panama)	0–6		Lara (Venezuela)	3–4*
1971	Licey (Dominican Republic)	6–0		Santurce (Puerto Rico)	1–3
	Hermosillo (Mexico)	2–4		Tijuana (Mexico)	1–3
	La Guaira (Venezuela)	2–4	1993	Santurce (Puerto Rico)	5–2†
	Santurce (Puerto Rico)	2–4		Aguilas Cibaeñas (Dominican)	4–3†
1973	Licey (Dominican)	5–1		Mazatlán (Mexico)	2–4
	Caracas (Venezuela)	3–3		Zulia (Venezuela)	2–4

Year	InterAmerican Series		Year	InterAmerican Series	
1962	Santurce (Puerto Rico)	8–1		Mayagüez (Puerto Rico)	4–5
	Caracas (Venezuela)	5–4		Marlboro (Panama)	1–8

*Licey defeated Lara two times in the final round of competition to win the series.
†Santurce defeated the Aguilas Cibaeñas in a one-game tie-breaker to win the series.

3. Regular Season City Championships, Santurce vs. San Juan, 1939–1999*

Season	Santurce Won–Loss	Season	Santurce Won–Loss	Season	Santurce Won–Loss
1939-40	3–5	1957-58	11–5	1984-85	6–6
1940-41	4–2	1958-59	10–5	1985-86	9–5
1941-42	4–2	1959-60	5–11	1986-87	5–7
1942-43	5–7	1960-61	6–10	1987-88	5–5
1943-44	10–6	1961-62	7–9	1988-89	3–9
1944-45	6–8	1962-63	4–10	1989-90	2–8
1945-46	5–9	1963-64	8–6	1990-91	5–6
1946-47	9–3	1964-65	8–6	1991-92	5–5
1947-48	8–4	1965-66	5–9	1992-93	7–5
1948-49	15–1	1966-67	11–3	1993-94	3–9
1949-50	8–8	1967-68	10–4	1994-95	2–10
1950-51	8–7	1968-69	12–2	1995-96	5–5
1951-52	8–10	1969-70	10–4	1996-97	6–4
1952-53	11–7	1970-71	8–4	1997-98	6–10
1953-54	12–8	1971-72	6–8	1998-99	7–3
1954-55	10–8	1972-73	9–5	Total	368–319
1955-56	12–6	1973-74	7–7		
1956-57	11–7	1983-84	6–6		

*The San Juan franchise became the Bayamón Cowboys from 1974-75 through 1982-83. The "City Championship" was discontinued during those nine seasons. San Juan moved to Carolina after the 1998-99 season.

4. Selected Santurce League Leaders, Hitting and Pitching, 1939–1999

Batting Average Champions

1941-42	Joshua Gibson	.480*
1943-44	Tetelo Vargas	.410
1946-47	Willard Brown	.390
1947-48	Willard Brown	.432
1949-50	Willard Brown	.354
1954-55	Willie Mays	.395
1956-57	Roberto Clemente†	.396
1957-58	Bill Harrell	.317
1958-59	Orlando Cepeda	.362
1964-65	Lou Johnson	.345
1966-67	Tany Pérez	.333
1971-72	Don Baylor	.324
1973-74	George Hendrick	.363
1984-85	Orlando Sánchez	.333

Home Run Champions

1939-40	Joshua Gibson	6
1941-42	Joshua Gibson	13
1942-43	Luis R. Olmo	4
1947-48	Willard Brown	27*
1948-49	Willard Brown	18^T
	Bob Thurman	18^T
1949-50	Willard Brown	16
1950-51	Buster Clarkson	18
1951-52	Johnny Davis	9^T
1957-58	Orlando Cepeda	13^T
1959-60	Al Nagel	10^T
1959-60	Jim McDaniel§	10^T
1961-62	Orlando Cepeda	19
1968-69	George Scott	13
1970-71	Reggie Jackson	20
1979-80	Ismael Oquendo	9^T
1983-84	Jerry Willard	18
1984-85	Jerry Willard	9
1992-93	Juan González	7
1995-96	Héctor Villanueva	8
1996-97	Héctor Villanueva†	11

RBI Champions

1942-43	Juan Sánchez	29
1944-45	Juan Sánchez	30
1946-47	Willard Brown	50^T
1947-48	Willard Brown	86
1949-50	Willard Brown	97*
1950-51	Willard Brown	76
1954-55	Buster Clarkson	61
1957-58	Orlando Cepeda	45
1961-62	Orlando Cepeda	53^T
1966-67	Tany Pérez	63
1968-69	George Scott	46
1983-84	Jerry Willard	48
1986-87	Tracy Woodson	41
1995-96	Héctor Villanueva	30
1996-97	José Cruz, Jr.	35^T
	Héctor Villanueva†	35^T
1997-98	Rubén Sierra	52

Runs Scored

1943-44	Tetelo Vargas	41
1945-46	Tetelo Vargas	40
1947-48	Willard Brown	79
1949-50	Bob Thurman	69^T
1951-52	Junior Gilliam	63
1952-53	Junior Gilliam	55
1954-55	Roberto Clemente	65
1955-56	Bill White	54
1957-58	Orlando Cepeda	49
1958-59	Orlando Cepeda	49
1962-63	Chico Ruíz	48
1966-67	Paul Blair	46^T
	Dave May	46^T
1970-71	Reggie Jackson	47
1983-84	Jerry Willard	51
1986-87	Jerry Browne	36^T
1995-96	José Muñoz	33^T
1996-97	James Mouton	36^T

*All-time league record.
†Played for Santurce and Caguas that season. None of Villanueva's 11 homers were with Santurce.
§Played for Ponce and Santurce that season.
^{T}=Tie.

Hits

1944-45	Juan Sánchez	61
1946-47	Willard Brown	99
1947-48	Bob Thurman	102^T
1949-50	Willard Brown	117
1950-51	Bob Thurman	112
1954-55	Roberto Clemente	94
1957-58	Orlando Cepeda	72
1966-67	Tany Pérez	87
1973-74	Mickey Rivers	90
1983-84	Steve Lubratich	81
1986-87	Tracy Woodson	63
1989-90	Albert Hall	61^T

Doubles

1942-43	Luis R. Olmo	11^T
1950-51	Bob Thurman	22
1958-59	Orlando Cepeda	15
1966-67	Tany Pérez	18
1967-68	Tany Pérez	20^T
1968-69	Leo Cárdenas	14^T
1969-70	Tany Pérez	17^T
1971-72	Don Baylor	19
1983-84	Juan Beníquez	22
1986-87	Tracy Woodson	15
1989-90	Terry McGriff	15
1992-93	Junior Ortíz	10
1993-94	Héctor Villanueva	10

Triples

1947-48	Bob Thurman	9
1951-52	Bob Thurman	8
1954-55	Willie Mays	7
1957-58	Bob Thurman	8
1958-59	Willie Kirkland	6^T
1960-61	Antonio Alomar	3^T
1961-62	Martín Beltrán	9
1962-63	Miguel de la Hoz	9
1977-78	Dell Alston	6
1981-82	Ivan de Jesús	3^T
1983-84	John Shelby	5^T
1985-86	Devon White	7
1988-89	Dwight Smith	4^T
1996-97	Russ Johnson	3^T

Stolen Bases

1942-43	Juan Sánchez	11
1944-45	Alfonso Gerard	12

1946-47	Cocó Ferrer	19^T
1975-76	Sandy Alomar, Sr.	14^T
1989-90	Albert Hall	22
1992-93	Gerald Williams	14
1996-97	James Mouton	20

Wins

1947-48	John Ford Smith	13
1948-49	John Ford Smith	13^T
1949-50	Rubén Gómez	14
1950-51	Rubén Gómez	14
1952-53	Bobo Holloman	15
1954-55	Sam Jones	14
1955-56	Steve Ridzik	14
1956-57	Marion Fricano	12^T
1958-59	Rubén Gómez	12
1963-64	Juan Pizarro	10^T
1966-67	Juan Pizarro	12^T
1967-68	Darrell Osteen	12
1971-72	Rogelio Moret	14
1972-73	Juan Pizarro	10^T
1982-83	Ken Dayley	9^T
1983-84	Rick Mahler	10
1987-88	Mike Pérez	6^T
1987-88	Bill Krueger	6^T
1990-91	Jaime Navarro	7^T
1991-92	Turk Wendell	7^T
1992-93	José Lebrón	7
1995-96	Bronswell Patrick	6^T

Earned Run Average

1952-53	Rubén Gómez	1.79
1954-55	Sam Jones	1.77
1964-65	Fred Talbot	1.30
1966-67	Dick Hughes	1.79
1982-83	Eduardo Figueroa	2.93
1995-96	Bronswell Patrick	1.66

Strikeouts

1944-45	Luis Cabrera	81
1945-46	Luis Cabrera	75
1952-53	Rubén Gómez	123
1954-55	Sam Jones	171
1959-60	Juan Pizarro	141
1960-61	Juan Pizarro	123
1961-62	Juan Pizarro	154

^{T}=Tie.

1967-68	Juan Pizarro	108
1971-72	Rogelio Moret	89
1977-78	Bob Galasso	71
1983-84	Julián González	72
1989-90	Rick Reed	53
1993-94	Dave Otto	38[T]

Saves

1964-65	Jim Dickson	3[T]
1969-70	William de Jesús	7[T]
1972-73	Ramon Hernández	9
1978-79	Tim Stoddard	10
1985-86	Brad Havens	9
1998-99	Juan (J.C.) Romero	11

[T]=*Tie.*

5. Santurce MVP Award Recipients, 1940–1999

MVP			MVP	
1940-41	Luis Cabrera		1954-55	Willie Mays
1941-42	Joshua Gibson		1958-59	Orlando Cepeda
1942-43	Luis R. Olmo[T]		1961-62	Orlando Cepeda
1947-48	Willard Brown		1966-67	Tany Pérez
1949-50	Willard Brown		1968-69	Elrod Hendricks
1950-51	Bob Thurman		1971-72	Rogelio Moret
1951-52	Rubén Gómez		1983-84	Jerry Willard

[T]=*Tie. Olmo shared the MVP Award with Pancho Coímbre of the Ponce Lions.*

6. Santurce Rookie of the Year Recipients, 1943–1999

1943-44	Jueyito Andrades		1955-56	José Pagán
1944-45	Alfonso Gerard[T]		1962-63	Kindo Geigel
1945-46	Víctor Cruz		1973-74	Ismael Oquendo
1947-48	Rubén Gómez		1984-85	Rubén Sierra
1948-49	Domingo Sevilla		1986-87	Jerry Browne
1950-51	Valmy Thomas		1997-98	Josué Espada
1952-53	William Figueroa			

[T]=*Tie. Gerard shared this award with Canena Márquez of Mayagüez.*

7. Selected Santurce Career Records, 1939–1999

The numbers in parentheses after players' names indicate the number of regular league seasons played with Santurce.

Batters

Willie Aikens (1)
BA   .284
HR   9
RBI   38

Angel Luis Alcaraz (5)
BA   .240
HR   8
RBI   71

Edwin Alicea (4)
BA   .215
HR   4
RBI   28

Gary Allenson (2)
BA   .218
HR   6
RBI   28

Ken Aspromonte (1)
BA   .272
HR   2
RBI   21

Sandy Alomar, Sr. (5)
BA   .257
HR   8
RBI   104
SB   34

Dusty Baker (1)
BA   .273
HR   4
RBI   20

Bobby Balcena (1)
BA   .282
HR   1
RBI   8

Don Baylor (3)
BA   .297

HR   22
RBI   84

Derek Bell (1)
BA   .227
HR   2
RBI   5

Jay Bell (1)
BA   .241
HR   4
RBI   20

Martín Beltrán (10)
BA   .238
HR   20
RBI   99

Juan Beníquez (18)
BA   .275
HR   69
RBI   427
SB   81

Paul Blair (3)
BA   .303
HR   7
RBI   75

Jackie Brandt (1)
BA   .349
HR   3
RBI   30

Willard Brown (9)
BA   .346
HR   97
RBI   447

Jerry Browne (1)
BA   .316
HR   0
RBI   15

Billy Bruton (1)
BA   .254
HR   2
RBI   24
SB   15

Tommy Butts (2)
BA   .271
HR   0
RBI   66

Roy Campanella (1)
BA   .294
HR   1
RBI   14

Casey Candaele (1)
BA   .276
HR   0
RBI   6

Leo Cárdenas (2)
BA   .233
HR   5
RBI   52

Ramón Castro (2)
BA   .232
HR   7
RBI   19

Danny Cater (1)
BA   .300
HR   3
RBI   31

Orlando Cepeda (13)
BA   .323
HR   89
RBI   340

Sammy Céspedes (4)
BA   .281

HR 2
RBI 67

Ron Cey (1)
BA .298
HR 7
RBI 43

Buster Clarkson (6)
BA .291
HR 52
RBI 245

Roberto Clemente (5)
BA .325
HR 16
RBI 117

Dennis Colón (3)
BA 232
HR 6
RBI 39

George Crowe (1)
BA .283
HR 12
RBI 40

José Cruz, Jr. (3)
BA .252
HR 19
RBI 83

Ray Dandridge (2)
BA .256
HR 2
RBI 32

Johnny Davis (2)
BA .239
HR 12
RBI 60

Iván de Jesús (12)
BA .236
HR 11
RBI 151
SB 78

Miguel de la Hoz (2)
BA .299
HR 8
RBI 63

Carlos Delgado (3)
BA .228
HR 4
RBI 22

Mike Devereaux (3)
BA .243
HR 6
RBI 40

Josué Espada (3)
BA .300
HR 1
RBI 12

Eric Fox (1)
BA .291
HR 2
RBI 25

Roger Freed (1)
BA .273
HR 9
RBI 40

Alfonso Gerard (14)
BA .303
HR 6
RBI 226

Joshua Gibson (3)
BA .355
HR 19
RBI 85

Junior Gilliam (3)
BA .278
HR 3
RBI 90
SB 47

Leo Gómez (6)
BA .270
HR 30
RBI 130

Fernando González (4)
BA .283
HR 9
RBI 53

Juan González (2)
BA .292
HR 14
RBI 39

Julio Gotay (5)
BA .273
HR 9
RBI 67

Chris Gwynn (1)
BA .295

HR 2
RBI 18

Larry Haney (2)
BA .206
HR 7
RBI 36

Bill Harrell (1)
BA .317
HR 4
RBI 28

Chuck Harrison (1)
BA .276
HR 6
RBI 20

Scott Hemond (1)
BA .287
HR 3
RBI 22

George Hendrick (1)
BA .363
HR 9
RBI 40

Elrod Hendricks (17)
BA .246
HR 105
RBI 349

Earl Hersch (1)
BA .279
HR 12
RBI 41

Joe Hicks (1)
BA .289
HR 4
RBI 25

Jack Howell (1)
BA .275
HR 3
RBI 19

Billy Hunter (1)
BA .229
HR 0
RBI 15

Raúl Ibañez (2)
BA .285
HR 11
RBI 44

Reggie Jackson (1)
BA   .272
HR   20
RBI   47
SB   9

Dave Johnson (1)
BA   .271
HR   6
RBI   30

Lou Johnson (1)
BA   .345
HR   6
RBI   41

Dave Kingman (1)
BA   .237
HR   6
RBI   24

Willie Kirkland (1)
BA   .284
HR   11
RBI   34

Rudy Law (2)
BA   .301
HR   4
RBI   22
SB   43

Mark Lemke (1)
BA   .347
HR   1
RBI   15

Sixto Lezcano (5)
BA   .262
HR   20
RBI   82

Luis López (4)
BA   .238
HR   1
RBI   40

Pedro López (4)
BA   .216
HR   8
RBI   24

Radamés López (2)
BA   .279
HR   0
RBI   19

Vidal López (1)
BA   .319

HR   6
RBI   28

Félix J. Maldonado (13)
BA   .256
HR   15
RBI   179

Dave May (4)
BA   .258
HR   36
RBI   129

Willie Mays (1)
BA   .395
HR   12
RBI   33
SB   10

Orlando Merced (3)
BA   .270
HR   11
RBI   49

Arturo Miranda (13)
BA   .224
HR   0
RBI   61

Bob Molinaro (1)
BA   .242
HR   5
RBI   36
SB   25

Guillermo Montañez (4)
BA   .265
HR   5
RBI   66

Jerry Morales (5)
BA   .260
HR   11
RBI   78

Joe Morgan (1)
BA   .229
HR   2
RBI   14

James Mouton (1)
BA   .250
HR   0
RBI   14
SB   20

José Muñoz (3)
BA   .247

HR   3
RBI   38

Al Nagel (1)
BA   .304
HR   10
RBI   33

Melvin Nieves (2)
BA   .256
HR   9
RBI   30

Otis Nixon (1)
BA   .267
HR   0
RBI   12
SB   24

José Olmeda (4)
BA   .229
HR   9
RBI   51

Luis R. Olmo (3)
BA   .278
HR   6
RBI   43

Rey Ordoñez (2)
BA   .322
HR   0
RBI   35

Junior Ortíz (5)
BA   .266
HR   6
RBI   73

Polilla Ortíz (3)
BA   .280
HR   0
RBI   15

José Pagán (4)
BA   .260
HR   13
RBI   78

Clarence Palm (2)
BA   .379
HR   1
RBI   26

Roy Partlow (1)
BA   .357
HR   1
RBI   22

Eduardo Pérez (5)
BA	.255
HR	12
RBI	49

Julián Pérez (7)
BA	.284
HR	2
RBI	68

Tany Pérez (10)
BA	.303
HR	65
RBI	319

Jorge Posada (3)
BA	.235
HR	4
RBI	24

Ron Pruitt (3)
BA	.291
HR	4
RBI	36

Jamie Quirk (1)
BA	.215
HR	1
RBI	26

Milton Ramírez (3)
BA	.270
HR	1
RBI	19

Fernando Ramos (6)
BA	.282
HR	18
RBI	168

Mickey Rivers (2)
BA	.346
HR	7
RBI	33
SB	24

Pinolo Rodríguez (11)
BA	.225
HR	25
RBI	128

Chico Ruíz (2)
BA	.271
HR	2
RBI	29
SB	33

Nolín Ruíz (12)
BA	.242

HR	12
RBI	129

José St. Clair (6)
BA	.202
HR	15
RBI	87

Juan Sánchez (5)
BA	.295
HR	0
RBI	83

Orlando Sánchez (16)
BA	.242
HR	37
RBI	175

George Scott (2)
BA	.292
HR	23
RBI	78

Dick Seay (4)
BA	.208
HR	1
RBI	21

John Shelby (2)
BA	.281
HR	7
RBI	42

Darrell Sherman (2)
BA	.290
HR	0
RBI	11
SB	15

Rubén Sierra (9)
BA	.274
HR	50
RBI	229

Dwight Smith (1)
BA	.286
HR	2
RBI	15

Tony Solaita (1)
BA	.245
HR	11
RBI	28

Charlie Spikes (1)
BA	.294
HR	3
RBI	17

Marv Staehle (1)
BA	.301
HR	1
RBI	15

Darryl Strawberry (1)
BA	.355
HR	6
RBI	10

Chris Stynes (1)
BA	.287
HR	1
RBI	15

Pat Tabler (2)
BA	.290
HR	3
RBI	18

Earl Taborn (3)
BA	.260
HR	15
RBI	107

José Tartabull (2)
BA	.286
HR	1
RBI	42

Valmy Thomas (13)
BA	.255
HR	23
RBI	332

Bob Thurman (11)
BA	.314
HR	117
RBI	555
SB	87

Tetelo Vargas (2)
BA	.374
HR	2
RBI	15

Edgard Velázquez (4)
BA	.270
HR	8
RBI	22

Héctor Villanueva (5)
BA	.248
HR	28
RBI	100

Danny Walton (1)
BA	.215

HR	12
RBI	35

Bill White (2)

BA	.308
HR	14
RBI	49

Devon White (1)

BA	.277
HR	4
RBI	17

Jerry Willard (3)

BA	.275

HR	28
RBI	90

Gerald Williams (4)

BA	.249
HR	4
RBI	53
SB	36

Artie Wilson (2)

BA	.220
HR	0
RBI	12

Tracy Woodson (2)

BA	.308

HR	7
RBI	42

Robin Yount (1)

BA	.306
HR	0
RBI	10

Don Zimmer (2)

BA	.283
HR	3
RBI	20

Pitchers

Kyle Abbott (1)

W–L	2–1
ERA	2.59
IP	31
K's	22

Doyle Alexander (1)

W–L	5–4
ERA	2.17
IP	100
K's	55

José Alvarez (2)

W–L	2–3
ERA	3.38
IP	64
K's	49

Larry Andersen (3)

W–L	6–6
ERA	3.38
IP	128
K's	50

Bud Anderson (2)

W–L	8–5
ERA	3.19
IP	124
K's	69

Craig Anderson (2)

W–L	7–10
ERA	3.04
IP	139
K's	82

Luis Aquino (2)

W–L	2–4
ERA	3.13

IP	63
K's	37

Scott Bailes (2)

W–L	3–2
ERA	3.34
IP	32
K's	15

Dan Bankhead (1)

W–L	7–1
ERA	3.71
IP	70
K's	40

Fred Beene (3)

W–L	9–8
ERA	2.84
IP	146
K's	96

Billy Brewer (1)

W–L	2–2
ERA	0.39
IP	23
K's	24

Raymond Brown (2)

W–L	11–12
ERA	2.87
IP	201
K's	na

George Brunet (1)

W–L	7–8
ERA	1.75
IP	118
K's	94

Tom Bruno (3)

W–L	10–14
ERA	4.06
IP	177
K's	95

Wally Bunker (1)

W–L	8–4
ERA	2.06
IP	109
K's	63

John Burgos (5)

W–L	6–4
ERA	3.90
IP	120
K's	58

Pete Burnside (1)

W–L	2–1
ERA	1.74
IP	46
K's	48

Billy Byrd (1)

W–L	15–10
ERA	1.97
IP	229
K's	158

Luis Cabrera (17)

W–L	105–98
ERA	3.35
IP	1,674
K's	863

José Calderón (5)

W–L	5–5

na: *Some individual statistics for selected players were not available.*

ERA	3.13
IP	112
K's	49

Rick Camp (1)

W–L	3–2
ERA	3.81
IP	26
K's	15

Bill Caudill (1)

W–L	6–2
ERA	2.34
IP	65
K's	49

Mike Cook (2)

W–L	9–4
EA	1.77
IP	81
K's	58

Ted Davidson (2)

W–L	7–5
ERA	2.12
IP	59
K's	34

Johnny Davis (2)

W–L	9–9
ERA	na
IP	na
K's	na

Leon Day (1)

W–L	1–2
ERA	5.25
IP	34
K's	20

Ken Dayley (1)

W–L	9–1
ERA	2.87
IP	73
K's	67

William de Jesús (9)

W–L	23–18
ERA	2.63
IP	332
K's	139

Carlos Díaz (5)

W–L	13–5
ERA	3.97
IP	186
K's	96

Jim Dickson (1)

W–L	6–3
ERA	3.95
IP	66
K's	30

Scott Elarton (1)

W–L	2–4
ERA	2.53
IP	53
K's	40

Eduardo Figueroa (3)

W–L	5–6
ERA	5.16
IP	120
K's	22

Dave Ford (1)

W–L	7–3
ERA	3.24
IP	103
K's	32

Mark Freeman (1)

W–L	8–8
ERA	3.64
IP	124
K's	75

Marion Fricano (3)

W–L	24–17
ERA	2.84
IP	348
K's	132

Gene Garber (1)

W–L	4–3
ERA	3.00
IP	93
K's	39

Kindo Geigel (10)

W–L	11–5
ERA	3.04
IP	249
K's	116

Bob Gibson (1)

W–L	6–8
ERA	2.12
IP	136
K's	142

Rubén Gómez (28)

W–L	173–118
ERA	2.94
IP	2,468
K's	1,386

Bill Greason (6)

W–L	45–30
ERA	2.90
IP	671
K's	371

Mike Grzanich (1)

W–L	2–1
ERA	1.73
IP	26
K's	12

Jim Hardin (2)

W–L	8–6
ERA	2.85
IP	123
K's	90

Greg Harris (1)

W–L	4–1
ERA	1.64
IP	66
K's	34

Mike Hartley (2)

W–L	2–5
ERA	2.39
IP	49
K's	45

Paul Hartzell (1)

W–L	8–2
ERA	2.92
IP	92
K's	37

Brad Havens (1)

W–L	6–3
ERA	1.97
IP	46
K's	39

LaTroy Hawkins (1)

W–L	3–1
ERA	1.96
IP	37
K's	12

Guillermo Hernández (3)

W–L	6–3
ERA	3.90
IP	108
K's	76

Ramón Hernández (7)

W–L	12–11
ERA	2.39
IP	188
K's	124

na: *Some individual statistics for selected players were not available.*

Bobo Holloman (2)

W–L	15–7
ERA	na
IP	na
K's	82

Chris Holt (2)

W–L	7–3
ERA	2.24
IP	64
K's	30

Dick Hughes (1)

W–L	11–2
ERA	1.79
IP	126
K's	79

Sam Jones (1)

W–L	14–4
ERA	1.77
IP	158
K's	171

Mike Kekich (1)

W–L	7–4
ERA	4.79
IP	94
K's	65

Bill Krueger (1)

W–L	6–3
ERA	3.17
IP	71
K's	44

Jim Lamarque (2)

W–L	13–10
ERA	2.59
IP	219
K's	99

Tom Lasorda (1)

W–L	7–6
ERA	3.60
IP	120
K's	55

José Lebrón (4)

W–L	7–6
ERA	3.27
IP	96
K's	48

Dave Leonhard (6)

W–L	26–21
ERA	3.44
IP	406
K's	229

Vidal López (1)

W–L	8–13
ERA	2.88
IP	178
K's	104

Sam McDowell (1)

W–L	6–8
ERA	3.75
IP	109
K's	85

Terris McDuffie (1)

W–L	2–3
ERA	3.39
IP	61
K's	na

Rick Mahler (1)

W–L	10–2
ERA	3.50
IP	113
K's	55

Duke Markell (1)

W–L	8–6
ERA	2.26
IP	119
K's	81

Carl Mathias (1)

W–L	7–4
ERA	2.65
IP	99
K's	61

Brian Maxcy (2)

W–L	7–3
ERA	3.71
IP	70
K's	37

Balor Moore (1)

W–L	3–2
ERA	2.37
IP	61
K	39

Rogelio Moret (16)

W–L	49–46
ERA	3.51
IP	780
K's	434

Jaime Navarro (4)

W–L	9–11
ERA	3.12
IP	164
K's	79

Julio Navarro (4)

W–L	14–16
ERA	3.16
IP	236
K's	126

David Nied (2)

W–L	4–4
ERA	2.71
IP	66
K's	44

Francisco J. Oliveras (2)

W–L	9–6
ERA	2.42
IP	127
K's	45

Rafaelito Ortíz (4)

W–L	8–7
ERA	na
IP	na
K's	na

Darrell Osteen (4)

W–L	19–13
ERA	2.38
IP	250
K's	177

Satchel Paige (1)

W–L	0–3
ERA	2.91
IP	34
K's	26

Jim Palmer (1)

W–L	5–0
ERA	2.79
IP	29
K's	33

Roy Partlow (1)

W–L	6–5
ERA	4.01
IP	103
K's	na

Bronswell Patrick (2)

W–L	10–1
ERA	1.93
IP	149
K's	65

Orlando Peña (2)

W–L	8–8
ERA	2.93
IP	144
K's	81

na: *Some individual statistics for selected players were not available.*

Troy Percival (1)
W–L	1–1
ERA	2.53
IP	21
K's	35

Mike Pérez (4)
W–L	10–7
ERA	3.58
IP	113
K's	98

Juan Pizarro (20)
W–L	134–95
ERA	2.58
IP	2,080
K's	1,476

Rick Reed (1)
W–L	6–4
ERA	3.12
IP	84
K's	53

Steve Ridzik (1)
W–L	14–3
ERA	2.61
IP	145
K's	89

Juan (J.C.) Romero (2)
W–L	5–4
ERA	3.46
IP	52
K's	50

Gilberto Rondón (9)
W–L	21–12
ERA	3.99
IP	430
K's	200

Pantalones Santiago (3)
W–L	10–15
ERA	3.87
IP	226
K's	97

Al Schroll (1)
W–L	9–6
ERA	3.03
IP	112
K's	74

Diego Seguí (1)
W–L	5–8

ERA	3.07
IP	120
K's	93

Al Severinsen (2)
W–L	5–0
ERA	0.26
IP	34
K's	14

Domingo Sevilla (5)
W–L	22–17
ERA	na
IP	na
K's	130

John Ford Smith (3)
W–L	31–15
ERA	na
IP	na
K's	218

Lee Smith (1)
W–L	3–2
ERA	2.85
IP	41
K's	44

Zane Smith (1)
W–L	6–2
ERA	2.01
IP	58
K's	28

Tim Stoddard (2)
W–L	8–10
ERA	2.44
IP	100
K's	78

Fred Talbot (1)
W–L	6–4
ERA	1.30
IP	83
K's	76

Esteban Texidor (8)
W–L	11–11
ERA	3.61
IP	327
K's	147

Bob Thurman (11)
W–L	39–32
ERA	na

IP	na
K's	261

Luis Tiant (1)
W–L	5–4
ERA	3.44
IP	65
K's	43

Manuel Velázquez (2)
W–L	15–12
ERA	2.67
IP	236
K's	na

Billy Wagner (1)
W–L	1–1
ERA	2.06
IP	35
K's	32

Murray Wall (1)
W–L	10–7
ERA	3.47
IP	158
K's	62

Colin Ward (1)
W–L	3–2
ERA	2.58
IP	66
K's	35

Turk Wendell (1)
W–L	7–1
ERA	0.94
IP	67
K's	45

David West (1)
W–L	5–4
ERA	3.55
IP	63
K's	39

John Wetteland (1)
W–L	3–6
ERA	5.09
IP	53
K's	40

Al Worthington (1)
W–L	9–2
ERA	2.66
IP	105
K's	39

na: *Some individual statistics for selected players were not available.*

8. Santurce Single Season Career Hitting and Pitching Records, 1939–1999

Single Season

Hitting	Player	Season	Total
At-Bats	Tommy Butts	1948-49	333
Runs	Willard Brown	1947-48	79
Hits	Willard Brown	1949-50	117
Doubles	Willard Brown	1946-47	25
Triples	Bob Thurman	1947-48	9
	Martín Beltrán	1961-62	9
	Miguel de la Hoz	1962-63	9
Home Runs	Willard Brown	1947-48	27*
RBI	Willard Brown	1949-50	97*
Average	Joshua Gibson	1941-42	.480*
Slugging	Joshua Gibson	1941-42	.959*
Stolen Bases	Bob Thurman	1949-50	26
Home Runs	Willard Brown	1947-48	1/8.7
Per Official	Juan González	1992-93	1/9.4
At-Bat	Joshua Gibson	1941-42	1/9.5

Pitching	Pitcher	Season	Total
Games	William de Jesús	1969-70	31
Games Started	Billy Byrd	1939-40	26
Complete Games	Billy Byrd	1939-40	24
Innings Pitched	Billy Byrd	1939-40	229
Wins	Billy Byrd	1939-40	15
	Bobo Holloman	1952-53	15
Losses	Luis Cabrera	1939-40	14
Strikeouts	Sam Jones	1954-55	171
Walks	Billy Byrd	1939-40	111
E.R.A.	Mike Cook	1992-93	0.70
Shutouts	Sam Jones	1954-55	7
Saves	Mike Hartley	1988-89	12

Career

Hitting	Player	Seasons	Total
At-Bats	Juan Beníquez	18	3,431
Runs	Bob Thurman	11	517
Hits	Juan Beníquez	18	944
Doubles	Juan Beníquez	18	159
Triples	Bob Thurman	11	60
Home Runs	Bob Thurman	11	117†

*All-time Puerto Rico Winter League record.
†All-time league team record.

Hitting	Player	Seasons	Total
RBI	Bob Thurman	11	555†
Average	Willard Brown	9	.346†
Slugging	Willard Brown	9	.611†
Stolen Bases	Bob Thurman	11	87
Home Runs	Juan González	2	1/12.7
Per Official	Willard Brown	9	1/18.7
At-Bat	Jerry Willard	3	1/18.7

Pitching	Pitcher	Seasons	Total
Games	Rubén Gómez	28†	409†
Innings Pitched	Rubén Gómez	28	2,468†
Wins	Rubén Gómez	28	173†
Losses	Rubén Gómez	28	118†
Strikeouts	Juan Pizarro	20	1,476†
Walks	Rubén Gómez	28	808†
E.R.A.	Juan Pizarro	20	2.58
Shutouts	Juan Pizarro	20	34†
Saves	Ramón Hernández	7	23

†*All-time Puerto Rico Winter League team record.*

9. Boxscores of No-Hitters by Santurce Pitchers

Jim Palmer's no-hitter at Mayagüez, December 22, 1968
CRABBERS 4, INDIANS 0

SANTURCE	ab	h	b	bi		MAYAGUEZ	ab	r	h	bi
Foy 3b	4	1	1	0		Medina rf	3	0	0	0
Gotay 2b	2	0	0	0		Ramos lf	3	0	0	0
May cf	2	1	0	0		Woods cf	2	0	0	0
Scott 1b	2	1	0	0		Derrick 1b	2	0	0	0
Hendricks c	3	1	2	2		Coggins 2b	2	0	0	0
Maldonado rf	3	0	1	1		Morales ss	2	0	0	0
Cárdenas ss	3	0	1	0		Brown 3b	3	0	0	0
Torres lf	2	0	0	1		Cepeda c	3	0	0	0
Palmer p	3	0	0	0		Virgil p	0	0	0	0
Totals	24	4	5	4		Aquino p	2	0	0	0
						Totals	22	0	0	0

Santurce	400 000 0–4
Mayagüez	000 000 0–0

E-Foy, Palmer. LOB-Santurce 3, Mayagüez 5. S-Gotay. SF-Torres. PB-Cepeda.

Santurce	IP	H	R	ER	BB	SO
Palmer W	7	0	0	0	3	10
Mayagüez						
Virgil L	⅓	3	4	4	2	0
Aquino	6⅔	2	0	0	0	3

Umpires: Home, McCoy; First, Montalvo; Third, Guasp. T 1:25. A 1,843.

Fred Beene's no-hitter at Santurce, January 17, 1970
WOLVES 0, CRABBERS 6

ARECIBO	ab	r	h	bi		SANTURCE	ab	r	h	bi
Rosario cf	3	0	0	0		Gotay 2b	4	0	0	0
Heidemann ss	4	0	0	0		May rf	2	1	1	3
Baker lf	3	0	0	0		Maldonado rf	1	0	0	0
Plaskett 1b	3	0	0	0		Scott 1b	4	0	0	0
Silva rf	2	0	0	0		Pérez 3b	3	1	1	0
Pacheco 3b	3	0	0	0		Hendricks c	2	1	1	0
Burgos 2b	3	0	0	0		G. Rodríguez lf	3	1	1	0
Isaac c	3	0	0	0		Rettenmund cf	3	0	1	1
Burchart p	0	0	0	0		Martínez ss	3	1	0	0
González p	1	0	0	0		Beene p	3	1	1	1
Alcaide ph	1	0	0	0		*Totals*	28	6	6	5
Domínguez p	0	0	0	0						
Ortíz ph	1	0	0	0						
Totals	27	0	0	0						

Arecibo	000 000 000–0
Santurce	060 000 00x–6

Arecibo	IP	H	R	ER	BB	SO
Burchart L	1⅓	5	5	5	0	0
González	3⅔	1	1	1	0	4
Domínguez	3	0	0	0	0	0
Santurce						
Beene W	9	0	0	0	2	4

Umpires — Home, Montalvo; First, Deegan; Third, Díaz. T 1:41. A 685. Scorer: Ramón L. Carrasquillo.

Scott Elarton's no-hitter at Santurce, December 14, 1997
CRIOLLOS 0, CRABBERS 3

CAGUAS	ab	r	h	bi		SANTURCE	ab	r	h	bi
López 2b	4	0	0	0		C. Gipson cf	5	0	1	0
Benítez cf	4	0	0	0		Stynes 3b	3	0	1	1
I. Rodríguez 1b	3	0	0	0		Posada 1b	3	0	1	0
Greene 3b	2	0	0	0		Sierra rf	3	1	1	0
Martínez dh	2	0	0	0		Pérez dh	3	1	1	1
Ochoa rf	3	0	0	0		D. Gibson lf	4	0	0	0
Candelaria lf	3	0	0	0		Castro c	4	0	3	1
Varitek c	3	0	0	0		Olmeda 2b	4	0	0	0
T. Rodríguez ss	2	0	0	0		V. Rodríguez ss	3	1	1	0
Crespo ph	1	0	0	0		*Totals*	32	3	9	3
Totals	27	0	0	0						

Caguas	000 000 000–0
Santurce	000 101 10x–3

E–I. Rodríguez, T. Rodríguez. LOB–Caguas 2, Santurce 9. 2B–Sierra,
Castro, Stynes, V. Rodríguez, HR–Pérez. SF–Stynes.

Caguas	IP	H	R	ER	HB	SO
Saier L	6⅔	8	3	3	2	3
Torres	⅓	0	0	0	0	1
Nye	1	1	0	0	2	3
Santurce						
Elarton W	9	0	0	0	2	8

Umpires — Home, Reyes; First, León; Second, Rey; Third, Guzmán. T 2:20. A 13,124. Scorer: Carlos Valero.

10. Santurce Team Rosters, 1939–1999

1939-40

P	Raúl Acosta
UT	Guillermo Angulo
P	Manuel Archeval
P	Billy Byrd
P	Luis Raúl Cabrera
1B	Guillermo "Wichie" Calderón
P	Ramón "Mon" Carrión
2B/SS	Rafael "Fellito" Concepción
OF	Ramón "Monchile" Concepción
3B	Agustín "Tingo" Daviú
C/MGR	Joshua Gibson
OF	Enrique González
C	Eduardo Nichols
OF	Oscar "El Brujo" Mangual
UT	Liborio Ramírez
OF	Manuel "El Indio" Ramírez
P	Manolín Rosario
2B/SS/ MGR	Dick Seay
OF	Joaquín "Nenaco" Vilá

1940-41

OF	Manuel Archeval
P/OF	Raymond Brown
P	Luis Raúl Cabrera
OF	Georgie Calderón
1B	Guillermo "Wichie" Calderón
2B	Rafael "Fellito" Concepción
3B	Agustín "Tingo" Daviú
OF	Enrique González
P	Cirico Machuca
OF	Oscar "El Brujo" Mangual
SS	Efraín "Pee Wee" Merced
C	Clarence Palm
OF	Pedro Jaime Reyes
SS	Vidal Richardson
UT	Antonio Rodríguez
2B/SS	Dick Seay
P	Fernando Solá
OF	Joaquín "Nenaco" Vilá
MGR	Pedrín Zorrilla

1941-42

OF	Manuel Archeval
P	Luis Raúl Cabrera
OF	Georgie Calderón
1B	Guillermo "Wichie" Calderón

2B	Rafael "Fellito" Concepción
3B	Ray Dandridge
C	Joshua Gibson
OF	Enrique González
OF	José González
P/OF	Vidal López
P	Cirico Machuca
OF	Oscar "El Brujo" Mangual
C	Clarence Palm
OF	Pedro Jaime Reyes
SS	Vidal Richardson
P	Gerardo Rodríguez
1B	José "Pepe" Santana
UT	Luis Santos
2B/MGR	Dick Seay
P	Fernando Solá
C	Joaquín "Nenaco" Vilá

1942-43

P	Santos Acosta
OF	Manuel Archeval
P	Luis Raúl Cabrera
1B	Guillermo "Wichie" Calderón
1B	Sammy Céspedes
UT	"El Rajao" Clemente
2B	Rafael "Fellito" Concepción
P	Jorge de Jesús
OF	Manolo García
C	Juan Ledeé
SS	Emilio "Millito" Martínez
OF/MGR	Luis R. Olmo
OF	Pedro Jaime Reyes
3B	Heriberto Rivera
OF	Juan Sánchez
1B	José "Pepe" Santana
3B	Lino Suarez
P	Manuel "Larú" Velázquez
C/UT	Santiago Velázquez
C	Joaquín "Nenaco" Vilá
P	Rogelio Wiscovitch

1943-44

3B	Félix "Jueyito" Andrades
OF	Manuel Archeval
OF	Efraín Blassini
P	Luis Raúl Cabrera
1B	Sammy Céspedes
2B	Rafael "Fellito" Concepción
P	Jorge de Jesús

OF	Manolo García
C	Juan Ledeé
SS	Emilio "Millito" Martínez
MGR	Luis R. Olmo
OF	Pedro Jaime Reyes
2B	Aniceto "Nenené" Rivera
3B	Heriberto Rivera
OF	Juan E. "Tetelo" Vargas
P	Manuel "Larú" Velázquez
P	Rogelio Wiscovitch

1944-45

3B	Félix "Jueyito" Andrades
P	Luis Raúl Cabrera
C	Roy Campanella
1B	Sammy Céspedes
MGR	Ramón "Monchile" Concepción
P	Percy Forrest
OF	Alfonso Gerard
SS/3B	Radamés López
P	Terris McDuffie
P	Guillermo "Momo" Pérez
OF	Pedro Jaime Reyes
2B	Aniceto "Nenené" Rivera
3B	Heriberto Rivera
1B/OF/P	Gerardo Rodríguez
OF	Juan Sánchez

1945-46

3B	Félix "Jueyito" Andrades
P	Kilpatrick Aponte
P	Luis Raúl Cabrera
OF/2B	Pedro "Perucho" Cepeda
P/1B	Sammy Céspedes
2B	Pedro "Millán" Clara
3B	Juan Cox
C/1B	Víctor "Vitín" Cruz
SS	Efigenio "Cocó" Ferrer
P	Joe Fillmore
OF	Alfonso Gerard
C	Joshua Gibson
SS	Manuel "Manache" Hernández
P	Gentry Jessup
3B	Radamés López
2B	Cirico Machuca
P	Rafael "Caró" Maldonado
SS	Emilio "Millito" Martínez
P	Rafaelito Ortíz
OF	Pedro Jaime Reyes
2B	Aniceto "Nenené" Rivera
1B	F. J. Rodríguez
1B/OF/P	Gerardo Rodríguez
2B/MGR	Dick Seay
OF	Juan E. "Tetelo" Vargas

1946-47

3B	Félix "Jueyito Andrades
P	Raymond Brown
OF	Willard Brown
P	Luis Raúl Cabrera
2B	Pedro "Millán" Clara
UT	Juan Cox
C	Víctor "Vitín" Cruz
P	Esteban "Teggy" Espinosa
SS	Efigenio "Cocó" Ferrer
C/3B	Alberto Flores
OF	Alfonso Gerard
C	Johnny Hayes
SS	Manuel "Manache" Hernández
P	Rafael "Caró" Maldonado
OF	Domingo Navarro
MGR	Clarence Palm
OF/P	Roy Partlow
P	José "Pepín" Pereira
3B	Luis F. Pérez
1B	Fernando Ramos
P	Gerardo Rodríguez
P	Fernando Solá
C	Joaquín "Nenaco" Vilá

1947-48

P	Julián Acosta
UT	Pablo Andino
3B	Félix "Jueyito" Andrades
3B	Pedro Juan Arroyo
OF	Willard Brown
P	Luis Raúl Cabrera
UT	Juan Cox
P	Esteban "Teggy" Espinosa
SS	Efigenio "Cocó" Ferrer
OF	Alfonso Gerard
P	Rubén Gómez
MGR	Vic Harris
SS	Manuel "Manache" Hernández
C	Reinaldo León
P	Rafael "Caró" Maldonado
OF	Domingo Navarro
P	Leroy "Satchel" Paige
P	José "Pepín" Pereira
3B	Luis F. Pérez
1B	Fernando Ramos
P	John Ford Smith
P	Fernando Solá
C	Earl "Mickey" Taborn
OF/P	Bob Thurman

1948-49

P	Manolo Alvarez
3B	Félix "Jueyito" Andrades

3B	Pedro Juan Arroyo
OF	Willard Brown
SS	Tommy Butts
P	Luis Raúl Cabrera
OF	Marzo Cabrera
C	Rafael Casanova
1B	Leonardo M. Chapman
C	Víctor "Vitín" Cruz
P	Rubén Díaz
P	Esteban "Teggy" Espinosa
SS	Efigenio "Cocó" Ferrer
OF	Alfonso Gerard
P	Rubén Gómez
MGR	Vic Harris
P	Efraín Hidalgo
P	Jim Lamarque
3B	Luis F. Pérez
1B	Fernando Ramos
P	Domingo "McDuffie" Sevilla
P	John Ford Smith
C	Earl "Mickey" Taborn
OF/P	Bob Thurman

OF	Willard Brown
P	Luis Raúl Cabrera
OF	Orlando Casellas
SS	James "Buster" Clarkson
C	Jaime Escalera
SS	Efigenio "Cocó" Ferrer
P	Enrique "Tite" Figueroa
OF	Alfonso Gerard
2B	Jim "Junior" Gilliam
P	Rubén Gómez
P	Walter James
P	Rafaelito Ortíz
P	William Powell
1B	Fernando Ramos
P	Henry Rementería
1B	José "Pepe Lucas" St. Clair
OF	Juan Sánchez
MGR	George Scales
P	Domingo "McDuffie" Sevilla
P	John Ford Smith
C	Valmy Thomas
OF/P	Bob Thurman
C	Manuel "Liquito" Traboux

1949-50

P	Manolo Alvarez
3B	Félix "Jueyito" Andrades
3B	Pedro Juan Arroyo
OF	Willard Brown
SS	Tommy Butts
P	Luis Raúl Cabrera
OF	Marzo Cabrera
1B	Leonardo M. Chapman
C	Víctor "Vitín" Cruz
2B/P	Leon Day
2B	Efigenio "Cocó" Ferrer
OF/P	Enrique "Tite" Figueroa
OF	Alfonso Gerard
P	Rubén Gómez
MGR	Vic Harris
P	Efraín Hidalgo
P	Walter James
P	Jim Lamarque
C	Eudah Napier
P	Rafaelito Ortíz
P	José "Pepín" Pereira
3B	Luis F. Pérez
1B	Fernando Ramos
1B	José "Pepe Lucas" St. Clair
OF	Juan Sánchez
P	Domingo "McDuffie" Sevilla
C	Earl "Mickey" Taborn
OF/P	Bob Thurman

1951-52

3B	Félix "Jueyito" Andrades
3B	Pedro Juan Arroyo
P	Dan Bankhead
OF	Willard Brown
P	Luis Raúl Cabrera
OF	Orlando Casellas
SS	James "Buster" Clarkson
P	Moisés Cohen
P	Eugene Collins
OF/P	Johnny Davis
SS	Efigenio "Cocó" Ferrer
OF	Alfonso Gerard
2B	Jim "Junior" Gilliam
P/OF	Rubén Gómez
P	Walter James
P	Angel Ortíz
P	Rafaelito Ortíz
1B	Fernando Ramos
1B	José "Pepe Lucas" St. Clair
OF	Juan Sánchez
MGR	George Scales
P	Pedro Seda
P	Domingo "McDuffie" Sevilla
C	Valmy Thomas
OF/P	Bob Thurman
C	Manuel "Liquito" Traboux
P	Murray Wall

1950-51

3B	Félix "Jueyito" Andrades
3B	Pedro Juan Arroyo

1952-53

3B	Félix "Jueyito" Andrades
3B	Pedro Juan Arroyo

OF	Willard Brown
OF	Billy Bruton
P	Luis Raúl Cabrera
OF	Orlando Casellas
3B/SS/ MGR	James "Buster" Clarkson
OF	Roberto Clemente
OF/1B/P	Johnny Davis
SS	Efigenio "Cocó" Ferrer
2B	William "Papi" Figueroa
OF	Alfonso Gerard
2B	Jim "Junior" Gilliam
P/OF	Rubén Gómez
P	Alba "Bobo" Holloman
P	Dick Hoover
SS	Billy Hunter
P	Walter James
P	Eleuterio "Tellito" López
P	Angel Ortíz
P	Benjamín Quintana
P	Milton Ralat
1B	José "Pepe Lucas" St. Clair
P	Pedro Seda
P	Domingo "McDuffie" Sevilla
C	Valmy Thomas
OF/P	Bob Thurman
C	Manuel "Liquito" Traboux

1953-54

P	Howard Anderson
3B	Félix "Jueyito" Andrades
3B	Pedro Juan Arroyo
OF	Roberto "Bobby" Balcena
1B	Wayne Belardi
OF	Willard Brown
P	Luis Raúl Cabrera
3B/SS/ MGR	James "Buster" Clarkson
OF	Roberto Clemente
3B	Ray Dandridge
2B	William "Papi" Figueroa
OF	Alfonso Gerard
P/OF	Rubén Gómez
P	Bill Greason
OF	Félix Guilbe
P	Alba "Bobo" Holloman
P	Walter James
P	Tom Lasorda
P	Eleuterio "Tellito" López
P	José "Pepín" Pereira
P	Ismael Pérez
P	Benjamín Quintana
P	Milton Ralat
2B/SS	Curtis Roberts
1B	José "Pepe Lucas" St.Clair

P	Jorge "Garabato" Sackie
C	Valmy Thomas
OF/1B/P	Bob Thurman
P	William Torres
C	Manuel "Liquito" Traboux
SS	Artie Wilson

1954-55

3B	Pedro Juan Arroyo
P	Pete Burnside
P	Luis Raúl Cabrera
C	Harry Chiti
3B	James "Buster" Clarkson
OF	Roberto Clemente
1B	George Crowe
2B	William "Papi" Figueroa
MGR	Herman Franks
SS	Billy Gardner
P/OF/PR	Rubén Gómez
P	Bill Greason
OF/P	Hal Jeffcoat
P	Sam Jones
SS	Billy Klaus
P	Eleuterio "Tellito" López
OF	Willie Mays
OF/PH	Luis R. Olmo
P	Benjamín Quintana
P	Milton Ralat
1B	José "Pepe Lucas" St. Clair
P	Jorge "Garabato" Sackie
2B	Ronnie Samford
C	Valmy Thomas
OF/P	Bob Thurman
C	Manuel "Liquito" Traboux
2B	Artie Wilson
SS	Don Zimmer

1955-56

3B	Pedro Juan Arroyo
OF	Félix Baez
P	Bud Byerly
P	Luis Raúl Cabrera
1B	Orlando "Peruchín" Cepeda
OF	Allie Clark
3B	James "Buster" Clarkson
OF	Roberto Clemente
P	Jim Constable
2B	William "Papi" Figueroa
MGR	Herman Franks
OF	Alfonso Gerard
P/OF	Rubén Gómez
P	Bill Greason
P	Angel Hernaíz

OF	Bob Lennon
P	Julio Navarro
OF	Luis R. Olmo
3B	José Pagán
P	Juan "Terín" Pizarro
P	William Powell
P	Milton Ralat
P	Steve Ridzik
2B	Ronnie Samford
SS	Darryl Spencer
C	Valmy Thomas
OF/P	Bob Thurman
C	Manuel "Liquito" Traboux
1B	Bill White
P	Al Worthington
SS/OF	Don Zimmer

1956-57

OF	Félix Baez
OF/1B	Willard Brown
1B	Orlando "Peruchín" Cepeda
OF	Roberto Clemente
MGR	Ramón "Monchile" Concepción
IF	Andrés Curet
2B	William "Papi" Figueroa
P	Marion Fricano
OF	Alfonso Gerard
OF/P	Rubén Gómez
P	Charles Gorin
P	Bill Greason
OF	Earl Hersch
P	David King
SS	Joe Koppe
P	Harry "Duke" Markell
UT	Félix Morales
P	Julio Navarro
MGR	Ted Norbert
3B	José Pagán
P	Juan "Terín" Pizarro
P	Milton Ralat
2B	Ronnie Samford
C	Valmy Thomas
OF	Bob Thurman
C	Manuel "Liquito" Traboux
1B	Bill White

1957-58

OF	Félix Baez
UT	José I. Carmona
1B	Orlando "Peruchín" Cepeda
MGR	Ramón "Monchile" Concepción
UT	Al Cruz Rodríguez
IF	Andrés Curet

P	Marion Fricano
2B	William "Papi" Figueroa
OF	Alfonso Gerard
P/OF	Rubén Gómez
P	Bill Greason
SS	Bill Harrell
P	David King
P	Marcelino Lissier
P	Luis Luzunaris
P	Salvador Martínez
P	Julio Navarro
3B	José Pagán
P	Antonio Quiñónes
P	Milton Ralat
P	Joaquín Santana
UT	Víctor Santos
C	Valmy Thomas
OF/P	Bob Thurman
C	Manuel "Liquito" Traboux

1958-59

2B/SS	Antonio Alomar
3B	Ken Aspromonte
OF	Jackie Brandt
2B	José I. Carmona
1B	Orlando "Peruchín" Cepeda
MGR	Ramón "Monchile" Concepción
2B	Al Cruz Rodríguez
IF	Andrés Curet
P	Marion Fricano
P	Rubén Gómez
P	Bill Greason
2B	Samuel "Sammy" Hernández
OF	Willie Kirkland
OF	Bob Lennon
P	Marcelino Lissier
OF	Félix Juan Maldonado
UT	Robert Morett
P	Julio Navarro
SS/3B	José Pagán
P	Antonio Quiñónes
P	Luis Sánchez
P	José "Pantalones" Santiago
C	Valmy Thomas
C	Manuel "Liquito" Traboux
P	Pete Wojey

1959-60

SS	Antonio Alomar
OF	Demetrio Alomar
P	Roberto Barbosa
OF	Félix Baez
OF	Celso Castro

OF/1B	Orlando "Peruchín" Cepeda		P	Ed Bauta
P	Clarence Churn		OF/1B	Martín Beltrán
UT	Al Cruz Rodríguez		MGR	Vern Benson
3B	Andrés Curet		SS	Leo Cárdenas
P/OF	Rubén Gómez		1B/OF	Orlando "Peruchín" Cepeda
P	Charlie Gorin		OF	Pedro Collazo Cepeda
2B	Samuel "Sammy" Hernández		3B	Cliff Cook
OF	Jim McDaniel		UT	Al Cruz Rodríguez
OF	Félix Juan Maldonado		P	Bob Gibson
MGR	Ray Murray		P/OF	Rubén Gómez
OF	Al Nagel		C/OF	Elrod Hendricks
P	Chris Nicolosi		2B	Samuel "Sammy" Hernández
MGR	Luis R. Olmo		2B	Julian Javier
P	Juan "Terín" Pizarro		3B	Ricardo Joseph
C	J. W. Porter		SS	Ron Kabbes
P	Luis Sánchez		OF	Félix Juan Maldonado
P	José "Pantalones" Santiago		P	Orlando "El Guajiro" Peña
C	Bernardo Schelmetty		P	Luis Peraza
C	Valmy Thomas		P	Juan "Terín" Pizarro
C	Manuel "Liquito" Traboux		P	Efigenio Rivera
			P	Al Schroll
			C	Valmy Thomas

1960-61

SS	Antonio Alomar			**1962-63**
OF	Demetrio Alomar			
OF	George Alusik		UT	Antonio Alomar
P	Roberto Barbosa		P	Craig Anderson
OF/1B	Martín Beltrán		1B	Martín Beltrán
1B	Orlando "Peruchín" Cepeda		IF/OF	Leo Burke
3B	Cliff Cook		OF	Pedro Collazo Cepeda
UT	Al Cruz Rodríguez		P	Bill Dailey
P	Mark Freeman		3B	Miguel de la Hoz
OF/P	Rubén Gómez		P	Frank Funk
C	Elrod Hendricks		C	Sixto "Tuta" García
2B	Samuel "Sammy" Hernández		P	José "Kindo" Geigel
OF	Joe Hicks		P	Rubén Gómez
OF	Miguel Lebrón		C	Elrod Hendricks
OF	Félix Juan Maldonado		2B	Samuel "Sammy" Hernández
P	Carl Mathias		MGR	Ray Katt
OF/C	Gene Oliver		P	Sam McDowell
MGR	Luis R. Olmo		OF	Félix Juan Maldonado
1B	Larry Osborne		SS	Arturito Miranda
P/OF	Juan "Terín" Pizarro		P	Luis Peraza
P	Efigenio Rivera		P	Juan "Terín" Pizarro
P	José "Pantalones" Santiago		P	Efigenio Rivera
C	Valmy Thomas		SS	Hiraldo "Chico" Ruíz
UT	Rafael Torruellas		OF	José Tartabull
			C	Valmy Thomas
			P	Dave Tyriver
			OF	Tony Washington

1961-62

2B	Antonio Alomar			
OF	Demetrio Alomar			**1963-64**
P	Craig Anderson			
P	Roberto Barbosa		OF/1B	Martín Beltrán
IF	Jim Baumer		C	Bill Bryan

C	J. M. Cepeda
1B	Orlando "Peruchín" Cepeda
C	José Cruz
3B	Miguel de la Hoz
P	Desiderio de León
IF/OF	Arlo Engel
OF	Al Ferrara
C	Sixto "Tuta" García
P	José "Kindo" Geigel
MGR	Preston Gómez
P	Rubén Gómez
C	Elrod Hendricks
2B	Samuel "Sammy" Hernández
P	G. McWilliams
OF	Félix Juan Maldonado
SS	Arturito Miranda
P	Aurelio Monteagudo
P	Phil Ortega
P	Orlando "El Guajiro" Peña
P	F. Ramón Pérez
P	Juan "Terín" Pizarro
P	Efigenio Rivera
SS	Hiraldo "Chico" Ruíz
P	Diego Seguí
OF	José Tartabull
OF	Luis Vilella
2B	Harry Watts

1964-65

C	Felipe Antonetty
OF/1B	Jim Beauchamp
OF/1B	Martín Beltrán
P	George Brunet
C	J. M. Cepeda
1B	Orlando "Peruchín" Cepeda
C	José Cruz
P	Desiderio de León
P	Jim Dickson
C	Sixto "Tuta" García
P	José "Kindo" Geigel
MGR	Preston Gómez
P	Rubén Gómez
C	Jesse Gonder
OF	Lou Johnson
P	Manly Johnston
OF	Félix Juan Maldonado
3B	José Martínez
SS	Arturito Miranda
MGR/ 3B/OF	Joe Morgan*
P	Phil Ortega
1B/3B	Atanasio "Tany" Pérez
P	Francisco "Mon" Pérez
P	Juan "Terín" Pizarro

*Interim manager.

UT	Arsenio "Pinolo" Rodríguez
2B	Marv Staehle
P	Fred Talbot

1965-66

2B	Angel Luis Alcaraz
C	Felipe Antonetty
OF/1B	Martín Beltrán
P	Danny Coombs
P	Antonio de Jesús
P	William de Jesús
UT	Félix de León
3B	Steve Demeter
C	Sixto "Tuta" García
P	José "Kindo" Geigel
P	Rubén Gómez
1B	Chuck Harrison
C	Elrod Hendricks
OF	Félix Juan Maldonado
P	Jerry Messerly
SS	Arturito Miranda
MGR	Luis R. Olmo
P	Darrell Osteen
1B	Atanasio "Tany" Pérez
P	Juan "Terín" Pizarro
P	Efigenio Rivera
UT	Arsenio "Pinolo" Rodríguez
OF	Bob Sadowski
OF	Art Shamsky
OF	Gilberto Torres
P	Israel Torres
P	Bob Wilson

1966-67

2B	Angel Luis Alcaraz
1B/PH	Martín Beltrán
OF	Paul Blair
1B	Orlando "Peruchín" Cepeda
P	Ted Davidson
P	William de Jesús
UT	Félix de León
3B	Steve Demeter
P	José "Kindo" Geigel
P	Rubén Gómez
C	Larry Haney
C/1B	Elrod Hendricks
P	Dick Hughes
OF	Félix Juan Maldonado
IF	Anselmo Martínez
OF	Dave May
SS	Arturito Miranda
P	Darrell Osteen
1B/3B	Atanasio "Tany" Pérez

P	Juan "Terín" Pizarro
UT	Arsenio "Pinolo" Rodríguez
OF	Gilberto Torres
P	Israel Torres
MGR	Earl Weaver

1967-68

OF	Javier "Terín" Andino
1B/PH	Martín Beltrán
OF	Paul Blair
P	Jaime Burgos
1B	Orlando "Peruchín" Cepeda
P	Ted Davidson
P	William de Jesús
P	José "Kindo" Geigel
P	Rubén Gómez
C	Larry Haney
P	Jim Hardin
C/1B	Elrod Hendricks
2B	Dave Johnson
P	Bob Lee
P	Dave Leonhard
OF	Félix Juan Maldonado
SS	Anselmo Martínez
OF	Dave May
SS	Arturito Miranda
P	Rogelio Moret
P	Darrell Osteen
1B/3B	Atanasio "Tany" Pérez
P	Francisco "Mon" Pérez
P	Juan "Terín" Pizarro
SS	Milton Ramírez
2B	Antonio Rodríguez
UT	Arsenio "Pinolo" Rodríguez
C/OF	Gerry Rodríguez
OF	Gilberto Torres
OF	Israel Torres
SS	Víctor Torruellas
IF/OF	J. Velilla
MGR	Earl Weaver

1968-69

OF	Javier "Terín" Andino
1B	Martín Beltrán
OF	Paul Blair
P	Wally Bunker
UT	José Candelaria
SS	Leo Cárdenas
P	J. Cisterna
P	William de Jesús
3B	Joe Foy
P	José "Kindo" Geigel
P	Rubén Gómez
2B	Julio Gotay
P	Jim Hardin

C	Elrod Hendricks
P	Dave Leonhard
P	Rosario "Papo" Llanos
OF	Félix Juan Maldonado
SS	Anselmo Martínez
OF	Dave May
UT	Arturito Miranda
P	Rogelio Moret
P	Jim Palmer
P	Juan "Terín" Pizarro
SS	Milton Ramírez
MGR	Frank Robinson
UT	Arsenio "Pinolo" Rodríguez
C	Gerry Rodríguez
1B	George Scott
P	Al Severinsen
OF	Gilberto Torres

1969-70

OF	Javier "Terín" Andino
P	Fred Beene
1B	Martín Beltrán
P	Frank Bertaina
P	Jaime Burgos
P	Bob Castiglione
P	William de Jesús
UT	Wilfredo García
P	José "Kindo" Geigel
P	Rubén Gómez
2B	Julio Gotay
C	Elrod Hendricks
P	Dave Leonhard
OF	Félix Juan Maldonado
SS	Anselmo Martínez
OF	Dave May
SS	Arturito Miranda
P	Rogelio Moret
OF	Curt Motton
3B	Atanasio "Tany" Pérez
P	Juan "Terín" Pizarro
OF	Merv Rettenmund
MGR	Frank Robinson
UT	Arsenio "Pinolo" Rodríguez
C/OF	Gerry Rodríguez
1B	George Scott
P	Al Severinsen
P	Thad Tillotson
OF	Gilberto Torres
SS	Víctor Torruellas
P	Fernando Vega
P	Bob Wolfe

1970-71

OF	Javier "Terín" Andino
OF	Don Baylor

P	Fred Beene
P	Bob Chlupsa
P	Joe Decker
P	William de Jesús
OF	Roger Freed
P	José "Kindo" Geigel
P	Rubén Gómez
2B	Julio Gotay
P	Larry Gura
C	Elrod Hendricks
OF	Reggie Jackson
P	Mike Kekich
P	Dave Leonhard
OF	Félix Juan Maldonado
2B/3B	Anselmo Martínez
C	John "Buck" Martínez
2B/SS	Arturito Miranda
P	Rogelio Moret
P	Darrell Osteen
1B	Atanasio "Tany" Pérez
P	Juan "Terín" Pizarro
SS	Milton Ramírez
MGR	Frank Robinson
OF/3B	Arsenio "Pinolo" Rodríguez
OF	Gilberto Torres
P	Fernando Vega

1971-72

P	Víctor Agosto
OF	Javier "Terín" Andino
OF	John "Dusty" Baker
OF/1B/3B	Don Baylor
P	Fred Beene
P	Rubén Castillo
1B	Orlando "Peruchín" Cepeda
P	Bob Chlupsa
OF	Rich Coggins
1B/OF	Terry Crowley
SS	Jerry DaVanon
P	Joe Decker
P	William de Jesús
P	Mike Garman
P	José "Kindo" Geigel
MGR	Rubén Gómez
2B	Julio Gotay
P	Dave Leonhard
P	Rosario "Papo" Llanos
UT	Anselmo Martínez
C	John "Buck" Martínez
UT	Arturito Miranda
P	Rogelio Moret
OF	Reyes Ortíz
P	Juan "Terín" Pizarro
IF	R. Quiñónes
2B/SS	Milton Ramírez
1B/3B	Arsenio "Pinolo" Rodríguez

C	Gerry Rodríguez
P	Esteban Texidor
P	Fernando Vega

1972-73

P	Víctor Agosto
P	Doyle Alexander
P	Lloyd Allen
OF	Javier "Terín" Andino
OF	Don Baylor
SS	Juan José Beníquez
P	Rubén Castillo
3B	Ron Cey
OF	Willie Crawford
2B	Jerry DaVanon
P	William de Jesús
OF	Gilberto "Bertín" Flores
P	Rubén Gómez
2B	Julio Gotay
C	Elrod Hendricks
P	Ramón "Mon" Hernández
P	Dave Leonhard
P	Rosario "Papo" Llanos
OF	Angel Mangual
SS	Arturito Miranda
P	Rogelio Moret
1B	Atanasio "Tany" Pérez
P	Juan "Terín" Pizarro
P	Bob Reynolds
MGR	Frank Robinson
UT	Arsenio "Pinolo" Rodríguez
C	Gerry Rodríguez
P	Don Rose
UT	Manuel "Nolín" Ruíz
P	Mike Strahler
P	Esteban Texidor
OF	Ron Woods

1973-74

P	Víctor Agosto
2B/DH	Angel Luis Alcaraz
P	Mel Behney
SS	Juan José Beníquez
2B/3B	Ron Cash
1B	Terry Crowley
P	William de Jesús
P	Steve Dunning
P	Ed Farmer
OF	Gilberto "Bertín" Flores
P	Rubén Gómez
OF	George Hendrick
C/DH	Elrod Hendricks
P	Ramón "Mon" Hernández

3B	Dave Kingman
OF	Angel Mangual
3B/SS	Arturito Miranda
P	Rogelio Moret
1B/DH	Ismael Oquendo
P	Juan "Terín" Pizarro
P	Bob Reynolds
OF	Mickey Rivers
MGR	Frank Robinson
UT	Arsenio "Pinolo" Rodríguez
C	Gerry Rodríguez
P	Gilberto Rondón
UT`	Manuel "Nolín" Ruíz
C	Charlie Sands
P	Dave Sells
P	Mike Strahler
OF	Champ Summers
P	Esteban Texidor

1974-75

P	Víctor Agosto
2B/DH	Angel Luis Alcaraz
2B	Santos "Sandy" Alomar, Sr.
OF	Juan José Beníquez
2B	Antonio "Tony" Bernazard
P	Mark Bomback
1B	Danny Cater
DH	Orlando "Peruchín" Cepeda
3B	Doug DeCinces
OF	Luis Delgado
P	Ed Farmer
SS	Luis Ferrer
P	Jim Fuller
P	Rubén Gómez
C	Elrod Hendricks
P	Ramón "Mon" Hernández
P	Jesse Jefferson
OF	Leron Lee
OF	Jerry Martin
P	Dyar Miller
3B/SS	Arturito Miranda
P	Rogelio Moret
P	Don Newhauser
1B/DH	Ismael Oquendo
OF	José "Polilla" Ortíz
P	Juan "Terín" Pizarro
OF	Mickey Rivers
MGR	Frank Robinson
3B/DH	Arsenio "Pinolo" Rodríguez
C	Gerry Rodríguez
P	Gilberto Rondón
SS/2B	Manuel "Nolín" Ruíz
P	Mike Strahler
P	Mark Willis
P	Esteban Texidor
SS	Robin Yount

1975-76

P	Glenn Abbott
2B	Angel Luis Alcaraz
2B	Santos "Sandy" Alomar, Sr.
P	Rick Baldwin
OF	Juan José Beníquez
OF	Luis Delgado
SS	Luis Ferrer
IF	Luis R. García
2B/SS	Rod Gilbreath
P	Rubén Gómez
C	Elrod Hendricks
P	Ramón "Mon" Hernández
DH/3B	Ron Jackson
P	Don Kirkwood
P	Dick Lange
MGR	Jack McKeon
SS	Mike Miley
SS	Arturito Miranda
P	Rogelio Moret
1B/DH	Ismael Oquendo
OF	José "Polilla" Ortíz
P	Juan "Terín" Pizarro
SS	Milton Ramírez
UT/DH	Arsenio "Pinolo" Rodríguez
C	Gerry Rodríguez
P	Gilberto Rondón
UT	Manuel "Nolín" Ruíz
C/DH	Orlando Sánchez
OF	Charlie Spikes
P	Ron Tate
P	Esteban Texidor
P	Hank Webb
OF	Jim Wohlford

1976-77

2B	Santos "Sandy" Alomar, Sr.
SS	Alan Bannister
OF	Juan José Beníquez
P	Tom Bruno
P	Rick Camp
2B	Julio Cruz
3B	Mike Cubbage
OF	Luis Delgado
IF	Luis R. García
3B	Wayne Gross
P	Paul Hartzell
C	Elrod Hendricks
P	Ramón "Mon" Hernández
C	Luis Isaac
OF	Orlando Isales
P	Frank LaCorte
MGR	Jack McKeon
P	Rogelio Moret
OF	José Oppenheimer

1B/DH	Ismael Oquendo
OF	José "Polilla" Ortíz
P	Mike Overy
P	Angel Pérez
3B/SS	Julián Pérez
P	Gerald Pirtle
P	Juan "Terín" Pizarro
C/3B/OF	Ron Pruitt
P	Gilberto Rondón
SS	Manuel "Nolín" Ruíz
C/DH/1B	Orlando Sánchez
3B	Tommy Sandt
1B	Tony Solaita
P	Esteban Texidor
P	Jackson Todd
DH/1B	Danny Walton

1977-78

2B	Santos "Sandy" Alomar, Sr.
OF	Dell Alston
P	Larry Andersen
OF	Juan José Beníquez
P	Tom Bruno
OF	Luis Delgado
P	Ed Farmer
P	Bob Galasso
C	Elrod Hendricks
P	Ramón "Mon" Hernández
C	Luis Isaac
OF	Orlando Isales
MGR	Jack Krol
PH	Manuel Limery
P	Balor Moore
OF	José Morales
P	Rogelio Moret
OF	José Oppenheimer
OF	Juan Oppenheimer
1B/DH	Ismael Oquendo
P	Antonio Pérez
3B/1B	Julián Pérez
3B	Jamie Quirk
P	Ken Reynolds
P	Luis Rodríguez
P	Gilberto Rondón
SS/2B	Manuel "Nolín" Ruíz
C/DH/OF	Orlando Sánchez
P	Jim Sutton
P	Esteban Texidor
OF	Gary Woods

1978-79

P	Larry Andersen
OF	Juan José Beníquez
P	Tom Bruno
2B	Julio Cruz

P	Rubén Cruz
OF	Paul Dade
OF	Luis Delgado
3B/OF	Rob Ellis
P	Dave Ford
C	Luis Isaac
OF	Orlando Isales
2B	Tim Johnson
P	Lynn McKinney
P	Rogelio Moret
1B/DH	Ismael Oquendo
P	Angel Pérez
DH	Atanasio "Tany" Pérez
3B/SS	Julián Pérez
C/OF	Ron Pruitt
P	Andy Replogle
SS	Carlos Ríos
MGR/DH	Frank Robinson
P	Gilberto Rondón
2B/SS	Manuel "Nolín" Ruíz
UT	Orlando Sánchez
P	José Sevillano
2B	Billy Smith
P	Randy Stein
P	Earl Stephenson
P	Tim Stoddard
P	Esteban Texidor
OF	Gorman Thomas

1979-80

1B/DH	Gary Alexander
C	Gary Allenson
P	Larry Andersen
2B	Santos "Sandy" Alomar, Sr.
IF	Edwin Aponte
P	Len Barker
3B	Kevin Bell
OF	Juan José Beniquez
P	Bill Caudill
P	David Clyde
P	Carlos Dávila
OF	Dick Davis
OF	Luis Delgado
P	Carlos Díaz
IF	Enrique Díaz
P	Wayne Garland
IF	Julián Gutierrez
P	Guillermo Hernández
P	Ramón "Mon" Hernández
C	Luis Isaac
OF	Orlando Isales
OF	Bob Molinaro
P	Rogelio Moret
1B/DH	Ismael Oquendo
P	Angel Pérez
DH/1B	Atanasio "Tany" Pérez

UT	Julián Pérez
C/OF	Ron Pruitt
2B/3B	Lenny Randle
SS	Carlos Ríos
MGR	Frank Robinson
P	Gilberto Rondón
2B/SS	Manuel "Nolín" Ruíz
UT	Orlando Sánchez
IF	Kurt Siebert
P	Tim Stoddard
OF	Mike Vail
OF	Roy White

1980-81

1B	Willie Aikens
C	Gary Allenson
OF/DH	Benigno "Benny" Ayala
3B	Kevin Bell
OF	Juan José Beníquez
P	Jaime Cocanower
2B	Julio Cruz
P	Carlos Dávila
SS	Iván de Jesús
IF	Luis de León
P	Carlos Díaz
P	Enrique Díaz
P	Gene Garber
IF/OF	Fernando González
OF	Dave Henderson
C	Terry Kennedy
OF	Rudy Law
P	Fred Martínez
P	Rogelio Moret
OF	Miguel Negrón
P	Bob Owchinko
UT	Julián Pérez
P	Joaquín Quintana
2B	Lenny Randle
SS	Carlos Ríos
MGR	Octavio "Cookie" Rojas
P	Gilberto Rondón
C	Luis "Papo" Rosado
UT	Manuel "Nolín" Ruíz
C/DH	Orlando Sánchez
P	Dave Schuler
P	Lee Smith
IF	Jerry Terrell
P	Steve Trout
P	John Urrea

1981-82

MGR	Jack Aker
P	Bud Anderson
OF/DH	Benigno "Benny" Ayala
P	Joe Beckwith

OF	Juan José Beníquez
P	Bob Blyth
3B	Fritz Connally
P	Joe Cowley
SS	Iván de Jesús
1F	Luis de León
P	Carlos Díaz
P	Eduardo Figueroa
MGR	Rubén Gómez
IF/OF	Fernando González
P	Guillermo Hernández
OF	Rudy Law
P	Charlie Leibrandt
OF	Carlos Lezcano
1B	Guillermo Montañez
OF	Jerry Morales
P	Rogelio Moret
P	Willard Mueller
OF	Miguel Negrón
P	Reggie Patterson
IF	Julián Pérez
P	Joaquín Quintana
2B	Kevin Rhomberg
SS	Carlos Ríos
C	Eliseo "Ellie" Rodríguez
P	Gilberto Rondón
C	Luis "Papo" Rosado
UT	Manuel "Nolín" Ruíz
C/DH	Orlando Sánchez
P	Paul Semall
3B	Pat Tabler

1982-83

MGR	Jack Aker
P	José Alvarez
IF	Edwin Aponte
P	Carlos Arroyo
OF/DH	Benigno "Benny" Ayala
C	Chris Bando
OF	Juan José Beníquez
P	Mark Brown
P	Ken Dayley
SS	Iván de Jesús
P	Carlos Díaz
P	Eduardo Figueroa
2B	Brian Giles
IF/OF	Fernando González
3B	Glenn Gulliver
P	Guillermo Hernández
P	Brian Kelly
OF	Sixto Lezcano
1B	Fernando Marín
1B	Guillermo Montañez
P	Edwin Morales
OF	Jerry Morales
P	Rogelio Moret

OF	Miguel Negrón
P	Reggie Patterson
DH	Atanasio "Tany" Pérez
IF	Julián Pérez
P	Joaquín Quintana
SS	Carlos Ríos
C	Eliseo "Ellie" Rodríguez
2B/SS	Víctor Rodríquez, Sr.
2B/SS	Manuel "Nolín" Ruíz
UT	Orlando Sánchez
IF	Eddie Santos
P	Mark Smith
3B/1B	Pat Tabler
P	Luis Tiant
DH/OF	Otoniel "Otto" Vélez

1983-84

P	José Alvarez
P	Bud Anderson
IF	Edwin Aponte
P	Carlos Arroyo
OF	Juan José Beníquez
P	Tom Brennan
P	Mark Brown
P	Carlos Cabassa
SS	Iván de Jesús
IF	Luis de León
P	Eduardo Figueroa
IF/OF	Fernando González
P	Julián González
P	Scott Holman
SS	Ed Jurak
P	Bob Lacey
3B	Steve Lubratich
P	Steve Luebber
P	Rick Mahler
MGR	Ray Miller
1B	Guillermo Montañez
P	Edwin Morales
OF	Jerry Morales
OF	Miguel Negrón
P	John Pacella
C	Eliseo "Ellie" Rodríguez
2B	Víctor Rodríguez, Sr.
UT	Manuel "Nolín" Ruíz
DH/1B	Orlando Sánchez
OF	John Shelby
P	Nate Snell
DH/OF	Otoniel "Otto" Vélez
P	Bob Walk
C	Jerry Willard
OF	Mike Young

1984-85

C	Santos "Sandy" Alomar, Jr.
P	Carmelo Alvarez

P	Carlos Arroyo
OF	Juan José Beníquez
P	Héctor Berríos
P	Rich Carlucci
P	Jeff Dedmon
SS	Iván de Jesús
IF	Luis de León
SS	Mario Díaz
P	Brian Fisher
P	Jerry Don Gleaton
3B/SS	Julio C. González
P	Tom Henke
P	Brad "The Animal" Lesley
P	Jim Lewis
P	Andy McGaffigan
P	Dennis Martínez
1B	Guillermo Montañez
OF	Jerry Morales
OF	Otis Nixon
SS	Dave Owen
P	John Pacella
3B	Kelly Paris
P	Mike Payne
P	Nelson Pedraza
P	Efraín Rodríguez
2B/3B	Víctor Rodríguez, Sr.
2B	Paul Runge
DH	Orlando Sánchez
UT	Rafael Sánchez
OF	John Shelby
OF	Rubén "El Indio" Sierra
P	Ulises "Candy" Sierra
P	Zane Smith
DH	Otoniel "Otto" Vélez
MGR	Frank Verdi
C	Jerry Willard
OF	Mike Young

1985-86

2B	Luis Aguayo
C	Santos "Sandy" Alomar, Jr.
MGR	Santos " Sandy" Alomar, Sr.
P	Jeff Barkley
OF	Juan José Beníquez
P	Rich Carlucci
IF	Luis Cruz
SS	Iván de Jesús
SS	Mario Díaz
P	Luis Faccio
P	Tony Ferreira
P	Brad Havens
3B	Jack Howell
OF	Carlos Lezcano
OF	Sixto Lezcano
2B	José "Chico" Lind
P	Tony Mack

2B	Mark McLemore		OF	Juan José Beníquez
C	Luis Martínez		P	John Burgos
OF	Jaime Moreno		P	José Calderón
OF	Pedro Muñoz		OF	Dave Clark
C	Al Pardo		SS	Iván de Jesús
UT	Nelson Pedraza		OF	Mike Devereaux
P	Craig Pippin		P	Mike Hartley
P	Reggie Ritter		OF	George Hinshaw
P	Geraldo Sánchez		P	Jeff Kaiser
C/DH/1B	Orlando Sánchez		MGR	Kevin Kennedy
OF	Rubén "El Indio" Sierra		P	Bill Krueger
P	Ulises "Candy" Sierra		P	Stan Kyles
IF	Roy Silver		OF	Sixto Lezcano
MGR	Frank Verdi		2B	José "Chico" Lind
OF	Devon White		P	Ron Mathis
P	Mitch "Wild Thing" Williams		IF	José Marzán
			P	Edwin Morales
			P	Jaime Navarro
	1986-87		P	Dave Oliveras
			P	Mike Pérez
2B	Luis Aguayo		P	Jeff Reece
C	Santos "Sandy" Alomar, Jr.		P	Reggie Ritter
OF	Juan José Beníquez		P	Geraldo Sánchez
2B	Jerry Browne		DH/1B/	Orlando Sánchez
P	John Burgos		OF	
P	Jaime Cocanower		P	Jack Savage
P	Glenn Cook		P	Rubén "El Indio" Sierra
IF	Luis Cruz		P	Ulises "Candy" Sierra
SS	Iván de Jesús		P	Eric Sonberg
OF	Mike Devereaux		P	Bob Stoddard
P	Jeff Edwards		IF	Amilcar Valdez
C	Jack Fimple		SS	José Valentín
P	Rusty Ford		C	Jerry Willard
OF	Chris Gwynn		P	Ed Wojna
P	Bob Hamilton		1B/3B	Tracy Woodson
P	Jimmy Jones			
MGR	Kevin Kennedy			
OF	Sixto Lezcano			**1988-89**
2B	José "Chico" Lind			
P	Manuel Mercado		P	Mike Basso
P	Rich Monteleone		OF	Juan José Beníquez
P	Mike Pérez		P	John Burgos
P	Víctor Quiles		P	Dennis Burtt
P	Gabalier Robles		P	José Calderón
P	Geraldo Sánchez		OF	Dave Clark
UT	Orlando Sánchez		OF	Tony Colón
1B	Larry See		P	Steve Davis
P	Steve Shirley		SS	Iván de Jesús
OF	Rubén "El Indio" Sierra		OF	Mike Devereaux
1B/DH	Jesús "Samarito" Vega		P	Mike Hartley
P	Colin Ward		P	Dwayne Henry
3B	Tracy Woodson		P	Mike Jones
			MGR	Kevin Kennedy
			OF	Carlos Laboy
	1987-88		OF	Sixto Lezcano
			2B	José "Chico" Lind
C	Santos "Sandy" Alomar, Jr.		UT	Luis López
SS	Jay Bell		3B	Jeff Manto

PH	José Marzán
PH	Jerry Morales
C/1B	Angel Morris
P	Mike Muñoz
P	Jaime Navarro
P	Jorge Ojeda
P	Dave Oliveras
UT	Javier Ortíz
P	Mike Pérez
2B/SS	Edgardo Romero
P	Geraldo Sánchez
DH/C	Orlando Sánchez
OF	Rubén "El Indio" Sierra
OF	Dwight Smith
IF	Amilcar Valdez
SS	José Valentín
P	John Wetteland
P	Rich Yett

1989-90

2B	José Angleró
OF	Juan Belbrú
UT	José Birriel
P	José Calderón
SS	Iván de Jesús
OF	Albert Hall
3B	Charlie Hayes
P	Shawn Holman
P	Jim Hvizda
P	Randy Kramer
OF	Carlos Laboy
P	José Lebrón
2B	José "Chico" Lind
OF	Luis López
SS	Luis López, Jr.
P	Morris Madden
UT	José Marzán
C	Terry McGriff
MGR	Ray Miller
1B/C	Angel Morris
P	Jaime Navarro
P	Jorge Ojeda
P	Bob Patterson
SS	Rey Quiñónes
P	Rick Reed
OF	José Rivera
P	Tomás Rodríguez
P	Mike Roesler
P	Scott Ruskin
1B	Mark Ryal
OF	Osvaldo Sánchez
P	Delvy Santiago
P	Bob Sebra
P	Ulises "Candy" Sierra

2B	José Valentín
DH	Osvaldo "Ozzie" Virgil, Jr.

1990-91

OF	Edwin Alicea
2B	José Angleró
OF	Eric Anthony
P	Luis Aquino
OF	Adán Ayala
OF	Juan Belbrú
DH/1B/OF	Juan José Beníquez
P	Kevin Brown
DH/OF	Tony Brown
OF	Jacob Brumfield
P	John Burgos
P	José Calderón
2B	Casey Candaele
1B	Edgard Castro
IF	Alan Cockrell
MGR	Mike Cubbage
OF	Mark Davis*
DH	Mike Davis
C/1B	Carlos Delgado
P	Tony Fossas*
P	Chris George
3B	Leo Gómez
P	Jack Lazorko*
P	José Lebrón
SS	Scott Leius
2B	Mark Lemke
P	José Meléndez
1B/DH	Angel Morris
P	Jaime Navarro
IF	Javier Ocasio
MGR	Max "Mako" Oliveras
C	Adalberto "Junior" Ortíz
OF	Darren Reed
1B/PH	Orlando Sánchez
OF	Osvaldo Sánchez
P	Delvy Santiago
P	Ulises "Candy" Sierra
P	Rick Thompson
OF	Andy Tomberlin
P	Colby Ward
P	David West
IF	Carlos Zayas

1991-92

P	Kyle Abbott
C/3B/OF	Troy Afenir
P	José Alberro

Played in the post-season only.

OF	Edwin Alicea
P	José Alvarez*
2B	José Angleró
P	Chris Beasley
1B	Jim Bowie
P	Jim Brennan
P	John Burgos
P	José Calderón
OF	Rubén Cruz
SS	Iván de Jesús
C/1B	Carlos Delgado
OF	Eric Fox
3B	Leo Gómez
SS/3B/C	Scott Hemond
1B	Dann Howitt
OF	Ryan Klesko
P	Jim Kramer
P	José Lebrón
2B	Luis López, Jr.
P	José Meléndez
P	Bob Moore
DH/1B/P	Angel Morris
P	David Nied
MGR	Max "Mako" Oliveras
C	Adalberto "Junior" Ortíz
OF	Nick Ortíz
OF	Ricky Otero
SS	Rey Quiñónes
1B	Nicko Riesgo*
P	Lino Rivera
IF	Luis Rodríguez
2B	Tony Rodríguez
1B/DH/PH	Orlando Sánchez
OF	Osvaldo Sánchez
P	Delvy Santiago
P	Ulises "Candy" Sierra
P	Heathcliff Slocumb
P	Bill Taylor
UT	José Trujillo
P	Steve "Turk" Wendell
OF	Gerald Williams

1992-93

2B	Luis Aguayo
P	José Alberro
OF	Edwin Alicea
P	José Alvarez*
P	Luis Arroyo
P	Scott Bailes
P	Billy Brewer
P	Tim Burcham
P	Mike Cook
P	Edwin Correa*
OF	Rubén Cruz

C/DH	Carlos Delgado
OF	Eric Fox*
P	Willie Fraser
P	Jay Gainer
OF/DH	Juan "Igor" González
P	Greg Harris
P	José Lebrón
2B	José "Chico" Lind
SS	Luis López, Jr.
OF	Damon Mashore
1B	Francisco Meléndez
C	Orlando Mercado
OF	Keith Mitchell
2B	José "Chepito" Muñoz
P	Francisco Javier Oliveras
MGR	Max "Mako" Oliveras
C	Adalberto "Junior" Ortíz
OF	Nick Ortíz
3B	Germán "Deportivo" Rivera
P	Lino Rivera
2B	Tony Rodríguez
P	Napoleon Robinson
P	Darryl Scott
OF	Darrell Sherman
DH	Dickie Thon
1B	Héctor Villanueva
OF	Gerald Williams

1993-94

P	José Alberro
OF	Edwin Alicea
P	Luis Arroyo
P	Mike Bielecki
P	Kevin Brown
P	Renay Bryand
OF	Damon Buford
DH	Iván Calderón
C	Raúl Casanova
P	Silvio Censale
P	Marty Clary
P	Mike Cook
2B	Erick Corps
P	Edwin Correa
UT	Miguel Correa
SS	Edgar Díaz
3B	Edwin Díaz
2B	Mario Díaz
P	Ken Edenfield
OF	John Fantauzzi
P	Héctor Fargas
P	Willie Fraser
P	John Fritz
OF	Juan "Igor" González
2B	Luis López, Jr.

Played in the post-season only.

OF	Damon Mashore
P	Héctor Mercado
C	Orlando Mercado
P	Francisco Javier Oliveras
MGR	Max "Mako" Oliveras
C	Adalberto "Junior" Ortíz
P	Dave Otto
2B	Tony Rodríguez
OF	Darrell Sherman
OF	Rubén "El Indio" Sierra
P	Dennis Springer
DH	Dickie Thon
OF	Edgard Velázquez
DH/1B	Héctor Villanueva
OF	Gerald Williams
P	Mark Zapelli*
P	Bart Zapoli

1994-95

P	Luis Arroyo
OF/1B	Derek Bell
P	Erik Bennett
P	Héctor Berríos
OF	Juan Cardona
C	Raúl Casanova
P	Frank Castillo
P	Kevin Coffman
2B/3B/SS	Erick Corps
P	John Cummings
P	Tim Delgado
OF	Carl Everett
P	Luis Galindez
3B/1B	Leo Gómez
P	Eddie Guardado
P	Eric Hill
P	Ryan Karp
OF	Ed Larregui
2B	Luis López, Jr.
OF	Terrell Lowery
3B	Luis Lucca
2B/3B	Gabriel Martínez
SS/3B/2B	Luis Martínez
DH	José Molina
OF	Johnny Monell
P	Oscar Muñoz
OF	Troy O'Leary
MGR	Max "Mako" Oliveras
SS	Rey Ordoñez
C/1B	Adalberto "Junior" Ortíz
P	Troy Percival
OF\1B\3B	Eduardo Pérez
P	Benny Puig
P	Lino Rivera
IF	Víctor Rodríguez, Jr.

2B	Víctor Rodríguez, Sr.
P	Rich Scheid
OF/DH	Rubén "El Indio" Sierra
DH/1B	Dickie Thon
P	Aristalco Tirado
OF	Edgard Velázquez
1B/C/DH	Héctor Villanueva
OF	Gerald Williams

1995-96

P	Dennis "Oil Can" Boyd*
P	Chris Brock
OF	Jarvis Brown
P	Duff Brumley
OF	José Camilo
P	Silvio Censale
P	Ramser Correa
OF	José "Cheito" Cruz, Jr.
MGR	José "Cheo" Cruz, Sr.
P	José "Flauta" de Jesús
P	Ken Edenfield
P	Osvaldo Fernández
3B/1B	Leo Gómez
P	Matt Grott
P	Mike Ignasiak
P	Mark Kiefer
C	Pedro López
3B	Luis Lucca
SS	Gabriel Martínez
C	Orlando Mercado
OF/1B	Orlando Merced
DH	José Molina
OF	Johnny Monell
2B	José "Chepito" Muñoz
P	David Nied
OF	Melvin Nieves
P	Rafael Novoa
IF/OF	José Olmeda
SS	Rey Ordoñez
P	Bronswell Patrick
1B/3B/OF	Eduardo Pérez
C	Jorge Posada
P	Roberto Rivera
OF	Noel Rodríguez
P	Jorge Roque
P	Bienvenido Sánchez
P	Carl Schutz
SS/1B	Dave Silvestri
2B/OF	Mitch Simmons
OF/DH	Darryl Strawberry
OF	Edgard Velázquez
DH/C/1B	Héctor Villanueva
P	Ismael Villegas

Played in the post-season only.

1996-97

P	Stevenson Agosto
P	Scott Bailes
C	Richie Borrero
P	Silvio Censale
1B	Dennis Colón
P	Ramser Correa
OF	José "Cheito" Cruz, Jr.
P	José "Flauta" de Jesús
SS	Josué Espada
MGR	Matt Galante
3B/1B	Leo Gómez
P	Mike Grzanich
P	Chris Holt
OF	Brian Hunter
SS/3B	Russ Johnson
C/1B	Randy Knorr
C	Jesse Levis
C	Pedro López
P	Andrew Lorraine
P	Tom Martin
SS	Gabriel Martínez
P	Brian Maxcy
1B/DH	Orlando Merced
OF	James Mouton
2B	José "Chepito" Muñoz
P	Oscar Muñoz
OF	Melvin Nieves
P	Rafael Novoa
IF/OF	José Olmeda
P	Bronswell Patrick
1B/3B	Eduardo Pérez
C	Jorge Posada
P	Roberto Rivera
P	Bienvenido Sánchez
P	Doug Simons
P	Mark Small
OF	Edgard Velázquez
1B/C/DH	Héctor Villanueva
P	Ismael Villegas

1997-98

P	Stevenson Agosto
P	Luis Aquino
P	Julio Ayala
P	Manuel Barrios
SS	David Berg
OF/2B	Hiram Bocachica
C	Richie Borrero
OF	José Camilo
C	Ramón Castro
1B	Dennis Colón
P	Ramser Correa
P	José "Flauta" de Jesús

P	Antonio Díaz
2B	Edwin Díaz
P	Billy Díaz
P	Scott Elarton
SS	Josué Espada
P	Steve Falteisek
OF	Derrick Gibson
OF	Charles Gipson
P	LaTroy Hawkins
OF	Raúl Ibañez
P	Ryan Karp
OF	Marc Lewis
P	Richie Lewis
1B	Luis López
C	Pedro López
3B	Lou Lucca
MGR	Pete Mackanin
SS	Gabriel Martínez
P	Brian Maxcy
P	Trever Miller
2B	José Olmeda
P	Russ Ortíz
1B	Eduardo Pérez
DH/1B	Jorge Posada
P	Roberto Rivera
2B	Víctor Rodríguez
P	Juan J.C. Romero
OF	Rubén "El Indio" Sierra
OF/3B	Chris Stynes
MGR	Frankie Thon
P	Luis Torres
OF	Edgard Velázquez
P	Ismael Villegas
P	Mike Walter
P	Paul Wilson

1998-99

P	Stevenson Agosto
P	José Bautista
C	Richie Borrero
P	Chris Brock
C	Ramón Castro
P	Jason Cole
DH/1B	Dennis Colón
3B	Cirilo Cruz
OF	José "Cheito" Cruz, Jr.
P	Antonio Díaz
2B	Edwin Díaz
P	Tim Dixon
3B	Josué Espada
DH/OF	Jesús Feliciano
P	Chris Holt
OF	Raúl Ibañez
P	Ken Juarbe
P	Steve Karsay
P	Rick Krivda

SS	Felipe López		1B	Eduardo Pérez
3B	Luis López		P	Bob Radlosky
C	Pedro López		C	Mike Redmond
P	Esteban Maldonado		P	Roberto Rivera
DH	Orlando Merced		P	Juan (J.C.) Romero
1B	Hensley Meulens		SS	Rico Rossy
P	Iván Montane		P	J. Sexton*
P	Steve Montgomery		OF	Rubén "El Indio" Sierra
P	Gerónimo Newton		MGR	Frankie Thon
2B/3B	José Olmeda		P	Mike Walter
P	Russ Ortíz		P	Scott Watkins

*Played in the post-season only.

11. Santurce Dream Team: "Imports" and "Natives," 1939–1999

"Imports"	Position	"Natives"
Joshua Gibson	Catcher	Elrod Hendricks
Clarence Palm	Catcher	Adalberto "Junior" Ortíz
Jerry Willard	Catcher	Valmy Thomas
George Scott	First Base	Orlando "Peruchín" Cepeda
Bill White	First Base	Fernando Ramos
Junior Gilliam	Second Base	Santos "Sandy" Alomar, Sr.
Mark Lemke	Second Base	Julio Gotay
Ron Cey	Third Base	Leo Gómez
Buster Clarkson	Third Base	José Pagán
Bill Harrell	Shortstop	Iván de Jesús
Rey Ordoñez	Shortstop	Efigenio "Cocó" Ferrer
Robin Yount	Shortstop	Milton Ramírez
Tany Pérez	DH	Orlando Merced
Darryl Strawberry	DH	Dickie Thon
Don Baylor	Outfield	Juan José Beníquez
Paul Blair	Outfield	Roberto Clemente
Willard Brown	Outfield	José "Cheito" Cruz, Jr.
George Hendrick	Outfield	Alfonso Gerard
Reggie Jackson	Outfield	Juan "Igor" González
Lou Johnson	Outfield	Luis Rodríguez Olmo
Willie Mays	Outfield	Juan Sánchez
Mickey Rivers	Outfield	Rubén "El Indio" Sierra
Bob Thurman	Outfield	Juan E. "Tetelo" Vargas
Pat Tabler	Utility	Manuel "Nolín" Ruiz
Don Zimmer	Utility	Orlando Sánchez

Pitchers

Fred Beene	Sam Jones	Luis Aquino	Jaime Navarro
Billy Brewer	Rick Mahler	John Burgos	Julio Navarro

Billy Byrd	Darrell Osteen	Luis Raúl Cabrera	Francisco J. Oliveras
Mike Cook	Jim Palmer	José Calderón	Mike Pérez
Ted Davidson	Bronswell Patrick	William de Jesús	Juan "Terín" Pizarro
Ken Dayley	Steve Ridzik	Carlos Díaz	Juan (J.C.) Romero
Scott Elarton	Al Severinsen	Kindo Geigel	Gilberto Rondón
Bob Gibson	John Ford Smith	Rubén Gómez	Pantalones Santiago
Bill Greason	Lee Smith	Guillermo Hernández	Domingo Sevilla
Bobo Holloman	Tim Stoddard	Ramón Hernández	Esteban Texidor
Dick Hughes	Turk Wendell	Rogelio Moret	Manuel Velázquez

Managers

Herman Franks	George Scales	Monchile Concepción	Mako Oliveras
Frank Robinson	Earl Weaver	Luis Rodríguez Olmo	Frankie Thon

12. Selected Major League Achievements Earned by Santurce Players through 1998

MVP Awards

American League

Frank Robinson,* 1966
Reggie Jackson, 1973
Don Baylor, 1979
Robin Yount, 1982, 1989
Guillermo Hernández,* 1984
Juan González,* 1996, 1998

National League

Roy Campanella,* 1951, 1953, 1955
Willie Mays, 1954, 1965
Frank Robinson,* 1961
Roberto Clemente,* 1966
Orlando Cepeda, 1967
Bob Gibson, 1968

World Series

Bob Gibson, 1964, 1967
Frank Robinson,* 1966
Roberto Clemente,* 1971
Reggie Jackson, 1973, 1977
Ron Cey, 1981
John Wetteland, 1996

No-Hitters

Sam Jones* (Chicago Cubs) vs. Pittsburgh, May 12, 1955
Jim Palmer (Baltimore) vs. Oakland, August 13, 1969
Bob Gibson (St. Louis) vs. Pittsburgh, August 14, 1971
Len Barker (Cleveland) vs. Pittsburgh, May 15, 1981†
Dennis Martínez* (Montreal) vs. Los Angeles, July 28, 1991†

Cy Young Awards

American League
  Miguel Cuéllar,* 1969
  Jim Palmer, 1973, 1975, 1976
  Guillermo Hernández,* 1984
National League
  Bob Gibson, 1968, 1970

Rookie of the Year

American League
Sandy Alomar, Jr.,* 1990
National League
Willie Mays, 1951
Junior Gilliam,* 1953

Frank Robinson,* 1956
Orlando Cepeda, 1958
Darryl Strawberry, 1983

3,000 Career Hits

Willie Mays   3,283
Robin Yount   3,142
Roberto Clemente* 3,000

*Played with other Puerto Rico League teams in addition to Santurce.
†Perfect game.

300 Career Homers

Willie Mays	660
Frank Robinson*	586
Reggie Jackson	563
Dave Kingman	442
Orlando Cepeda	379
Tany Pérez	379
Don Baylor	338
Darryl Strawberry	332
Ron Cey	308
Juan González*	301

1,500 Career RBI

Willie Mays	1,907
Frank Robinson*	1,812
Reggie Jackson	1,702
Tany Pérez	1,652

.300 Career Batting Average

Roberto Clemente*	.317
Willie Mays	.302

1,500 Career Runs

Willie Mays	2,062
Frank Robinson*	1,829
Robin Yount	1,632
Reggie Jackson	1,551

300 Career Steals

Otis Nixon*	594
Julio Cruz	343
Willie Mays	338
Devon White	306

2,000 Career Strikeouts

Bob Gibson	3,117
Sam McDowell	2,453
Luis Tiant	2,416
Jim Palmer	2,217
Dennis Martínez	2,149

200 Career Wins

Jim Palmer	286
Bob Gibson	251
Dennis Martínez	245
Luis Tiant	229

200 Career Saves

Lee Smith	478†
Tom Henke	311
John Wetteland	253
Gene Garber	218

Golden Glove Awards (Partial List)

American League
- Paul Blair (8)
- George Scott (8)
- Devon White (7)
- Jim Palmer (4)
- Dave Johnson (3)
- Sandy Alomar, Jr.* (1)
- Juan José Beníquez* (1)
- Sixto Lezcano*(1)
- Robin Yount (1)

National League
- Roberto Clemente* (12)
- Willie Mays (12)
- Bob Gibson (9)
- Bill White (7)
- Rey Ordoñez (2)
- Jackie Brandt (1)
- José Lind (1)

Cooperstown Inductees, 1969–1999

Roy Campanella*	1969
Satchel Paige*	1971
Josh Gibson	1972
Roberto Clemente*	1973
Willie Mays	1979
Bob Gibson	1982
Frank Robinson*	1982
Ray Dandridge	1987
Jim Palmer	1990
Reggie Jackson	1993
Leon Day*	1995
Earl Weaver	1996
Tom Lasorda*	1997
Orlando Cepeda	1999†
Robin Yount	1999

Single Season RBI Record by a Santurce Player

Juan González (157 RBI)	1998
A former Santurce player	

Played with other Puerto Rico League teams in addition to Santurce.
†*All-time Major League record.*

13. Puerto Rico Professional Baseball Hall of Fame Inductees with a Santurce Connection, 1991–1996*

1991 Inductees

Willard Brown
Orlando Cepeda
Perucho Cepeda
Roberto Clemente
Rubén Gómez
Juan Pizarro
Bob Thurman

1992 Inductees

Luis R. Olmo
Rafaelito Ortíz
Tetelo Vargas
Pedrín Zorrilla

1993 Inductees

Pito Alvarez de la Vega
Leon Day
Manolo García
Pantalones Santiago
Artie Wilson

1996 Inductees

Raymond Brown
Buster Clarkson
Joshua Gibson
Satchel Paige
Tany Pérez
George Scales

These inductees played with or managed Santurce one or more seasons with the exception of Pito Alvarez de la Vega who was Santurce's broadcaster after his playing career ended. Pedrín Zorrilla managed the team one season during his tenure as the team owner. The last ceremony took place in Aguadilla, Puerto Rico, on October 20, 1996.

14. Pedrín Zorrilla Award Recipients, 1981–1998*

Manolo Guzmán	1981	Tany Pérez	1992
José "Cheo" Cruz, Sr.	1982	Orlando Cepeda	1993
Sixto Lezcano and Mambo de León	1983	Mako Oliveras	1994
Guillermo Hernández	1984	Javier López	1995
José "Cheo" Cruz, Sr.	1985	Roberto Alomar and Bernie Williams	1996
Luis R. Mayoral	1986	Sandy Alomar, Jr., and Terry García	1997
Guigo Otero Suro	1987	Rubén Gómez and Ricky Ledeé	1998
Pito Alvarez de la Vega	1988		
José "Pepito" Méndez	1989		

The Pedrín Zorrilla award was not given in 1990 or 1991.

15. Santurce and Other League Teams and Stadiums, 1939–1999

Teams/Franchises	Stadiums and Seasons
Aguadilla Tiburones (Sharks)	Parque Colón (1939–1942, 1946–1951)
Arecibo Lobos* (Wolves)	Luis Rodríguez Olmo (1961–1981, 1982–1999) Juan Ramón Loubriel (1999–)
Caguas Criollos† *(There is no perfect English translation for the term "Criollos" which refers to individuals who are natives of, and indigenous to, Puerto Rico. Thus, "Criollos" is a source of pride)*	José Gautier Benítez (1938–1942) Ildefonso Solá Morales (1946–1974, 1976–1991, 1994–present) Hiram Bithorn (1974–1976) Juan Ramón Loubriel (1991–1992)
Guayama Brujos (Witches)	Parque Ina Calimano (1938–1942)
Humacao Grises Orientales (Oriental Grays)§	Jáyase Hernández (1938–1942)
Mayagüez Indios (Indians)	Liga París (1938–1949) Isidoro García (1949–present)
Ponce Leones/Piratas Kofresí (Lions/Kofresí Pirates)	Parque Charles H. Terry/ Liga del Castillo (1938–1949) Paquito Montaner (1949–present)
San Juan Senadores/Metros** (Senators/Metros)	Sixto Escobar (1938–1962) Hiram Bithorn (1962–1974, 1983–1999)
Bayamón Vaqueros** (Cowboys)	Juan Ramón Loubriel (1974–1983)
Carolina Gigantes** (Giants)	Roberto Clemente Stadium (1999–)
Santurce Cangrejeros (Crabbers)	Sixto Escobar (1939–1962) Hiram Bithorn (1962–1982, 1989–present) Juan Ramón Loubriel (1982–1989)

*The Arecibo Wolves were not in the League in 1981-82. Arecibo moved to Bayamón after the 1998-99 season.
†Caguas was called Bayamón–Rio Piedras in 1991-92.
§The Humacao franchise moved to Arecibo during the 1941-42 season, but Arecibo did not have a home ballpark.
**San Juan was known as the Metros from 1984-85 through 1992-93. They were the Senators from 1938 to 1974 and from 1993 to 1999. The franchise moved to Bayamón in 1974-75 and were the Cowboys through 1982-83. Their new name as of October 1999 is the Carolina Giants, based on their move to the Roberto Clemente Stadium.

NOTES

1. It Began with Pedrín

1. Biographical data on Pedrín Zorrilla, courtesy of Diana Zorrilla, 1997.

2. Ibid.

3. Carlos Pieve, *Los Genios de la Insuficiencia* (Santo Domingo, Dominican Republic: Alfa y Omega, 1984), p. 246.

4. *El Mundo*, April 8, 1940.

5. *Don Q Baseball Cues* (Ponce, Puerto Rico: Destilería Serrallés, Inc., 1951), no. 10, p. 101.

6. *El Mundo*, October 9, 1939.

7. Rafael Costas, *Enciclopedia Béisbol Ponce Leones* (Santo Domingo, Dominican Republic: Editorial Corripio, 1989), p. 35.

8. Ibid., p. 56.

9. *El Mundo*, October 22, 1939.

10. *El Mundo*, October 23, 1939.

11. Ibid.

12. *El Mundo*, November 6, 1939.

13. José A. Crescioni Benítez, *El Béisbol Profesional Boricua* (San Juan, Puerto Rico: First Book Publishing, 1997), p. 196.

14. *El Mundo*, December 11, 1939.

15. Ibid.

16. *El Mundo*, December 27, 1939.

17. *El Mundo*, October 20, 1940.

18. *El Imparcial*, January 26, 1941.

19. Ibid.

20. *El Imparcial*, February 3, 1941.

21. *El Imparcial*, February 17, 1941.

22. *El Imparcial*, March 3, 1941.

23. *El Imparcial*, March 17, 1941.

24. *El Imparcial*, March 24, 1941.

25. *El Imparcial*, March 31, 1941.

26. Víctor Navarro, *Crónicas de las Series Finales: Béisbol Profesional de Puerto Rico, 1938–39 a 1947–48* (Aguadilla, Puerto Rico: Navarro's Publishing Services, 1991), Serie 3, p. 9.

27. Ibid.

28. *El Imparcial*, October 6, 1941.

29. Costas, p. 58.

30. *El Imparcial*, November 3, 1941.

31. *El Imparcial*, October 11, 1941.

32. Phone conversation with Juan Vené, January 13, 1998.

33. *El Imparcial*, October 14, 1941.

34. *El Imparcial*, October 22, 1941.

35. *El Mundo*, October 27, 1941.

36. *El Mundo*, November 3, 1941.

37. *El Mundo*, November 5, 1941.

38. *El Imparcial*, November 10, 1941.

39. *El Imparcial*, November 17, 1941.

40. *El Imparcial*, December 10, 1941.

41. Roy Campanella, *It's Good to Be Alive* (New York: Signet, 1974 reprint), p. 85.

42. *El Imparcial*, December 27, 1941.

43. Víctor Navarro, *Los Juegos de Estrellas* (Aguadilla, Puerto Rico: Navarro's Publishing Services, 1992), p. 5.

44. *El Mundo*, January 2, 1942.

45. Phone conversation with Ismael Trabal, March 3, 1998.

46. *El Imparcial*, January 12, 1942.

47. *El Mundo*, February 8, 1942.

48. *El Mundo*, March 3, 1942.

49. William Brashler, *Josh Gibson in the Negro Leagues* (New York: Harper & Row, 1978), p. 142.

50. Roberto Inclán, *Senadores de San Juan, 1938–39 a 1982–83* (San Juan, Puerto Rico: San Juan Baseball Club, 1983), p. 7.

51. Crescioni, p. 373.

52. Navarro, *Juegos*, p. 6.

53. Navarro, *Series*, Serie 4, p. 3.

54. Ibid., p. 6.

55. Crescioni, p. 67.
56. Navarro, *Juegos*, p. 7.
57. Campanella, p. 84.

58. *El Vocero*, January 30, 1979.
59. Crescioni, p. 69.
60. Ibid., p. 70.

2. A League Anchor

1. Héctor Barea, *Libro Oficial Béisbol Profesional de Puerto Rico* (Guaynabo, Puerto Rico: Art Printing, 1981), pp. 52, 54, 56, 58.
2. Anibal Sepúlveda and Jorge Carbonell, *Cangrejos* (San Juan, Puerto Rico: Carimar Research Center, Puerto Rico Office of Historic Preservation, 1987), p. 20.
3. Ibid., p. 10.
4. Ibid., p. 17.
5. Ibid., p. 29.
6. Various publications and sources.
7. Sepúlveda & Carbonell, p. 32.
8. Crescioni, p. 73.
9. James A. Riley, *The Biographical Encyclopedia of the Negro Baseball Leagues* (New York: Carroll & Graf Publishers, 1994), p. 128.
10. Fufi Santori, *Con Pantalones* (Aguadilla, Puerto Rico: Quality Printers, 1987), p. 20.
11. Riley, p. 128.
12. Barea, p. 54.
13. Crescioni, p. 237.
14. Costas working papers.
15. Crescioni, p. 368.
16. Ibid., p. 76.
17. *Don Q Baseball Cues* (Ponce, Puerto Rico: Destilería Serrallés, Inc., 1949), no. 6, p. 96.
18. Ibid., p. 38.
19. *El Nuevo Día*, January 11, 1987.
20. *Don Q Baseball Cues*, no. 6, pp. 54–55.
21. Ibid., p. 56.
22. Ibid.
23. *El Mundo*, February 18, 1949.
24. *The Sporting News*, November 23, 1949.
25. Crescioni, p. 368.
26. *The Sporting News*, January 18, 1950.
27. *The Sporting News*, December 28, 1949.
28. Crescioni, p. 79.
29. *Don Q Baseball Cues* (Ponce, Puerto Rico: Destilería Serrallés, Inc., 1950), no. 8, 108.
30. *El Listín Diario*, January 10, 1981.
31. *Don Q Baseball Cues*, no. 8, p. 77.
32. Ibid., p. 78.
33. Ibid.
34. *The Sporting News*, March 1, 1950.
35. Sepúlveda & Carbonell, p. 31.
36. *The Sporting News*, October 25, 1950.
37. Crescioni, p. 81.
38. Navarro, *Juegos*, p. 11.
39. *Don Q Baseball Cues*, no. 10, p. 59.
40. Ibid., p. 101.

41. *The Sporting News*, February 28, 1951.
42. *El Mundo*, February 16, 1951.
43. *Don Q Baseball Cues*, no. 10, p. 12.
44. *El Mundo*, February 19, 1951.
45. *Don Q Baseball Cues*, no. 10, p. 78.
46. *The Sporting News*, February 28, 1951.
47. *El Mundo*, February 28, 1951.
48. *The Sporting News*, October 31, 1951.
49. *The Sporting News*, December 26, 1951.
50. *The Sporting News*, January 16, 1952.
51. *The Sporting News*, February 13, 1952.
52. *The Sporting News*, February 20, 1952.
53. *The Sporting News*, February 27, 1952.
54. *The Sporting News*, March 5, 1952.
55. Luis R. Mayoral, *Roberto Clemente Aún Escucha las Ovaciones* (Hato Rey: Ramallo Brothers Printing, 1987), p. 11.
56. Ibid.
57. *El Mundo*, December 17, 1954.
58. Navarro, *Juegos*, pp. 12–14.
59. *The Sporting News*, January 21, 1953.
60. *The Sporting News*, February 18, 1953.
61. *The Sporting News*, February 25, 1953.
62. *El Mundo*, February 15, 1953.
63. *The Sporting News*, February 25, 1953.
64. Edgardo Rodríguez Juliá, *Peloteros* (Rio Piedras: Editorial de la Universidad de Puerto Rico, 1997), p. 28.
65. John Thorn, and Peter Palmer, with David Reuther, eds., *Total Baseball* (New York: Warner, 1991), p. 600.
66. *The Sporting News*, March 4, 1953.
67. *El Mundo*, February 26, 1953.
68. *The Sporting News*, March 4, 1953.
69. Various publications and sources.
70. Barea, p. 58.
71. *The Sporting News*, December 9, 1953.
72. Thorn & Palmer, p. 1380.
73. Luis R. Mayoral, "Lasorda Recuerda a Pedrín Zorrilla," *El Vocero*, May 17, 1986.
74. *Resúmen Final del Campeonato de 1953–54* (San Juan, Puerto Rico: Liga de Béisbol Profesional de Puerto Rico, 1954), p. 76.
75. Mayoral, *Roberto Clemente*, p. 13.
76. Navarro, *Juegos*, pp. 15–16.
77. *The Sporting News*, January 13, 1954.
78. *The Sporting News*, February 10, 1954.
79. Mayoral, *Roberto Clemente*, p. 13.
80. *The Sporting News*, March 3, 1954.

3. Rubén Gómez, #22

1. *Don Q Baseball Cues*, no. 6, p. 55.
2. Ibid., p. 56.
3. Costas working papers.
4. Armada working papers.
5. Crescioni, pp. 213–214, 369.
6. Various newspapers and publications.
7. *The Sporting News*, October 13, 1954.
8. Crescioni, p. 327.
9. *Don Q Baseball Cues*, no. 8, p. 34.
10. *Don Q Baseball Cues*, no. 10, p. 78.
11. *Don Q Baseball Cues*, no. 8, pp. 35, 78, 87–90.
12. *Don Q Baseball Cues*, no. 10, pp. 58–59.
13. Ibid., pp. 63–64.
14. Navarro, *Juegos*, p. 11.
15. *Don Q Baseball Cues*, no. 10, pp. 77–78.
16. *The Sporting News*, January 30, 1952.
17. *El Mundo*, October 12, 1954.
18. Costas working papers.
19. Crescioni, p. 369.
20. *The Sporting News*, February 27, 1952.
21. *The Sporting News*, October 29, 1952.
22. *The Sporting News*, February 11, 1953.
23. Ibid.
24. *El Mundo*, February 14, 1953.
25. *The Sporting News*, February 18, 1953.
26. *The Sporting News*, February 25, 1953.
27. *The Sporting News*, March 4, 1953.
28. Crescioni, p. 327.
29. *El Mundo*, October 27, 1953.
30. *El Mundo*, February 22, 1954.
31. *The Sporting News*, October 13, 1954.
32. Thorn & Palmer, pp. 152, 156–158.
33. *The Sporting News*, October 13, 1954.
34. *The Sporting News*, November 11, 1954.
35. *The Sporting News*, January 19, 1955.
36. *El Mundo*, January 27, 1955.
37. Navarro, Juegos, p. 17.
38. *El Mundo*, February 5/7, 1955.
39. *The Sporting News*, February 23, 1955.
40. Ibid.
41. Ibid.
42. *The Sporting News*, January 9, 1957.
43. Ismael Trabal, "Dos Boricuas en la Historia," Revista Deportiva, *El Vocero*, October 29, 1983, p. 11.
44. Ibid.
45. Costas working papers.
46. *The Sporting News*, December 17, 1958.
47. *The Sporting News*, February 4, 1959.
48. *The Sporting News*, February 11, 1959.
49. *The Sporting News*, February 25, 1959.
50. Ibid.
51. *The Sporting News*, December 23, 1959.
52. Crescioni, p. 327.
53. *The Sporting News*, December 30, 1959.
54. *The Sporting News*, January 6, 1960.
55. Costas working papers.
56. *The San Juan Star*, January 13, 1962.
57. Costas working papers.
58. *The Sporting News*, November 10, 1962.
59. *The San Juan Star*, January 29, 1963.
60. *The Sporting News*, February 22, 1964.
61. *The San Juan Star*, November 8, 1964.
62. *The San Juan Star*, December 24, 1964.
63. *The San Juan Star*, January 27, 1965.
64. *The Sporting News*, December 25, 1965.
65. Panchicú Toste, *Paloviejo en los Deportes* (Camuy, Puerto Rico: Barceló Marqués & Co., 1966), p. 34.
66. *The Sporting News*, November 20, 1965.
67. Toste, p. 22.
68. *Juegos*, p. 30.
69. Crescioni, p. 327.
70. Panchicú Toste, *Paloviejo en los Deportes* (Camuy, Puerto Rico: Barceló Marqués & Co., 1967), p. 35.
71. *Juegos*, p. 30.
72. *The San Juan Star*, January 20, 1967.
73. *The San Juan Star*, January 30, 1967.
74. *Don Q Baseball Cues* (Ponce, Puerto Rico: Destilería Serrallés, Inc., 1969), no. 25, p. 98.
75. *Juegos*, p. 31.
76. *The San Juan Star*, January 10, 1968.
77. Various publications and sources.
78. Ibid.
79. *Don Q Baseball Cues*, no. 25, p. 44.
80. Ibid.
81. *Juegos*, p. 32.
82. *Don Q Baseball Cues*, no. 25, pp. 60–61.
83. Panchicú Toste and Rafael Pont Flores, *Palo Viejo–Estadísticas de Béisbol Profesional Temporada 1969* (Hato Rey, Puerto Rico: Ramallo Brothers Printing, 1970), p. 46.
84. Ibid., p. 16.
85. *Juegos*, p. 33.
86. Toste & Pont Flores, p. 33.
87. Crescioni, p. 327.
88. *Juegos*, p. 34.
89. *The Sporting News*, February 27, 1971.
90. Various publications and sources.
91. *Compilación Oficial*, 1972–73.
92. Costas working papers.
93. *The San Juan Star*, December 21, 1973.
94. Armada working papers.
95. Costas working papers.
96. Navarro, *Juegos*, p. 39.
97. Various publications and sources.

4. From Caracas to Caracas

1. *El Imparcial*, October 8, 1954.
2. *El Imparcial*, October 16, 1954.
3. Tom Meany, "Señor Mays — Big Hit in San Juan," *Collier's*, January 7, 1955, p. 49.
4. Dick Clark and Larry Lester, eds. *The Negro Leagues Book* (Cleveland: Society for American Baseball Research, 1994), p. 305.
5. *El Mundo*, October 18, 1954.
6. *The Sporting News*, October 27, 1954.
7. Meany, p. 48.
8. Ibid., p. 51.
9. Ibid.
10. *The Sporting News*, December 1, 1954.
11. *The Sporting News*, December 8, 1954.
12. Meany, p. 51.
13. Thorn & Palmer, p. 494.
14. *The Sporting News*, December 22, 1954.
15. *El Mundo*, December 10, 1954.
16. Navarro, *Juegos*, pp. 18–19.
17. *El Mundo*, December 28, 1954.
18. *El Mundo*, January 15, 1955.
19. *El Mundo*, January 11, 1955.
20. Crescioni, p. 89.
21. Ibid., p. 90.
22. *El Mundo*, February 4, 1955.
23. *El Mundo*, February 5, 1955.
24. Harry T. Paxton, "Baseball's Hothouse," *The Saturday Evening Post*, February 14, 1959, p. 81.
25. *El Mundo*, February 7, 1955.
26. *The Sporting News*, February 16, 1955.
27. *El Mundo*, February 9, 1955.
28. *The Sporting News*, February 23, 1955.
29. *El Mundo*, February 11, 1955.
30. *El Mundo*, February 14, 1955.
31. Ibid.
32. *The Sporting News*, February 23, 1955.
33. *El Mundo*, February 18, 1955.
34. *El Mundo*, February 16, 1955.
35. *El Mundo*, February 18, 1955.
36. Ibid.
37. Meany, p. 51.
38. Crescioni, p. 368.
39. *The Sporting News*, October 26, 1955.
40. *The Sporting News*, November 2, 1955.
41. *The Sporting News*, November 9, 1955.
42. *The Sporting News*, November 16, 1955.
43. *The Sporting News*, November 30, 1955.
44. Navarro, *Juegos*, p. 21.
45. *The Sporting News*, December 14, 1955.
46. *The Sporting News*, December 28, 1955.
47. *El Mundo*, January 10, 1956.
48. *El Mundo*, January 7, 1956.
49. *The Sporting News*, February 8, 1956.
50. *The Sporting News*, February 15, 1956.
51. Ibid.
52. *The Sporting News*, October 10, 1956.
53. *The Sporting News*, November 14, 1956.
54. *The Sporting News*, November 28, 1956.
55. Luis R. Mayoral, "Fue Importante en Mi Vida," *El Vocero*, February 11, 1989.
56. *The Sporting News*, December 19, 1956.
57. *The Sporting News*, December 26, 1956.
58. *The Sporting News*, January 9, 1957.
59. *El Mundo*, January 2, 1957.
60. *El Mundo*, January 11, 1957.
61. *The Sporting News*, November 6, 1957.
62. *The Sporting News*, November 27, 1957.
63. José Seda and Jorge Fernández, *Béisbol Semiprofesional, 1938–1941* (Caguas, Puerto Rico: Imprenta Aguayo), p. 57.
64. *The Sporting News*, December 11, 1957.
65. *The Sporting News*, February 19, 1958.
66. Crescioni, p. 95.
67. Ibid., pp. 95–96.
68. *El Mundo*, January 24, 1958.
69. *The Sporting News*, February 12, 1958.
70. Ibid.
71. Paxton, p. 83.
72. *The Sporting News*, November 5, 1958.
73. *The Sporting News*, January 14, 1959.
74. *The Sporting News*, February 11, 1959.
75. *The Sporting News*, February 25, 1959.
76. Ibid.
77. Ibid.

5. Escobar Gives Way to Bithorn

1. *The Sporting News*, October 14, 1959.
2. *The Sporting News*, October 21, 1959.
3. *The Sporting News*, December 9, 1959.
4. *The Sporting News*, November 25, 1959.
5. Barea, p. 78.
6. *The Sporting News*, January 20, 1960.
7. Santori, p. 92.
8. Navarro, *Juegos*, p. 21.
9. *The Sporting News*, February 3, 1960.
10. *The Sporting News*, February 24, 1960.
11. *The Sporting News*, November 2, 1960.
12. Crescioni, p. 101.
13. *The Sporting News*, December 7, 1960.
14. *The Sporting News*, January 4, 1961.
15. Navarro, *Juegos*, p. 23.
16. *The Sporting News*, January 25, 1961.
17. *The Sporting News*, February 15, 1961.
18. *The Sporting News*, February 22, 1961.

19. *The Sporting News*, November 1, 1961.
20. Navarro, *Juegos*, p. 24.
21. *The San Juan Star*, January 10, 1962.
22. *The San Juan Star*, January 15, 1962.
23. Various publications and sources.
24. *The Sporting News*, January 24, 1962.
25. Crescioni, p. 104.
26. *The San Juan Star*, January 25, 1962.
27. *The San Juan Star*, January 26, 1962.
28. *The Sporting News*, February 7, 1962.
29. *The San Juan Star*, January 29, 1962.
30. *The San Juan Star*, January 30, 1962.
31. *The San Juan Star*, January 31, 1962.
32. *The San Juan Star*, February 1, 1962.
33. *The San Juan Star*, February 2, 1962.
34. *The San Juan Star*, January 31, 1962.
35. *El Mundo*, February 7, 1962.
36. *The Sporting News*, February 21, 1962.
37. *The San Juan Star*, February 9, 1962.
38. *The San Juan Star*, February 10, 1962.
39. *The Sporting News*, February 21, 1962.
40. *El Mundo*, February 12, 1962.
41. *The Sporting News*, February 21, 1962.
42. Ibid.
43. Crescioni, p. 368.
44. *The Sporting News*, November 24, 1962.
45. Navarro, *Juegos*, p.26.
46. *The San Juan Star*, January 26, 1963.
47. *The San Juan Star*, January 27, 1963.
48. *The San Juan Star*, January 28, 1963.
49. *The Sporting News*, February 16, 1963.
50. *The San Juan Star*, January 30, 1963.
51. *The San Juan Star*, January 31, 1963.
52. *The San Juan Star*, February 1, 1963.
53. *The Sporting News*, February 23, 1963.
54. *The San Juan Star*, January 3, 1964.
55. *The San Juan Star*, January 4, 1964.
56. *The San Juan Star*, January 6, 1964.
57. Navarro, *Juegos*, p. 27.
58. *The San Juan Star*, January 9, 1964.
59. *The San Juan Star*, January 12, 1964.
60. *The Sporting News*, February 22, 1964.
61. *The San Juan Star*, October 20, 1964.
62. *The San Juan Star*, November 5, 1964.
63. *The San Juan Star*, November 9, 1964.
64. *The San Juan Star*, January 2, 1965.
65. *The San Juan Star*, December 31, 1964.
66. Navarro, *Juegos*, 28.
67. *The San Juan Star*, January 12, 1965.
68. *El Mundo*, January 14, 1965.
69. *The San Juan Star*, January 13, 1965.
70. *The San Juan Star*, January 21, 1965.
71. *The Sporting News*, February 6, 1965.
72. *The San Juan Star*, January 24, 1965.
73. *The San Juan Star*, January 26, 1965.
74. *The San Juan Star*, January 27, 1965.
75. *The San Juan Star*, January 29, 1965.
76. Ibid.
77. *The San Juan Star*, January 30, 1965.
78. *The San Juan Star*, January 31, 1965.
79. *The San Juan Star*, February 1, 1965.
80. *The San Juan Star*, February 2, 1965.
81. *The San Juan Star*, February 3, 1965.
82. Toste, 1966, p. 47.
83. *The Sporting News*, November 6, 1965.
84. *The Sporting News*, November 20, 1965.
85. *The Sporting News*, December 25, 1965.
86. *The Sporting News*, January 22, 1966.
87. Toste, 1966, p. 47.

6. *Baltimore Comes to Town*

1. Toste, 1967, p. 9.
2. Ibid., p. 7.
3. Ibid.
4. Costas, p. 66.
5. Crescioni, p. 113.
6. Costas, p. 66.
7. Toste, 1967, p. 53.
8. Ibid., p. 46.
9. Ibid.
10. *El Mundo*, January 20, 1967.
11, Ibid.
12. Toste, 1967, p. 40.
13. Ibid., p. 31.
14. Ibid., p. 42.
15. Ibid.
16. Ibid.
17. Ibid., p. 40.
18. *The Sporting News*, December 26, 1967.
19. *The Sporting News*, January 16, 1968.
20. *El Mundo*, January 19, 1968.
21. *Compilación Oficial*, 1967–68.
22. Various publications and sources.
23. *The Sporting News*, November 9, 1968.
24. Crescioni, p. 117.
25. *Don Q Baseball Cues*, no. 25, pp. 122–123.
26. *The San Juan Star*, January 2, 1968.
27. *Don Q Baseball Cues*, no. 25, p. 61.
28. Toste and Pont Flores, 1970, p. 14.
29. *The Sporting News*, December 13, 1969.
30. *The Sporting News*, January 3, 1970.
31. Navarro, *Juegos*, p. 34.
32. Toste and Pont Flores, 1970, p. 63.
33. *The Sporting News*, February 7, 1970.
34. *Compilación Oficial*, 1969–70.
35. Costas, p. 66.
36. *Compilación Oficial*, 1969–70.

37. *The Sporting News*, January 2, 1971.
38. Ibid.
39. Navarro, *Juegos*, p. 34.
40. *The Sporting News*, February 6, 1971.
41. *El Mundo*, January 25, 1971.
42. *El Mundo*, January 27, 1971.
43. *The San Juan Star*, February 2, 1971.
44. *The San Juan Star*, February 4, 1971.
45. Ibid.
46. *The San Juan Star*, February 6, 1971.
47. *The Sporting News*, February 20, 1971.
48. *The Sporting News*, February 27, 1971.

49. *The San Juan Star*, October 22, 1971.
50. Navarro, *Juegos*, p. 35.
51. *Compilación Oficial*, 1971–72.
52. *The Sporting News*, February 19, 1972.
53. *The San Juan Star*, January 17, 1972.
54. *Compilación Oficial*, 1972–73.
55. *The Sporting News*, January 20, 1973.
56. Navarro, *Juegos*, p. 36.
57. *Compilación Oficial*, 1972–73.
58. Ibid.
59. *The Sporting News, February 17, 1973*.
60. *Compilación Oficial*, 1972–73.

7. The Dry Spell Begins

1. Thorn & Palmer, p. 1229.
2. *The San Juan Star*, October 21, 1973.
3. *The San Juan Star*, October 25, 1973.
4. *The San Juan Star*, November 27, 1973.
5. *The San Juan Star*, November 7, 1973.
6. *The San Juan Star*, November 12, 1973.
7. *The San Juan Star*, November 17, 1973.
8. Barea, p. 63.
9. *The San Juan Star*, December 16, 1973.
10. Navarro, *Juegos*, p. 37.
11. *El Mundo*, January 8, 1975.
12. Costas, p. 335.
13. Navarro, *Juegos*, p. 38.
14. *The San Juan Star*, January 16, 1976.
15. *The San Juan Star*, December 18, 1975.
16. Pieve, p. 88.
17. Ibid., p. 90.
18. Ibid., pp. 91–92.
19. Barea, p. 78.
20. Pieve, pp. 40–41.
21. *El Nuevo Día*, January 16, 1977.
22. Lloyd Johnson, and Miles Wolff, eds., with Steve McDonald, assoc. ed., *The Encyclopedia of Minor League Baseball* (Durham, North Carolina: Baseball America, Inc., 2nd edition, 1997), p. 530.
23. Costas, p. 105.
24. Barea, p. 17.
25. Navarro, *Juegos*, p. 39.
26. Ibid., p. 40.
27. Johnson & Wolff, pp. 502, 528, 536.
28. *The San Juan Star*, October 25, 1977.
29. *Compilación Oficial*, 1977–78.
30. *The San Juan Star*, January 7, 1978.
31. Ibid.
32. *The San Juan Star*, October 24, 1977.

33. *Compilación Oficial*, 1977–78.
34. Mario A. Rodríguez, "El Gran Pedrín," *El Mundo*, June 7, 1979.
35. *El Mundo*, October 23, 1978.
36. Navarro, *Juegos*, p. 42.
37. *The San Juan Star*, January 17, 1979.
38. *The San Juan Star*, January 23, 1979.
39. *Compilación Oficial*, 1978–79.
40. Luis R. Mayoral, *Mas Allá de un Sueño* (Hato Rey, Puerto Rico: Ramallo Brothers Printing, 1981), p. 71.
41. *Anuario Cangrejero*, Edición 1980–81 (Hato Rey, Puerto Rico: Ramallo Brothers Printing, 1981), p. 39.
42. *The San Juan Star*, October 23, 1979.
43. Navarro, *Juegos*, p. 42.
44. *Compilación Oficial*, 1979–80.
45. Thorn & Palmer, p. 224.
46. *Compilación Oficial*, 1980–81.
47. Ibid.
48. *The San Juan Star*, January 4, 1981.
49. Costas, p. 334.
50. *The San Juan Star*, January 4, 1981.
51. *The San Juan Star*, January 7, 1981.
52. *The San Juan Star*, January 24, 1981.
53. Luis R. Mayoral, "Pedrín Zorrilla Had the Common Touch," *The San Juan Star*, April 12, 1981.
54. *Anuario Cangrejero*, Edicíon 1982–83 (San Juan, Puerto Rico: Art Printing, 1982), p. 27.
55. *The San Juan Star*, October 30, 1981.
56. *Anuario Cangrejero*, 1982–83, p. 31.
57. Ibid., p. 28.
58. Ibid., p. 37.
59. Navarro, *Juegos*, p. 44.
60. *Anuario Cangrejero*, 1982–83, p. 42.

8. The Dry Spell Continues

1. José A. Toro Sugrañes, *Almanaque Puertorriqueño* (Rio Piedras, Puerto Rico: Editorial Edil, 1990), p. 87.

2. *Revista Cangrejera*, Edición 1983–84 (Miami, Florida: Trade Litho Inc., 1983), p. 2.
3. Thorn & Palmer, p. 1536.

4. *El Nuevo Día*, November 3, 1982.
5. *Revista Cangrejera*, Edición 1983–84, p. 56.
6. Ibid., p. 57.
7. Navarro, *Juegos*, p. 44.
8. *Revista Cangrejera*, 1983–84, p. 72.
9. Ibid., p. 74.
10. *The San Juan Star*, January 24, 1983.
11. Pieve, p. 273.
12. *Revista Cangrejera*, 1983–84, p. 76.
13. *Compilación Oficial*, 1982–83.
14. *Revista Cangrejera*, 1983–84, p. 2.
15. Crescioni, p. 208.
16. Barea, p. 77.
17. Crescioni, p. 370.
18. *Compilación Oficial*, 1983–84.
19. Navarro, *Juegos*, p. 45.
20. *Revista Cangrejera*, Edición 1984–85 (Miami, Florida: Trade Litho, Inc., 1984), p. 71.
21. Ibid., p. 74.
22. Ibid., p. 75.
23. *Compilación Oficial*, 1984–85.
24. *El Mundo*, January 20, 1985.
25. Navarro, *Juegos*, p. 46.
26. *El Nuevo Día*, January 18, 1985.
27. *El Vocero*, January 18, 1985.
28. *Revista Cangrejera*, Edición 1985–86 (Miami, Florida: Trade Litho, Inc., 1985), p. 78.
29. Ibid., p. 79.
30. Ibid., p. 80.
31. Ibid.
32. Ibid., p. 81.

33. Ibid., p. 84.
34. *The San Juan Star*, October 20, 1985.
35. *The San Juan Star*, October 23, 1985.
36. *Revista Cangrejera*, Edición 1985–86, p. 38.
37. *The San Juan Star*, January 13, 1986.
38. *El Nuevo Día*, January 5, 1986.
39. *The San Juan Star*, January 23, 1986.
40. *Revista Cangrejera*, Edición 1986–87 (Miami, Florida: Trade Litho, Inc., 1986), pp. 12–13, 92–93.
41. *Compilación Oficial*, 1986–87.
42. Ibid.
43. Crescioni, p. 374.
44. *The San Juan Star*, January 9, 1988.
45. Navarro, *Juegos*, p. 47.
46. *Compilación Oficial*, 1987–88.
47. *The San Juan Star*, January 11, 1988.
48. *The San Juan Star*, January 18, 1988.
49. *The San Juan Star*, January 25, 1988.
50. *The San Juan Star*, January 27, 1988.
51. *The San Juan Star*, January 30, 1988.
52. *Compilación Oficial*, 1988–89.
53. Ibid.
54. Thorn & Palmer, p. 1860.
55. Navarro, *Juegos*, p. 48.
56. Crescioni, p. 368.
57. *Compilación Oficial*, 1989–90.
58. Ibid.
59. *The San Juan Star*, December 16, 1989.
60. *Compilación Oficial*, 1989–90.

9. A New Decade

1. Alex W. Maldonado, "Nobody Came to the Funeral of Fomento," *The San Juan Star*, January 2, 1998.
2. Ibid.
3. *Compilación Oficial*, 1990–91.
4. *El Nuevo Día*, December 3, 1990.
5. *El Nuevo Día*, January 14, 1991.
6. Ibid.
7. Carlos Pieve, "Ganará el Equipo de Mako Oliveras," *El Nuevo Día*, January 23, 1991.
8. *The San Juan Star*, January 31, 1991.
9. *El Nuevo Día*, January 31, 1991.
10. Ibid.
11. Ibid.
12. *Compilación Oficial*, 1990–91.
13. *El Vocero*, February 3, 1991.
14. *Compilación Oficial*, 1990–91.
15. *USA Today Baseball Weekly*, November 15–21, 1991.
16. *Compilación Oficial*, 1991–92.
17. *El Nuevo Día*, November 4, 1991.
18. *The San Juan Star*, November 22, 1991.

19. Ibid.
20. *The San Juan Star*, January 4, 1992.
21. *El Vocero*, December 3, 1991.
22. *Compilación Oficial*, 1991–92.
23. *El Nuevo Día*, December 15, 1991.
24. *El Nuevo Día*, December 19, 1991.
25. *El Nuevo Día*, December 22, 1991.
26. *El Vocero*, January 9, 1992.
27. *The San Juan Star*, February 7, 1992.
28. *Compilación Oficial*, 1991–92.
29. *The San Juan Star*, February 10, 1992.
30. *Recuento Cronológico Temporada 1992–93* (Rio Piedras, Puerto Rico: Liga de Béisbol Profesional de Puerto Rico, 1993), pp. 69–70.
31. Ibid., p. 34
32. Crescioni, p. 165.
33. Ibid., p. 370.
34. *The San Juan Star*, January 5, 1993.
35. *The San Juan Star*, January 21, 1993.
36. *The San Juan Star*, January 27, 1993.
37. *Recuento 1992–93*, pp. 105 & 108.
38. *El Diario*, February 11, 1993.

39. *The San Juan Star*, February 10, 1993.

40. *Recuento 1992–93*, p. 111.

41. *USA Today Baseball Weekly*, December 29, 1993–January 11, 1994.

42. *El Nuevo Día*, December 27, 1993.

43. Ibid.

44. Crescioni, p. 167.

45. *Compilación Oficial*, 1993–94.

46. *Baseball America*, February 21–March 6, 1994.

47. Crescioni, p. 368.

48. Leigh Montville, "A Latin Beat," *Sports Illustrated*, January 16, 1995, p. 44.

49. *Compilación Oficial*, 1994–95.

50. *Recuento Temporada 1994–95* (Rio Piedras, Puerto Rico: Liga de Béisbol Profesional de Puerto Rico, 1995), pp. 153–159.

51. Ibid., p. 22.

52. Armada working papers.

53. *The San Juan Star*, February 9, 1995.

54. *El Nuevo Día*, February 4, 1995.

55. Crescioni, p. 368.

56. Ibid., p. 171.

57. *Recuento Temporada 1995–96* (Rio Piedras, Puerto Rico: Liga de Béisbol Profesional de Puerto Rico), p. 58.

58. Ibid., pp. 59–60.

59. Various publications and sources.

60. *Recuento 1995–96*, p. 108.

61. Ibid., pp. 133–134.

62. Ibid., p. 140.

63. Ibid., p. 143.

64. Ibid., p. 150.

65. Ibid., pp. 181–182.

66. *Recuento Temporada 1996–97* (Rio Piedras, Puerto Rico: Liga de Béisbol Profesional de Puerto Rico), p. 101.

67. Ibid., p. 124.

68. Ibid., pp. 135–140.

69. *Itinerario Oficial Temporada 1997–98* (Rio Piedras, Puerto Rico: Liga de Béisbol Profesional de Puerto Rico).

70. Eric's Unofficial Web Site of the Caguas Criollos.

71. Ibid.

72. *El Nuevo Día*, January 14, 1998.

73. Various publications and sources.

74. *The San Juan Star*, February 27, 1998.

75. Ibid.

76. *El Nuevo Día*, February 27, 1998.

77. Ibid.

10. Thanks for the Memories

1. *Baseball America's 1998 Almanac* (Durham, NC: Baseball America, 1997), pp. 122–123.

2. *USA Today Baseball Weekly 1997 Almanac* (New York: Henry Holt and Company, Inc., 1997), p. 372.

3. *Baseball America's 1996 Directory* (Durham, NC: Baseball America, 1996), p. 132.

4. *Bleacher Creature* (New Orleans: Zephyrs Monthly Newsletter, May 1998), p. 5

5. *Compilación Oficial*, 1997–98.

6. *Baseball America's 1998 Almanac*, pp. 122–123.

7. *USA Today Baseball Weekly 1997 Almanac*, pp. 242 & 358.

8. *Recuento Temporada 1992–93*, p. 111.

9. *Houston Chronicle*, May 17, 1998.

10. Various publications and sources.

11. Ibid.

12. *Dallas Morning News*, June 8, 1998.

13. *The Washington Post*, June 21,1998.

14. *Texas Rangers Media Guide 1998* (Arlington, TX: Tarrant Printing, 1998), p. 313.

15. Ibid., p. 18.

16. Ibid., p. 19.

17. *Compilación Oficial*, 1983–84.

18. *Texas Rangers Media Guide 1998*, p. 25.

19. Ibid.

20. Ibid.

21. *Fort Worth Star-Telegram*, June 11, 1998.

22. Joaquín Monserrate Matienzo, "El Relato del 'Divino Loco'," *El Nuevo Día*, November 1, 1998.

SELECTED BIBLIOGRAPHY

Newspapers

Puerto Rico

El Imparcial, 1939–55
El Mundo, 1939–79
El Nuevo Día, 1974–99
El Vocero, 1974–99
The San Juan Star, 1959–99

U.S.A.

Baseball America, 1994–98
El Diario, 1993
The Sporting News, 1949–73
USA Today, 1995–99
USA Today Baseball Weekly, 1991–99

Books

Barea, Héctor. *Libro Oficial Béisbol Profesional de Puerto Rico*. Guaynabo, Puerto Rico: Art Printing, 1981.

Brashler, William. *Josh Gibson in the Negro Leagues*. New York: Harper & Row, 1978.

Campanella, Roy. *It's Good to Be Alive*. New York: Signet, 1974 reprint.

Clark, Dick, and Larry Lester, eds. *The Negro Leagues Book*. Cleveland: Society for American Baseball Research, 1994.

Costas, Rafael. *Enciclopedia Béisbol Ponce Leones*. Santo Domingo, Dominican Republic: Editorial Corripio, 1989.

Crescioni Benítez, José A. *El Béisbol Profesional Boricua*. San Juan, Puerto Rico: First Book Publishing, 1997.

Inclán, Roberto. *Senadores de San Juan, 1938–39 a 1982–83*. San Juan, Puerto Rico: San Juan Baseball Club, 1983.

Johnson, Lloyd, and Miles Wolff, eds., with Steve McDonald, assoc. ed. *The Encyclopedia of Minor League Baseball*. Durham, North Carolina: Baseball America, Inc., 2nd edition, 1997.

Mayoral, Luis R. *Mas Allá de un Sueño*. Hato Rey, Puerto Rico: Ramallo Brothers Printing, 1981.

_____. *Roberto Clemente Aún Escucha las Ovaciones*. Hato Rey, Puerto Rico: Ramallo Brothers Printing, 1987.

Navarro, Víctor. *Crónicas de las Series Finales: Béisbol Profesional de Puerto Rico, 1938–39 a 1947–48*. Aguadilla, Puerto Rico: Navarro's Publishing Service, 1991.

_____. *Los Juegos de Estrellas*. Aguadilla, Puerto Rico: Navarro's Publishing Services, 1992.

Pieve, Carlos. *Los Genios de la Insuficiencia*. Santo Domingo, Dominican Republic: Alfa y Omega, 1984.

Riley, James A. *The Biographical Encyclopedia of the Negro Baseball Leagues*. New York: Carroll & Graf Publishers, 1994.

Rodríguez Juliá, Edgardo. *Peloteros*. Rio Piedras, Puerto Rico: Editorial de la Universidad de Puerto Rico, 1997.
Santori, Fufi. *Con Pantalones*. Aguadilla, Puerto Rico: Quality Printers, 1987.
Seda, José, and Jorge Fernández. *Béisbol Semiprofesional, 1938–1941*. Caguas, Puerto Rico: Imprenta Aguayo.
*Sepúlveda, Anibal, and Jorge Carbonell. *Cangrejos*. San Juan, Puerto Rico: Carimar Research Center, Puerto Rico Office of Historic Preservation, 1987.
Thorn, John, and Pete Palmer, with David Reuther, eds. *Total Baseball*. New York: Warner, 1991.
*Toro Sugrañes, José A. *Almanaque Puertorriqueño*. Rio Piedras, Puerto Rico: Editorial Edil, 1990.

Articles

Maldonado, Alex W. "Nobody Came to the Funeral of Fomento." *The San Juan Star*, January 2, 1998.
Mayoral, Luis R. "Lasorda Recuerda a Pedrín Zorrilla." *El Vocero*, May 17, 1986.
Mayoral, Luis R. "Pedrín Zorrilla Had the Common Touch." *The San Juan Star*, April 12, 1981.
Meany, Tom. "Señor Mays — Big Hit in San Juan." *Collier's*, January 7, 1955.
Monserrate Matienzo, Joaquín. "El Relato del 'Divino Loco.'" *El Nuevo Día*, November 1, 1998.
Montville, Leigh. "A Latin Beat." *Sports Illustrated*, January 16, 1995.
Paxton, Harry T. "Baseball's Hothouse." *The Saturday Evening Post*, February 14, 1959.
Pieve, Carlos. "Ganará el Equipo de Mako Oliveras." *El Nuevo Día*, January 23, 1991.
Rodríguez, Mario A. "El Gran Pedrín." *El Mundo*, June 7, 1979.
Trabal, Ismael. "Dos Boricuas en la Historia." *El Vocero*, October 29, 1983.

Other Publications

Anuarios Cangrejeros and *Revistas Cangrejeras*. Santurce Baseball Club yearbooks and magazines, 1979–80 through 1986–87.
Baseball America's 1998 Almanac.
Baseball America's 1996 Directory.
Bleacher Creature. New Orleans Zephyrs Monthly Newsletter, 1998.
Compilaciones Oficiales de la Liga de Béisbol Profesional de Puerto Rico. Puerto Rico Winter League official statistics, 1967–68 through 1997–98.
Don Q Baseball Cues. Statistical booklets focusing on Puerto Rico Winter League seasons, 1945–46 through 1968–69.
Guía de Prensa, Vaqueros de Bayamón. Media Guide for Bayamón Cowboys, 1978–79.
Itinerarios Oficiales. Official League Schedules, 1982–83 through 1997–98.
Panchicú Toste, ed. *Paloviejo en los Deportes*. Detailed Statistical Booklets on the 1965–66 and 1966–67 Puerto Rico Winter League seasons.
Panchicú Toste, and Rafael Pont Flores, eds. *Palo Viejo–Estadísticas de Béisbol Profesional Temporada 1969*. Detailed Statistical Booklet on the 1969–70 Puerto Rico Winter League season.
Recuentos de la Liga de Béisbol Profesional de Puerto Rico. Puerto Rico Winter League recounts, 1992–93 and 1994–95 through 1996–97.
Resúmen Final del Campeonato de la Liga de Béisbol Profesional de Puerto Rico. Puerto Rico Winter League final summary, 1953–54.
Texas Rangers Media Guide 1998.
USA Today Baseball Weekly 1997 Almanac.

Unpublished Working Papers

Also helpful in preparing this book were works in progress by Angel Armada, Rafael Costas and Víctor Navarro. Their unpublished sources are refererenced as working papers.

These are not baseball books.

INDEX